TIMELINES FOR WESTERN CHRISTIANITY

(1) CHRONOLOGICAL THEOLOGY

Companion Volume
(2) GEOGRAPHIC HISTORY

Thomas P. Johnston

Evangelism Unlimited, Inc.
Liberty, Missouri
2016

Printed in the United States of America

Thirteen-Digit ISBN: 9780983152682

Published by Evangelism Unlimited, Inc.
Liberty, Missouri

Dewey Decimal Classification: 270
Subject Heading: CHRISTIAN CHURCH HISTORY

Cover artwork by Stephan J. Albin

INTRODUCTION TO COMBINED VOLUMES

The complexity of writing on these subjects is related to seeking a balance between being wise as a serpent and gentle as a dove (Matt 10:16). Christ, when He walked on earth, was able to bridge these difficult approaches: "For the Law was given through Moses; grace and truth were realized through Jesus Christ" (John 1:17). This difficult balance is the challenge of this subject.

Furthermore, there are two very different purposes or reasons for selecting such a topic. One reason might be to convince a Catholic audience to turn toward Evangelical Christianity. This writing does not share this purpose. The second reason is to train Evangelicals and Baptists the historical points of deviation between the Church of Rome and Historic Evangelicalism. This second purpose is the goal of the present work. The first reason relates to evangelizing, while the second focuses on training believers in the faith.

Likewise, evangelism relates to the beginning of the Great Commission in Matthew, "Go, win disciples of all nations." It must be done with humility and gentleness, focusing on the gospel of salvation. Training believers in the faith relates to discipleship or the second part of Matthew's Great Commission, "teaching them to observe all that I have commanded you" (Matt 28:19-20). Training persons about Western Christianity or Roman Catholicism within the context of a Baptist institution ascribes to the latter purpose. The content and issues addressed in these books are neither intended as an evangelism tool nor as a conciliatory tool. Rather, these historical notes are intended to inform Baptists about points of differentiation between the *Baptist Faith and Message* (2000)* and the theology of the Church of Rome as described in their writings.

The acute reader will notice that primary writings have often been cited, and secondary sources have been referenced as such. Therefore it is left up to the reader to decide if the sources are trustworthy or if the concept being expressed is cogently argued. The purpose for these pages is to examine what may often be censored in select Histories of the Churches.

While grace is needed in the communication of any topic, it must not be exercized at the expense of truth. Both need to be maintained simultaneously. Perhaps it has been the case that mainstream U.S. histories of the churches in the past 50-100 years have tended to gloss over certain glaring aspects of the history of Christianity, even those that led to the forming of the United States as a nation. Furthermore, a misunderstanding of the history of the churches has tended towards theological naiveté and broadness of mind, and has often resulted in freethinking in the area of denominational and theological distinctives.

At stake is actually the Gospel itself, freedom to verbalize the Gospel, and even freedom of conscience.

Before the larger chart, "Chronological Theology," I have included eleven charts that have been in process for quite some time. It is my desire that students will gain a unique grasp of historical issues in a chronological and contextual format, while being mindful of the problems of historiography. These charts are meant to prepare the reader for the material found in "Chronological Theology" and in Volume 2, "Chronological History." For further insights, I would guide the reader to the introductory comments to these other sections.

Maranatha. Even so come Lord Jesus!

Thomas P. Johnston, Ph.D.
March 2016.

*By the way, this author does not claim any authority to speak on behalf of Baptists or any Baptist group. The opinions here expressed a personally derived through study.

TABLE OF CONTENTS

Chart One: Views of Church History One (98-1517 A.D.)

The following chart identifies the varieties of approaches to the study of Church History One (CH1). It is historiographic. Some blurring and overlap is to be expected within the chart.

Views of Catholicism	Views of Reformation	Views of Monasticism	Approaches to Church History One	Views of Baptist Origins[1]
Ignatius Loyola's View The Church has always been holy and immaculate; She cannot and will never err (cf. Eph 5:27)	The Church of Rome never needed to be "reformed" from outside; it has performed its own internal reformations over the years	Monasticism is the ideal Christian life of holiness (Benedictine Vows: Poverty, Abstinence, and Obedience, cf. Gregory I)	Proper understanding of doctrinal developments in CH1 are rightly communicated by Peter the Lombard and Thomas Aquinas	**Baptists Are an Innovation** Baptists are an innovative sect, a heretical aberration of the truth, and enemies of the gospel
Erasmus' Soft Critique The Church has had minor ups and downs, but for doctrine She continues as its Guiding Star	Reformation may have benefitted the Catholic Church in some ways, as it recalibrated itself through the Counter-Reformation	Monasticism is the ideal Christian life of holiness (Benedictine Vows: Poverty, Abstinence, and Obedience, cf. Gregory I)	The Roman State Church provides the Guiding Star of doctrinal clarity through the maze of Early Church heretical movements	**Baptists Are Mistaken** Baptists misinterpret the Bible on many points; while their baptism may be valid, they are at best "departed brethren"
Reformed Adaptation of Erasmus Rome carried the torch of the Truth until prior to the Reformation period when the sale of Indulgences (Sixtus IV in 1471) or the sexual exploits of the Borgia family tarnished aspects of papal leadership	Reformation was needed as a clean break for lifestyle issues and doctrinal deviations; especially the doctrine of justification by faith	Monastic teachings are helpful for New Testament Christians to understand personal spiritual disciplines	Unlikely any believed or practiced Particular Baptist principles any time during CH1; Medieval Christianity is considered a less important time period of church history with neither protagonists or antagonists	**1. Outgrowth of English Separatism** Doctrinal truth traveled through the Early Church creeds, through Medieval Catholicism, emerging in the Reformers that themselves were monks or priests (e.g. Luther and Calvin)
Mainstream 20th Century Evangelical Rome deviated from biblical doctrine sometime from A.D. 1000 to the pre-Reformation period (Gregory VII, Urban II, Lombard, Aquinas, Innocent III)	Reformation needed to happen, but did not go far enough; it remained married to infant baptism and the State Church model	Monastic teachings are helpful for New Testament Christians to understand personal spiritual disciplines	The Anabaptists clearly practiced Baptism by immersion; they baptized themselves when Grebel baptized Blaurock at the home of Manz on 21 Jan 1525	**2. Anabaptist Influence** Doctrinal truth traveled through the Early Church creeds, through Medieval Catholicism, emerging in the Reformers that themselves were monks or priests (e.g. Menno Simons)
Rome Is the Antichrist Rome became the Antichrist when the church was wed with the state under Constantine. Some need to heed the admonition of Rev 18:4, "Come out of her."	Reformation needed to happen, but did not go far enough; it remained married to infant baptism and the State Church model	Monastic teachings are an aberration of the true New Testament life of godliness and holiness, as found in marriage and supporting one's own family	The true church during the time of CH1 were those who were faithful to the Word of God, while usually found among various dissenting church groups, in some cases it was found within the State Church	**3. Continuation of Biblical Teachings** Baptist principles are lodged in Scripture and not in some type of human succession, rather a spiritual succession wrought by the Word of God bearing fruit in hearts and lives (cf. Col 1:5-6)
Rome Is the Antichrist Rome became the Antichrist when the church was wed with the state under Constantine.	Reformation needed to happen, but did not go far enough; it remained married to infant baptism and the State Church model	Monastic teachings are an aberration of the true New Testament life of godliness and holiness, as found in marriage and supporting one's own family	Unbroken succession of Baptist witness throughout CH1, often considered to begin with Jesus being baptized by John the Baptist; often see truth flowing through dissenting church movements (Cathars, etc.)	**4. Succession of Baptist Churches** Possibly a reaction to the hierarchical successionism of Rome; believe in an unbroken line of people baptized by immersion (cf. Acts 14:17)

---

[1]The four numbered views of Baptist origin are taken from H. Leon McBeth, *The Baptist Heritage: Four Centuries of Baptist Witness* (Nashville: Broadman, 1987), 56-57.

Chart Two: Fifteen Approaches to the Study of Christian History

	1	2	3	4	5	6	7
APPROACHES	Secular History	Secular History of Christianity	**Salvation History I** OT History	**Salvation History II** Life, Death, and Resurrection of Christ	**Salvation History III** Apostolic Age	Church History	**Particular Histories I** History of Individual Churches or Groups of Churches
EXPLANATION	Must by its very framing focus on a language and territory	Focus on kings, rulers, territories; bishops, patriarchs, popes; approved councils and creeds	The OT Scriptures	The inspired testimony of the Gospels	The inspired testimony of the Book of Acts and the other NT books	Fallacious nomen-clature; The myth of the unified "Church" that can be objectively studied in history	Considered due to language or territory
EXAMPLES	Including the secularization of the history of the churches, via various approaches to historical criticism	From a secular approach: Cicero's history of the city of Rome (with rulers, generals, and wars)	OT	Matthew, Mark, Luke, John	The Book of Acts and all the remaining NT books	Church History One is normally the non-evan-gelistic development of THE Western Church	Antiochian Greek Orthodox, Egyptian Coptic, Roman Catholic, Baptist, etc.
SELECTED CITIES	Babylon, Alexandria, Athens	Jerusalem, Antioch, Athens, Rome, Cons-taninople, London, Moscow, etc.	Babylon, Nineveh, Bethel, Jerusalem, Babylon	Bethlehem, Nazareth, Jerusalem	In Acts: Jerusalem Antioch Ephesus Rome	Jerusalem, Rome, etc.	Jerusalem, Rome, etc.
EMPHASES	Kings, wars, culture	Kings, wars, culture				Portrayal of a type of pre-Reformation idyllic ecumenical spirit (i.e. "Christian Charity")	Prioritative Apostolic Succession
RESULT	God's working left out of history	The Gospel and evangel-ism left out of church history	Often focus is either only OT, or only OT in relation to Christ	Focus on earthly ministry of Jesus		Usually does not consider the Gospel or evangelism	Depends on distinctive of group being studied

Salvation History = German *Heilsgeschichte*; Church history = "The history of a church's self-understanding"; the issue for teaching the history of the churches becomes: how do columns 10-11 relate to 1-2, 6-9 and/or 13-14?

Chart Two: Fifteen Approaches to the Study of Christian History

	8	9	10	11	12	13	14	15
APPROACHES	Particular Histories II	Particular Histories	Salvation History IV		Prophetic Orientations			
	History of a Theological Under-standing	History of a Methodolo-gical Under-standing	History of Evangelizing	History of Christ's Blood-Bought Church	Aligning OT predictive prophecies into NT history	Aligning OT and NT prophecy with Church Age and Eschaton	Seeking and Finding Daily Fulfillments of Prophecy	Prophetic Emphasis Divorced from the Great Commission
EXPLANATION	Considered because of a overarching theological *a priori*	Views of Baptism; Views of the Great Commission; Views of Christian sanctification	New Testament evangelizing; New Testament missions; i.e. the history of spreading the Gospel	Matt 16:18; Rev 5:9-10; the history of the reception of the Gospel	OT prophecies, such as: Gen 9-10, 49; Dan 2, 7-12	OT and NT prophecies, such as: Gen 9-10, 49; Dan 2, 7-12; Matt 24-25; Mark 13; Luke 21; 2 Thess 2; 1 Tim 4; Rev 2-3, 6-18	Scouring the Scriptures daily to line up biblical prophecies with the day's headlines, particularly in regard to Israel and the Holy Land	Based on the same OT and NT prophe-cies, in 19th century cultic groups were born from an approach to predictive prophecy
EXAMPLES	Sacerdotalism (sacramental-ism); Mariology; Justification by faith	From Monasticism to Gospel preaching and everything in between	Includes a jump from the NT Book of Acts to the First Great Awakening with very little in between		NT authors did this, and so do conservative commentators on the Bible books	19th Century U.S. Prophecy Conferences, sometimes considered "Dispensa-tional"	During and after World War Two numerous ministers aligned biblical prophecy with daily news	Adventists? Herbert W. Armstrong; Jehovah's Witnesses; Mormons; etc.
SELECTED CITIES	Dependent on the emphasis	Dependent on the emphasis	Jerusalem, Samaria, Rome... London, Northhamp-ton, MA, upper New York, etc.	Figuratively: the true heavenly "Zion"	Jerusalem; etc.	Babylon versus the New Jerusalem	Jerusalem and daily events around "Holy Land" (usually very little about Rome)	
EMPHASES	Jesus instating perpetual priesthood; Paul's approach to justification	From the ascetic lifestyle of some biblical prophets to a Matt 10 style of evangelism	Open air preaching, personal evangelism on the street, and church evangelism	Conversion; true church; signs of a NT church; etc.	Prophecies about the first coming of Jesus and the coming of the church	John Darby; Niagara Bible Conferences; etc.	Perhaps some TV evangelists could be included in this list?	Interpreting predictive prophecy become more important than the Gospel of salvation
RESULT	Interesting to focus on one theology	Interesting to focus on one methodology	Good; should not be segmented from history of the churches	Is not this, in fact, true "church history"?	Keeps OT authority alive with its NT links; affirms NT	Keeps focus on return of Christ, 1 Thess 1:9-10	May press Scripture beyond its mysterious interpretation	Emphasizes another gospel, and socio-political issues

Chart Three: History and Prophecy: Pre-19th Century Protestant Conceptions of History

In their desire to interpret church history according to the Scriptures, early Protestant historians developed views of the history based on the four monarchies in Dan 2, 7 (John Sleidan [1506-1556], *The Key of History or the Four Chief Monarchies*, two books in one binding [Strasbourg, 1556; London, 1627]).

Rev. 11:15, "The kingdoms of this world" (cf. Mark 10:42)
Babylon → Persia → Greece → Rome → Rome and the Kingdom of Christ

Four Monarchies of Daniel*	John Sleidan Reformed (1506-1556)	Daniel 7	Edward Gibbon English Enlightenment (1737-1794)	Tom Johnston Considering Megatrends in Church History
(1) Babylon Dan 2:32, 37-38; Dan 7:4 (from Gen 10:10 to Dan 5:30)	Head of gold = Babylon; From Nimrod To Belshazzar ~2177-530 B.C. Or from 1787 to 3434 ~1647 years Flood was in ~1656	First Beast Like a lion with eagle's wings... [Babylon destroyed, never to be rebuilt, Jer 25:9; 51:37]	For a short time converting to Roman Catholicism, and then returning to Anglicism, Gibbon wrote **The Rise and Fall of the Roman Empire** in six volumes from 1776-1788. Interestingly, the title seems to presuppose a "fall" of Daniel's fourth monarchy. Gibbon's did not trace the downfall of Rome, but that of Byzantium. So, did Constantine's moving the capital of the empire really move Rome's prophesied seat of power? For if the "Roman Empire" truly "fell," than so does biblical prophecy's usefulness for history.	Do the four monarchies not only represent earthly powers, but also spirits and worldviews (Eph 6:12)? (1) **Babylon**: Lucifer-type, Isa 14:12; enemy, Rev 17-18; Religion: emperor worship; (2) **Persia**: demonic prince, Dan 10:13, 20; Religion: Zoroastrian dualism, morphing into Islam? (3) **Greece**: demonic prince, Dan 10:20; Religion: Greek pantheon of gods and/or perhaps Greek philosophical thought? (4) **Rome**: OT, no mention; NT, addressed only as a city; Religion: Emperor worship, military and political power?
(2) Persia Dan 2:32, 39; Dan 7:5; Dan 8:20 (Isa 45:1)	Chest of silver = Persia; From Cyrus To Darius; ~530-330 B.C. Or from 3434 to 3609 ~200 yrs (*p37*)	Second Beast Suddenly, like a bear with three ribs in its teeth [country, not city]	Today, 560 years after the fall of Constantinople to the Turks, Daniel's fourth monarchy, Rome, continues on as a major player in world affairs! Likewise, Rome still considers herself the cradle of Western Civilization (Gregory XVI, *Inter Praecipuas* [1844]); further, keeping alive (albeit sometimes by a thread) the Latin language with its world-conquering power and its world-dominating politics (politics absorbed in religious fervor with adaptable political leadership by proxy), forming an irrefutable linguistic link between the Roman Empire and its emperor worship, and the "Universal" Church of Rome.	Are there not, in fact, five major periods in Rome's "second" monarchy, as can be noted up to this point in Christianity in the Western World: (1) **Constantine**'s "conversion" to his hasty move to Constantinople; (2) The **edicts** that gave church political authority over Rome (launching centuries-long investiture contr.); (3) **Charlemagne**'s crowning and the investiture ordeals; (4) **Napoleon**'s Conquests and their impact on Rome? (5) **Hitler**'s Third Reich and its impact on European politics?
(3) Greece Dan 2:32, 39; Dan 7:6; Dan 8:20-22 (during the 400 "silent years")	Belly and thighs of bronze = Greece; From Alexander the Great To Pompey ~330-27 B.C. Or from 3609 to 3925 ~303 years - - - - - Sleidan's dates (based on Cicero): 3212, Rome first founded (*p44*); 3954, Birth of Christ (*p116*)	Another Beast Like a leopard with four wings and four heads and dominion [country, not city]	Could it be that the German Enlightenment period (Immanuel Kant; Friedrich Schleiermacher) had a secularizing effect upon all study, including the study of history, leading 19th Century mainstream Protestants to overlook or ignore teachings from prophecy in the study of Church History, as imported to the U.S. by Philip Schaff in the late 1800s?	In fact, it even appears that after the 1789 French revolution, Some Evangelical Christians thought that the Millennial age had arrived, perhaps because: (1) They had experienced Rome's long war against the Huguenots (cf. Rev 13:7) (2) They had experienced the breaking of Rome's power in the Napoleonic wars (Napoleon as a Messiah-type); (3) They had experienced a new era of worldwide Protestant missionary activity, partly owing to the *Pax Britannica* of the 19th Century. And yet, as history would have it, Rome made a significant comeback in the 19th and 20th Centuries.
(4) Rome I Dan 2:33, 40; Dan 7:7-8, 19-25	Legs of iron = Rome I; From Octavian (Caesar Augustus□) To Flavius Constant.; ~27 B.C.-312 A.D. Or from 3925□ to 4264 ~339 years □Received title of "Perpetual Dictator"***	Fourth Beast: Dreadful and terrible and exceedingly strong With iron teeth Ten horns; another horn emerged; three plucked up; one horn spoke pompous words [city for empire]	Could it be that the impact of this secularizing tendency made its way into mainstream U.S. Evangelical histories after the 1950s through: (1) Gaining control of major British and U.S. printing presses, first secular, then Evangelical (e.g. Pius X, *Pascendi* [1907], via its regulation of *nihil obstat*); (2) Gaining control of the major U.S. faculties in church history (Harvard, Penn State, and Univ. of Chicago), shaping research, doctoral studies, and writing;	Even so, three U.S. ecclesial shifts took place in 1900: (1) An almost imperceptible historiographic shift amongst Evangelicals as regards Church History in general, and especially pre-Reformation Rome in particular; (2) Simultaneously, Rome's silent takeover of the worldwide translation activities of the United Bible Society; and (3) A conciliatory wave arising from within Evangelicalism as regards working together with Rome on many levels, including in evangelism.
(4+) Rome II (describes a blended kingdom) Dan 2:33, 41-44; Dan 7:18, 21-22, 24-26 Of anti-Christ? Dan 8:23-25	Feet of iron and clay = Rome II (as state + church) From Constantine (or Theodosius) 312 A.D.-present; ~1700 years; Does the mixture relate to the true and false church or to the blending of sacred and secular? Being broken to pieces: politically? Religiously?	The one horn begins to make war against the saints, and prevails upon them Until the Ancient of Days comes and judges in favor of the saints - - - - Either Rome fits into the end time picture, or it has some mighty strong "karma" [city for authority]	(3) Discovering and developing Janissaries for history positions in prominent Evangelical schools? Consider P. Jenkins: "Christianity became predominantly European not because this continent had any obvious affinity for that faith, but by default: Europe was the continent where it was not destroyed" (*The Lost History of Christianity* [2008], 3).	This last shift has once again made one's feeling toward Rome (*nihil obstat*) a new academic litmus test. One wonders if the following quote rightly explains Rome's feeling towards those not willing to submit to their leadership: "For at this time almost all the nations from *Illyricum* to *Gallia*, conspired against the name of the Romanes." (Sleidan, 130). Anyway, does the U.S. fit into a prophetic view of the 19th and 20th Century? May the U.S. be the one horn in Dan 7:8, 21? Maybe... maybe not? .... Of the seven churches in Revelation 2-3: (1) Notice that Rome was not one of these churches, even though a church existed there at the time of its writing; (2) Nor is Babylon listed as a church, although there were churches in that part of "Asia"; (3) The seven churches were groups of churches named by their respective cities, all existing simultaneously.

*It is interesting to note that none of these four chief monarchies is Israel (under David or Solomon), unto which God promised an eternal reign to David in 2 Sam 7:12-13.

***He [Caesar] assumed the offered title and authority of Perpetual Dictator, and swayed the Senate according to his own will. He, in a manner of having sole bestowing of

Chart Three: History and Prophecy: Pre-19th Century Protestant Conceptions of History

Some divide the 7 churches in Rev. 2-3 into 7 chronological churches. Jurieu critiqued this methodology showing its tendency to subjectivity (Pierre Jurieu, *The Accomplishment of the Scriptures* [Rotterdam & London, 1687], 1:7-18). Could not the 4 horsemen of Rev 6 be distinct but overlapping eras in the 4th Monarchy?

"have become the kingdoms of our Lord and of His Christ"   **"And He will reign forever and ever!"**

Ephesus→Smyrna→Pergamum→Thyatira→Sardis→Philadelphia→Laodicea   Rome I&II   Church History and Fall of Babylon

and Seven Churches of Rev 2-3	Patrick Forbes Scottish Presbyterian (1564-1635)	Cocceius Dutch Covenant Theologian (1603-1669)	Henry More English Jesuit Priest (1614-1687)	Pierre Jurieu Fr. Reformed Pastor (1637-1713)	Four Horsemen, Rev 6	The Great Sign from Heaven Rev 12	Beast Out of the Sea Rev 13°	Fall of Babylon Rev 16-18
(1) Ephesus	0-300 A.D., "Primitive Church"	0-110 A.D., Apostolic Church	0-tenth year of Nero's Empire	Praises to Thyatira greater than to Apostolic church?	(1) Horseman on White Horse	(1) Woman clothed with the sun		Great city divided into 3 parts
What of the Nicolaitans (v 6)?	Nicolaitans may signify all the heretics	Nicolaos = conqueror of the people, thus speaking of heretics			"Conquering and to conquer"	She gave birth to child		Woman arrayed in purple and scarlet, sitting on scarlet beast
(2) Smyrna	400-500 A.D., Period of the Arians, Macedonians, Nestorians, and Eutychians	Signifies the suffering Church of all ages, especially of the first three Centuries under pagan rulers	Tenth year of Nero's Empire to 324, Constantine and the Council of Nicaea	Of Forbes: Why is high praise be given to a church during a time of growing apostasy? Was persecution merely imprisonment?	312 A.D., Constantine: "Conquer with this!" or 800 A.D., Charlemagne	(2) Fiery dragon with seven heads and ten horns and seven diadems on his heads	Beast out of the sea having seven heads and ten horns and ten crowns	Her name, "Mystery, Babylon the Great, the Mother of the Harlots of the Earth"
Its 10 days of persecution (v 10)?	Church persecuted by Arian Emperors	The ten Roman persecutions under pagan Emperors	Tenth year of Nero's reign	A stretch or chance	(2) Horseman on Fiery Red Horse	Threw a 3rd of the stars of heaven to the earth	Beast like leopard, feet of a bear, mouth of a lion (cf. Dan 7)	The beast had seven heads and 10 horns
(3) Pergamum	600-1100 A.D., period of the Antichrist	From Constantine to the birth of Antichrist	324-1242, the Empire of the Antichrist, including the extinguishing of the Waldenses and Albigenses	Of Forbes: Can praise be given to this time period? Does not "you have those" imply a minority? Of Cocceius: How negative of this time!	"To take peace from the earth, that people should kill one another, given a great sword"	Stood ready to devour the child at his birth	Mortally wounded, wound healed	She was drunk with the blood of the saints
What is meant by Antipas (v 13)?	Antipas = Anti-papa, an Enemy opposing the Pope	Antipas = those believing Consubstantiation; Antipas for Antipatros or Isopatros or equal to the Father	Antipas = Antipope, or contrary to the Pope		1073 A.D., Gregory VII (Hildebrand) or 1198 A.D., Innocent III	(3) Child was to rule all nations with a "rod of iron"	Worshipped the dragon who gave his authority to the beast	Rev 17:9, the 7 heads are 7 mountains upon which woman sits
What is meant by Pergamus (v 12)?		Pergamus = the famous fortress, Troy; Rome signifies strength or fortress			(3) Horseman on Black Horse	He was caught up to heaven; Woman fled to the wilderness		Also 7 kings: 5 have fallen, 1 is, & the other has not yet come
(4) Thyatira	1100-1517 A.D., from the Albigenses to Luther	The church under the reign of Antichrist	1242-1517 A.D., From destruction of the Albigenses to the abandonment of Rome	The Albigenses and Waldenses could hardly be blamed for Rome's Jezebel	"A pair of scales in his hands" (for communism?)	(4) War in heaven between Michael the Archangel and the dragon and his angels		The 10 horns are 10 kings; sea is the multitude of people
What of Jezebel (v 20)?	Unclear	Sickness of Jezebel = disasters that befell Roman Catholic Church			Vlad. Lenin, Jos. Stalin, Bar. Obama?	Dragon cast to the earth, where he persecuted the Woman		10 horns on the beast will hate the harlot and burn her with fire
(5) Sardis	1517-1600, The Reformed Church	The Reformed Church	1517 A.D. to the ruin of Antichrist, the period of the Reformation	How could the nascent Reformed church be told, "you are dead," where Thyatira receives not such a rebuke?	(4) Horseman on Pale Horse	The Dragon then made war with her offspring	Granted him to make war against the saints and overcome them	The woman (harlot) is the great city which reigns over the kings of the earth
(6) Philadelphia	1600-1700 A.D., Church that shall carry Reformation to its greatest height	Church of brotherly love; this church shall be persecuted	Antichrist ruined and infidel nations converted	Necessitates a 8th time period for the 1000 year reign, after the apostasy of Laodicea	Power over 1/4th of earth to kill		3rd beast (666), two horns like a lamb; causes all to receive mark of the beast	What great city in world history could be said to rule over kings of the earth?
(7) Laodicea	1600-1700 A.D., Backslidden Protestant church reverts back to formalism and duty	Church immediately preceding the judgment of God, and when Christ shall reign on the earth	The decay immediately preceding the Second Coming of Jesus Christ	Did not like the need for a general apostasy after the Philadelphia church	e.g. China is 1/6th of world population	What of **Islam** and its history of **Jihad**? Or what of **China** or **India** with their histories? How do these religious or political world powers fit to prophecy? Is **Russia** part of the European 10, or are these Western European language group countries? **Israel** and **Egypt** are not listed in four Monarchies		

all honors, and public offices, conferring them upon whom he pleased, thereby incurring many men's ill-will" (Sleidan, 108). Sleidan ended his Book 1 with the murder of Julius Caesar; Book 2 considers this fourth monarchy. °*Actes and Monuments of John Foxe*, 4th edition (London: The Religious Tract Society, n.d.) 1: xxx-xxxii.

	Issues	64-325 A.D.	325-451	451-604	604-787	787-1066
Biblical-Denominatinoal	**Believer's Baptism** (encouraged or discouraged)		Augustine decried the rebaptism of Catholics by Donatists (*Contra Donatisten*); baptismal regeneration is enshrined in Nicene Creed			
	Evangelization (encouraged or discouraged), including the **Expansion of the Church** (acknowledging different schemes to evangelize at that time, and to measure growth of the true church by historians)	**10 Persecutions** of Rome against Christians: Nero in 64; Domitian in 95; Trajan (98-117); Hadrian (117-138); Marcus Aurelius (161-180); Septimus Severus (222-235); Maximinus the Thracian (235-238); Decius (250-251); Valerian (253-260); Diocletian (303-305)	Augustine seemed to attack Evangelicals as (1) Manichean (spiritually, due to non-sacramental views) and (2) Donatists (separatistic)	Council of Orange (529), against freedom to choose (i.e. against decisional preaching), without first baptism, and then continued efforts, assurance of salvation is vainglory, predestination is decried		
	Conversion Theology: By grace through faith through preaching or Through sacraments regardless of knowledge of recipient or holiness of administrator		With Augustine, the sacramental side of the Latin church won out against the Evangelical side of the church			
	Biblical Authority: Constant struggle between Scriptures and traditions of the territorial churches 1000 reign of Jerome's Vulgate in Medieval Europe (link between text and theology no coincidence, esp. concept "do penance")		Canon partially formulated at Nicea (325); Jerome's Vulgate commissioned by Bishop of Rome, Damasus (383), to counter Donatist translations?	Chalcedon (451) finalized the remaining books of the NT canon		
Ecumenical-Theological	**Trinitarian Theology** (debate about the deity of three persons of the Trinity)		Council of Nicea (325) called by Constantine, voted against Arius; Constantinople 1 (381) on the divinity of the Holy Spirit			
	Christology (debate about the interaction of human and divine natures in Christ)		Council of Ephesus (431) condemned Nestorius, proclaimed Mary as "Mother of God"	Chalcedon (451) defined the two natures of Christ against Eutyches, who was excommunicated	Constantinople 3 (680-681) put an end to "monothelitism" by defining two wills in Christ, the Divine and the human	

Chart Four: Issues in the First 1,000 Years of Western Christianity

	Issues	64-325 A.D.	325-451	451-604	604-787	787-1066
Ecumenical-Theological	**Soteriology** (means of salvation)	Cyprian (200-258) linked salvation to the hierarchical church	Council of Ephesus (431) renewed condemnation of Pelagius	Council of Orange (529): against "semi-Pelagianism", for Natural Headship of Adam, against "faith alone", for baptismal regeneration		
	Worship (what is done in the public service of the Church as a result of the theology of salvation; shows what is important)				Gregory I centralized the Latin territorial church with use of the Gallican Missal, his calendar, and his chants (borrowed from Eastern Monasticism)	
State-Church Relations	**Ecclesiastical Controversy** (what and who is the true church?)	Cyprian (200-258) made clear that there was no salvation outside the Catholic church; Constantine gave Rome the edge on the political organization of the "Church"	Rome began to consolidate its authority, Augustine argued against the "schismatic" Donatists of North Africa	With the Council of Ephesus' vote against Nestorius (431), the territorial Greek and Latin church bodies began to split; Constantinople 2 (553) reaffirmed the first four general councils		Pope and Patriarch of Constantinople mutually excommunicate each other (1066)
	Iconoclastic Controversy (on the use of statues for prayer and worship)	The sale of relics began early in the church	Constantine's mother, Helena, encouraged worship of relics, found the real cross of Christ (326); Rome began using images (statues) for prayer and worship, and began using images to worship angels and dead saints (375)		Gregory I wrote the Abbott Mellitus to place relics of the saints in the Temples of the English druids, and to emulate their feast days	At the Council of Nicea II (787), the Latin territorial church favored the use of statues in worship, whereas the Eastern church did not
	Investiture Controversy (on church or state [local] control of church appointments)					Pope crowns Charlemagne "Holy Roman Emperor" (Christmas 800), thereby establishing the Church over the crown
Secular History	**Political Issues**: Kings, Wars, Major Battles, and Political Philosophies		Constantine moved the capital of the Roman Empire to Byzantium, aka. Constantinople (330), by 395, when the kingdom was split in two, a war for primacy began East vs. West			
	Segmented Issues: Scientific discoveries, Women's Rights, Homosexual Rights, Economic advance					

Chart Five: Ten Roman Persecutions and Early General Councils

Foxe	Sleidan	N.S. Gill[1]	Emperor (dates of rule)	Dates	Location of persecution	Miscellaneous
1	1	1	Nero (54-64)	64	Rome	It was reported that the Christians were responsible for a fire that destroyed part of the city of Rome, thus they were persecuted; Tradition says that Peter and Paul were killed in Rome during this persecution
2	2	2	Domitian (81-96)	95	Rome and vicinity	Apparently, persecution broke out because the Jews refused to pay the poll tax in support of Capitalonus Jupiter; It was at this time that John was exiled to the island of Patmos
3	3	3	Trajan (98-117)		Bithynia	Organized under the governorship of Pliny the Younger; in a letter of Pliny to Trajan, he outlined the procedure when someone informed on a Christian, they were arrested, and if they answered three questions in the positive, they were put to death; It was during this persecution that Ignatius lost his life
		4	Hadrian (117-138)		Smyrna [?]	**Polycarp** lost his life by an enraged mob in Smyrna in the middle of the Second Century
						Montanism rose up in Asia Minor; "Tertullian becoming one of its ablest proponents"
4		5	Marcus Aurelius (161-180)		General, esp. Lyons and Vienna	Marcus was a devout stoic, biased against Christianity; ascribed calamities to the Christians, ordering persecution; Property of Christians should be given to their accusers; **Justin Martyr** lost his life in this persecution
5	4	6	Septimus Severus			Reigned from (222-235)
6		7	Maximinus the Thracian			Reigned from (235-238)
7	5	8	Decius (250-251)		General or universal	Severest persecution (for one year); Ordered an annual offering to the Roman gods; those who did received a *libellus*, those in the church often did not; Origen suffered leading to his death; The church then had to decide on what to do with lapsed members
8	6	9	Valerian (253-260)			Led to **Novatian schism**, on account of the reinstatement of lapsed Christians; two separate Bishops of Rome were elected: Cornelius and Novatian; the Novatian party, or the pure church, became considered "schismatic"
9	7		Aurelian (270-275)			Listed in Sleidan
10	8	10	Diocletian (284-305)	303-305; 4 edicts: 303, 303, 304, 305		Led to the **Donatist schism** (note letter of Gregory I to the Tetrarch of Numidia); Decree that all Christian services should cease, Bibles should be burned, all churches should be destroyed, all who held offices or posts in the army were to sacrifice to the gods, lose all rights of citizenship, prisoners who sacrificed to gods to be released, All Christians to be compelled to sacrifice; Labor camps (in mines) used as a punishment of some Christians
	9[2]		Maximian (286-305)			Co-emperor with Diocletian

---

[1]See about.com; available at: http://ancienthistory.about.com/od/earlychurch/f/10persecutions.htm (online); accessed: 28 Feb 2013; Internet.
[2]Sleidan did not seem to be looking for the number "10," as did Foxe and others due to Rev 2:10.

Chart Five: Ten Roman Persecutions and Early General Councils

7 ecum	Others	Leaders	Emperor and/or Pope; -dates of rule	Dates	Desired Breadth of Councils	Miscellaneous
		1	Galerius (305-311)	311		Deathbed Edict of Toleration, provided Christians did not disturb the peace of the Empire
		2	Constantine (306-337)	313		312, Constantine accepted Christianity under [Pope] Sylvester I, leading to the much argued "Donation of Constantine"; 313, Edict of Milan reaffirmed the 311 Edict of Toleration; 323, Constantine became the sole emperor; 337, baptized on his deathbed by the Arianizing bishop Eusebius of Nicomedia
		3	Livinius (308-324)			"Many write that the cause of this war was, for that Licinius did bitterly persecute the professors of Christianity, although he had been very often entreated and admonished to the contrary by Constantine" (Sleidan, 151)
1			Constantine [Pope] Sylvester	325	"Universal"	**Council of Nicea**, included 318 bishops, against Arius; produced Nicene Creed
			Constantine	330		Moved capital of Roman Empire to Constantinople (Byzantium), forming a division between the Eastern (Greek and Orthodox) and the Western (Latin and Catholic) Roman Empires
	1			340	?	**Synod of Gangra**, anathematized the shunning of marriage, forbidding the eating of meats, special dress, etc.
2			Theodosius I; Pope Damasus	381	"Universal"	**Council of Constantinople 1**, 150 bishops, against followers of Macedonius
		4	Theodosius	391; 393		Banned visits to pagan shrines; Banned pagan sacrifices
	2		Aurelius, Bishop of Carthage	418	?	**Council of Carthage**, against Pelagians and Donatists
3			Pope Celestine I	431	"Universal"	**Council of Ephesus**; more than 200 bishops present, Cyril of Alexandria presiding; against Nestorius' Christotokos (banished); condemned Pelagius
4			Marcian; Pope Leo I	451	"Universal"	**Council of Chalcedon**; 150 bishops present; defined two natures of Christ; against Eutyches, who was excommunicated
	3		30 bishops present	473	?	**Council of Arles**, against total depravity, particular atonement, and predestination
	4		Caesarius of Arles	529	"Universal"	**Second Council of Orange**, condemned so called semi-Pelagianism; affirmed sacramental view of infant baptism; received papal sanction
5			Justinian I Pope Vigilius	553	"Universal"	**Council of Constantinople 2**; Condemned errors of Origen; confirmed first four "general" councils as Chalcedon was contested by some heretics
		5	Pope Gregory I	590-604		Very prominent pope in first 1000 years of church; established Gregorian Calendar, Gallican Missal [using Latin language]; reorganized church offices (extra-NT titles); Emperor Maurice assassinated in 602; Papacy became Western Roman Empire's chief political office
6			Constantine Pogonatus Pope Agatho	680-681	"Universal"	**Council of Constantinople 3**; 174 Bishops, including Patriarchs of Constantinople and Antioch and the emperor; ended monothelitism, anathematized a number of people
7			Constantine VI; Pope Adrian I	787	"Universal"	**Second Council of Nicaea**; 300-367 bishops present; regulated veneration of holy images

Chart Six:

A Century by Century Quick View of Developments in Western Christianity

"There is therefore now no condemnation to those who are in Christ Jesus, who do not walk according to the flesh, but according to the Spirit. For the law of the Spirit of life in Christ Jesus has made me free from the law of sin and death. For what the law could not do in that it was weak through the flesh, God did by sending His own Son in the likeness of sinful flesh, on account of sin: He condemned sin in the flesh, that the righteous requirement of the law might be fulfilled in us who do not walk according to the flesh but according to the Spirit. For those who live according to the flesh set their minds on the things of the flesh, but those who live according to the Spirit, the things of the Spirit. For to be carnally minded is death, but to be spiritually minded is life and peace. Because the carnal mind is enmity against God; for it is not subject to the law of God, nor indeed can be. So then, those who are in the flesh cannot please God." Romans 8:1-8

As in a well-played game of Chess, now entering a third millennium, the major players in the game of Christian history have faced their opponent's moves and countermoves. While political maneuvering and battles are fairly simple to chart and plot, charting God's moves brings in another complexity. If one is open to the fact that God does move in history, and is, in fact, moving in and through Christian history, and if one is open to the fact that God moves through His Word proclaimed, through the Gospel of His Son received by faith alone, and through a wide variety of revivals and awakenings in history, then one is forced to leave the natural world of politics and wars to enter the world of spiritual warfare, fought with spiritual weapons wielded by prophets, evangelists, pastors, and teachers.

More disconcerting, then, become choosing sides. "Who is on the Lord's side" (Exod 32:26) and who is not? When, if ever, did the territorial state churches actually counter the moves of God through revivals and awakenings by promulgating decrees (Creeds) and by endorsing, encouraging, and exercising persecution? If they did not, then what do we do with revivals in history? In this case revivals in history were either human fabrication or clever deceptions from the Evil One. It is a matter of perspective deducing physical weapons or spiritual weaponry.

If territorial churches did counter God's actions in history through awakenings and revivals, then why follow their development in the name of Church History? While being mindful of the varieties of state church systems metamorphosing in different ways and at different rates throughout history, the following chart seeks to plot the seminal lines of drift of the Western territorial state church system away from the gospel and towards becoming a chief opponent of the movements of God in history.

The final page of this section includes a contemporary perspective of Roman Catholicism by Leonardo De Chirico, Pastor of a Reformed Baptist Church in Rome, Italy, Breccia di Roma.

Issue-Year	0-100		
Heresies[1]— Identified[a]	**Docetism**, first century, Christ's body was an illusion, He was primarily Spirit (thus Docetics are defined as having denied the humanity of Christ); **Gnosticism**: Requiring a special or mysterious knowledge for salvation; the material world is considered evil; but the spiritual world is considered good; Christ is the key to unlocking the mysteries to enter the spiritual world; some understand John's writings as having gnostic tendencies (1 John 2:15-17), as does also portions in the Pauline epistles (Gal 5:16-17; Col 1:27)		
Secondary Applications of Identified Heresies	**Docetism**: Can/has the above definition be leveled against those who believe that salvation has no "physical" or sacramental element, but is complete through hearing and believing alone? **Gnosticism**: Is not Gnosticism a guised attack on individual interpretation, especially being its 19th Century provenance? Positing a gnostic audience seems to force an allegorical interpretation of some Scripture, forcing it to be allegorized through a presupposed or imagined interpretive grid. Could not Gnosticism be attached to anyone who requires a "born again" experience to properly understand the Scriptures? Also positing an anti-gnostic hermeneutic could undermine individual interpretation (Freedom of Conscience), by which the individual believer has both the privilege and obligation to interpret Scripture for himself, quite apart from the dictates of a hierarchy or other authoritative person or body.		
Heresies— Unidentified[b]	That Peter and Paul founded the church in Rome appears contradicted by the biblical text of Romans and Acts. The book of Acts states that Paul wanted to go to Rome (Acts 19:21; 23:11) and finally did arrived there (Acts 28:14). Whereas, Paul wrote to the church of Rome prior to his ever being there (Rom 1:15). Neither does the name Peter [or Cephas] was ever used by Paul in the book of Romans.		
Early Councils	**Jerusalem Assembly**, ~49AD (cf. Acts 15): appears to be descriptive and not prescriptive; but its text is used to provide the precedent for: (1) Binding church councils; (2) An example of "going up" to a city [e.g. Rome] to receive apostolic insight into doctrinal matters in dispute (cf. Deut 17); (3) The writing of binding extra-biblical injunctions on any number of items: worship, lifestyle, or theological, with apostolic weight, using the precedent of the Acts 15 letter, as later cited in Acts 21		
"Heresies" in Communion	Paul spoke of disruptions in local church fellowship from rival factions in 1 Cor 1 to discord at the Lord's Supper in 1 Cor 11. The New Testament records the existence and prominence of false prophets and false teachers in its time, describing them in great detail in a number of places, and sometimes giving their names. John the Apostle also spoke of the Antichrist and of numerous antichrists. Further the Bible records a number of disorderly figures in the church at that time, such as Simon, Elymas, Alexander, and Diotrephes. So in conclusion, then, we have no pristine Apostolic Church during the time of the Apostles, nor do we have a pristine Early Church after the time of the Apostles (cf. Deut 31:27; Matt 24:4-5, 11, 24; Acts 20:29-30; 1 Tim 4:1-5; 2 Pet 2:1ff.).		
[Given] Bishops of Rome (later taking the title of Pope)[2]	St. Peter (32-67) St. Linus (67-76)	St. Anacletus (Cletus) (76-88) [presumably announced Church of Rome as head over all other churches[sl]]	St. Clement I (88-97) St. Evaristus (97-105)
Roman Emperors[3]	ROME ONLY[c]		
	Caesar Augustus (27BC-14AD)[d] Tiberius (14-37) Caligula (37-41) Claudius (41-54)	Nero (54-68) **Galba** (68-69) Otho (69) Vitellius (69) Vespasian (69-79)	Titus (79-81) Domitian (81-96) **Nerva** (96-98) Trajan (98-117)

[a]Like any political entity (e.g. U.S. Department of Transportation), does not an Emperor-sponsored church, by virtue of its very existence, affirm its authority by creating binding policies and procedures, unwavering rules and regulations, and through finding, arresting, and either fining, incarcerating, exiling, or executing all who disobey its absolute authority (cf. Rom 12)? No opposition to its policies can exist from a political-hierarchical point-of-view (e.g. one cannot have two opposing sets of "Rules of the Road"), Deut 17.

[b]Notice the not so subtle move away from preaching Jesus and the "Pauline Gospel" to fostering a proper intellectual assent to the "Orthodox View" of the Trinity—an important doctrine, but a shift none-the-less. What ever happened to the primary issues such as the reality of sin, the need for conversion, the substitutionary atonement, and justification by faith?

[c]It is quite impossible to list all competing senators and generals from various regions who fought, betrayed, poisoned, and killed for the title of Roman Emperor.

[d]Bold letters indicate a new change in dynasty of Roman Emperors, either a new dynasty, no dynasty, or the renewal of a previous dynasty.

[sl]all "sl" in this document indicates citations or references from Johannes Sleidan, *of the four chiefe Monarchies. Or, the key of History*; translated by Abraham Darcie [1550; London: M. Fletcher, 1627).

---

[1]Expanded from "List of Christian Heresies"; available at: http://en.wikipedia.org/wiki/List_of_Christian_heresies (online); accessed: 10 Sept 2012; Internet.

[2]"The List of Popes" available at: http://www.newadvent.org/cathen/12272b.htm (online); accessed: 1 July 2003; Internet. Annotations by author.

[3]"List of Roman Emperors"; available at: http://en.wikipedia.org/wiki/List_of_Roman_emperors (online); accessed: 12 Dec 2012; Internet.

Issue-Year	100-200		
Heresies—Identified	**Adoptionism**: Belief that the human body of Jesus was adopted at some point in time in His life by the Godhead taught by Theodotus of Byzantium around A.D. 190 (a.k.a. Psilanthropism and Dynamic Monarchianism); **Marcionism**: Marcion of Sinope, a type of gnostic, arrived in Rome, in 144AD, took Paul as chief apostle, rejected Hebrew Bible (OT); founded rival church; Tertullian wrote against his doctrine; **Monarchianism**: "Emphasis on the indivisibility of God (Father) at the expense of the other 'persons' of the Trinity tending toward either Saballianism (Modalism) or to Adoptionism."		
Secondary Applications of Identified Heresies	**Marcionite**: Applied to anyone with Dispensational tendencies, who may emphasize things like NT evangelism, NT theology, or a NT church; these ideas may be considered Marcionite; **Monarchianism**: Applied to those who differentiate the workings of the members of the Trinity: to the point of preaching "Christ"; being born of or filled with the "Holy Spirit"; consider: "Most evangelists have Monarchial tendencies!"		
Heresies— Unidentified	**Monasticism**: The retreat of **Monks (Cenobytic and Communal)** from the world marked a shift away from Christ's Great Commission, wherein followers of Jesus are specifically commanded to go out into the world to preach the gospel to nations and the people therein. For example, it was Gregory I (Pope from 590-604) that published and promoted the life of the cenobitic [lonely] monk Benedict of Nursia as an example of the truly consecrated Christian life. **Infant baptism** appears to have been opposed by Montanists; believer's baptism appears removed from early extant texts; Making the **Sign of the Cross**[4] was established[e] **Justin Martyr** (100-165) is typically put forward as the premier "Apologist" of the post-apostolic era of the church. Rarely is it mentioned that his type of apologetics does not correspond to that of the Apostle Paul, where the Greek verb ἀπολογέομαι (apologeomai) is twice used in Acts 26:1-2, followed by a description of how Paul shared the gospel with King Agrippa. Paul never provided ethical or philosophical arguments, never complained of his unlawful arrest, of his many beatings, nor of his long detention. Nor did Paul seek to prove the rational superiority of Christianity. Paul acted in accordance with his doctrinal position as explained in Rom 5:3, "And not only *that*, but we also glory in tribulations," as well as 1 Cor 1:17, "Christ did not send me to baptize but to evangelize." Putting forward Justin Martyr as a post-apostolic example of rational discourse in fulfillment of Christian mission displays an unbiblical shift in church-state relationships, and a move away from the Great Commission as found in Mark 16:15 and Luke 24:46-47. It is the first step in a series of steps that moves the student of Early Church history away from Evangelical convictions.		
Early Councils	**Council of Rome**, 155 A.D.[sl] **Council of Rome**, 193 A.D.[sl] **Council of Ephesus**, 193 A.D.[sl]		
"Heresies" in Communion	**Montanism**: Considered a charismatic-type sub-group, joined by the noted early church theologian Tertullian; given the territorial church's downgrade toward a sacramental view of the Holy Spirit in conversion, this division is hardly surprising **Ecclesiology**: Hierarchical church began to develop (under the pretext of combatting heresy) using OT organizational structures, Deut 17:9-13;		
[Given] Bishops of Rome (later taking the title of Pope)[5]	St. Evaristus (97-105) St. Alexander I (105-115) [Add pinch of salt to water][sl] St. Sixtus I (115-125)—also called Xystus I	St. Telesphorus (125-136) St. Hyginus (136-140) St. Pius I (140-155) St. Anicetus (155-166)	St. Soter (166-175) St. Eleutherius (175-189) St. Victor I (189-199) St. Zephyrinus (199-217)
Roman Emperors[6]	ROME ONLY		
	Trajan (98-117) Hadrian (117-138) Antoninus Pius (138-161)	Lucius Verus (161-169) Marcus Aurelius (161-180) Commodus (177-192) **Pertinax** (193)	Didius Julianus (193) Septimus Severus (193-211) Caracalla (198-217)

[e]Eventually prayers began to be addressed beyond "in the name of Jesus," but rather in the name of the Blessed Trinity, almost as a type of mantra, spell, or magic utterance. Further, as a focus on the Trinity overtook faith in Jesus (Rom 10:11) and His cross as the message (1 Cor 2:2), so justification by the Sacraments overtook justification by faith: Rom 10:4, "For Christ *is* the end of the law for righteousness to everyone who believes."

---

[4]Lorraine Boettner places this addition closer to A.D. 300 (Lorraine Boettner's "Chronological Listing of Roman Catholic Heresies and Inventions," *Roman Catholicism*, 5th ed. [Presbyterian and Reformed, 1962, 1967, 1976, 1985, 1989; Banner of Truth Trust, 1962, 1966; Baker, 1983], 7).
[5]Taken from website with the addition of notations; from: http://www.newadvent.org/cathen/12272b.htm; Accessed: 1 July 2003; Internet.
[6]From http://en.wikipedia.org/wiki/List_of_Roman_emperors; accessed: 12 Dec 2012.

Issue-Year	200-300			
Heresies—Identified	**Manicheanism**: a supposed dualistic doctrine said to be based on teachings of a certain Mani (210-276AD), condemned by Emperor Theodosius I decree in 382AD; **Sabbelianism**: "Belief that the Father, Son, and Holy Spirit are three characterizations of one God, rather than three distinct 'persons' in one God."			
Secondary Applications...	**Manicheanism**: was this used against those denying the fetishism of relics or the sacraments,[f] or misplaced holiness (Holy Water, Oil, Host), believing rather in new birth? "Evangelicals have Manichean tendencies" (Noll)[7]			
Heresies— Unidentified	**Ecclesiological Controversy**: congregational vs. bishop rule; local vs. non-local rule (of distant bishops), etc. **Missional Controversy**: Was the Great Commission verbalized by Christ to or for the collective whole of the church, hence under the direct authority of the increasingly complex web of church leaders (Patriarchs, Archbishops, and Bishops), or was it spoken to each individual obedient Christian to be obeyed as he was gifted and felt inclined? Moreover do the warnings about and examples of false teachers in the OT and NT also relate to false teaching about the fulfillment of the Great Commission? **Parish organization**: "The city of Rome had forty fully organized parish churches before the end of the third century"; France, 5th; England, 10th (Schaff-Herzog); e.g. Deut 21:1-9 **Titles for Church Leaders**: Not only did the office of "**bishop**" become a spiritual parallel to mayors, governors, senators, and/or emperors, but soon other non-NT names were used or invented, such as priest, Archbishop, Patriarch, Cardinal, etc. Battles over preeminent titles became intense between autocephalous territorial churches **Apostolic Successionism**: Churches sought a superior market niche by arguing along lines of human succession, sparking a debate over which church could prove its most ancient existence (Antioch) or most prominent early bishop (Rome, Peter; Constantinople, Andrew); authority shifted from which church truly preached the gospel in the power of the Holy Spirit to who was anointed with the proper oil of succession by the proper human organizational leader. **Fellowship Controversy**: Cyprian of Carthage (200-258) appeared to make fellowship with "the Church" a sign of theological orthodoxy above conformity to biblical doctrine; his famous line being: "outside the [Catholic] Church there is no salvation" [*extra Ecclesiam nulla salus*] reduced orthodoxy to approval from one particular church hierarchy—Rome. Other than circular reasoning, this statement of Cyprian begs the question, "which church?" Of what assembly or gathering are we speaking? Jesus in Revelation 2-3 identifies several very negative churches, that Christ called "churches," for example, to the church in Sardis, Jesus said, "but you are dead" (Rev 3:1).			
Other Councils	**Synod of Carthage**, 220 A.D.[sh] **Synod at Lambese** (Numidia), 240 A.D.[sh] **Council of Carthage**, 251 A.D.[sl] **Easter Synod** (Carthage), 252, 253, etc.[sh]	**Council of Carthage**, 255 A.D. (attended by 31 bishops)[sh] **Council of Carthage**, 256 A.D. (attended by 71 bishops)[sh]	**Council of Carthage**, 256 A.D. (attended by 87 bishops)[sh] **Council of Iconium**, 258 A.D.[sl] **Council of Antioch**, 264 A.D.[sl]	
"Heresies" in Communion	**Novatian schism**: two competing Bishops of Rome, Cornelius and Novatus; Cornelius' apparently denied being a Christian when faced with persecution in order to avoid death; **Donatists**: a similar 4-5th C. schism from Carthage in N. Africa; Augustine argued for the use of force against them			
Bishops of Rome	St. Zephyrinus (199-217) St. Callistus I (217-222) St. Urban I (222-230) St. Pontain (230-235)	St. Anterus (235-236) St. Fabian (236-250) St. Cornelius (251-253) "Anti-pope": Novatus (251-258)	St. Lucius I (253-254) St. Stephen I (254-257) St. Sixtus II (257-258) St. Dionysius (260-268)	St. Felix I (269-274) St. Eutychian (275-283) St. Caius (283-296), or: Gaius St. Marcellinus (296-304)
Roman Emperors	ROME ONLY			
	Septimus Severus (193-211) Caracalla (198-217) Geta (209-211) Macrinus (217-218) Elagabalus (218-222) Severus Alexander (222-235) **Maximinus I** (235-238) Gordian I (238)	Gordian II (238) Pupienas (238) Balbinus (238) Gordian III (238-244) Philip I (244-249) Trajan Decius (249-251) Hostilian (251)	Trebonianus Gallus (251-253) Aemilian (253) Valerian (253-260) Gallienus (253-268) Claudius Gothicus (268-270) Quintillus (270) Aurelian (270-275)	Tacitus (275-276) Florian (276) Probus (276-282) Carus (282-283) Numerian (283-284) Carinus (283-285) **Diocletian** (284-305)

[f]The fetishism of the sacraments is based on the fact that the Holy Spirit is made to pass in, with, and by the physical nature of the sign or symbol involved, such as water in Baptism, the host in communion, or the oil in Consecration or Extreme Unction. Hence, the two natures in Christ argument is leveraged to prove the need for a material to accompany the spiritual activity in operation in whatever sacrament is being applied.

[sh]All "sh" in this document stand for the *Schaff-Herzog Encyclopedia of Religious Knowledge*; available at www.ccel.org (online); accessed 18 Dec 2015.

[7]"Modifying the evangelical tendency to Manichaeism may cost some of the single-minded enthusiasm of activism, but it will be worth it in order to be able to worship God with the mind" (Mark Noll, *The Scandal of the Evangelical Mind* [Grand Rapids: Eerdmans, 1994], 245).

Issue-Year	300-400—Turning Point (TP) #1: Conquer with Earthly Sword				
Heresies—Identified	**Arianism**: declared heresy in 325, by Arius; presumably denied full deity of Christ; **Macedonians** or **Pneumatomachians** ("Spirit fighters"); "identified with 4th Cent. Bishop Macedonius I of		Constantinople, Eustathius of Sebaste their main theologian"; **Apollinarism**: declared heresy in 381		
Secondary Applications...	**Having Donatist Tendencies**: used for anyone who did not submit to Rome's interpretation as a final authority? **Problem**: Where does ultimate Church authority lay, Bible, the Crown, or the Bishop of Rome?				
Heresies— Unidentified	**Prayers to the dead**, as apparently taught in the Apocryphal Books; **Use of relics**, encouraging a theology of signs and symbols; **Conversion via infant Baptism** = reception of Holy Spirit due to the symbolic (spiritual) nature of the water? **Sign of the cross** became: 1. Constantine's sign by which to conquer; 2. Catholic special sign for prayer to a variety of recipients; 3. Sign later worn by those sworn to join a crusade **Emperor constitutes the true church**; Empire-controlled; non-local; non-congregational; disobeying church = treason contra emperor/king; Later, in A.D. 800, in a reflexive way, **the Church will constitute the true emperor**		**The Church Militant**" (used by Loyola and others) was a concept derived from Constantine seeing a cross in the sky and hearing "conquer with this"—the sign later used by those who joined in Holy Crusades **Veneration of angels and dead saints**; with an increase in the list of recipients of and respondents to prayer **Leaders called priests**, initiating the use of non-NT titles; **Mass** as daily celebration; bread gains spiritual power; Shift from preaching **"Jesus"** to emphasizing the **Trinity**; also shift from **particular atonement** to **general atonement**		
"Ecumenical" Councils[f]	1. **Council of Nicaea**,[g] 325 A.D.		2. **Council of Constantinople**, 381 A.D.		
Other Councils	**Council of Carthage**, 312 A.D., 70 bishops, excommunicated Caecilian[sh] **Council of Carthage**, 330 A.D., gathering 270 Donatist Bishops[sh]	**Synod of Gangra**, 340 A.D., anathematized the shunning of marriage, forbidding the eating of meats, special dress...[sl]	**1st Council at Carthage**, 345-48 A.D.[h] **Council of Antioch**, 363 A.D., replied to Pope's claims of Roman primacy[sl] **The Praetorium**, 389 A.D.[sh]	**2nd Council at Hippo**, 390 A.D.[h] **Hadrumetum**, 394 A.D. (et al.)[sh] **Council of Carthage**, 397 A.D.[sh]	
"Heresies" in Communion	**Centralized church government**, see Deut 17:9-13; 13:13-18.				
Bishops of Rome	St. Marcellinus (296-304) St. Marcellus I (308-309)[h] St. Eusebius (309 or 310)	St. Miltiades (311-14) St. Sylvester I (314-35) St. Marcus (336)	St. Julius I (337-52), pressed his primacy in convocating councils and weighty causes[sl]	Liberius (352-66) St. Damasus I (366-83)[i]	St. Siricius (384-99) St. Anastasius I (399-401)
The Fourth Century Splitting of Power	WESTERN WORLD			EASTERN WORLD	
	[in 330 A.D.] FROM ROME...[j]			...TO BYZANTIUM[j]	
Roman Emperors	Diocletian (284-305) Maximian (286-305) Constantius Chlorus (305-306) Galerius (305-311) Severus II (306-307)	**Constantine I** (306-337) Co-ruler: Licinius (308-324) Constantine's empire divided (A.D. 337) 1. Constantine II: Moroc-co, Spain, France, Britain	2. Constans: Carthage, Italy, Austria, Balkans 3. Dalmatius: Greece, et al. 4. Constantius: Egypt, Israel, Lebanon, Turkey	**Constantine I** (306-337) Maxentius (306-312) Maximinus II (311-313) Licinius I (308-324) Constantine II (337-340) Constantius II (337-361)	Constans I (337-350) Vetranio (350) Julian II (360-363) **Jovian** (363-364) **Valentinian I** (364-375) Valens (364-378)	Gratian (367-383) Valentinian II (375-392) **Theodosius I**, Great (379-395) Arcadius (383-408) Honorius (393-423)

[f]Renaming certain councils as "Ecumenical" allows historians to frame the question as to which are primary and worthy of study and which not, thereby limiting discussion by positing the need for certain number of bishops and/or those called by the Roman Emperor. Quite a few pre-Nicene councils did take place. It appears that few other councils are discussed unless they are deemed useful for some special reason, such as the Second Council of Orange (A.D. 529).

[g]It appears that the state began ruling over church in calling "Ecumenical" Councils, cf. 1 Cor 4:8. Who decided that the Nicene Creed was to become the "Rule of Faith" for the remainder of the history of the church? Nicaea did not restrain the church from drifting into the heresy of sacramentalism [a.k.a. Sacerdotalism].

[h]That Nicaea was not the first synod of Bishops was noted in Marcellus I's decree (308 A.D.) that Bishops of Rome alone had authority to call synods of Bishops (Sleidan, 149-150). The historiographic question is, who has the right to call a council, and/or to number or count them as official councils?

[i]Saying of Damasus, "Whoever the Bishop is, be it at *Rome, Eugubius, Constantinople, Rhegium,* or *Alexandria,* he is of the same demerit and Priesthood."[sl]

[j]Consider the ongoing political and religious impact of the one decision of Constantine in 330 A.D. to move the Capital of Rome to Byzantium or Constantinople! In effect Constantine divided the fourth monarchy of Daniel 2, 7, 9 into two large monarchies, East and West, that splintered into many other subgroupings.

Issue-Year	400-450			
Heresies—Identified	Nestorianism:[k] Nestorius taught that Mary was *Christotokos*, Mother of Christ, or mother of the human side of Jesus, but not Mother of God; he was accused of dividing the substance of Christ; a corollary issue may relate to the human role in salvation via giving and receiving the Sacraments			
Secondary Appl.	Nestorian: Anyone shunning Mary as "Mother of God" is considered to have Nestorian tendencies			
Heresies—Unidentified	Augustine, growing champion of politically-controlled church, fiercely condemned a Donatist 'priest' for rebaptizing a Catholic Began use of coercion against rival churches; Freedom of conscience deeded to Bishop of Rome as centralized authority (as in OT); Augustine's just war ideas seem to have been later used to justify crusades and inquisition; Sacramental salvation: Augustine, as a devotee of Ambrose, loaned his intellectual prowess to further the cause of salvation through the Sacraments, with a focus on "signs and symbols" However, the focus of faith in Rom 1:16 is not the symbol of the sacrament, but the content of the gospel; Then, strange as it may seem, the "Symbol of Faith" grew to be considered the Nicene Creed, which never mentions sin, substitution, or justification by faith, all of which are very important to the Book of Romans Further, the Nicene Creed did not halt the church of Rome from drifting into a sacramental salvation, thus it did not inhibit heresy—or at least not sacramentalism Latin and "Rule by forced linguistic conformity or uniformity": Greek with Alexander then Latin with Caesar	Jerome's Latin Vulgate,[l] commissioned in 382 by Pope Damasus, formalized and codified sacramental salvation/worship: Restricted freedom of conscience in choosing a Latin Bible translation; Provided the means by which the Church of Rome (1) maintained authority over the text of Scripture, as they own the copyright over Jerome's Vulgate, (2) maintained its monopoly as a church—the ongoing power of the church of Rome through Latin—and the Latin alphabet—demonstrates that we are still experiencing the fourth "chief monarchy" of Dan 2 and 7, and (3) seek to maintain a level of control over doctrine; Latin as Interloper: Preeminence given to Latin language; yet God never assigned Latin as an original language as He did Hebrew and Greek?[m] With language comes the cultural mantle to protect the text: so the Masoretes protected the Hebrew Scriptures, as the Greeks monks did the NT and LXX—further, the spoken language protects interpretation; Restricting education to Latin accentuated the divide between the clergy (who knew Latin) and the laity (who did not); Transfer the complexity of learning Latin to the complexity of properly understanding the Scriptures, further limiting the Bible's readership; Highlighting that a language is "dead" released it from the interpretive shackles of common cultural usage of thousands or millions of mother tongue speakers—interpretations of a "dead" language can be manipulated and tweaked to fit predetermined breadth of thought; Language (especially a "dead" one that has to be learned by everyone) is combined with religion, culture, and politics to form a powerful mix; Teaching a language (like Latin) frames the thoughts of the learner (e.g. like using Peter the Lombard's *Four Books of Sentences* to teach Latin); E.g. Mohammed seems to have learned the power of a unified language (as did Gregory I) when he restricted the study of the Koran to Arabic only; Mary raised to the title of "Mother of God"; Bishop of Rome took name "Peter, Prince of the Apostles" Emperor Valentinian III gave unilateral power over church affairs to the Bishop of Rome [which power he had no biblical authority to give]			
"Ecum." Council	3. Council of Ephesus, 431AD			
Other Councils	Council of Mileve, 402 A.D.[sh] General Synod, 403 A.D., Laid down formula to be accepted by Donatists[sh] Synod of 404 A.D., Led to repression of schismatics[n]	3rd Council of Carthage, 411 A.D., Largest African Council; led to violent suppression of the Donatists. 4th Council of Carthage, 418 A.D., Voted in favor of Augustine and against Pelagian and Donatists.		6th Council of Carthage, 419 A.D., Boniface of Rome sought primacy based on Council of Nice, was proven wrong by official decrees from Alexandria and Constantinople.
Bishops of Rome	St. Anastasius I (399-401) St. Innocent I (401-17)	St. Zosimus (417-18) St. Boniface I (418-22)	St. Celestine I (422-32) St. Sixtus III (432-40)	St. Leo I (the Great) (440-61)
Roman, Byzantine,[8] or Holy Roman Emperors[9]	BYZANTIUM (aka. East)		ROME (aka. West)	
	Arcadius (383-408) Honorius (393-423)[o]	Theodosius II (402-450)	Honorius (393-423)[o] Constantius III (421)	Joannes (423-425) Valentian III (424-455)

[k] "Any history of Christianity that fails to pay due attention to these Jacobites and Nestorians is missing a very large part of the story" (Jenkins, *The Lost History*, xi).

[l] E.g. consider, Jerome's "do penance" instead of "repent" 69 times (DRA), the sin of luxury instead of licentiousness (Gal 5:19), ceremonies (Deut 4:8), etc.

[m] Language wars ensued, "Latin must increase, Hebrew and Greek must decrease"; Hebrew eventually disappeared, yet Greek remained a dominant world language because of Byzantium for another 1,000 years.

[n] Many other synods and councils were held against the Donatist Controversy, who by repressive measures were forced to capitulate to the views of Augustine.

[o] Gray highlighting indicates that a particular ruler ruled over both Eastern and Western Empires—after Constantine moved the capital from Rome to Byzantium.

[8] From: http://en.wikipedia.org/wiki/List_of_Byzantine_Emperors; accessed: 20 Dec 2012.

[9] From: http://en.wikipedia.org/wiki/List_of_holy_roman_emperors; accessed: 20 Dec 2012; Apparently, the word "Holy" derives from the 1157 AD precedent of Frederick Barbarossa.

Issue-Year	450-500—TP #2: Mainstreaming a Works Salvation			
Heresies—Identified	[The state-church system began to mainstream a works salvation, thereby stumbling over Christ, Rom 9:33; to cover their error they framed numerous heresies focused against the "Scriptures alone, faith alone, and grace alone" group, apparently using the **fallacy of composition**]			
Secondary Applications...	**Christological controversy** required physical elements as media for spiritual effect; cf. *ex opere operato*, "from the work worked" [from the physical elements rightfully used and applied the Holy Spirit's work is actually effectuated]			
Heresies—Unidentified	Greatest debate of the time: **sacramental versus evangelical salvation**—appears debate is hidden by reframing issues; **Predestination** and **limited atonement** anathematized; Rome adopted a general atonement approach to salvation, sympathetic to both state church rule and infant baptism; **Bishop of Rome** took control over the two powers, ecclesial and political: this battle over church/state control raged until Gregory VII (1073-85) and Boniface VIII (1294-1303); became catalyst for 1st Amendment of U.S. Constitution; **Sacraments** provided Rome its monopoly **Simon Stylites** (388-459) is venerated as a saint, a Syrian ascetic who sat on top of a pillar for 37 years; the prominence of his life in histories portrays the historian's redefinition of the Great Commission away from the NT precedent as found in the Book of Acts (cf. Luther's Commentary on Galatians 1:8-9).			
Ecum Councils	4. Council of Chalcedon, 451AD°			
Other Councils	**Council of Arles**, 473AD, condemned total depravity, particular atonement, predestination, and double predestination, as well as teaching that baptism does not save. **Synod of Carthage**, 484 A.D., called by Vandal King Huneric, to impose Arianism on certain African Sees.			
Bishops of Rome	St. Leo I (the Great) (440-461)p St. Hilarius (461-468) St. Simplicius (468-483)	St. Felix III(II) (483-492) St. Gelasius I (492-496)		Anastasius II (496-498) St. Symmachus (498-514)
Roman Emperors, Byzantine Emperors, or Holy Roman Emperors	BYZANTIUM		ROME	
	Marcian (450-457) **Leo I** (457-474) Leo II (474)	Zeno (474-475, 476-491) Basiliscus (475-476) Anastasius I (491-518)	Valentian III (424-455) **Petronius Maximus** (455) **Avitus** (455-456) **Maiorian** (457-461) Libius Severus (461-465) Anthemius (467-472) Olybrius (472); Glyrecius (473-474)	**Julian Nepos** (474-475 [480]) **Romulus Augustus** (475-476) Leo I (457-474); Leo II (474) Zeno (474-475, 476-491) Basiliscus (475-476) Anastasius I (491-518)

pLeo I requested that the general councils be in Italy rather than in Asia, so that he could attend, "but he obtained nothing"sl

Issue-Year	500-600			
Heresies—Identified	**Monothelitism**: taught that Jesus had two natures but only one will; leaving room for spiritual salvation without the physical nature of a Sacrament; **Pelagianism**: said to oppose predestination, emphasized man's freewill—without the divine aid of [infant] baptism?			
Secondary Applications...	**Pelagian**: anyone who evangelizes and calls people to repent and believe without the aid of prior Baptism			

Heresies— Unidentified	**Infant Baptism** equated with **spiritual rebirth**, a general atonement approach to conversion; rather than each person repenting and believing for himself, physical water affects spiritual result, conversion and Great Commission redefined;
	Evangelization of those previously infant baptized deemed heretical;
	Benedictine vows: spiritual maturity redefined away from a NT model:
	  Voluntary poverty (living from alms),
	  Required sexual abstinence, and
	  Obedience to a human superior.
	Forged Document Gives Rome Authority: In a [forged] document to Rome, Justinian "calls him, the Head of all the Churches, and subjects all to him"[sl]
	On Gregory's Mission to the Britons: Did Gregory I leverage Briton slaves, finding their culture already evangelized, to Rome's ecumenical and territorial gains?			

Ecumenical Councils	5. **2nd Council of Constantinople**, 553AD			
Other Councils	**North African Synod**, 525 A.D., attended by 60 bishops.[sh] **Second Council of Orange**, 529AD, affirmed [infant] baptism alone as initial reception of grace, anathematized double-predestination **North African Synod**, 535 A.D., attended by 217 bishops.[sh]			

Bishops of Rome	St. Symmachus (498-514)
	St. Hormisdas (514-23)
	St. John I (523-526)
	St. Felix IV/III (526-530)
		Boniface II (530-532)
		John II (533-535)
		St. Agapetus I (535-536),[q]
		  aka. Agapitus
			St. Silverius (536-537)[n]
			Vigilius (537-555)[n]
			Pelagius I (556-561)
			John III (561-574)
				Benedict I (575-579)
				Pelagius II (579-590)
				St. Gregory I (the Great)
				  (590-604)

	BYZANTIUM		**ROME**	
Roman Emperors, Byzantine Emperors, or Holy Roman Emperors	Anastasius I (491-518) **Justin I** (518-527) Justinian I, the Great (527-565) Editor of Justinian's Code Empress Theodora removed three Bishops of Rome during this time[n]	Justin II (565-578) Tiberius II Constantine (578-582) Maurice (582-602)	Anastasius I (491-518) **Justin I** (518-527) Justinian I, the Great (527-565), editor of Justinian's Code	Justin II (565-578) Tiberius II Constantine (578-582) Maurice (582-602)

[q]The Empress Theodora was said to have removed all three popes, Agapetus, Silverius, and Virgilius, for their dealings with Anthemius, Patriarch of Constantinople.[sl]

Issue-Year	600-700—TP #3: Dividing Eastern-Western Europe				
Heresies—Identified	A controversy erupted between Gregory I and Patriarch John IV of Constantinople, who had claimed the title of "Universal Bishop"[r]; Emperor Phocas, after massacring his predecessor and family,* to the praise of Gregory I, later removed the title from Constantinople, giving it to Boniface III of Rome in 607				
Secondary Applications…	*The death of Emperor Maurice ended the unified Roman Empire, resulting in an East-West scenario—where it remains today!				
Heresies—Unidentified	Gregory I decried destruction of **druid and pagan holy places** in Britain, contra Matt 17:4; commended use of "holy water"; Gregory I taught **Purgatory** as a place to purge sin after death; **Seven Cardinal Sins** expounded;[s] **Latin required**:[t] leveraged linguistic control of church, state, and education vs. mother tongue or Bible in Greek or Hebrew;		**Prayers** to Mary, angels, and dead saints: developing large levels of Roman Catholic pantheon acceptable for prayer; **Title of Pope** ("Father") given to Bishop of Rome, further moving the Western Church away from a New Testament church model		
Ecumenical Councils	6. **3rd Council of Constantinople**, 680-681AD				
"Heresies" in Communion	Gregory I turned his pen against the Donatists of North Africa, requesting use of economic prejudice and political force; Queen Theodolinda gave Gregory I a crown of iron, later placed on Charlemagne as 1st Holy Roman Emperor[10] 649, **Lateran Council** included 20 canons for anathematizing all who disagreed with all the details of first five Ecumenical Councils				
Bishops of Rome	St. Gregory I (the Great) (590-604), often considered the first Pope of the **Medieval era** or **Dark Ages** Sabinian (604-606)	Boniface III (607) St. Boniface IV (608-615) St. Deusdedit (Adeodatus I) (615-618) Boniface V (619-625)	Honorius I (625-638) Severinus (640) John IV (640-642) Theodore I (642-649) St. Martin I (649-655)	St. Eugene I (655-657) St. Vitalian (657-672) Adeodatus (II) (672-676) Donus (676-678) St. Agatho (678-681)	St. Leo II (682-683) St. Benedict II (684-685) John V (685-686) Conon (686-687) St. Sergius I (687-701)

Roman Emperors, Byzantine Emperors, or Holy Roman Emperors	BYZANTIUM		ROME	
	Maurice (582-602)[u] **Phocas** (602-610) **Heraclius** (610-641)- Heraclian Dynasty Constantine III (641) Heraklonas (641) Constans II (641-668)	Constantine IV, the Bearded (668-685) Justinian II, the slit nosed (685-695) **Twenty Years Anarchy Leontios** (695-698) Tiberius III (698-705)	Maurice (582-602)[q]	

[r]Was Gregory I jealous in saying that a person taking that title was "blasphemous, antichristian, and diabolical, by whomsoever assumed" (H.T. Hudson, *Papal Power*, 31)?

[s]These seven cardinal sins are: pride, greed, envy, anger, luxury, gluttony, and laziness. These are virtually opposite to the Seven Virtues of the Greek Stoics.

[t]With the monopoly of use of Latin for higher education in the Western World: "All [educational] roads [must-needs] lead to Rome." Monopolizing education by the use of Latin ensured Rome's future dominance culturally, historically, economically, and spiritually [compare with Islam's use of Arabic]. Simultaneously thwarting any serious competition to this centralized dominance. Thus, while each Western tongue has its place, Latin where they all meet. Linguistically, the Greeks have nothing to prove.

[u]Maurice killed by his general Phocas (602)—was the Bishop of Rome an innocent bystander? His death splintered the **Western Roman Empire** and ended the **Classical era** [Greek dominated era]; yet the **Byzantine Empire** (ruled from Constantinople), increased in strength and territory for another Five Centuries; the Bishop of Rome, receiving the title of Universal Bishop, later applied the title of Emperor to territorial warriors; had Gregory I foreseen the possibilities of such power for Latin conquest? Could he have imagined the complexity of ruling the world by proxy through leaders in different lands or through Bishops acting as vice-regents to young kings and queens? Did God foresee him as a ruler above other city-states, choosing emperors to his own liking and for his own purposes (e.g. Dan 2 & 7)?

---

[10]Of crowning: "He [Pompey] caused King *Tigranes* to yield himself over into his hands, and seeing him abased and forlorn in his camp, advanced him, as *Cicero* writes, and placing the Diadem upon his head again which he had taken from him, under certain cautions commanded him to reign again" (Sleidan, *of the four chiefe Monarchies*, 95; spelling modernized).

Chart Six: A Century by Century Quick View of Developments in Western Christianity

Issue-Year	700-800			
Heresies—Identified	Iconoclastic Controversy from 730-1054: over **veneration of statues** (East vs. West), including the use of statues versus what became Holy Icons; the result was mutual excommunication; Augustine had already joined the First and Second Commandments into one, dividing the tenth into two			
Secondary Applications...	Those who were against statues and images were vilified as not submitting to the Bishop of Rome			
Heresies—Unidentified	**Kissing of Pope's foot** established; **Worship of cross, images, and relics**: further leading to fetishism and a theology of signs and symbols, later codified in Peter the Lombard's *Four Books of Sentences* (c. 1161 AD);		**Successionism Questions**: did the anointing oil ever fail in allowing for proper godly apostolic succession when some Popes lived in obvious sin? Can physical oil maintained and handled by men ever be deemed infallible in its application (*ex opere operato*)? Does not the existence of named wicked men in the lineage of Jesus not undermine the holy nature of any succession?	
Ecumenical Councils	7. **2nd Council of Nicaea**, 787AD			
"Heresies" in Communion	752, Childeric was dethroned by Pope Zachary;v that year Pepin, grandfather of Charlemagne was crowned king by [St] Boniface, Bishop of Mainz; 754, Pepin was recrowned king of the Franks by Pope Stephen,w rewarding his assistance in a war against the Lombards for protection of the Eternal City (Rome)			
Bishops of Rome	St. Sergius I (687-701) John VI (701-707) Sisinnius (708) Constantine (708-715)	St. Gregory II (715-731) St. Gregory III (731-741) St. Zachary (741-752)x	Stephen II (752) Stephen III (752-757) St. Paul I (757-767)	Stephen IV (767-772) Adrian I (772-795) St. Leo III (795-816)
	BYZANTIUM		ROME	
Roman Emperors, Byzantine Emperors, or Holy Roman Emperors	Tiberius III (698-705) Justinian II, the slit nosed (705-711) Philippikos Bardanes (711-713) Anatasios II (713-715) Theodosios III (715-717) **Leo III, the Isaurian [Dynasty] (717-741)**	Constantine V, the dung-named (741-775) Artabasdos (741-743) Leo IV, the Khazar (775-780) Constantine VI (780-797) Irene of Athens (797-802)	[n.a.]	

vBy the pope dethroning a King, it testified that he had perceived, revered, and accepted his power over the king.

wLikewise the Pope crowning a king did two things: (1) Placed Pope above the king; (2) Made king a fief of the Pope; and (3) made the king's estates a fiefdom of Pope (as spiritual tributaries). Now the kings and their states became an arm of the church; which explains the later indulgences as a form of taxation.

x"Zacharias satisfied his requests [Bishop Boniface] and permitted Bishoprics at Merburgh, Bamberg, and Erphord; and also gave him leave to go to Charlemagne, Charles Martel his son, who was desirous to have a Council held in his presence in some city of the French Kingdom and that he might diligently reform the abuses of the Church, but most especially remove adulterers" (Sl., 221-22).

Issue-Year	800-900—TP #4: The Return to an Earthly Sword: Transubstantiation First Taught		
Heresies—Identified			
Secondary Applications...	Appears that early church Trinitarian and Christological arguments were being used against the Paulicians		
Heresies—Unidentified	**Church constituted an existing state**: Pope Leo III crowned Charlemagne as Holy Roman Emperor (H.R.E.)[11] Several **Pseudonymous** creeds and works authored, such as the "Creed of Athanansius" which promoted intellectual assent to a specific belief in the Trinity as synonymous to salvation **Records destroyed** in Rome; Rome began rewriting history and eliminating any negative records from this point; applying "Nihil Obstat"—or "nothing opposing"	**Salt** added to "Holy Water," adding a touch of Druidism to the rite of Baptism, as the water was now deemed to be holy and intrinsically spiritual (having new spiritual powers), plus giving this water salvific powers **Transubstantiation** added to Sacrifice of the Mass: the same qualities (as Holy Water) were conjured with the bread at Mass, accomplishing two things: making Rome the only proper source of a true "Holy Host" and necessitating that people, if they wanted true spiritual food, had to attend Mass at a "Catholic" Church	
Ecumenical Councils	8. Fourth Council of Constantinople, 869AD		
"Heresies" in Communion	Paulicians, repressed by Emperess Theodora II in 843		
Bishops of Rome	St. Leo III (795-816) Stephen V (816-817) St. Paschal I (817-824) Eugene II (824-827) Valentine (827) Gregory IV (827-844)	Sergius II (844-847) St. Leo IV (847-855) Benedict III (855-858) St. Nicholas I (858-867)[y] Adrian II (867-872) John VIII (872-882)	Marinus I (882-884) St. Adrian III (884-885) Stephen VI (885-891) Formosus (891-896)—6 popes in 3 yrs; 3 in 1 year! Formusus exhumed and excommunica-ted in "Cadaver Synod" (897) Boniface VI (896)	Stephen VII (896-897) Romanus (897) Theodore II (897) John IX (898-900)
Byzantine Emperors or Holy Roman Emperors	BYZANTIUM		WEST [Germanic Roman Empire][z]	
	Irene of Athens (797-802) **Nikephoros I** (802-811) Staurakios (811-812) Michael I (812-813) **Leo V** (813-820)	**Michael II** (820-829) Theophilos (829-842) Micheal III (842-867) **Basil I** (867-886) Leo VI (886-912)	**Charles I** (800-814), Holy Roman Empire founded Louis I (816-840) Lothair I (823-855) Louis II (850, 872-875) Charles II, "le gros" (875-877)	Charles III (881-888) **Guy** (891-894) Lambert (892-898) **Arnulf** (896-899) **Louis III** (901-905)

[y]There seems an interesting stretch of time when no pope is called "saint" after St. Nicholas (858-867).

[z]The "Holy Roman Empire" was boldly established and sanctioned by the Pope Leo III 470 years after Constantine had moved the capital to Byzantium; from 602-800 there was sporadic Eastern rulership; the French call this new empire the "Holy Germanic Roman Empire" (*Saint Empire Romain Germanique*), the Germans call it the "Holy Roman Empire of the German Nation" (*Heiliges römisches Reich deutscher Nation*), the First Kingdom (First Reich), or the Old Empire (see Wikipedia.fr).

[11]When the Church of Rome formally identified itself with the historic Roman Empire by using the term "Holy Roman Empire" (H.R.E.), it appears that they made a decision that Jesus decried in Matt 23:29-33, wherein the Jews of His day were adorning the monuments of the prophets, and saying, "if we had lived in those days of our fathers, we would not have participated with them in the blood of the prophets" (v. 30). In 800, when it formed the political H.R.E., the Church of Rome identified itself with that which was formerly a persecutor of the church, including the illegal trial and murder of Christ and the city where Paul was in prison, as well as the many Martyrs in the major persecutions before Constantine. It was not a big surprise that its predecessor was already a persecutor of the Evangelical church.

Issue-Year	900-1000			
Heresies—Identified				
Secondary Applications...	Appears that early church Trinitarian and Christological arguments also used against the early Cathars			

Heresies—Unidentified	**College of Cardinals** established—further moving the Church of Rome away from a NT church leadership model
	Fasting on Fridays and lent—church forcing food regulations on the cultures it controlled (as a spiritual theocracy), contra Rom 14 and 1 Tim 4:
	  Those not submitting to food laws became guilty of high treason against the emperor or king
	  Ecclesiastical codes were designated with the highest level of criminal activities
	Historical Revisionism by means of extant sources: Significant historical revisionism took place in the 800s-900s in the area of destroying papal archives and only reproducing sources suitable to promote viewpoints acceptable to the church at that time; sources not complementing official views were either (1) not reproduced or (2) were destroyed outright
	Homosexuality Mainstreamed: Given its divisive nature in U.S. churches today, it is amazing that homosexuality never led to any major canonical actions. Rather Pope Leo IX merely responded to the complaint of Pierre Damien by slapping the wrists of certain homosexuals in *Ad splendidum nitentis* ["On Brightly Shining"] as reported in the Symbols and Creeds of the Church[12]			

Early Ecumenical Councils				
"Heresies" in Communion	[Byzantine Emperor and Archbishop of Constantinople offered Tomislav the realm of Croatia in 923 AD, then crowned by Pope John X in 925 AD, expanding Rome's Western influence further Eastward]			
Bishops of Rome	Benedict IV (900-903) Leo V (903) Sergius III (904-911) Anastasius III (911-913) Lando (913-914) John X (914-928)	Leo VI (928) Stephen VIII (929-931) John XI (931-935) Leo VII (936-939) Stephen IX (939-942) Marinus II (942-946)	Agapetus II (946-955) John XII (955-963) Leo VIII (963-964) Benedict V (964) John XIII (965-972) Benedict VI (973-974)	Benedict VII (974-983) John XIV (983-984) John XV (985-996) Gregory V (996-999) Sylvester II (999-1003)

	BYZANTIUM		WEST [Germanic Roman Empire]	

Byzantine Emperors or Holy Roman Emperors	Leo VI (886-912)
	Alexander III (912-913)
	Constantine VII (913-959)
	Romanos I (920-944)
		Romanos II (959-963)
		Nikophoros II (963-969)
		John I (969-976)
		Basil II (976-1025)
			Louis III (901-905)
			  Conrad (911-918)[t]
			Berengar (915-925)
			  Henry (919-936)[aa]
				Otto I (962-973)
				  [coronation dates]
				Otto II (967-983)
				Otto III (996-1002)

[aa]Election date cited, since there was apparently no coronation by a Pope for these emperors.

---

[12]"But because we act with a great humanity, we desire and we command, confident of divine mercy, that those who, ... [the text then details three of four positions of homosexual deviancy], and who have not done it by long habit or with several, if they have refrained from their sexuality and if they have expiated their infamous acts by just penitence, be admitted to the same position in which they could not have remained forever had they remained in their misdeed" (DS 688).

Issue-Year	1000-1100—TP #5: Millennialism: Take Up the Heavenly Sword[bb]			
Heresies—Identified	Numerous regional and local councils were held against heretics The non-celibacy of priests became an issue			
Heresies—Unidentified	**Burning Alive Heretics** began in 1002AD,[13] which eventually included the turning over of heretics to be put to death by secular hands, much like Jesus was killed by the Roman guards **Attendance at Mass** (along with its financial support) became obligatory for all citizens within the realm of Catholic rulers	**Transubstantiation** canonized; thus the bread of the Eucharist was worshiped as the very body of Christ, and the wine for being the very blood of Christ, following the prayer of consecration **Celibacy of all priests** decreed in **1st Lateran Council** **Sexual immorality** of celibate priests was a problem [DS 688] **Rosary Beads** with prayer invented for use by Rome's faithful		
Medieval Western Councils	Numerous regional and local councils were held against heretics			
"Heresies" in Communion	1054AD, Mutual excommunication: Pope and Eastern Patriarch **English Crusade**: church and crown returned to Rome by crusade under Archbishop Lanfranc and William the Conqueror			
Bishops of Rome (later taking the title of Pope)	Sylvester II (999-1003) John XVII (1003) John XVIII (1003-09) Sergius IV (1009-12) Benedict VIII (1012-24) John XIX (1024-32) Benedict IX (1032-45) Sylvester III (1045) [considered "anti-pope" in 1044?] "Three contended for the Papacy, and what they attempted was by all sinister practices"[sl]	Benedict IX (1045) –Benedict IX, second of three reigns? Gregory VI (1045-46) Clement II (1046-47) Benedict IX (1047-48) Damasus II (1048) St. Leo IX (1049-54) Victor II (1055-57) Stephen X (1057-58)	Benedict X, deposed[sl] Nicholas II (1058-61) Alexander II (1061-73) St. Gregory VII (1073-85): transubstantiation; "Dictatus Papae" Clement III, "anti-pope" (1080-1100) Blessed Victor III (1086-87) Blessed Urban II (1088-99), famous for preaching crusades Paschal II (1099-1118)	
	BYZANTIUM		WEST	
Holy Roman Emperors	Basil II (976-1025) Constantine VIII (1025-1028) Zoe (1028-1050) Romanos III (1028-1034) Michael IV (1034-1041) Michael V (1041-42) Theodora (1042-56) Constantine IX (1042-1055)	**Michael VI** (1056-57) **Isaac I** (1057-1059) **Constantine X** (1059-1067) Michael VII (1067-1078) Romanos IV (1068-1071) Nikephoros III (1078-1081) **Alexios I** (1081-1118)	Otto III (996-1002) [...] Henry II (1014-1024) [...]**Conrad II** (1027-1039)	[...] Henry III (1046-1056) [...] Henry IV (1084-1105)

[bb]One gets the impression that the new millennium marked a massive change in vision for the Church of Rome—she becomes much more aggressive and hostile up until the time of Napoleon (1800); Rome becomes adept at ruling over several kingdoms simultaneously, using the Western Emperor to regain lost territories and to increase its territorial acquisitions—hence the most militant leaders appeared to become Holy Roman Emperors (as good "Defenders of the Faith"), much as a preview to the colonialism of the 15th-19th Centuries.

---

[13]Was there not some kind of nunc-millennial [now-millennial] ethos among the Bishops of Rome (the "Eternal City") that led to their burning of heretics not long after the turn of the second millennium (cf. Rev 21:8)? If Christ was truly present in the person of the Pope, then he could not abide sin (Rev 21:27; 22:15; Amos 7:12-13), ergo must send heretics to literal flames!

Issue-Year	1100-1200—TP #6: Take Up the Sword of Justice; Sacramental Theology Codified				
Heresies— Identified	**3rd Lateran Council**: dealt with problem of competing popes ("anti-Popes"), condemned named heretics in Southern France (§23)		**Local Financial Support** of a church disallowed (self-supporting) **Marriage of Clergy** condemned		
Heresies— Unidentified	**The Four Books of Sentences** of **Peter [the] Lombard** (d. 1160) became the central reference point for doctrinal study and for determining doctrinal faithfulness to the "Faith once and for all delivered to the saints" "**Signs and symbols**" became the Central Interpretive Motif (CIM) for salvation and theology in Lombard's *Sentences* (Bk. 1, Dist. 1, Ch. 1)[14] The emotive term, "**Anti-Pope**," so-named for church leaders being locally appointed or elected as autocephalous (self-ruling) hierarchies within the Western Church territorial region, presupposes (1) that there can only be one Pope, or representative of Christ on earth, and (2) that regional self-rule is to be "anti" the Church, its unity, and its love		**Seven Sacraments** made necessary under pain of anathema "**Baptism of Desire**" established as a downgrade of true baptism **Inquisitors** protected from reprisals of any local people (2LC, §15) Pope assumed **Dual Power** (over entirety of church and all states) **Episcopal Inquisition** established by Alexander III—Bishop responsible to eliminate all heretics from their diocese **Matilda of Tuscany** bequeathed her territory to the temporal rule of the bishop of Rome[15] **Papal Inquisition** established by Innocent III (travelling teams with papal authority to travel from diocese to diocese)		
Medieval Western Councils	9. **1st Lateran Council**, 1123AD		10. **2nd Lateran Council**, 1139AD		11. **3rd Lateran Council**, 1179AD
"Heresies" in Communion	**Henricians** and **Petrobusians** multiplied in Southern France **Synod of Saint-Félix** (France): in 1167 **Orthodox Bishop Nicetas** anointed six Cathar bishops in Southern France: Bernard Raimond, Bishop of Toulouse; Guiraud Mercier, Bishop of Carcassonne; Raimond de Casals, Bishop of Agen; Robert d'Epernon, Bishop of France; Sicard Cellerier, Bishop of Albi; and Marc, Bishop of Lombardy[16] **Waldenses** (Poor men of Lyons) were anathematized				
Bishops of Rome (later taking the title of Pope)	Paschal II (1099-1118) Gelasius II (1118-1119), driven to France Callistus II (1119-1124), First Lateran Council Honorius II (1124-1130)	Innocent II (1130-1143), at first considered an "anti-pope"; 2nd Lateran Council, followers of the monk Henry condemned in this time (Cathars in Laurangais, France) Celestine II (1143-1144) Lucius II (1144-1145)	Blessed Eugene III (1145-1153) Anastasius IV (1153-1154) Adrian IV (1154-1159) Alexander III (1159-1181); called **3rd Lateran Council**, which sanctioned the Inquisition Lucius III (1181-1185)	**Sporadic Multiple Popes during this Time** **-In Rome** Anacletus II (1130-1138), at first considered properly elected pope, died in battle Victor IV (G. Conti, 1138)	**-Guelph Dynasty (Viterbo, Italy)** Victor IV (Octavian of Rome, 1159-1163) Paschal III (1164-1168) Callistus III (1168-1178)	**-Roman Papacy (cont.)** Urban III (1185-1187) Gregory VIII (1187) Clement III (1187-1191) Celestine III (1191-1198) Innocent III (1198-1216), took title of "vicar of Christ"
Holy Roman Emperors	BYZANTIUM			WEST		
	Alexios I Komnenos (1081-1118) John II Komnenos (1118-1143) Manuel I Kmonenos (1143-1180) Alexios II Komnenos (1180-1183)	Andronikos I Komnenos (1183-1185) Isaac II Angelos (1185-1195) Alexios III Angelos (1195-1203)		Henry IV (10[53]84-1105); 3 yrs old when made King; government ruled by mother, then clergy vice-regents; Henry became licentious	Henry V (1111-1125) **Lothair III** (1133-1137) **Frederick I [Barbarossa]** (1155-1190) Henry VI (1191-1197)	

---

[14]"While considering the contents of the Old and New Law again and again by diligent chase [*indagine*], the prevenient grace of God has hinted to us, that a treatise on the Sacred Page is [*versari*] chiefly about things and/or signs. For as Augustine, the egregious Doctor, says in the book *on Christian Doctrine*: 'Every doctrine is of things, and/or signs. But even things are learned through signs. But here [those] are properly named things, which are not employed to signify anything; but signs, those whose use is in signifying'" ("The Four Books of Sentences"; from http://www.franciscan-archive.org/lombardus/opera/ls1-01.html; on 16 May 2006).

[15]"At the investiture of Lothair as Emperor he gained the territories belonging to Matilda of Tuscany in return for an annuity to be paid to the pope, in consequence of which the curial party based the contention that the Emperor was a vassal of the Papal see" ("Innocent II"; from www.wikipedia.org; on 5 Jan 2013). Interesting when governments pay tribute to Rome!

[16]See Monique Zerner, *L'histoire de catharisme en discussion* (Nice 2001) and Jean Odol, *Le Lauragais cathare, terre de feu et de sang* (to have appeared, 2005); noted in the article of Jean Odol, "L'acte de naissance des échêvés Cathares: La charte de niquinta, Saint-Félix, 1167" [the birthing act (or articles of inc.) of the cathar bishoprics: the chart of Niquinta, Saint Felix, 1167], by Jean Odol; from: http://www.couleur-lauragais.fr/pages/journaux/2005/cl69/histoire.html; 21 Sept 2007.

Issue-Year	1200-1300 Sword of Justice Exonerated Theologically by Aquinas			
Heresies—Identified	Further heretics named, condemned, with a call to take up arms against them (**4th Lateran Council**, §1); The Waldensian Durand d'Osca reconverts to Catholicism; Innocent III writes up a confession for him to say to recant his Waldensian beliefs (Confession of Durand d'Osca, DS792ff.)			
Secondary Applications...	**Holy Crusades** were turned against Christian people of other denominations, much as had been already done to regain Britain through William the Conqueror in 1066 AD			
Heresies—Unidentified	Apparent first public use of the **Rosary** by [St] Dominic (founder of the Dominican Order, O.F.P. or O.P.) to give "courage" to crusaders before they wiped out whole Cathar towns in France; **Aquinas**, building from **Lombard**'s sacramental salvation, gave guidelines for when Catholicism was in a minority position;cc **Confessional system** established as part of Sacrament of Penance;	**Adoration of Host** during the Mass instituted; **Bible** forbidden to laymen; **Devotional Artifacts**, called "scapulars," to be worn for protection; **"Extirpation of heretics"** unto death was defended by Thomas Aquinas in Paris; **Special haircuts** only for approved clergy on pain of anathema		
Medieval Western Councils	**12. 4th Lateran Council**, 1215AD	**13. 1st Council of Lyons**, 1245AD	**14. 2nd Council of Lyons**, 1274AD	
"Heresies" in Communion	**16 Denominations of the Cathars** were listed by an Inquisitor in 1250, being called variously, e.g. Albigensian Church, Church of the Latins of Constantinople, etc.; and then as a separate group, the Leonists, Poor Men of Lyons, or Waldenses;dd			
Bishops of Rome (later taking the title of Pope)	**Papacy in Rome** Innocent III (1198-1216), took "vicar of Christ" as new title Honorius III (1216-27), political issues in Serbiaee Gregory IX (1227-41) Celestine IV (1241) Innocent IV (1243-54)	**Viterbo Papacy Period** Alexander IV (1254-61), moved papal court to Viterbo, Italy in 1257 Urban IV (1261-64) Clement IV (1265-68) Blessed Gregory X (1271-76)	**Viterbo Papacy (cont.)** Blessed Innocent V (1276) Adrian V (1276) John XXI (1276-77) Nicholas III (1277-80)	**Papacy Back in Rome** Martin IV (1281-85) Honorius IV (1285-87) Nicholas IV (1288-92) St. Celestine V (1294) Boniface VIII (1294-1303), wrote the Bull *Unum Sanctam*, speaking of the "Two Swords"
Holy Roman Emperors	BYZANTIUM		WEST	
	Alexios III Angelos (1195-1203) Isaac II Angelos (1203-1204) Alexios IV Angelos (1203-1204) Alexios V (1204) **Theodore I Laskaris** (1205-1221/22)	John II Doukas Vatatzes (1221/22-1254) Theodose II Laskaris (1254-1258) John IV Lakaris (1258-1261) **Michael VIII** (1259-1282) Andronikos II (1282-1328)	Otto IV (1209-1215) [...]	**Frederick II** (1220-1250) [...]

ccRome in a political minority is uncomfortable with its territorial approach to spiritual rule since the time of Constantine, Aquinas' advice is important (cf. Summa, II-II).

ddThe extinction of the memory of these 16 Cathar denominations listed by Rainerio Sacchoni in his 1250 "On the Cathars and the Poor Men of Lyons" is quite a remarkable feat, reminiscent of Rome's taking Deut 25:17-19 to apply to those they deemed heretics, as Rome in fact later commanded for Wycliffe and others.

eeStephen Nemanjic was first crowned King of Serbia in 1217 by a Catholic legate; and then recrowned king of Serbia by his brother, an Orthodox Archbishop, in 1222.

Issue-Year	1300-1400 Wycliffe Ministers in England			
Heresies—Identified	Wycliffe (1320-1384) first condemned in 1377 by Gregory XI, who censured 19 of Wycliffe's articles related to the Investiture Controversy (King vs. Pope). He wrote a Bull against Wycliffe that year.			
Secondary Applications...	Later John Huss was burned at the stake for being a Wycliffite and Luther was said to have Wycliffite tendencies.			
Heresies—Unidentified	**Power of Pope** identified as the "Two Swords" (absolute power over church and state); **Avignon Papacy**, where the Pope moved the Church of Rome's headquarters to Avignon, France (about 1,000 km to the northwest in the center of the **Cathar-infested** region of Provence, Laurangais, and Albi); **Bank of Merits**ee in heaven developed, whose blessings are controlled and distributed exclusively by the Church of Rome			
Medieval Western Councils	**15. Council of Vienne**, 1311-1313AD			
"Heresies" in Communion	John Wycliffe's doctrines considered dangerous to church control and unity; He was considered an "Arch-Heretic"; 150 years later Luther was called a "Wycliffite" or follower of Wycliffe; There were two simultaneous and official popes holding each having worldwide spiritual and political authority during most of this century			

Bishops of Rome (later taking the title of Pope)	**Roman Papacy**		**Poitiers Papacy (1305-1309)**	**Avignon Papacy (1309-1415)**	
	Boniface VIII (1294-1303) Blessed Benedict XI (1303-04) When was Benedict X? Was he not later considered as an "anti-pope" in 1058?	[The City of Rome was vacated of Papal authority for about 70 years]ff Urban VI (1378-89)[17] Boniface IX (1389-1404)	Pope Clement V (1305-1314), Raymond Bertrand de Got was French	Pope Clement V (1305-1314) Pope John XXII (1316-1334) Pope Benedict XII (1334-1342) (French Inquisitor Jacques Fournier) Pope Clement VI (1342-1352)	Pope Innocent VI (1352-1362) Pope Urban V (1362-1370) Pope Gregory XI (1370-1375) Clement VII (1378-1394) Benedict XIII (1394-1423)

Holy Roman Emperors	**BYZANTIUM**		**WEST**		
	Andronikos II Paliologos (1282-1328) John V Palaiologos (1341-1376) John VI Kanta-kouzenos (1347-1354) Andronikos IV Palaiologos (1376-1379)	John V Palaiologos (1379-1390) John VII Palaiologos (1390) John V Palaiologos (1390-1391) Manuel II Palaiologos (1391-1425)	**Henry VII (1312-1313)** [...]		**Louis IV (1328-1347)** [...] **Charles IV (1355-1378)**

eeClement VI, in his *Unigenitus Dei Filius* (27 Jan 1343), developed for the first time (according to Denzinger, *Symboles et définitions de la foi catholique* [Paris: Cerf, 2005]) the concept of a "Bank of Merits" in heaven, whose merits are distributed by the [Roman Catholic] "Church" (cf. DS1025-1027).
ffHence Luther's *Babylonian Captivity of the Church* (1520), in which Luther described the Seven Sacraments of the Church as a spiritual captivity; cf. Jer 25:11-12; 29:10.

[17]"Some sources suggest that Giovanni di Bicci de' Medici introduced this method [double-entry accounting] for the Medici bank in the 14th century" (http://en.wikipedia.org/ wiki/Double-entry_bookkeeping_system). The Medici bank was used by some popes after the return of the "seat" of the Papacy from Avignon, France to Rome, Italy.

Issue-Year	1400-1500—TP #7: Western Colonialism: Global Political Dynamics Recalibrated after Fall of Constantine—leading to a Beginning of Colonialism Invention of the Printing Press (1455)—and Huss Ministers in Bohemia			
Heresies—Identified	The **Council of Constance** condemned as arch-heretics: **John Wycliffe** (posthumously) condemned for believing: That the **Host** is true bread in nature (#1-5); Aspects of **Baptism** (#6, #57); On the solemnity of **consecrating bishops** (#7); That **oral confession** is unnecessary, but rather harmful to those hearing them (#9-10); Priests and deacons are holy (**saints**) by their conduct, not their ordination (on necessity for human instrumentalities) (#13);		Condemnations of Wycliffe (continued): About the pope (#17-23); The dress of modern religious is hypocrisy (#32); On the folly of the religious orders (#33-37, #39); On the free giving of tithes (#38, #41); On predestination (#56, #58). **John Huss** was burned at the stake for being a disciple of Wycliffe, and also believing: On predestination (#1-3, #5-6); Papacy emanated from prior imperial power (#9-13), etc.	
Secondary Applications...	In the **Council of Constance**, it appears that Rome began anathematizing more directly central doctrines of Evangelicalism			
Heresies—Unidentified	**Cup** of the Lord's Supper forbidden to laity; **Purgatory** proclaimed as official church teaching; **Seven Sacraments** confirmed as church teaching; **Church constitutes non-existent states** as its tributaries, calling it **"Colonization"**; **Indulgences** (representing forgiveness of sins) sold for profit; e.g. NT money changers and Simon the Sorcerer?		**Papal indiscretion** appeared to reach one of its peaks in this century: **Sixtus IV** had many children and welcomed them into the Vatican; **Innocent VIII** organized wedding parties for his children and admitted his 13-year-old nephew into the college of cardinals; **Alexander VI** (Rodrigo Borgia) had many illegitimate sons.	
Medieval Western Councils	16. **Council of Constance**, 1414-1418AD; where Jon Hus was burned alive;		17. **Council of Basle**, Ferrara, Florence, 1431-1439AD.	
"Heresies" in Communion	Three simultaneous **approved** popes for six years: Consider then the praise given when a single sitting Pope was chosen in 1417, "Gaudium Magnum: Habemus Papam!" (e.g. Luke 2:10)—especially important since the Pope was considered the living wellspring of salvation		Jan Huss burned alive, as was Jerome of Prague, the Hussites subdued; Augustine of Rome, archbishop of Nazareth anathematized.	
Bishops of Rome (later taking the title of Pope)	**Avignon Papacy**	**Pisan Papacy**	**Roman Papacy**	
	Avignon Papacy Benedict XIII (1394-1423)	Alexander V (1409-1410) John XXIII (1410-1415), a 20th Century pope (1958-1963) took the same name	Boniface IX (1389-1404) Innocent VII (1404-06) Gregory XII (Rome, 1406-15) Martin V (1417-31) Eugene IV (1431-47) Nicholas V (1447-55)	Callistus III (1455-58) Pius II (1458-64) Paul II (1464-71) Sixtus IV (1471-84) Innocent VIII (1484-92) Alexander VI (1492-1503)
Holy Roman Emperors	BYZANTIUM		WEST	
	Manuel II Palaiologos (1391-1425) John VIII Palaiologos (1425-1448) Constantine XI Paliologos (1449-1453) **Byzantine Empire fell to Ottoman Empire in 1453**	[Claimants to empire in exile] Demetrios Palaiologos (1453-1460) Thomas Paliaologos (1453-1465) Andreas Paliologos (1465-1502)	Sigismund (1433-1437) [...]	**Frederick III** (1452-1493) [...] Maximilian I (1486[99]-1519)

[99]Election date cited, since there was apparently no coronation by a Pope for these emperors.

Chart Six: A Century by Century Quick View of Developments in Western Christianity

Issue-Year	1500-1600—TP #8: Protestant Reformation Some Western States Pull Away from Rome Certain Freedom of the Press in Select Countries	
Heresies—Identified	In the **Fifth Lateran Council** issues included: Proper **management of funds** coming into the Church of Rome (largely to keep from the theft of indulgence moneys) Dealing with **education of children** and **blasphemy** against Jesus Christ, the Virgin Mary, and the saints (speaking against any of these, or against the false worship given to any of these). In the **Council of Trent**: Non-acceptance of **Apocryphal Books** condemned as heresy; **Justification by faith alone** condemned as a heresy (incl 18 canons menacing and decreeing death for various beliefs);	In the Council of Trent (cont.): On the **Sacraments** (incl. 13 canons for various beliefs); On **Baptism** (14 canons, incl. one requiring infant baptism); On **Confirmation of Priests** (3 canons); On **Reformation** (Session 23, Canon 15, "Although at their ordination priests receive power to forgive sins"; Canon 18, on raising support for a seminary in each diocese); On **Marriage** (incl. 12 Canons).
Secondary Applications...	In the **Council of Trent**, it appears that Rome, removing all guile, attacked and anathematized the most important doctrines of Evangelicalism (Justification by faith, Bible alone)	
Heresies—Unidentified	After Reformation: church history is often considered differently after 1517, admitting that Luther had some valid concerns: Meanwhile, Rome, portrays itself as always in a state of Reformation, putting forth its own Reforming efforts, usually meaning tighter financial control, further Medieval-type theology, and providing for new ways to repress "heretics" Fires of martyrdom continued to burn Baptists and Protestants	
Medieval Western Councils	18. **5th Lateran Council**, 1512-1517; 19. **Council of Trent**, 1545-1563, held during the papacies of five popes and two emperors, held to examine and condemn the errors of Luther and other Protestant Reformers.	
"Heresies" in Communion	Protestant Reformation led to freedom of the press in some countries of Europe, and to significant development of territorial churches rivaling Rome's self-defined and enforced monopoly.	

	Rome			
Bishops of Rome (later taking the title of Pope)	Alexander VI (1492-1503) Pius III (1503) Julius II (1503-13) Leo X (1513-21), wrote Bull of excommunication burned by Luther	Adrian VI (1522-23), was inquisitor-general before becoming Pope Clement VII (1523-34) Paul III (1534-49) Julius III (1550-55) Marcellus II (1555)	Paul IV (1555-59) Pius IV (1559-65) St. Pius V (1566-72) Gregory XIII (1572-85), made gold medallion to commemorate Paris' St. Bartholemew Massacre in 1572	Sixtus V (1585-90) Urban VII (1590) Gregory XIV (1590-91) Innocent IX (1591) Clement VIII (1592-1605)

	WEST	
Holy Roman Emperors	Maximilian I (1486[hh]-1519) [...] Charles V (1530-1556), apparently the "last to be crowned [Holy Roman] emperor" [...]	Ferdinand I (1531[hh]-1564) Maximilian II (1562[hh]-1576) Rudolph II (1575-1612)

[hh]Election date cited, since there was apparently no coronation by a Pope for these emperors.

Issue-Year	1600-1700 Strong Polemical Century in Western Europe		
Heresies—Identified			
Secondary Applications...			
Heresies—Unidentified			
Modern Western Councils			
"Heresies" in Communion	1685, Louis XIV of France famously revoked the Edict of Nantes [which was an edict giving limited allowances or "toleration" to the Huguenots]; it suddenly became illegal to be Protestant in France.		
Bishops of Rome (later taking the title of Pope)	Clement VIII (1592-1605) Leo XI (1605) Paul V (1605-21) Gregory XV (1621-23)	Urban VIII (1623-44) Innocent X (1644-55) Alexander VII (1655-67) Clement IX (1667-69)	Clement X (1670-76) Blessed Innocent XI (1676-89) Alexander VIII (1689-91) Innocent XII (1691-1700)
Holy Roman Emperors	WEST		
	Rudolph II (1575-1612) Matthias (1612-1619)	Ferdinand II (1619-1637) Ferdinand III (1637-1657)	Leopold I (1657-1705)

Issue-Year	1700-1800 First Great Awakening Impacts NW Europe And U.S.A.			
Heresies—Identified	14 June 1761, on the heels of the First Great Awakening, Clement XIII publishes *In Dominico Agro*, explaining how to deal with heretics and heretical teaching: • Cautiously balance between not seeming to turn their backs to, while shunning and condemning at the same time; • The faithful should only "know in moderation"; and • Remove faithful from proximity to error. 25 Nov 1766, Clement XIII in his *Christianae Reipublicae* derided the idea of Christian republics, based on "human reasoning" (i.e. from the Bible and not from the "Holy Fathers")	25 Dec 1775, Pius VI in his *Inscrutabile* ordered every diocese to found a college or assist an adjoining diocese in the founding of a college as a way to stop the spread of heresy (building on Benedict XV). Citing Pope Leo, Paul VI quoted: "We can rule those entrusted to us only by pursuing with zeal for the Lord's faith those who destroy and those who are destroyed and by cutting them off from sound minds with the utmost severity to prevent the plague spreading" (Epistles 7-8, chap. 2, to the bishops throughout Italy). 28 Aug 1794, Pius published *Auctorem fidei* to right the errors of the 1786 Synod of Pistoia, and its Jansenist tendencies		
Secondary Applications...	Founded after the teachings of Cornelius Jansen of Old Louvain, Jansenists were a groups that leaned toward Calvinistic teachings while remaining within the Catholic church; for example, the philosopher and mathematician Blaise Pascal was considered a Jansenist			
Heresies—Unidentified	1708, promulgation of the immaculate conception of Mary (that is, that she was born without a sin nature, i.e. original sin; something akin to the immaculate conception of Jesus) by Clement XI in 1708, later confirmed by Pius IX in 1854). "Since the 1740s, Popes have regularly sent encyclicals."[18] These encyclicals are deemed infallible Tradition, as well as being considered inerrant.[19]			
Modern Western Councils				
"Heresies" in Communion	1789, French Revolution defeated the French crown and the tyranny of the Catholic Church through the power of the crown, ushered in the "Enlightenment" period (known for its "rationalism") a Napoleonic period of democratic republics. 1798, 20 Feb, Pope Pius VI was arrested by French forces for refusing to renounce his temporal power, and placed in Florence; in 1799 he was moved to Valence, France, where he died after 6 weeks.			
Bishops of Rome (later taking the title of Pope)	Clement XI (1700-21) Innocent XIII (1721-24) Benedict XIII (1724-30)	Clement XII (1730-40) Benedict XIV (1740-58)	Clement XIII (1758-69)—died the night before a conclave to disband the Jesuits	Clement XIV (1769-74)—died not long after he disbanded the Jesuits[ii] Pius VI (1775-99)
Holy Roman Emperors	WEST			
	Leopold I (1657-1705) Joseph I (1705-1711) Charles VI (1711-1740)	[...] Charles VII (1742-1745)	**Francis I** (1745[ii]-1765) Joseph II (1765-1790)	Leopold II (1790[ii]-1792) Francis II (1792-1806)

[ii]The Jesuits, in fact, were reinstated as an approved order 41 years later in 1814 by Pius VII. Apparently, the Jesuits were expelled from numerous countries at various times for their revolutionary approach in seeking to promote papal primacy: "England (1581, 1604), France (1594, 1606, 1762-1763), Portugal (1598, 1759), Russia (1717), Spain (1767), Genoa (1767), Venice (1767), Naples (1768), Malta (1768), and Parma (1768)" (cited in Richard Bennett, "Pope Francis Shows His True Colors" *The Trinity Review* [July-August 2013], 2).
[ii]Election date cited, since there was apparently no coronation by a Pope for these emperors.

---

[18]Leonardo De Chirico, *A Christian's Pocket Guide to Papacy* (Ross-Shire, Scotland: Christian Focus, 2015), 24.
[19]Leo XIII, *Providentissimus Deus*; available at: http://www.catholic-forum.com/saints/pope0256b.htm; accessed 8 March 2002; Internet.

Issue-Year	1800-1900—TP #9: Protestant Great Century of Missions: Extends Worldwide Political Influence of Western European States		
Heresies—Identified	Napoleon inaugurated an era of constitutional republics in the Western world that remained throughout Western Europe and the colonized world through the end of the 20th Century "Less than two years before, in February 1798, French troops had marched into Rome and taken Pope Pius VI prisoner. They placed the sickly pontiff in the citadel of Valence where he died on August 29, 1799. … [In 1800] Few in the conclave that elected Pius VII could have anticipated the severity of the struggle that awaited the pope and the Church in the coming decades, for the new Vicar of Christ spent the next 15 years in battle with the dictator openly cursed as an Antichrist and an enemy of civilization: Napoleon Bonaparte."[20] The Bible societies were also repeatedly anathematized by Pius IX, in Section IV of his Syllabus of Errors.		
Secondary Applications...	Leo XIII propagated the inerrancy of the Bible, along with the inerrancy of Catholic Holy Tradition in his encyclical, *Providentissimus Deus* (18 Nov 1893)		
Heresies—Unidentified	Infallibility of Pope Assumption of Mary Pilgrimages to various Marian sites encouraged, including supposed healings, purchase of Holy Water, jewelry to which indulgence power is given, etc. Rather than a list of censored books, Rome decided to require an "imprimatur" on all books acceptable for Catholics; the imprimatur was to come from a Bishop in good standing with Rome The [Blessed] Cardinal John Henry Newman strongly argued for the biblical Peter as implicitly filling the role of the office of the Papacy in his "An Essay on the Development of Christian Doctrine" (1845).		
Modern Western Councils	20. 1st **Vatican Council**, 1869-1870; perhaps a response to dealing with constitutional republics; an important decree of this council was the infallibility of the pope when speaking *ex cathedra*		
"Heresies" in Communion	Old Catholic churches (mainly in Germany) separated from Rome primarily over the doctrine of the infallibility of the Pope In light of talks between the Anglicans and Eastern Orthodox (called the Lambeth Conferences), the Anglicans were anathematized as having an invalid ordination (rendering all the Sacraments from their hands invalid in the eyes of Rome)		
Bishops of Rome (later taking the title of Pope)	Pius VII (1800-23), a relative of Pius VI's mother Leo XII (1823-29)	Pius VIII (1829-30) Gregory XVI (1831-46)	Blessed Pius IX (1846-78) Leo XIII (1878-1903)
	WEST		
Holy Roman Emperors	Francis II (1792-1806) **Emperor Napoleon** (1804-1815)[kk] ushered in Constitutional Republics in the European lands he conquered, ushered in the **Modern era**; necessitating clandestine control by the pope, who could no longer control politically through monarchs alone		

[kk]Election date cited, since there was apparently no coronation by a Pope for this emperor.

[20]"Catholic Answers: The Pope Who Outlasted a Tyrant"; available at: http://www.catholic.com/magazine/articles/the-pope-who-outlasted-a-tyrant (online); accessed 28 Oct 2014.

Issue-Year	1900-2000—TP #10: Catholic Consolidation of Power: Rome Gathers Western Ecclesiastical and Political Influence into its Fold		
Heresies—Identified	Protestant ecumenical movement decried, with prohibitions against attending its conferences (1928): 1934, apparent change of heart in Rome toward the budding ecumenical movement; 1960, John XXIII created the SPCU, the Secretariat for the Promoting Christian Unity, since 1988 they are called the Pontifical Counsel for Promoting Unity among Christians; 1961, Vatican sent observers to Third General Assembly of the World Council of Churches in New Delhi, India		
Secondary Applications...	1907, Pius X in his encyclical, *Pascendi*, §55, ordered the forming of secret "Councils of Vigilance" against heresy in every diocese, to meet every two months in the presence of the bishop; 1910, Pius X's oath against modernist—Protestant theology; 1943, Pius XII then taught a limited infallibility of the Bible in his *Divino Afflante Spiritu*; 1964, Eugene Nida penned "Guidelines for Interconfessional Cooperation in Translating the Bible," signed in 1968 both by Rome's SPCU and by the United Bible Society: 1987 revised guidelines are now housed on Vatican website, as Vatican gained majority control of the United Bible Society translation and publication apparatus		
Heresies—Unidentified	Added to the requirement of the "imprimatur", also in *Pascendi* (1907), Pius X required that a "Nihil Obstat" be receive for approved books from the hand of a Censor Deputatis assigned by Rome; **French President** bestowed honors which were a part of the French monarchy[21] (a church and state issue)		
Modern Western Councils	**21. 2nd Vatican Council**, 1962-1965; among important decrees were Lumen Gentium's approach to Protestants and other religions and Dei Verbum's opening the door to Roman Catholics work with various Bible societies		
"Heresies" in Communion	World Council of Churches at first deemed a "pan-Christian" group attendance was prohibited (1928) Was Billy Graham deemed to have "invincible ignorance" ("Letter to the Archbishop of Boston," 8 Aug 1949)?		
Bishops of Rome (later taking the title of Pope)	Leo XIII (1878-1903) St. Pius X (1903-14) Benedict XV (1914-22)	Pius XI (1922-39) Pius XII (1939-58) Blessed John XXIII (1958-63)	Paul VI (1963-78) John Paul I (1978) John Paul II (1978-2005)[II]
Holy Roman Emperors	Pius IX in 1907 instituted secret "Councils of Vigilance" to maintain *nihil obstat* in all matters civil and ecclesiastical within every diocese worldwide.		

[II]First polish pope.

[21]"In 1953... As a sign of his esteem, the President of France, Vincent Auriol, claimed the ancient privilege possessed by French monarchs and bestowed the red hat [of a cardinal] on Roncalli at a ceremony in the Elysee Palace" ("Pope John XXIII"; available at: http://en.wikipedia.org/wiki/John_xxiii [online]; accessed: 5 Jan 2013; Internet).

Issue-Year	2000-2100		
Heresies—Identified			
Secondary Applications...			
Heresies—Unidentified	Pope Francis I on the role of women (ordination and Mary): "As far as the ordination of women, the Church has already spoken out and the answer is no. John Paul II made the Church's stance definitive. The door is closed. But let me tell you something, Our Lady, was more important than the apostles, bishops, deacons and priests. Women play a role that's more important than that of bishops, or priests. How? This is what we have to explain better publicly"[22] In good Jesuit fashion, Pope Francis appears to thrive on the rhetorical edge of populism in his approach to many controversial issues.		
Modern Western Councils			
"Heresies" in Communion			
Bishops of Rome (later taking the title of Pope)	John Paul II (1978-2005) Benedict XVIII (2005-2013 resignation)[mm] Francis I (2013-)[nn]		
Holy Roman Emperors	**EAST** Vladimir Putin,[oo] the de facto head of the Eastern Block countries (since 2012, it appears that Putin reaffirmed the role of the Orthodox Church in Russia life)		**WEST** Barack Obama,[pp] as president of the U.S. is the de facto 1st political head of the Western world, with Merkel of Germany (2nd) and Holland of France (3rd)

[mm]Benedict resigned in 2013, the prior Pope who resigned was Gregory XII in 1415.

[nn]The first Jesuit pope, the first pope from the Americas, and the first pope from the Southern hemisphere; he was the son of Italian immigrants to Argentina, and apparently speaks Italian very well, as well as Spanish.

[oo]"Power of religion: With Putin's help, Russian church grows as political force"; available at: http://www.foxnews.com/world/2013/07/12/power-religion-with-putin-help-russian-church-grows-as-political-force/?test=latestnews (online); accessed: 16 Jul 13; Internet.

[pp]A first, U.S. President Woodrow Wilson met with Pope Benedict XV in 1919. Next Dwight D. Eisenhower met with John XXIII in 1959. Then came the avalanche. Since Paul VI became Pope in 1963 there have been 26 meetings of reigning Popes with sitting U.S. Presidents. Paul VI's policy of *Aggiornamento* (Italian for "updated"), seemed to mark a political shift of Western power after World War II from the Continent of Europe to the U.S., a religious shift from dealing with European state churches to the free market churches of the U.S. Since 1963, Paul VI met 6 times with 4 U.S. Presidents, John Paul II 15 times with 5, Benedict XVI met 4 times with 2, and Francis I has met once with one.

[22]Francis I, "Pope Francis talks to press about Benedict XVI, Vatican Bank and 'gay lobby'"; available at: http://www.romereports.com/palio/pope-francis-talks-to-press-about-benedict-xvi-vatican-bank-and-gay-lobby-english-10723.html#.UmPNDhZ5lII; accessed: 20 Oct 2013; Internet.

A Contemporary Perspective
Interview with Reformed Baptist Pastor of Breccia di Roma (Rome, Italy)
Leonardo De Chirico[23]

1. Did you grow up in the Catholic Church? If so, what drew you to become an evangelical Christian?

My family was an ordinary Italian family, nominally Christian and devout to Saint Antony, but with little grasp of basic gospel truths. One day we were visited by a Swiss couple from the local evangelical church that was going door to door. They asked if we were Christians. The answer was "yes, of course." They further asked if we had ever read the Bible. The answer was "no." Catholics were not supposed to read the Bible.

They then replied, "How can you be Christian if you don't read what Christ has done for you?" It was as if a light was switched on in the darkness. It was the beginning of a journey that led my father to become a believer, then the rest of the family followed at different stages of life.

2. What is the main doctrinal divide, in your estimation, between Roman Catholics and Protestants?

In Roman Catholicism the tendency is to idolize the church. The distinction between Creator and creature is blurred by way of conferring to the church what ultimately belongs to the triune God alone. The church is elevated to a position that makes it an idol, stemming out of a non-tragic view of sin, the conviction that in significant ways the church continues the incarnation of Jesus Christ resulting in an abnormally conflated ecclesiology. The great bullet points of the Protestant Reformation, i.e. Scripture alone, Christ alone, grace alone, are all biblical remedies against the idolatrous tendency of a self-referential church, which sadly have been rejected so far.

3. In your ongoing interaction with Roman Catholics in Italy, what approach have you taken and found to be effective when witnessing to them?

Exposing them to Scripture as much as possible and not assuming they already grasp the basics of the gospel. They may know some Christian vocabulary, but it is generally marred, distorted by traditions and deviant cultural baggage. Most Catholics in Italy are of the "pick-and-choose" variety and so they blend unbiblical traditions and secular unbelief. It is also important to show the personal and the communal aspects of the faith in order to embody viable alternatives for their daily lives.

4. You have written a very helpful little book on the papacy. So tell us, what are positive and negative aspects of this new pope Francis?

There is much sentimentalism about Pope Francis. He is a champion of the gospel of "welcoming all" and "showing compassion." Many secular people, as well as many evangelicals, are fascinated by it. We should ask: What about repentance and faith in Christ alone? What about turning back from idolatry and following Christ wholeheartedly? What about putting the Word of God first? Some of the language of the Pope seems to resemble gospel emphases, yet the substance of it is still heavily sacramental and Marian, leaning towards a liberal form of Catholicism. He is the first Jesuit to become Pope and we should never forget that the Jesuit order was founded to fight against the Protestant Reformation by learning its secrets and using them against it.

5. Let's address the elephant in the room: Is the Pope the Anti-Christ?

Luther, Calvin, the seventeenth-century Protestant confessions, the Puritans, Wesley, Spurgeon, et al., believed that the papacy (not this or that Pope) is the institution out of which the Anti-Christ will eventually come. I share this broad protestant consensus. The papacy claims christological and pneumatological titles and prerogatives (e.g. vicar of Christ, infallible teacher, supreme head of the church with full, immediate and universal power), coupling them with earthly political power. Remember that Popes are monarchs of a sovereign political state. In the papacy what belongs to God and what belongs to Caesar tragically intermingle. This poisoned mixture is the potential milieu for the Anti-Christ to rise from.

6. You are a pastor of a Reformed Baptist Church in Rome. Is a church like yours extremely rare? How has the culture perceived your congregation?

Evangelicals are 1% of the population in Italy and Rome is no different from the rest of the country. We still struggle with the centuries-long prejudice of evangelicals being perceived as a cult. What makes our church distinct is that it is confessional (holding to the 1689 London Confession of Faith and belonging to a Reformed Baptist association of churches), urban (impacting the cultural, political, media, and academic institutions of the city with the gospel), and missional (living to the glory of God in all vocations and initiatives). Unlike cults, we cherish church history and claim to belong to the catholic (not necessarily Roman Catholic!) church. Unlike cults, the gospel we believe in is for the whole of life. Unlike cults, we encourage constructive and critical cultural engagement. Thankfully, there is a growing number of churches like that.

[Read the remainder of the interview at: http://vaticanfiles.org/2015/11/115-rome-the-pope-and-gospel-work-in-italy-10-questions-with-leonardo-de-chirico/

---

[23]"115. Rome, the Pope and Gospel Work in Italy. 10 Questions With Leonardo De Chirico"; available at: http://vaticanfiles.org/2015/11/115-rome-the-pope-and-gospel-work-in-italy-10-questions-with-leonardo-de-chirico/ (online); accessed 27 Nov 2015; Internet.

Chart Seven: The Genius and Impact of Gregory the Great, Bishop of Rome (590-604 A.D.)
Original Visionary of What Became Western Europe
The Contemporary Western World Being the Result of the Protestant Reformation, Enlightenment Era, and Napoleonic Revolution

	Impact	Before	After
Worship	**Worship**	**Pluriform**	**Uniformity**
	Calendar[1]	Culturally guided	Gregorian Calendar
	Songs	Religious-regional	Gregorian Chants
	Missal	Religious-regional	Gallican Missal
	Language	Indigenous	Latin
Organization	**Organization**	**Decentralized**	**Centralization**
	Monasticism	Cenobitic monks (Eastern)	Communal monasteries (Western)—Gregory's was an abbot[2] Authoring "The Life of Saint Benedict"
	Church	Rome one of five Patriarchates (Jerusalem, Antioch, Rome, Alexandria, Constantinople)	One Western Pope (Bishop of Rome) Parish systems developed in Rome
	Politics	Maurice as Emperor over East and West (murdered in 602 A.D.)	No Western Emperor for two Centuries (Charlemagne crowned in 800 A.D.)
Foreign Affairs	Byzantium	Political threat through rule by Greek-speaking foreigners in Byzantium	Cut ties with Eastern Roman Empire by breaking the alliance of rulership, after the murder of Maurice
	Lombards	Political threat to Rome northern Italy	Used church funds as ransom to save Rome
	Donatists	Schismatic threat in Carthaginian Empire	Writing Exarch of Africa, various types of repression*
	Visigoths	Heretical threat in Spain	Accommodation by allowing validity of Arian Baptism
	Franks	Degenerate clergy in the Frankish (Gallican) Church	Using Gallican Missal
	Britons	Strategy for absorbing the 7/8 evangelized Kingdoms of the Celts into Kingdom of Northumbria	Sending Augustine with letters to various leaders: Later sending him the *pallium* (of a Bishop) Accommodating the use of Pagan Temples to Christian use, including feast days, and depositing relics of saints*
Theology[3]	Biblical interpretation	Philo of Alexandria also taught allegorical interpretation	Propounded allegorical view[4]
	Sacraments		
	Baptism		Gregory taught that Baptism cleansed from Original Sin
	Penance		Sacrament of Penance
	Holy Orders		Three Benedictine vows applied to monks
	Defining sin	Four Cardinal sins discussed	Seven Cardinal Sins delineated, as well as Venial Sins
	Mary	Mary's role not yet emphasized in Western Church	Prayer to and worship of Mary
	Relics		Relics encouraged
	After Life		Promoted the doctrine of Purgatory
Strategies	Territorial	Emperors and kings exerted control over what bishops were chosen in their realms	Evangelization = territorial expansion through strategic political partnerships
	Romanizaton		Evangelism = Christianization or Romanization[5] (religious-cultural-political consent and enforcement)
	Ambassadors	Evangelism or Romanization through influencing heretical kings via their families (Visigoths and Lombards)	Influencing the influencers: sending bishops as ambassadors to kings and queens
	Accommodation		Theological accommodation where necessary
	Sacramentary		Discipleship through his *Sacramentary* (controlling what is read and preached in liturgy), and through music
	Precursor to the "Dark Ages"?		Limiting availability of scholarship to royalty, aristocrats, or those with Sacrament of Holy Orders living in monasteries?

*Consider respective letters attached.

---

[1]"He was the first to date events by the day of the month as we do now..." (Frederick H. Dudden, *Gregory the Great* [London: Longmans, Green & Co., 1905; New York: Russell and Russell, 1967], 2:443)

[2]'To the Abbot, Benedict gave absolute authority. ... He was obeyed in all things. ... No one must question his orders or appeal from his decision. ... As a restraint upon the Abbot, it was provided that when a vacancy in post arose, he should be elected by the community and from its own members, and they were to be guided by the virtue, learning and practical wisdom of the candidate' (Henry H. Howorth, *Gregory the Great* (London, England: John Murray, 1912), 66-67).

[3]"He does consolidate and strengthen the Catholicism he found, preparing the matter for future elaboration. ... He gives to theology a tone and an emphasis which cannot be disregarded. And from his time to that of Anselm no teacher of equal eminence arose in the Church. For a period of nearly four centuries the last word on theology rested with Gregory the Great" (Dudden, 1:v).

[4]Based on his lifelong study of Job, titled *Magna Moralia*, in which he combined mysticism and allegorism (Howorth, xxxvii).

[5]"Often these [Franks] had become Romanized and, as a corollary, had professed Christianity" (Kenneth S. Latourette, *A History of the Expansion of Christianity* [Grand Rapids: Zondervan, 1970], 1:206).

Chart Seven: Select Letters of Gregory the Great

To the Abbot Mellitus [addresses Syncretism]

"To our well loved son Abbot Mellitus: Gregory, servant of the servants of God.

"Since the departure of those of our fellowship who are bearing you company, we have been seriously anxious, because we have received no news of the success of your journey. Therefore, when by God's help you reached our most reverend brother, Bishop Augustine, we wish you to inform him that we have been giving careful thought to the affairs of the English, and have come to the conclusion that the temples of the idols among that people should on no account be destroyed, but the temples themselves are to be aspersed with holy water, altars set up in them, and relics deposited there. For if these temples are well-built, they must be purified from the worship of demons and dedicated to the service of the true God. In this way, we hope that the people, seeing that their temples are not destroyed, may abandon their error and, flocking more readily to their accustomed resorts, may come to know and adore the true God. And since they have a custom of sacrificing many oxen to demons, let some other solemnity be substituted in its place, such as a day of Dedication or the festivals of the holy martyrs whose relics are enshrined there. On such occasions they might well construct shelters of boughs for themselves around the churches that were once temples, and celebrate the solemnity with devout feasting. They are no longer to sacrifice beasts to the Devil, but they may kill them for food to the praise of God, and give thanks to the Giver of all gifts for the plenty they enjoy. If the people are allowed some worldly pleasures in this way, they will more readily come to desire they joys of the spirit. For it is certainly impossible to eradicate all errors from obstinate minds at one stroke, and whoever wishes to climb a mountain top climbs gradually step by step, and not in one leap. It was in this way that the Lord revealed Himself to the Israelite people in Egypt, permitting the sacrifices formerly offered to the Devil to be offered thenceforward to Himself instead. So He bade them sacrifice beasts to Him, so that, once they became enlightened, they might abandon one element of the sacrifice and retain another. For, while they were to offer the same beasts as before, they were to offer to God instead of to idols, so that they would no longer be offering the same sacrifices. Of your kindness, you are to inform our brother Augustine of this policy, so that he may conduct consider how he may best implement it on the spot. God keep you safe, my very dear son.

"Dated the seventeenth of June, in the nineteenth year of the reign of our most pious Lord and Emperor Maurice Tiberius Augustus, and the eighteenth after his Consulship: the fourth indiction."[6]

To All the Bishops of Numidia [regarding the Donatists]

"Gregory to all the Bishops of Numidia.

"If ever, most dear brethren in Christ, a troublesome mixture of tares intrudes itself among green corn, it is necessary for the hand of the husbandman to root it up entirely, lest the future fruit of the fertile corn should be obstructed. Wherefore let us too, who, however unworthy, have undertaken the cultivation of the field of the Lord, hasten to render the corn pure from all offence of tares, that the field of the Lord may fructify with more abundant increase. Now you requested through Hilarus our chartulary (2) from our predecessor of blessed memory that you might retain all the customs of past time, which, from the beginnings of the ordinances of the blessed Peter, Prince of the apostles, long antiquity has so far retained. And we, indeed, according to the tenour of your representation, allow your custom (so long as it clearly makes no claim to the prejudice of the catholic faith) to remain undisturbed, whether as to constituting primates or as to other points; save that with respect to those who attain to the episcopate from among the Donatists, we by all means forbid them to be advanced to the dignity of primacy, even though their standing should denote them for that position(3). But let it suffice them to take care of the people committed to them, without aiming at the topmost place of the primacy in preference to those prelates whom the Catholic faith hath both taught and engendered in the bosom of the Church. Do you, therefore, most dear brethren, anticipate our admonitions in the zeal of the charity of the Lord, knowing that the strict Judge will bring into examination all we do, and will approve every one of us with regard not to the prerogative of a higher rank, but to the merits of our works. I beseech you, therefore, love ye one another mutually, having peace among yourselves in Christ, and with one purpose of heart oppose ye heretics and enemies of the Church. Be ye solicitous for the souls of your neighbours: persuade all ye can to faith by the preaching of charity, holding before them also the terror of the future judgment; inasmuch as ye are appointed to be shepherds, and the Lord of the docks expects from the shepherds to whom He has committed them the fruit of a multiplied flock.

"And if He should foresee an augmentation of His own flock through your bestowal of more diligent care upon it, He will assuredly adorn you with manifold gifts of the heavenly kingdom. Furthermore, addressing to you the greeting of fraternal love, I pray the Lord that He would make you, whom He has chosen to be shepherds of souls, worthy in His sight, and Himself so order our deeds here that He may accept them as they deserve in the future life."[7]

---

[6]Bede, *A History of the English Church and People*, trans. L. Sherley-Price, rev. R. E. Latham (Harmondsworth, Middlesex, England: Penguin Books, 1979), 86-87.

[7]Gregory I, Pope, *Epistle LXXVII*, "To All the Bishops of Numidia"; accessed: 8 September 1997; from: www.ccel.wheaton.edu/Gregory/Register/E24.htm.

Chart Eight: Gregory VII's *Dictatus Papae* (1075)—A Comparative

Introduction from Halall (with the Henderson translation): "The Dictatus Papae was included in Pope's register in the year 1075. Some argue that it was written by Pope Gregory VII (r. 1073-1085) himself, others argues that it had a much later different origin. In 1087 Cardinal Deusdedit published a collection of the laws of the Church which he drew from [m]any sources. The Dictatus agrees so clearly and closely with this collection that some have argued the Dictatus must have been based on it; and so must be of a later date of compilation than 1087. There is little doubt that the principals below do express the pope's principals [principles]."

Introduction to the Loud translation: "This set of 27 propositions is included in Gregory VII's Register, and appears to have been promulgated at the Lenten synod at the beginning of March 1075. Their significance has been much debated. It has been suggested that they were intended from the first as the headings for a 'Gregorian' canon law collection, and while such a collection was never compiled in this exact form, Cardinal Deusdedit drew heavily on them for his important canonical collection, completed in 1086. Alternatively, they may have been simply a statement in principle of papal rights and powers, as envisaged by Gregory. Most of them seem to have been drawn up in response to contemporary debates and problems."

Prior to reading this important document, it is helpful to read and understand the level of authority given to the high priest (pontifex) in the Book of Deuteronomy, in addition to the death penalty for disobeying his command:

> Deut 17:8-13 (NKJ), "If a matter arises which is too hard for you to judge, between degrees of guilt for bloodshed, between one judgment or another, or between one punishment or another, matters of controversy within your gates, then you shall arise and go up to the place which the LORD your God chooses. And you shall come to the priests, the Levites, and to the judge *there* in those days, and inquire *of them*; they shall pronounce upon you the sentence of judgment. You shall do according to the sentence which they pronounce upon you in that place which the LORD chooses. And you shall be careful to do according to all that they order you. According to the sentence of the law in which they instruct you, according to the judgment which they tell you, you shall do; you shall not turn aside *to* the right hand or *to* the left from the sentence which they pronounce upon you. Now the man who acts presumptuously and will not heed the priest who stands to minister there before the LORD your God, or the judge, that man shall die. So you shall put away the evil from Israel. And all the people shall hear and fear, and no longer act presumptuously."

The Dictates of the Pope

#	Latin Original*	Henderson Translation**	Brian Pullan°°	Other
1	Quod Romana ecclesia a solo Domino sit fundata	That the Roman church was founded by God alone.	That the Roman church was founded by God alone.	[Implication] That the Roman church is the only truly valid church founded by the Lord.
2	Quod solus Romanus pontifex iure dicatur universalis	That the Roman pontiff alone can with right be called universal.	That only the Bishop of Rome is by law called universal.	Loud°: That only the Roman pontiff can by right be called universal.
3	Quod ille solus possit deponere episcopos vel reconciliare	That he alone can depose or reinstate bishops.	That he alone may depose or reinstate bishops.	
4	Quod legatus eius omnibus episcopis presit in concilio etiam inferioris gradus et adversus eos sententiam depositionis possit dare	That, in a council his legate, even if a lower grade, is above all bishops, and can pass sentence of deposition against them.	That his legate may preside over all the bishops in council, even should he be of inferior rank, and may pronounce sentence of deposition against them.	Loud°: That in a council his legate takes precedence over all bishops, even if he is of a lower grade to them, and he can pass a sentence of deposition against them.
5	Quod absentes papa possit deponere	That the pope may depose the absent.	That the Pope may depose persons in their absence.	
6	Quod cum excommunicatis ab illo inter cetera nec in eadem domo debemus manere	That, among other things, we ought not to remain in the same house with those excommunicated by him.	That, among other things, we must not stay under the same roof with persons whom he has excommunicated.	
7	Quod illi soli licet pro temporis necessitate novas leges condere, novas plebes congregare, de canonica abbatiam facere et e contra, divitem episcopatum dividere et inopes unire	That for him alone is it lawful, according to the needs of the time, to make new laws, to assemble together new congregations, to make an abbey of a canonry; and, on the other hand, to divide a rich bishopric and unite the poor ones.	That he alone may establish new laws to meet urgent needs of the time, found new dioceses [novas plebes congregare] or make a canonry into an abbey; and, on the other hand, divide a rich bishopric and combine poor ones.	Loud°: That for him alone is it permitted to make new laws, according to the needs of the time, to gather together new congregations, to make an abbey of a canonry, and on the other hand to split up a rich bishopric and to unite poor ones.

#	Latin Original*	Henderson Translation**	Brian Pullan°°	Other
8	Quod solus possit uti imperialibus insigniis	That he alone may use the imperial insignia.	That he alone may use the imperial insignia.	Cf. Queen Theodolinda gave Gregory I the imperial crown (later given to Charlemagne)
9	Quod solius pape pedes omnes principes deosculentur	That of the pope alone all princes shall kiss the feet.	That the Pope is the only man whose feet shall be kissed by all princes.	Loud°: That all princes shall kiss the feet of the pope alone.
10	Quod illius solius nomen in ecclesiis recitetur	That his name alone shall be spoken in the churches.	That his title alone shall be read out in churches.	Is the Pope is taking Acts 4:12 and Eph 4:5 to refer to himself? [e.g. see Deut 13:4]
11	Quod hoc unicum est nomen in mundo	That this is the only name in the world.	That this title is unique in all the world.	Wylie°°°: the pope's name is the chief name in the world
12	Quod illi liceat imperatores deponere	That it may be permitted to him to depose emperors.	That he may depose Emperors.	Wylie°°°: it is lawful for him to depose emperors
13	Quod illi liceat de sede ad sedem necessitate cogente episcopos transmutare (CIC c. 416: Sedes episcopalis vacat Episcopi dioecesani morte, renuntiatione a Romano Pontifice acceptata, translatione ac privatione Episcopo intimata)	That he may be permitted to transfer bishops if need be.	That for urgent reasons he may transfer bishops from one see to another.	Loud°: That it may be permitted to him to translate bishops from one see to another, when need dictates.
14	Quod de omni ecclesia quocunque voluerit clericum valeat ordinare	That he has power to ordain a clerk of any church he may wish.	That he may ordain a clerk from any church, wherever he wishes.	Loud°: That he has the power to ordain a cleric from any church, should he so wish.
15	Quod ab illo ordinatus alii ecclesie preesse potest, sed non militare; et quod ab aliquo episcopo non debet superiorem gradum accipere	That he who is ordained by him may preside over another church, but may not hold a subordinate position; and that such a one may not receive a higher grade from any bishop.	That one ordained by him may hold a commanding but not a subordinate position in another church, and must not accept higher rank from any other bishop.	Loud°: That someone who is ordained by him can rule over another church, but not serve therein; and that person should not accept a higher grade from another bishop.
16	Quod nulla synodus absque precepto eius debet generalis vocari	That no synod shall be called a general one without his order.	That no council may be called "general" without his commandment.	Loud°: That no synod should be called a general one without his order.
17	Quod nullum capitulum nullus que liber canonicus habeatur absque illius auctoritate	That no chapter and no book shall be considered canonical without his authority.	That no chapter or book may be recognized as canonical without his authority.	[Does this place him above the canon of Scripture? What then of translation, interpretation, and application?]
18	Quod sententia illius a nullo debeat retractari et ipse omnium solus retractare possit	That a sentence passed by him may be retracted by no one; and that he himself, alone of all, may retract it.	That no sentence of his may be retracted by anyone, and he is the only one who can retract it.	Loud°: That his sentence ought not to be rescinded by anyone else and he alone of all can retract it. Wylie°°°: "his decision is to be withstood by none, but he alone may annul those of all men"
19	Quod a nemine ipse iudicari debeat	That he himself may be judged by no one.	That he must not be judged by anyone.	Loud°: That he ought to be judged by no one. Wylie°°°: "he can be judged by no one" [cf. Self-proclaimed absolute dictatorial power and authority]
20	Quod nullus audeat condemnare apostolicam sedem appellantem	That no one shall dare to condemn one who appeals to the apostolic chair.	That no one shall dare to condemn one who appeals to the Apostolic See.	Loud°: That nobody may dare to condemn one who has appealed to the Apostolic See.
21	Quod maiores cause cuiuscunque ecclesie ad eam referri debeant	That to the latter should be referred the more important cases of every church.	That the more important lawsuits of any church must be referred to the Apostolic See.	Loud°: That the more important cases of every church ought to be referred to it. [cf. Deut 1:17]

#	Latin Original*	Henderson Translation**	Brian Pullan°°	Other
22	Quod Romana ecclesia nunquam erravit nec imperpetuum scriptura testante errabit	That the Roman church has never erred; nor will it err to all eternity, the Scripture bearing witness.	That the Roman church has never erred, nor, as witness Scripture, will it ever do so.	Loud°: That the Roman Church has never erred, nor, as Scripture bears witness, will it ever err. [cf. Loyola's "Rules for Thinking within the Church," No. 13]
23	Quod Romanus pontifex, si canonice fuerit ordinatus, meritis beati Petri indubitanter efficitur sanctus, testante sancto Ennodio Papiensi episcopo ei multis sanctis patribus faventibus, sicut in decretis beati Symachi pape continetur	That the Roman pontiff, if he have been canonically ordained, is undoubtedly made a saint by the merits of St. Peter; St. Ennodius, bishop of Pavia, bearing witness, and many holy fathers agreeing with him. As is contained in the decrees of St. Symmachus the pope.	That the Bishop of Rome, if he has been canonically ordained, is undoubtedly sanctified by the merits of St. Peter, on the testimony of St. Ennodius, Bishop of Pavia, with the support of many holy Fathers - as it says in the decrees of the blessed Pope Symmachus.	Loud°: That the Roman pontiff, if he shall be canonically ordained, is undoubtedly made a saint through the merits of the Blessed Peter, as St. Enodius, Bishop of Pavia, bears witness with many holy fathers agreeing with him, as is contained in the decrees of the Blessed Pope Symachus.
24	Quod illius precepto et licentia subiectis liceat accusare	That, by his command and consent, it may be lawful for subordinates to bring accusations.	That by his commandment and with his permission, subordinate persons may bring accusations.	
25	Quod absque synodali conventu possit episcopos deponere et reconciliare	That he may depose and reinstate bishops without assembling a synod.	That he may depose and reinstate bishops without summoning a council.	Loud°: That he may oppose and reinstate bishops without assembling a synod.
26	Quod catholicus non habeatur, qui non concordat Romane ecclesie	That he who is not at peace with the Roman church shall not be considered catholic.	That no one may be regarded as a catholic if he is not in agreement with the Roman church.	Loud°: That he who is not at peace [in accord] with the Roman Church shall not be considered catholic.
27	Quod a fidelitate iniquorum subiectos potest absolvere	That he may absolve subjects from their fealty to wicked men.	That the Pope can absolve the subjects of the wicked from their fealty to them.	

*Latin from: http://faculty.cua.edu/pennington/Canon%20Law/GregorianReform/ Dictatuspapae.htm (online); accessed 4 July 2011.

**Translated in Ernest F. Henderson, *Select Historical Documents of the Middle Ages*, (London: George Bell and Sons, 1910), 366-367; available at: http://www.fordham.edu/halsall/source/g7-dictpap.html (online); accessed: 4 July 2011. This text is part of the "Internet Medieval Source Book." The Sourcebook is a collection of public domain and copy-permitted texts related to medieval and Byzantine history. Unless otherwise indicated the specific electronic form of the document is copyright. Permission is granted for electronic copying, distribution in print form for educational purposes and personal use. If you do reduplicate the document, indicate the source. No permission is granted for commercial use. (c)Paul Halsall Jan 1996 halsall@murray.fordham.edu.

°G. A. Loud. Unpublished translation. Translation of *Das Register Gregors VII.*, ed. E. Caspar (M.G.H. *Epistolae Selectae* 2, Berlin 1920-1923), 202-08; available at: http://faculty.cua.edu/pennington/churchhistory220/topicfive/DictatusPapae2.html (online); accessed: 4 July 2011; Internet.

°°Brian Pullan, *Sources for the History of Medieval Europe from the Mid-Eighth to the Mid-Thirteenth Century* (Oxford: Basil Blackwell, 1971), document no. III 9, translated from Gregory VII's *Register*, no. II 55a.; available at: http://faculty.cua.edu/pennington/ churchhistory220/topicfive/DictatusPapaePullan.htm (online); accessed 4 July 2011; Internet.

°°°J. A. Wylie, *The History of Protestantism*, Vol 1, Book 1, Chap 4; available at: http://www.doctrine.org/history/HPv1b1.htm; Accessed 10 Feb 2010; Internet.

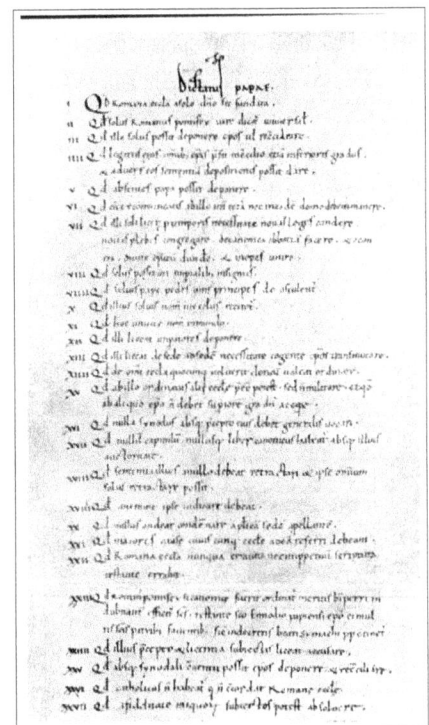

Chart Nine: Crusades of the Holy Roman Empire

Introduction:

The Holy Roman Empire was founded when Pope Leo III placed the iron crown (Queen Theodolinda had given to Pope Gregory I two centuries before) upon the head of Charlemagne in 800 A.D. However, the crusades listed below do not include any of the military activities of Charlemagne, the first Holy Roman Emperor (800 AD), nor of any of his successors, until just prior to start of the "official" crusading period. Analyzing this chart gives new meaning to Constantine's conversion experience, when he apparently saw a cross in the heavens and heard a voice saying "conquer with [for] this"—a statement perhaps reminiscent of Rev 6:1-2:

> "Now I saw when the Lamb opened one of the seals; and I heard one of the four living creatures saying with a voice like thunder, 'Come and see.' And I looked, and behold, a white horse. He who sat on it had a bow; and a crown was given to him, and he went out conquering and to conquer." (Rev 6:1-2)

The difference in official and non-official crusades lies in definition. If the term crusade is limited to meaning only crusades wherein Catholic princes travel from Europe to re-conquer territories of the Palestine from Muslim rule, then they number approximately nine crusades. If the term crusade includes any preached or sanctioned Catholic military exploits to re-conquer lands or dominions ruled by non-Catholics, then the number of crusades increases dramatically.

The chart below was expanded from information found at: http://en.wikipedia.org/wiki/Crusades (online); accessed 28 Feb 2013; Internet. The numbering of the "official" crusades follows Wikipedia. The varying crusades are divided into five time periods to provide assistance in historical-chronological comparison.

A. Select Early "Non-Official" Crusades

Official Crusades	Unofficial Crusades	Year	Name/Location	Other
	1	1066	England	William the Conqueror invaded England and installed as Archbishop of Canterbury, Lanfranc
	2	1072	Sicily	The Norman Robert Guiscard conquered northern Sicily
	3	1085	Spain	Christian princes from Basques invade take the Moorish (Muslim) ruled city of Toledo, in what is described the *Reconquista* (reconquering)

B. "Nine" Official Crusades + Select Other Non-Official Crusades

Official Crusades	Unofficial Crusades	Year	Name/Location	Other
1st	4	1095-1099	Holy Land	Preached by Pope Urban II; called to retake the Holy Land for the Holy Roman Empire and Church of Rome
	5	1101	Holy Land	Unsuccessful, defeated by the Turkish Kilij Arslan
	6	1107-1110	Holy Land, Norwegian Crusade	Sigurd, 60 ships and 5,000 men sailed from Norway, and made their way to the Holy Land via England, Portugal, and many other stops on the way to Jerusalem; assisted King of Jerusalem, Baldwin I, in taking Sidon; returned by way of Constantinople
	7	1142	First Crusade against Orthodox Novgorod	"The major turning point into more permanent conflict between Sweden and Novgorod arrived with Sweden's firmer organization into the Catholic Church in the 12th century and papal requests for crusades against lands controlled by the Orthodox church" (Wikipedia, "Swedish–Novgorodian Wars")
2nd	8	1147-1149	Holy Land	Preached by Bernard of Clairvaux, French Louis VII and German Conrad III marched to Jerusalem; returning home, they stopped in Portugal and helped Alfonso I of Portugal retake Lisbon from the Muslims
	9	1147-1149	Wendish Crusade	Saxons and Danes unsuccessfully fought the Polabian Slavs
		1154	Great Schism	Pope and Patriarch of Constantinople excommunicate each other

#	#	Year	Name/Location	Other
	10	1155	First Swedish Crusade	When the King of Sweden conquered Finland
	11	1155	The Taking of Ireland	Pope Adrian IV's encyclical *Laudabiliter*, using the "Donation of Constantine" as a basis, gave the Norman King Henry II the authority to invade Ireland to establish the Irish Church under the authority of the Papal See[1]
		1075	Decree of Gregory VII	Gregory VII published his *Dictatus Papae*, which affirmed the Church of Rome as the only true church, and proclaimed the pope's supreme authority over all the churches, synods, books, sentences proclaimed, and requires that princes kiss his feet
	12	1181	First Albigensian Crusade	Led by Papal Legate Henry Abbot of Clairveaux with Catholic knights; to rid Southern France of the "Manichean" Cathars
		1187	Saladin's counter-attack	Muslims under Saladin, retook all the Crusader territories, with the exception of several coastal towns
3rd	13	1187-1192	Holy Land	Called by Pope Gregory VIII, in his *Audita tremendi*, and organized by Frederick I Barbarossa of Germany (who died on route), Philip II Augustus of France (returned home to try to take Normandy from Richard), and Richard the Lion-Hearted of England; Richard captured the Island of Cyprus from Byzantium in 1191; after taking some coastal towns, including Jaffa, Richard made a deal to allow Europeans to trade in the Holy Land and make pilgrimages to Jerusalem
	14	1190	Teutonic Order of knights founded	This order over the next hundred years subjugated much of northeast Europe, fought against the Danish and Swedes, the Slavs, and invaded Orthodox Russia
	15	1198-1212	Baltic Crusades: Livonians	Campaign of German and Swedish Catholic princes against the Livonians.
	16	1199	Siege of Jerusalem	Was a earthly Millennial hope, with a rule by the Holy Roman Empire driving the crusaders?
	17	1201-1290	Baltic Crusades: Curonians and Semigallians	Campaign of German and Swedish Catholic princes against the Curonians and Semigallians
4th	18	1202-1204	Constantinople invaded	Preached by pope Innocent III, sought to invade Israel via Egypt; went to Constantinope, and upon capture, Innocent III crowned Baldwin IX, Count of Flanders as first Latin Emperor in Constantinople
	19	1206-1261	Baltic Crusades: against Saaremaa	Campaign of German and Swedish Catholic princes against Saaremaa.
	20	1208-1224	Baltic Crusades: Latgallians and Selonians	Campaign of German and Swedish Catholic princes against the Latgallians and Selonians.
	21	1208-1224	Baltic Crusades: Estonians	Campaign of German and Swedish Catholic princes against the Estonians.
	22	1209-1227	Second Albigensian Crusade	Led by Simon de Montfort, then picked up several Louis' (Prince and King); to rid Southern France of the "Manichean" Cathars
	23	1212	"Children's Crusade"	Unsuccessful, French peasant children, most never got past the Alps, remnant returned home
5th	24	1217-1221	Holy Land	Another attempt to retake Jerusalem (that had been lost to the Muslims), [St] Francis of Assisi took part in this crusade; leading to the "Franciscan Custody of the Holy Land"; forces from Austria, Hungary, former king of Jerusalem, and the Prince of Antioch

---

[1]"Legitimacy for the Norman invasion of Ireland was derived from a Papal Bull of 1155—*Laudabiliter*. The bull gave King Henry II of England authority to invade Ireland ostensibly as a means of reforming the Church in Ireland more directly under the control of the Holy See. The authorisation from the Holy See was based upon the Donation of Constantine which made every Christian island in the western Roman Empire the property of the Papacy. By the time of the English Reformation, the Donation had been exposed as a papal forgery" (available at: http://en.wikipedia.org/wiki/Church_of_Ireland; accessed 29 Mar 2013).

#	#	Year	Name/Location	Other
				attacked Jerusalem; great loss of crusader lives; not successful
	25	1219, 1222	Prussian Crusade	Duke of Masovia, Konrad I, at the behest of the Catholic Bishop of Prussia launched several unsuccessful crusades against Prussia; these efforts helped launch the Crusading Monastic order, the Teutonic Knights who ruled Prussia (Germany) for several centuries
6th	26	1228-1229	Holy Land	Again over Jerusalem ("Pray for the peace of Jerusalem") Frederick II went to Jerusalem, and through diplomacy won considerable control over portions of Jerusalem, married the young heiress to the kingdom (in 1225), and upon her death in 1228, became king of Jerusalem
	27	1232-1234	Sledinger Crusade	Against the Frisians (Netherlands/Germany), to bring them under the Archbishop of Bremen-Hamburg
	28	1240	Third Albigensian Crusade	To rid Southern France of the "Manichean" Cathars (see Chart book)
		1244	Muslims regain Jerusalem	This seems to mark the end of the Kingdom of Outremer (beyond the sea)
7th	29	1248-1254	Holy Land: Egypt	Against Egypt; Louis IX attacked Egypt, his crusaders were defeated and he was captured and held for a huge ransom
	30	1249	Second Swedish Crusade	Against Finland
	31	?	Third Swedish Crusade	Against Novgorod
	32	1255	Fourth Albigensian Crusade	To rid Southern France of the "Manichean" Cathars
	33	1259	Frist Crusade against the Tatars	Pope Alexander IV tried unsuccessfully to create a crusade against the Blue Horde, i.e. the Mongol invasion of Poland
8th	34	1270	Holy Land: Tunisia, former land of the Donatists and the Carthaginian Empire	Against Tunisia in North Africa; fought by King Louis IX of France; his army devastated by disease; the king died while trying to take the Holy Land
9th	35	1271-1272	Holy Land	Against Egypt; fought by the future King Edward I of England; it was deemed a failure and ended the crusades in the Middle East

C. Select Medieval Crusades Following the Holy Land Crusading Period

	#	Year	Name/Location	Other
	36	1284	Aragonese Crusade	Peter I of Cyprus fought against Muslim Alexandria
		1291	Cleansing of Franks from Middle East	By 1291, after the fall of Antioch (1268), Tripoli (1289), and Acre (1291), all traces of French rulership disappeared from the Middle East (until the end of the 19th Century colonization, with the work of Cardinal Lavigerie, founder of the White Fathers)
	37	1383	Norwich Crusade	Henry le Despenser, Bishop of Norwich, against Antipope Clement VII
	38	1390	Mahdian Crusade	French-Genoese fight against pirates from Mahdia; led by Louis II, Duke of Bourbon
	39	1396	Crusade of Nicopolis	Organized by Sigismund of Luxemburg; against the Balkans
	40	1398-1399	Second Crusade of the Tatars	Ended with the Tatars victorious besieging of Kiev; "and Christian blood flowed like water, up to the Kievan walls" (Wikipedia)

D. Select Pre-Reformation Crusades

	#	Year	Name/Location	Other
	41	1420	First Hussite Crusade	To bring Hussites back into submission to the Pope
	42	1421	Second Hussite Crusade	

#	#	Year	Name/Location	Other
	43	1424	Third Hussite Crusade	
	44	1426	Fourth Hussite Crusade	
	45	1433-1434	Fifth Hussite Crusade	
	46	1444	Crusade of Varna	Led by Polish-Hungarian king, Wladyslaw; against the Balkans
	47	1452	Hussite town of Tabor captured	

E. Select Reformation and Post-Reformation Crusades

#	#	Year	Name/Location	Other
	48	1524-1529	Subduing so-called "Peasants' Revolt," including Waldshut	Austria and Germany, crushed those who dared to leave state churches
	49	1529	First Kappel War	Switzerland, to bring non-Catholic departments (cantons) back under Catholic church
	50	1531	Second Kappel War	Switzerland, to bring non-Catholic departments (cantons) back under Catholic church
	51	1534-1535	Crusade against Anabaptists of Munster	Beseiged a town that have voted to remove itself from Catholic hierarchy (as did Bern, Neuchatel, Zurich, Wittenberg, and Geneva)
	52	1539-1540	Crusade against Anabaptists of Steinborn, Austria	Ferdinand sent his marshal to Steinborn to arrest Anabaptists of the Steinborn area
	53	1545	Massacre of Waldensian-Lutherans in Merindol and Cabriere, France	Destroying the entire populations of these towns
	54	1546-1547	Schmalkadic War	Germany
	55	1555-1558	Bloody Mary's internal crusade against non-Catholics	Systematic cherry-picking of hundreds of leaders and regular folk sentenced to the fire
	56	1561	Duke of Savoy Crusade	Duke of Savoy sent in 4-5,000 troops to crush the Waldensians in several Alpine valleys
	57	1562-1598	French Wars of Religion	Duke of Guise began attacking various Reformed towns in France
	57	1568-1648	Eighty Years War	The Netherlands
	58	1572	St. Bartholomew Massacre	Began in Paris when a cardinal of killed the Huguenot Admiral Colligny, from 30,000 to 100,000 were killed in several days in towns of France
	60	1618-1648	Thirty Years War	Austria, Bohemia, France, Denmark, Sweden
	61	1639-1651	Wars of Three Kingdoms	England, Scotland, and Ireland
	62	1681-1759	Les Dragonnades	France; multiple inter-related anti-Lutheran wars, especially fierce after Protestantism was made illegal in 1685 by Louis XIV
	63	1688-1697	Nine Years War	Louis XIV of France versus William III of Orange

Chart Ten: Timeline of the Holy Germanic Roman Empire's Colonization
The Fall of the Byzantine Roman Empire in 1453
The Beginning of Rome's Colonization in 1455
[Consider also the simultaneous invention of Offset Printing in 1455, the "Gutenberg Bible" in Mainz, Germany]

Rome's longtime rival, the Eastern Empire, and the seat of the Eastern Patriarch of Constantinople, weakened by the Roman crusaders, was finally defeated by the hand of Arab Muslims. A similar fate at the hand of Islamic Jihad had already destroyed the Carthanagian empire, seat of the Donatist churches of North Africa, in the 7th Century.

While the Eastern Churches still remained, fragmented by language groups, the Bishop of Rome's stature as unique and unrivaled head over world affairs was confirmed by this long-awaited fate. Further, whether intentional or unintentional, it appears that this fate of Constantinople "gave permission" to or removed an obstacle for Rome to act on its claim of "catholicity" or "universality":

- 579 A.D.: Gregory, to become Pope Gregory I in 590, was sent to Constantinople as an envoy to monitor relations between these two historic State-Church Patriarchates;

- 800 A.D., Pope Leo III decided that there needed to be a Western Empire, and so he crowned Frankish king Charlemagne emperor of the "Holy Roman Empire" or "Holy Roman Empire of the Germanic Nation."
  - It seems that Leo III followed the precedent of the prophet Ahijah in 1 Kings 11, who anointed Jeroboam as King over Israel, thus dividing the kingdom of Israel into Israel and Judah;
  - Leo III was likewise intentionally dividing the Roman Empire into two states:
    - One under the authority of the Bishop of Rome or Pope (as the person who placed the crown) and the other under the divine right of the Emperor, under the tutelage of the Patriarch of Constantinople;
    - One called "Holy Roman Empire"; and by implication, the other the "Secular Roman Empire."

- 806-810 A.D., the newly crowned Charlemagne, Frankish Emperor of the Germanic Roman Empire went to war with Byzantium over rulership of Venice, a disputed territory in debates over the boundaries between the now two Roman Empires, as discussed in the Pax Nicephori.
  - It appears that Roman Emperor Nikopheros I did not consider Charlemagne a rightful emperor, not accepting "Pope" Leo III as having the authority to crown an emperor over his empire;

- 1054 A.D.: The mutual anathema [curse] further gave Rome the spiritual authority to act on its own, without deference to the Patriarch of Constantinople, as he no longer had any spiritual authority, either in matters of salvation or in matters of world politics;

- 1167 A.D.: With Rome's view of state-church inter-relations, the fact that a bishop from Constantinople, the Bulgarian Bishop Nicetas, had the audacity to travel to France and anoint four bishops of the "Cathar Churches" in Saint-Félix-de-Caraman, France, was seen as an act of war, eventually leading to the multiple Albigensian crusades in Southern France and the genocide of their civilization.

- 1453 A.D.: With the fall of Constantinople to Muslims, Rome's historic rival was out of the way; it could now set up its own one "Kingdom of God on earth":
  - Not as a strange two-headed monster, or worse yet, a multiple-headed monster (as is much discussed in a number of papal encyclicals and writings).

In 1455, Rome then began to colonize the world (establishing earthly political realms under its triple authority):

1. Its authority to sanction explorers and partition the world into States, dividing them between committed Catholic rulers (Princes, Kings, or Emperors);

2. Its authority to send missionaries to these states to establish either by conversion, by political means, or by military force the Catholic Church as the State Church over those colonies;

3. Its ongoing authority to monitor and oversee the theology and politics of these states that it allowed, encouraged, and established.

These states include the colonization of:

- Central and South America, beginning in the 15th-16th Centuries;

- North America in the 17th Century;

- Africa in the 19th Century.

Chart Eleven: Considering the Reverse Chronological Study of Western Christianity

The Problem—Stair Step Content

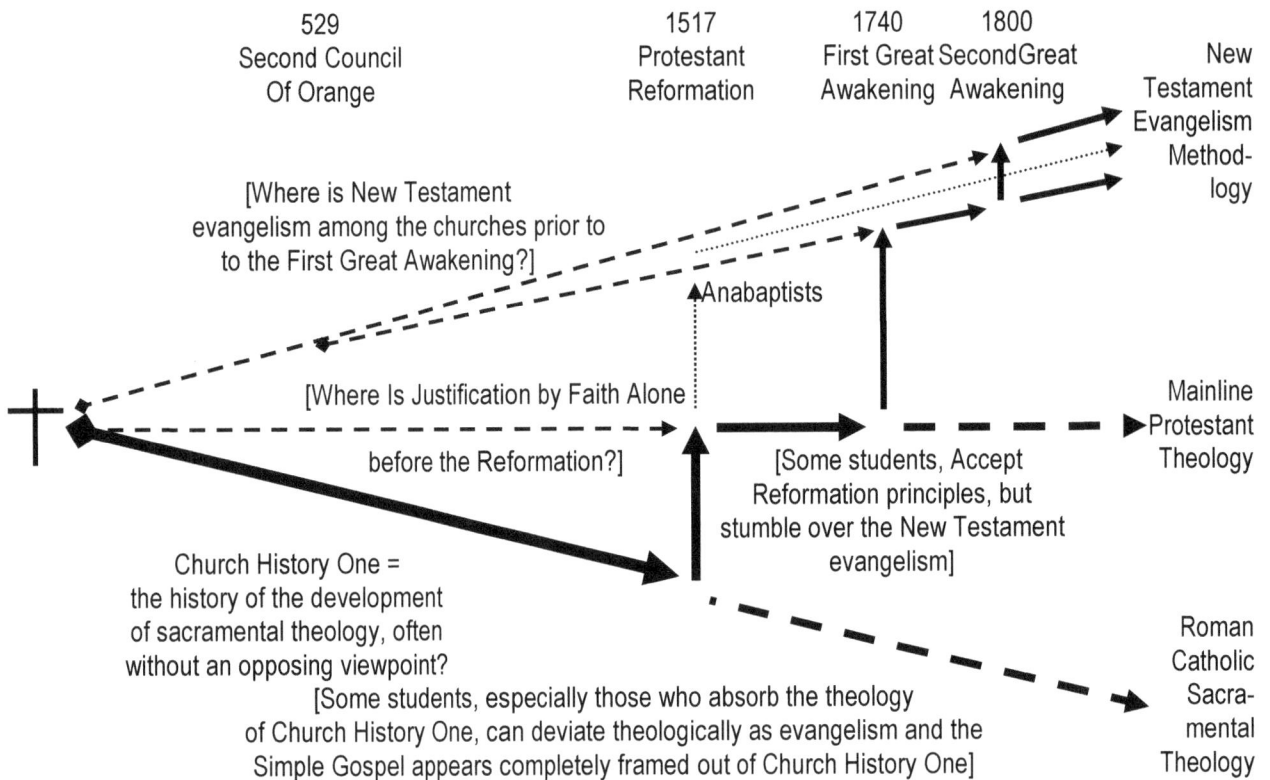

529
Second Council
Of Orange

1517
Protestant
Reformation

1740
First Great
Awakening

1800
Second Great
Awakening

New
Testament
Evangelism
Method-
logy

[Where is New Testament
evangelism among the churches prior to
to the First Great Awakening?]

Anabaptists

[Where Is Justification by Faith Alone

before the Reformation?]

Mainline
Protestant
Theology

[Some students, Accept
Reformation principles, but
stumble over the New Testament
evangelism]

Church History One =
the history of the development
of sacramental theology, often
without an opposing viewpoint?

Roman
Catholic
Sacra-
mental
Theology

[Some students, especially those who absorb the theology
of Church History One, can deviate theologically as evangelism and the
Simple Gospel appears completely framed out of Church History One]

A Solution

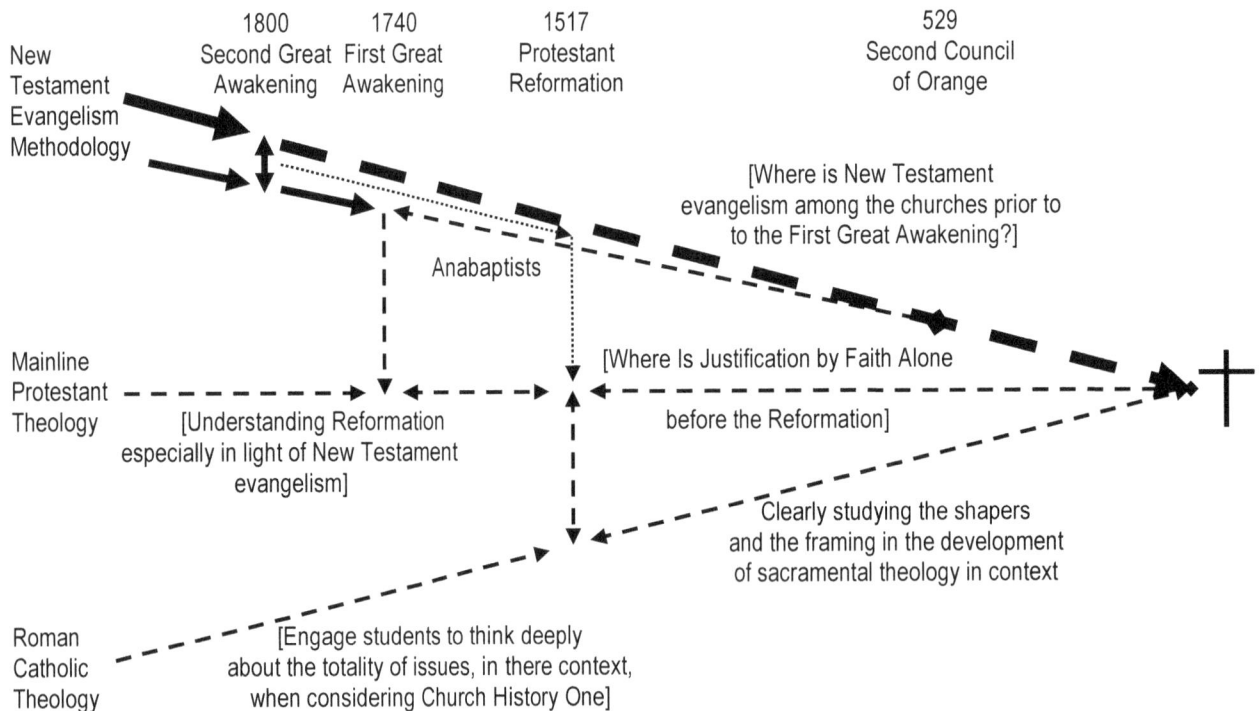

1800
Second Great
Awakening

1740
First Great
Awakening

1517
Protestant
Reformation

529
Second Council
of Orange

New
Testament
Evangelism
Methodology

[Where is New Testament
evangelism among the churches prior to
to the First Great Awakening?]

Anabaptists

Mainline
Protestant
Theology

[Where Is Justification by Faith Alone

before the Reformation]

[Understanding Reformation
especially in light of New Testament
evangelism]

Clearly studying the shapers
and the framing in the development
of sacramental theology in context

Roman
Catholic
Theology

[Engage students to think deeply
about the totality of issues, in there context,
when considering Church History One]

44

Chart Eleven: Select Reverse Chronological Historical-Theological Barriers and Disconnects

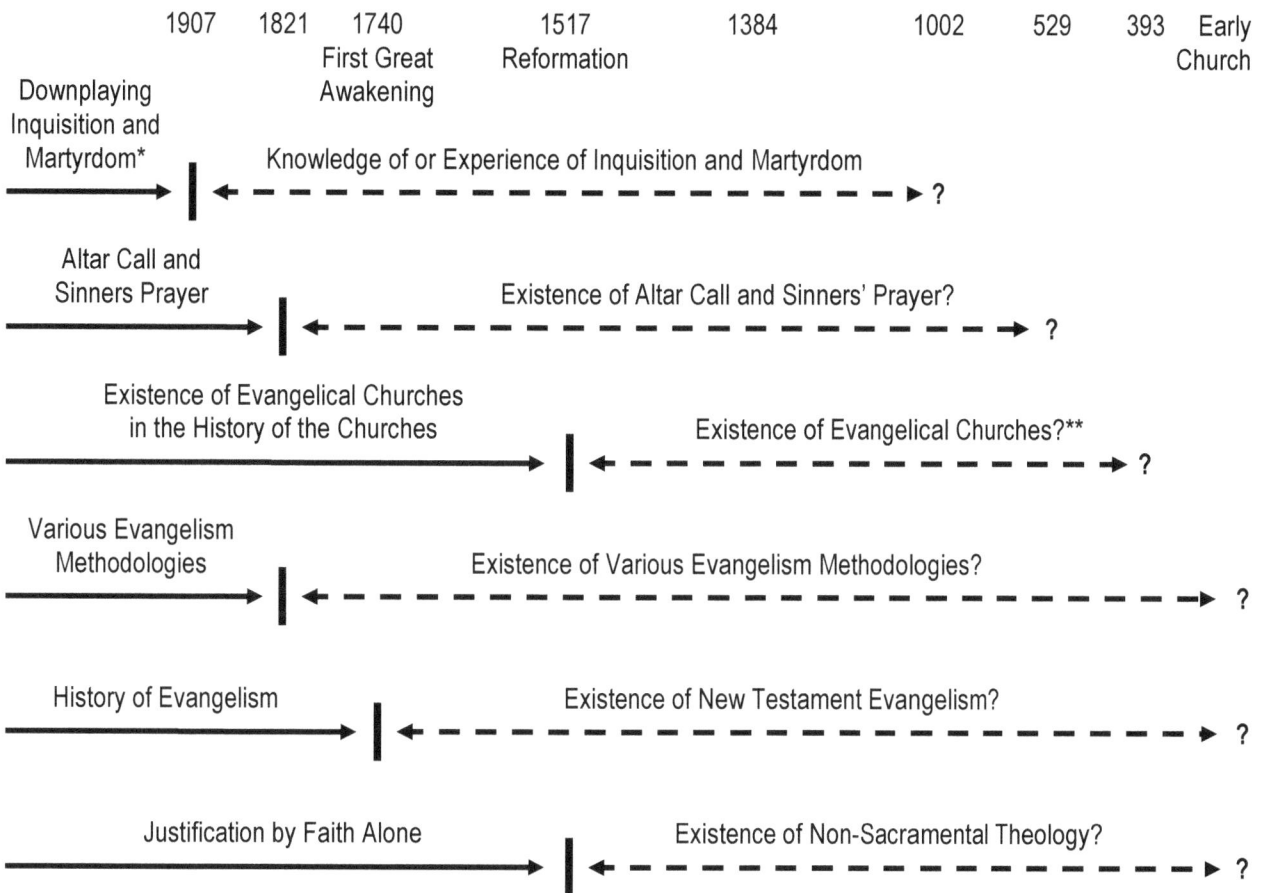

1907	1821	1740	1517	1384	1002	529	393	Early
		First Great	Reformation					Church
		Awakening						

Downplaying Inquisition and Martyrdom*

Knowledge of or Experience of Inquisition and Martyrdom → ?

Altar Call and Sinners Prayer

Existence of Altar Call and Sinners' Prayer? → ?

Existence of Evangelical Churches in the History of the Churches

Existence of Evangelical Churches?** → ?

Various Evangelism Methodologies

Existence of Various Evangelism Methodologies? → ?

History of Evangelism

Existence of New Testament Evangelism? → ?

Justification by Faith Alone

Existence of Non-Sacramental Theology? → ?

Proposed History of Influences upon U.S. Evangelical Theological Curriculum

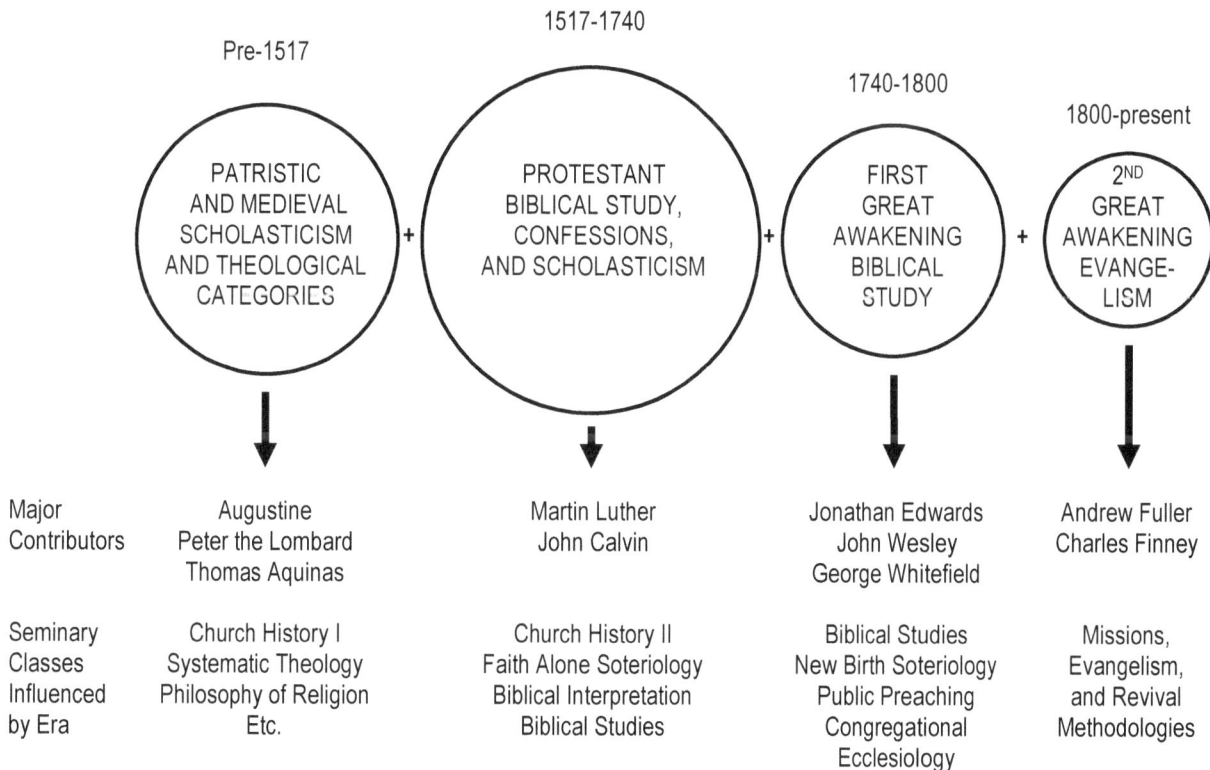

Pre-1517

1517-1740

1740-1800

1800-present

(PATRISTIC AND MEDIEVAL SCHOLASTICISM AND THEOLOGICAL CATEGORIES) + (PROTESTANT BIBLICAL STUDY, CONFESSIONS, AND SCHOLASTICISM) + (FIRST GREAT AWAKENING BIBLICAL STUDY) + (2ND GREAT AWAKENING EVANGE-LISM)

Major Contributors	Augustine Peter the Lombard Thomas Aquinas	Martin Luther John Calvin	Jonathan Edwards John Wesley George Whitefield	Andrew Fuller Charles Finney
Seminary Classes Influenced by Era	Church History I Systematic Theology Philosophy of Religion Etc.	Church History II Faith Alone Soteriology Biblical Interpretation Biblical Studies	Biblical Studies New Birth Soteriology Public Preaching Congregational Ecclesiology	Missions, Evangelism, and Revival Methodologies

INTRODUCTION TO CHRONOLOGICAL THEOLOGY

This chronology began with the 45 heresies and inventions listed in Lorraine Boettner's "Chronological Listing of Roman Catholic Heresies and Inventions," *Roman Catholicism*, 5th ed. (Presbyterian and Reformed, 1962, 1967, 1976, 1985, 1989; Banner of Truth Trust, 1962, 1966; Baker, 1983), 7-9. This author, seeking to verify Boettner's list, gradually reorganized and expanded it with primary and secondary material, thereby providing a historical-chronological approach, rather than a thematic approach to the study of the Church of Rome and its teachings. This author has also benefited from two Reformation-era historians published in Geneva and elsewhere: Johannes Sleidan and Jean de Hainault. To Boettner's list of 45 was also added 62 items from Jean [de] Hainault's "Tables of Popes" in his *State of the Church, with Discourses from the Time of the Apostles* (Alberges sur le Zoom: Jacques Canin, 1605; translation from the French mine). De Hainault's book was originally published in several French editions (Geneva: 1556, 1557, 1558, 1561, 1562) by Jean Crespin, the famed Reformation Geneva publisher who published 53 of Calvin's works, as well as printing several editions of the English Geneva Bible (1569, 1570). The original lists of Boettner and de Hainault are identified by their name, followed by the number of the listing. Sleidan was the official special collections scribe and librarian of the Protestant Reformation, copying and safeguarding Reformation manuscripts for progenity. He was salaried by Philip of Hess, and along with his collection of documents, wrote *The Key of History or the Four Chief Monarchies*, three books in one binding (Strasbourg, 1556; Geneva: 1556, 1557 [4 eds.], 1558 [6 eds.], 1559 [3 eds.], 1561, 1563, 1566; London, 1627).

When Martin Luther wrote that Jerome in a preface to his 435 A.D. Vulgate had made Christ into a Moses (another lawgiver) the ramifications of this teaching were immense. For example, when the Pope took the name "Vicar of Christ," it further affirmed him as supreme lawgiver, anyone disagreeing in his laws was deemed defiant to Christ Himself. This role of lawgiver led to gradual developments in church government and distinctive theology, including the sacramental system of salvation. These doctrines are part of Rome's "living tradition," which, according to Leo XIII's *Provenditissimus Deus* (1893) is "without error." Yet it is difficult to understand when and how such changes could take place. This chart seeks to search out this question. Over the years there came to be significant deviation from such doctrines as justification by Scriptures alone, grace alone, and faith alone, not to speak of compromises in many biblically-forbidden practices, such as worship of the Host [the bread in Communion], paying money for the forgiveness of sins [indulgences], prayers to Mary, the saints, and various statues of the same, bowing and genuflecting before men, the kissing of rings and feet, etc.

The following chronology also includes quotes from various primary sources. The first source for official Catholic symbols and creeds is Heinrich Denzinger, Peter Hünermann (ed., original edition), and Joseph Hoffmann (ed., French edition), *Symboles et définitions de la foi catholique: Enchiridion Symbolorum*, 38th ed. (37th ed., Freiburg: Herder, 1997; Paris: Cerf, 2005). This book and its numbering system provided the 1994 *Catechism of the Catholic Church* its "DS" notations, which system is also used for citations in this chronology. The second tier of primary sources comes from encyclicals and councils of the Church available through various media. Peter the Lombard's *Sentences* and Thomas Aquinas' *Summa Theologica* provided interesting insight into medieval use of the Patristic authors (particularly Augustine). Another secondary source was the Schaff-Herzog *Encyclopedia of Religious Knowledge*, 3rd ed., 4 vols. (New York: Funk and Wagnalls, 1891).

It is not the wish of this author to be negative or judgmental, but rather seek to understand (and to "rightly divide" the annals of history). At the request of several students, I have also provided an introductory biblical assessment of the issues as it seemed palatable to me. The esteemed reader is encouraged to form his own understanding of the issues found herein. This chronology and its various assessments are only a beginning. The issues are multitudinous, pluriform, and deeply substantial. Disclaimer: this author does not presume to speak on behalf of any Baptist group.

Thomas P. Johnston, Ph.D.
Liberty, Missouri, U.S.A., 2016.

~Date	Prayer, Veneration, Sacraments and Other Doctrines	Ecclesiology/Politics	Rival Churches and Movements, Named by Their Antagonists	Biblical Assessment of Rome's Doctrines and Practices
~55	Paul debunks the naïve ideal of a pristine apostolic church: 1 Cor 6:7 (KJV), "Now therefore there is utterly a fault among you" 1 Cor 6:7 (TPJ), "Already therefore there is a total fault among you" Use of the word "fault" is also found in the following translations: Tyndale, Bishops, Webster, Young's, Darby (cf. Rom 11:12; compare with Deut 32:5). The historiography on the translation of this verse is quite fascinating! If the apostolic church was already faulty, then they were not holy and immaculate, as will be the case at the Second Coming of Christ as prophesied by Paul: Eph 5:27, "that He might present her to Himself a glorious church, not having spot or wrinkle or any such thing, but that she should be holy and without blemish."	Jerusalem Council gave the Church a new set of regulations (Acts 15:27-29), that was "to abstain from: • Things sacrificed to idols • Blood • Things strangled • Fornication. They were repeated by James in Acts 21: "But concerning the Gentiles who believe, we have written and decided that they should observe no such thing, except that they should keep themselves from things offered to idols, from blood, from things strangled, and from sexual immorality" (Acts 21:25) From that idea, it was postulated that Christ and His church were in essence givers of a "New Law," cf. Peter the Lombard (1160 A.D.), Four Books of Sentences, Book 1, Distinction 1, Paragraph 1, Sentence 1: "While considering the contents of the Old and New Law again and again by diligent chase [indagine], the prevenient grace of God has hinted to us, that a treatise on the Sacred Page is [versari] chiefly about things and/or signs. For as Augustine, the egregious Doctor, says in the book on Christian Doctrine:[1] 'Every doctrine is of things, and/or signs. But even things are learned through signs. But here (those) are properly named things, which are not employed to signify anything; but signs, those whose use is in signifying.'"[1] [Footnote 1: "Chapter 2, n. 2; here and in the next passage, but with many words omitted by Master (Peter) and not a few added or changed."]	Those called "some men from Judea" (Acts 15:1), "certain ones of the sect of the Pharisees" (Acts 15:5), and later even "certain men from James" (Gal 2:12) Versus Paul and Barnabas: • On behalf of the non-circumcised or Hellenistic Christians • On behalf of the pure proclamation of the Gospel	Just as James gave a decree of laws to the believing Gentiles in Acts 15:27-29: • "Therefore we have sent Judas and Silas, who themselves will also report the same things by word of mouth. For it seemed good to the Holy Spirit and to us to lay upon you no greater burden than these essentials: that you abstain from things sacrificed to idols and from blood and from things strangled and from fornication; if you keep yourselves free from such things, you will do well. Farewell" (cf. Acts 21:25). And based on the interpretation that Jesus was in fact the initiator of a New Law, Acts 15:16: • "After these things I will return, And I will rebuild the tabernacle of David which has fallen, And I will rebuild its ruins, And I will restore it" Of which Rome alone [feels it] holds the keys (vis-à-vis their interpretation of Matt 16:19; 18:18). The keys apparently referring to the fact that: 1. Rome was like the new chosen place as mentioned in Deut 17:9-13: "And you shall come to the priests, the Levites, and to the judge there in those days, and inquire of them; they shall pronounce upon you the sentence of judgment. You shall do according to the sentence which they pronounce upon you in that place which the LORD chooses. And you shall be careful to do according to all that they order you. According to the sentence of the law in which they instruct you, according to the judgment which they tell you, you shall do; you shall not turn aside to the right hand or to the left from the sentence which they pronounce upon you. Now the man who acts presumptuously and will not heed the priest who stands to minister there before the LORD your God, or the judge, that man shall die. So you shall put away the evil from Israel. And all the people shall hear and fear, and no longer act presumptuously" 2. Rome saw itself headed by the new leader of the church, the representative not only of Peter (Matt 16:18), but of Jesus Himself! 3. Rome saw itself as the new lawgiver. Especially after Constantine, the Church of Rome (guided by its Pope) began to understand itself as the new lawgiver, the only infallible interpreter of biblical revelation, and the divinely-ordained arbitrator of all ecclesiastical matters (Pontifex meaning "high priest," and the Pope considering himself, using this OT passage, the chosen "Pastor of the Universal Church"). 4. Rome saw itself as the new law-enforcer. It was when the Church of Rome was wed to the state, after Constantine, it appears that Rome began to rely more heavily on the civil laws of the OT, which gave their decrees supreme power, the breaking of which resulted in the death penalty. As Rome leveraged these powers, using its

---

[1]Peter the Lombard, Four Books of Sentences, Book 1, "On the Unity and Trinity of God," Distinction 1, Chapter 1, "Every doctrine concerns things and/or signs"; available at: http://www.franciscan-archive.org/lombardus/opera/ls1-01.html (online); accessed: 16 May 2006; Internet.

~Date	Prayer, Veneration, Sacraments and Other Doctrines	Ecclesiology/Politics	Rival Churches and Movements, Named by Their Antagonists	Biblical Assessment of Rome's Doctrines and Practices
				political and military prowess, as prophesied in Dan 2:33, 40-44; 7:7-8, 18-26; and 8:23-25, they sought and have basically achieved ecclesiastical world domination. As to adding to the Law of God via "canonical" laws or codes, Moses qualified the unique Laws He was giving in Deuteronomy both temporally and in terms of content: The phrase "Which I command you today" (Deut 27:10) is found 22 times in Deuteronomy, placing a temporal qualification on which laws were meant to be followed with divine authority; The dual command "You shall not add to the word which I command you, nor take from it" (Deut 4:2 NKJ) limits the content of the law to those things specifically given by Moses, this same dual admonition being repeated in Deut 12:32. Further, Deuteronomy is imminently clear that the curses and blessings of the Old Covenant are limited to what "is written in this book": o "All the words of this law that are written in this book, Deut 28:58 o Including that "which *is* not written in this Book of the Law," Deut 28:61 o "And every curse that is written in this book would settle on him," Deut 29:20 o "According to all the curses of the covenant that are written in this Book of the Law," Deut 29:21 o "To bring on it every curse that is written in this book," Deut 29:27 o "If you obey the voice of the LORD your God, to keep His commandments and His statutes which are written in this Book of the Law," Deut 30:10 So one ongoing theme underlying these notes becomes, when did Rome begin to make additions to the Scriptures, which are not found in Scriptures, with are outside of Scriptures (from some strain of Tradition), and which are contrary to the Scriptures? Consider, for example, the teaching on the immaculate conception of Mary within St. Anne, the mother of the Virgin Mary. From whence comes that teaching from the Bible (promulgated by Clement XI in 1708)? Notice how the immaculate conception of Mary diminishes the uniqueness of the Isa 7:14 miracle of the immaculate conception of Christ. "You shall not add, nor shall you subtract," taught throughout Scripture, is an important teaching related to the doctrine of Scripture, its sufficiency, unity, harmony, integrity, and finality. As to Christ initiating a new law, Rom 8:15 clarifies that this was not the case. True believers are not slaves to a new law, but sons, guided by the Holy Spirit (Rom 8:14): Rom 8:15, "For you did not receive the spirit of bondage again to fear, but you received the Spirit of adoption by whom we cry out, 'Abba, Father.'" This verse summarizes the idea initiated in Rom 8:1:

~Date	Prayer, Veneration, Sacraments and Other Doctrines	Ecclesiology/Politics	Rival Churches and Movements, Named by Their Antagonists	Biblical Assessment of Rome's Doctrines and Practices
				Rom 8:1 (NKJ), "*There is* therefore now no condemnation to those who are in Christ Jesus, who do not walk according to the flesh, but according to the Spirit."
67		Ignatius of Antioch (aka. Ignatius Theophorus) became Bishop of Antioch at the death of Evodius (who presumably succeed the Apostle Peter). Ignatius of Antioch wrote a number of letters, still extant, and is the first example of a leader who presumably served to oversee a group of churches taking or receiving the title "Bishop."		The title and developed role of a "Bishop" creates a number of problems for New Testament Church government.[2] Six will be enumerated: • Removes responsibility from the people of the local church over their own officials, as described in 1 Tim 3, in which qualifications are given for choosing local church leaders; • Removes the accountability of the local church official to their local congregation, both in matters of life and doctrine; • Inserts an outside authoritarian voice into the governing of the local church; • Gives one person power over multiple local churches, both for good (political efficiency and expediency) and for ill (such as greed, abuse of power, and the unaccountable insertion of false doctrine); • Allows church government to reflect human governing principles which are against the teaching of Christ in Mark 10:42-45: Mark 10:42-45, "But Jesus called them to *Himself* and said to them, 'You know that those who are considered rulers over the Gentiles lord it over them, and their great ones exercise authority over them. Yet it shall not be so among you; but whoever desires to become great among you shall be your servant. And whoever of you desires to be first shall be slave of all. For even the Son of Man did not come to be served, but to serve, and to give His life a ransom for many.'" • Prepared the way for the centralization of power in the church in the OT program with a Chief Priest in the chosen city (cf. Deut 17:8-13). Of interest related to the evolution of the use of the term "bishop" are the words of Christ, "it shall not be so among you" (Mark 10:43). It appears that this straight forward command of Jesus has been abrogated for expediency in the early history of the territorial churches. Three lessons on spiritual succession from the historical books of the OT: • **Spiritual succession does not pass through the lines of the prophets(Prophet):** ○ "Then *Micaiah* said, 'Therefore hear the word of the LORD: I saw the LORD sitting on His throne, and all the host of heaven standing by, on His right hand and on His left. And the LORD said, "Who will persuade Ahab to go up, that he may fall at Ramoth Gilead?" So one spoke in this manner, and another spoke in that manner.

---

[2]"While the title of 'bishop' hardened its meaning and was put in a hierarchical framework of church government, the see of Rome and the bishops that came after Peter were increasingly seen as special leaders" (Leonardo De Chirico, *A Christian's Pocket Guide to Papacy* [Ross-Shire, Scotland: Christian Focus, 2015], 29).

~Date	Prayer, Veneration, Sacraments and Other Doctrines	Ecclesiology/Politics	Rival Churches and Movements, Named by Their Antagonists	Biblical Assessment of Rome's Doctrines and Practices
				Then a spirit came forward and stood before the LORD, and said, "I will persuade him." The LORD said to him, "In what way?" So he said, "I will go out and be a lying spirit in the mouth of all his prophets." And the LORD said, "You shall persuade *him*, and also prevail. Go out and do so." Therefore look! The LORD has put a lying spirit in the mouth of all these prophets of yours, and the LORD has declared disaster against you.' Now Zedekiah the son of Chenaanah went near and struck Micaiah on the cheek, and said, "Which way did the spirit from the LORD go from me to speak to you?" (1 Kings 22:19-24) ○ "Thus says the LORD of hosts: 'Do not listen to the words of the prophets who prophesy to you. They make you worthless; They speak a vision of their own heart, Not from the mouth of the LORD'" (Jer 23:16). • **Spiritual succession does not pass through the priestly anointing oil (Priest):** ○ "Then Nadab and Abihu, the sons of Aaron, each took his censer and put fire in it, put incense on it, and offered profane fire before the LORD, which He had not commanded them. So fire went out from the LORD and devoured them, and they died before the LORD" (Lev 10:1-2); ○ "Now the sons of Eli *were* corrupt; they did not know the LORD. And the priests' custom with the people *was that* when any man offered a sacrifice, the priest's servant would come with a three-pronged fleshhook in his hand while the meat was boiling. Then he would thrust *it* into the pan, or kettle, or caldron, or pot; and the priest would take for himself all that the fleshhook brought up. So they did in Shiloh to all the Israelites who came there. Also, before they burned the fat, the priest's servant would come and say to the man who sacrificed, 'Give meat for roasting to the priest, for he will not take boiled meat from you, but raw.' And *if* the man said to him, 'They should really burn the fat first; *then* you may take *as much* as your heart desires,' he would then answer him, '*No*, but you must give *it* now; and if not, I will take *it* by force.' Therefore the sin of the young men was very great before the LORD, for men abhorred the offering of the LORD" (1 Sam 2:12-17). • **Spiritual succession does not pass on through hereditary lines (King):** ○ "Ahaziah the son of Ahab became king over Israel in Samaria in the seventeenth year of Jehoshaphat king of Judah, and reigned two years over Israel. He did evil in the sight of the LORD, and walked in the way of his father and in the way of his mother and in the way of Jeroboam the son of Nebat, who had made Israel sin; for he served Baal and worshiped him, and provoked the LORD God of Israel to anger, according to all that his father had done" (1 Kings 22:51-53). ○ So also says John in John: "But as many as received Him, to them He gave the right to become children of God, to those who believe in

~Date	Prayer, Veneration, Sacraments and Other Doctrines	Ecclesiology/Politics	Rival Churches and Movements, Named by Their Antagonists	Biblical Assessment of Rome's Doctrines and Practices
				His name: who were born, not of blood, nor of the will of the flesh, nor of the will of man, but of God" (John 1:12-13).
105-115	"Alexander: They attribute to him the benediction of [holy] water with [a pinch of] salt. Item: the mixture of water with the wine at consecration. That they no longer consecrate leavened bread" (de Hainault, #1).[3]			Consider the words of the first official Protestant Historian, Johannes Sleidan (circa 1556) and his skepticism toward most of the pre-Constantinian decrees of the Bishops of Rome.[4]
				Regarding adding a pinch of salt, see 850 A.D. (cf. Boettner, #16).
125-136	"Telesphorus: They attribute to him fasting prior to Easter" (de Hainault, #2).			Turning days in the so-called "Christian Calendar" into Old Covenant-style ritualistic commemorations.
				Consider the Byzantine reading of Rom 14:5-6:
				Rom 14:5-6 (NKJ), "One person esteems *one* day above another; another esteems every day *alike*. Let each be fully convinced in his own mind. He who observes the day, observes *it* to the Lord; and he who does not observe the day, to the Lord he does not observe *it*. He who eats, eats to the Lord, for he gives God thanks; and he who does not eat, to the Lord he does not eat, and gives God thanks."
				This supposed command of Telesphorus is against Rom 14:5-6 on two counts:
				• Forcing all Christians (and eventually entire societies) to follow special days, specifically prohibited in Rom 14;
				• Forcing all Christians (and eventually entire societies) to follow special food related laws, also prohibited in Rom 14, Col 2, and 1 Tim 4.
				The eventual enforcement of specific laws on fasting [through use of the secular arm] negated not judging in Romans (cf. the "Sausage Affair" in Zurich, 1522):
				• "Let not him who eats despise him who does not eat, and let not him who does not eat judge him who eats; for God has received him" (Rom 14:3);
				• "For the kingdom of God is not eating and drinking, but righteousness and peace and joy in the Holy Spirit" (Rom 14:17).
				Notice the very clear question of Paul:
				• "But why do you judge your brother? Or why do you

[3]Jean de Hainault, *L'Estat de l'Eglise, avec Discours des Temps depuis les Apotres* ["The State of the Church, with Discourses from the Times since the Apostles] (Aberges sur le Zoom: Jacques Canin, 1605); translation mine.

[4]"The first of all began the Bishops of *Rome* to live in safety; for till then, almost all of them, (who from *Peter*, whom they reckon to be their first, are reckoned to thirty-three) were tormented with persecutions. Their decrees are inserted in the books of the Counsels but to the greatest part of them are so sleight, triviall, and quite different from the sacred Scriptures, as makes it credible that they were a long time after forged by some others. But if they be true, and proceeded from them, then indeed that which *Paul* by prophesie foretold, seemes most rightly to be applied to this place, that then the sonne of perdition and man of sinne beganne to work the mysterie of iniquity. That decree yet extant goes under *Anacletus* his name, the fourth from *Peter*, as they reckon; wherein he ordaineth the Church of *Rome* to be (by Christ's command and institution) the head of the other Churches.

"To *Alexander* the next after him, is that decree attributed, where he commands, that the water should be consecrated with salt to purge the people, and to avoid the snares of the Devil. But judge I pray you how far those differ from the Majestie of the Apostles, how farre from the writings of St. John the Evangelist who almost lived to this very time. I have onely set down these two decrees, that by them wee may judge of the rest, for they are almost of the same molde, and cary open colour of ambition, and not onely the speech wants of grace, but also the matter it selfe hath no salt in it, both which Paul requires of ministers of the Church" (John Sleidan [1506-1556], *The Key of History or the Four Chief Monarchies*, two books in one binding [Strasbourg, 1556; London, 1627], 152-154).

~Date	Prayer, Veneration, Sacraments and Other Doctrines	Ecclesiology/Politics	Rival Churches and Movements, Named by Their Antagonists	Biblical Assessment of Rome's Doctrines and Practices
				show contempt for your brother? For we shall all stand before the judgment seat of Christ" (Rom 14:10). These questions from Romans 14:10 do not make sense in a State-Church system for several reasons: • Since the state exists to make and enforce civil law, being that is constantly making rules, regulations, and judgments for people to follow; • Since, also, the hierarchy required in a state-church system (e.g. citizens versus state functionaries) was then Christianized through special us of the OT as "laity and clergy"; • Wherein the role of clergy becomes to "rule over" and "judge" the activities of their underlings (against Rom 14:4), i.e. the laity—even to the point of: ○ The pontifical court ruling over and judging Kings and Princes—and giving Kings and Princes specific civil laws that they must needs impose upon their citizens; ○ Inquisitors ruling over and judging the consciences of ordinary citizens, telling them what they are to believe and how they are to believe it, with use of the secular power of capital punishment if necessary to keep citizens in submission to the regulations of the Church of Rome! ○ Sellers of Indulgences entering countries with its "Taxes of the Roman Ministry" as evaluated by approved indulgence sellers an as coded for numerous specific sins, further adding to the tax burden of the various Western societies wherein they were sent or went[5] • Rome offers a pragmatic answer to this *non-sequetor* (i.e. pragmatism): "Our Western Civilization is the master of the world, precisely because of our state-church construct" [in which various Christian rules and regulations are imposed upon the people]. ○ Read, for example, the assertion of Brian Van Hove, a Jesuit author, that the authority and severity of Inquisition from Roman Cathollicism is largely a myth[6] ○ Or, consider French Medievalist, Anne Brenon, explaining the standard historiography that the destroyed civilization of the Cathars (in Southern France), being quite Manichean, would not have survived regardless of the crusades and Inquisition set up against them.[7]

[5]See 1471 A.D.

[6]"After the original crisis, more significantly, it just happened that the Inquisition outlived its purpose and lingered on. Some have always insisted that at any time the Catholic Church could re-activate this institution which they allege rests on torture and the extraction of confessions by coercion, among other ugly features. Honest students of history regard this assertion as mere propaganda. ...

"With the publication of Henry Charles Leas A History of the Inquisition of the Middle Ages in 1887, the golden age of inquisition history was barely opened. We are now enjoying it more fully, and it is still in its early stages. Sources and methods have been improved, confessional bickering has been bypassed, and legends have been set aside. But in the popular imagination, the old myth lingers, in Europe as well as in America. Until the work of Chadwick, Kamen, Peters, Henningsen, and their associates is made more widely known, we will not be able to appreciate that ours is such a golden age" (Fr. Brian Van Hove, S.J., "Beyond the Myth of Inquisition: Ours Is the Golden Age"; available at: http://www.catholiceducation.org/en/controversy/the-inquisition/beyond-the-myth-of-the-inquisition-ours-is-the-golden-age.html [online]; accessed: 8 Dec 2014; Internet).

[7]"Founding themselves upon this one-sided Medieval documentation, the modern theologians (from Döllinger to Father Dondaine, O.P.), the historians of religion (from Söderberg to Runciman), and the historians (from Arno Post to Christine Thouzellier) who studied and wrote on the subject up to the middle of the 20th Century, ended quite naturally to one consensal opinion, leaving the phenomena of the Cathars as a well-ordered question: catharism was a foreign body in Western Christianity and, as such, it was given over to failure. Heirs of Persian Manichaeanism and of the intervening *Mazdéism* of the Paulicians and

~Date	Prayer, Veneration, Sacraments and Other Doctrines	Ecclesiology/Politics	Rival Churches and Movements, Named by Their Antagonists	Biblical Assessment of Rome's Doctrines and Practices
				In a brother-to-brother local church system, this kind of judgment is not proper, as per Paul in Romans 14, but in a state-church hierarchical system, it is not only permissible to judge, but appropriate and necessary!
136-140	"Hyginus: They attribute to him accomplices [godparents?] for Baptism" (de Hainault, #3).			Turning the concept of Baptism on its head, by removing from it the prior repentance on the part of the individual being baptized (Acts 2:38), as well as the prior need for faith (Mark 16:16; Acts 8:12, 13, 36-37; 18:8; 19:4-5). Rather, infant baptism became a cycle of life ritual for maximum church influence and power over believers and non-believers, involving family, believing relatives, or other influential friends.
140-155	"Pius I: That Easter be celebrated on Sunday" (de Hainault, #4)	Bishop of Rome [later considered "Pope"] had/took the name "Pius"; later when new names were taken by Popes upon consecration, eleven other Pius' followed this name.	Montanist movement [supposedly] originated by Montanus; emphasized gifts of the Holy Spirit [and the new birth?], opposed infant baptism	"There is none good but God," Matt 19:17; Mark 10:18; "For all have sinned," Rom 3:23; etc. Infant baptism proved to be the most difficult of the supra-NT "sacraments" for NT Christians to shun: • It became ingrained into the culture of the family system as a "Rite of Passage" ceremony to be celebrated by all; • It became a stumbling block to NT conversion, NT evangelism, and NT evangelists. Infant Baptism appears to be based on a false transference of the OT rite of passage of circumcision, whose true significance Paul had to bring to light in Romans 4: • Abraham's righteousness was imputed prior to circumcision, based on faith alone in Gen 15:6; • The rite of circumcision was given later, almost as a sign of his prior faith, Gen 17:23-27; • This sign was then commanded to be given to all male children at eight days old, Gen 17:10-14 As is common, the outward ritual continued, but the inner faith did not. Therefore, many times, Stephen rebuked the Jews of His day for having an uncircumcised heart, Acts 7:51. Further, circumcision became a big issue in the apostolic church, as relates to a works salvation, necessitating God to bring Peter to the house of Cornelius to prove that salvation was not related to outward circumcision, Acts 10; 15: • The same arguments which disqualified circumcision as part of salvation, also disqualify infant baptism as being necessary, efficient, or a corollary to salvation; • Nevertheless, infant baptism continues as a stumbling block within many Evangelical churches. The 529 AD Second Council of Orange underscored that Baptism (primarily infant baptism in context), as applied by a human being,

Bogomils, it was characterized by a dualist doctrine of Oriental origin which it taught. Unrealistic, pessimistic, fundamentally anti-social, it had no chance of surviving in Western Christianity and very understandable repression of which it was the object—crusade and Inquisition—had only but accelerated the process of internal degeneration which would have without a doubt led to its disappearing.

   "Paradoxically, it was in the publication and study of the inquisition archives that opened the first flaw of this wall of certainty." (Anne Brenon, *Les Archipels Cathares* [Cahors, France: Dire, 2000], 13. Translation mine).

~Date	Prayer, Veneration, Sacraments and Other Doctrines	Ecclesiology/Politics	Rival Churches and Movements, Named by Their Antagonists	Biblical Assessment of Rome's Doctrines and Practices
				therefore being a work, was the means of receiving grace.[8]
				It is surprising, therefore, that Calvin in his antagonism to the Anabaptists, used circumcision as the precedent for infant baptism, leaving this precedent for Protestant churches that use this rite to initiate their children into their churches.[9]
				This author is not yet aware of why Easter was not celebrated on Sunday, as is presupposed by this decree.
				Church Government One: As far as the centralization of power in church government with the Bishop of Rome, this appears to be step one. The question follows, to whom was this decree made? And who was mandated to follow this decree? Was not Carthage equally or more significant than Rome for much of the first three centuries of the Christian era?
150/160-220/240			Tertullian, sometimes called the "Father of Latin Theology" wrote from Carthage many volumes, which have come down to the present day. Two of these volumes later helped frame NT Christians as heretics: ○ *Adversus Marcionem*, and ○ *De praescriptione haereticorum* His conversion to Montanism in 202 A.D. appears to be linked to the laxity of religion that he saw in the mainstream hierarchical church (*or perhaps even his rejection of the sacramental system of salvation which was high jacking the*	Two sides into which the churches were splitting was: • The sacramental salvation, with its focus on the outward signs, symbols, and rituals of the "new law," and its government being territorial and political, versus • Salvation by faith alone through grace alone outside of works, with their focus on the Gospel, and being non-territorial in spirit, but rather the gathered out from among the nations, cf. Rev 5:9-10 The latter side was being skewered by accusations of numerous errors and many doctrinal heresies. It seems likely that Tertullian's writings became a linchpin for later attacks on the Gospel-preaching portion of the churches of the Living God—setting up, as it were, the great apostasy of the Roman church, which reached its culmination by the 11th Century, after the collapse of power of the Byzantine Empire and the Eastern church How these writings of Tertullian were/are used: • The "Marcionite" label is used against Christians

---

[8]"According to the catholic faith we also believe that after grace has been received through baptism, all baptized persons have the ability and responsibility, if they desire to labor faithfully, to perform with the aid and cooperation of Christ what is of essential importance in regard to the salvation of their soul" ("Conclusion"; Second Council of Orange; available at: http://www.reformed.org/documents/index.html?mainframe=http://www.reformed.org/documents/canons_of_orange.html (online); accessed: 5 June 2009; Internet).

[9]"There is no doubt that doctrine must precede, by which man is instructed to be converted unto God, with faith and repentance. We see that our Lord acted in the same fashion towards Abraham, as regarding Circumcision. For before giving him this sign, He received him into His Covenant, and instructed him in His Word.

"But we have now to note, that when a man is received of God into the company of the faithful, the promise of salvation is given to him, not only for his person, but also for his children. For it is said to him: "I am your God, and the God of your children after you" (Gen 17:7). Therefore for the man, who has not been received into the Covenant of God from his youth, is as a stranger to the Church, up to the time when by the doctrine of salvation he is brought to faith and repentance. But at that point his offspring likewise at the same time become [members of] the Church. And for this cause the little children of the faithful are baptized by virtue of this Covenant, which is established with their fathers, in their name, and for their profit. Behold thus where these poor Anabaptists abuse themselves. That the doctrine must precede the Sacrament, we do not resist" (John Calvin, "Brief Instruction to Arm the Good Faithful Ones against the Errors of the Communal Sect of the Anabaptists" ["Brieve Instruction pour Armer tous Bons Fideles contre les Erreurs de la Secte Commune des Anabaptistes"] (Geneva: Jehan Girard, 1544); in *Corpus Reformatorum*, vol 35; Ioannis Calvini, *Opera Quae Supersunt Omnia*, vol. 7 (Brunsvigae: Schwetschke, 1868), 45-142; translation mine).

~Date	Prayer, Veneration, Sacraments and Other Doctrines	Ecclesiology/Politics	Rival Churches and Movements, Named by Their Antagonists	Biblical Assessment of Rome's Doctrines and Practices
			mainstream church in his day). Thus toward the end of his life, Rome considered him schismatic—rejecting the charity and unity of the church—and therefore a heretic. However, because his writings proved valuable to Rome for its early anti-heretical question-framing and its rhetoric of primacy, some of his writings remain available to this day; thus Tertullian is said to be the teacher of Cyprian, who was the predecessor of Ambrose, who was the mentor of Augustine, the mot important theologian of the Church of Rome.	who are more Dispensational in their theology, one part of which is not adapting the OT rites, ceremonies, vestments, and architecture for the NT church, as was being done by the sacramental side of the church • The label "heretic" was and is sometimes assigned to groups through the "Fallacy of Composition," wherein an emphasis of the teaching of an identified person or group is implied, therefore labeling that person or group as guilty of the entire system of heretical teaching as explained by Tertullian. It appears that the sacramental system parallels the issue discussed in the Book of Hebrews, whereby Hebraic Christians wandered back into the shadows of OT ritual, abandoning the light of the Gospel: • Heb 10:1, "For the law, having a shadow of the good things to come, *and* not the very image of the things, can never with these same sacrifices, which they offer continually year by year, make those who approach perfect" In the context of this verse, the concept of "make perfect" is parallel to the idea of "make holy" from which is derived the term "sacrament." Notice the author's emphatic use of "can never" [οὐδέποτε]. According to this verse, the Sacraments of the Catholic church can never sanctify anyone who relies on them—they are not even a shadow of redemption in Christ, as was the OT Law. Of the OT, Paul made it very clear. Although the OT is old (Rom 7:6) and the NT Christian is no longer bound to it, just as the widow is no longer bound to her deceased husband (Rom 7:1-4), yet the Law is not sin (Rom 7:7), although it convicts of sin and increases the power of temptation to sin (Rom 7:7-11). Paul concluded with the moral characteristics and qualities of the Law: • Rom 7:12, "Therefore the law *is* holy, and the commandment holy and just and good." By the way, this topic is deep and complex. This author has numerous pages of notes on the distinctions and comparatives between the OT and NT, including about 15 ways in which the two can either be compared or contrasted. Paul in Romans 11:6 makes a very interesting argument concerning grace and works: • Rom 11:6, "And if by grace, then *it is* no longer of works; otherwise grace is no longer grace. But if *it is* of works, it is no longer grace; otherwise work is no longer work." Herein, we may find why the Church of Rome has decided to title the Sacraments as "means of grace." There appears to be a word game in which grace is received by a work, but that very work is called a "means of grace." Confusing, but very effective to keep many confused as to the true means of grace, repentance and verbal

~Date	Prayer, Veneration, Sacraments and Other Doctrines	Ecclesiology/Politics	Rival Churches and Movements, Named by Their Antagonists	Biblical Assessment of Rome's Doctrines and Practices
				confession of Christ as Savior.
				Notice what the NT says about nullifying the grace of God through "the Law [of Moses]," or "the law [of Christ, so called]": • Rom 4:14 (NAS), "For if those who are of the Law are heirs, faith is made void and the promise is nullified" • Gal 2:21 (NAS), "I do not nullify the grace of God; for if righteousness *comes* through the Law, then Christ died needlessly"
				How is teaching that the work of the Holy Spirit taking place through (a) the proper words vocalized by a priest and (b) through the "spiritual" intermediary of the physical substance of the sacrament not become blasphemy against the Holy Spirit and His sovereign working (John 3:8)?
155-166	"Anicetus: The crown of priests is attributed to him by not a few" (de Hainault, #5).			Note, first of all the use of the word "priest" for a leader in the church. Territorial church leaders borrowed and revived this OT title formerly held by the opponents of Jesus in the NT.
				The priests primary function is that of being an intermediary between God and the people, by offering up prayers and sacrifices (Heb 5:1-4). Note the two Persons in the NT that have this intermediary prayer function: the Holy Spirit (prayer) and Christ Himself (one sacrifice and prayer): • Rom 8:26, "Likewise the Spirit also helps in our weaknesses. For we do not know what we should pray for as we ought, but the Spirit Himself makes intercession for us with groanings which cannot be uttered." • Heb 7:25, "Therefore He is also able to save to the uttermost those who come to God through Him, since He always lives to make intercession for them." • Heb 9:12, "Not with the blood of goats and calves, but with His own blood He entered the Most Holy Place once for all, having obtained eternal redemption."
				So then, according to Hainault, priests and other religious people began to gather special vestments in OT fashion, contra Matt 23:5; note the misuse of Acts 21:24 to proof-text a special clerical haircut.
				For power hungry church leaders, the name priest in the OT wielded greater power. See for example, the level of authority of the Levite, which NT authority was wielded only by Christ Himself (e.g. Mark 13:31; John 5:24, 47; 8:51; 12:48; 14:23-24), and to a lesser extent the words of the apostles who transcribed the words of Jesus (Acts 2:44): • Deut 24:8, "Take heed in an outbreak of leprosy, **that you carefully observe and do according to all** that the priests, the Levites, **shall teach you**; just as I commanded them, **so you shall be careful to do**."
				Further, if heresy is considered a "plague" worse

~Date	Prayer, Veneration, Sacraments and Other Doctrines	Ecclesiology/Politics	Rival Churches and Movements, Named by Their Antagonists	Biblical Assessment of Rome's Doctrines and Practices
				than leprosy. This idea provided deadly authority to the historic church in the case of heresy, which authority was vested in the "approved" state-church priesthood.
				The necessary blood lineage of the OT Levites was replaced by the anointing oil of the "Sacrament of Holy Orders" rightly administered by a bishop in proper submission to the authority of the Roman See.
161-180				During the rule of the Emperor of Rome, Diocletian, there were severe general persecutions of Christians
189-199	"Victor I: The day to celebrate Easter was a great question that agitated under this one" (de Hainault, #6).			Regarding fighting over days, see Rom 14:5-6.
				The approved date for the celebration of Easter became the focal issue (*cause célèbre*) by which Bishop Wilfrid gave Rome control over the Celtic churches in Northumbria, England, at the Synod of Whitby in 664 A.D. Wilfrid became Archbishop of Canterbury in 668 A.D.
190		"Polycrates, bishop of Ephesus, *c.* A.D. 190, says that St. John was a priest, wearing a mitre (or 'golden plate,' petavlon); but the meaning is not clear. ... Tertullian at the end of the second century speaks of the bishop as 'high priest', and, in reference to the Christian ministry, speaks of 'functions of priesthood.'" Hippolytus, early in the 3rd cent., uses similar language: 'We being their [the apostles] successors and participators in this grace of high-priesthood,' etc."[10]		Herein we have the beginning of the novel word "priest" to describe the ministry of a Christian leader. The word priest is not found for any Christian leader in the NT.
				On this topic speaks the 1994 *Catechism of the Catholic Church*:
				"in virtue of the sacrament of Holy Orders, after the image of Christ, the supreme and eternal priest, they are consecrated in order to preach the Gospel and shepherd the faithful as well as to celebrate divine worship *as true priests of the New Testament*" (*Catechism*, §1564).
				Use of the term "priest" to describe the Catholic leader eventually forced Rome's hand to equate their ministry with Heb 5:1-3 and the offering of sacrifices, the Sacrifice of the Mass being the most important.[11]
				The use of the word "priest" to describe the functions of a Christian leader:
				• Undermines the unique mediatory position of Christ, 1 John 2:1-2
				• Is used in the NT for antagonists of the Gospel, e.g. the high priests who condemned Jesus and Stephen to death, as well as the priest of Zeus who opposed Paul prior to his being stoned and left for dead in Lystra (Acts 14)

---

[10]James Hastings, *Encyclopedia of Religion and Ethics* (New York: Scribner's, 1928), 8:662.

[11]"1366 The Eucharist is thus a sacrifice because it re-presents (makes present) the sacrifice of the cross, because it is its *memorial* and because it *applies* its fruit:

"[Christ] our Lord God, was once and for all to offer himself to God the Father by his death on the altar of the cross, to accomplish there an everlasting redemption. But because his priesthood was not to end with his death, at the Last Supper 'on the night he was betrayed', [he wanted] to leave to his beloved spouse the Church a visible sacrifice (as the nature of man demands) by which the bloody sacrifice which he was to accomplish once for all on the cross would be re-presented, its memory perpetuated until the end of the world, and its salutary power be applied to the forgiveness of sins we commit daily.

"1367 The sacrifice of Christ and the sacrifice of the Eucharist are *one single sacrifice*: 'The victim is one and the same: the same now offers through the ministry of the priests, who then offered himself on the cross; only the manner of the offering is different.' 'In this divine sacrifice which is celebrated in the Mass, the same Christ who offered himself once in a bloody manner on the altar of the cross is contained and is offered in an unbloody manner'" (*Catechism of the Catholic Church*, ed. by Joseph Cardinal Ratzinger [Rome: Libreria Editrice Vaticana, 1994; London: Geoffrey Chapman, 1994], §1366-1367).

~Date	Prayer, Veneration, Sacraments and Other Doctrines	Ecclesiology/Politics	Rival Churches and Movements, Named by Their Antagonists	Biblical Assessment of Rome's Doctrines and Practices
				• Renders the ministry of the leaders wholly other than that of the NT pastor or evangelist, in conformity with the Great Commission, as the priest considers his chief role mediatorial in offering sacrifices (Heb 5, e.g. the sacrifice of Jesus on the cross as contained in the 9th Century Eucharistic sacrifice)[12] and in listening to confessions and granting absolution, called the Sacrament of Penance. The same is true of calling the role of bishops or of the pope that of a "high priest."
199-217	"Zephyrinus: That the consecration [of the wine] was done in a glass chalice; which was corrected by the Council of Rheims" (de Hainault, #7).			Beginning to add regulations concerning proper vessels to be used in worship, again in Old Testament fashion.
200-258		[St] Cyprian of Carthage said, "outside the [Catholic] Church there is no salvation"; for example, note Leo XIII's use of Cyprian in his *Satis Cognitum* (1896): 5: "Whosoever is separated from the Church is united to an adulteress. He has cut himself off from the promises of the Church, and he who leaves the Church of Christ cannot arrive at the rewards of Christ....He who observes not this unity observes not the law of God, holds not the faith of the Father and the Son, clings not to life and salvation" (S. Cyprianus, *De Cath. Eccl. Unitate*, n. 6). The term for this "one church" underwent a series of revisions over the years: 1. "The Holy Catholic Church" (Apostle's Creed) 2. "One Holy Catholic and Apostolic Church" (325 A.D. Nicene Creed) 3. "Only one Church... the Holy Roman Catholic [and] Apostolic Church," (1208 A.D. Confession of Durand d'Osca [de Huesca]	Likewise, Aquinas quoted Cyprian in answer to the question "Whether Schismatics Have [Spiritual] Power?" (SS, Q[39], A[3]): "He who observes neither unity of spirit nor the concord of peace, and severs himself from the bonds of the Church, and from the fellowship of her priests, cannot have episcopal power or honor" (in Ep. lii, quoted vii, qu. 1, can. Novatianus) Notice that the following paragraph from Sleidan (1560) shows that Cyprian taught the primacy of the local bishop over Rome: "In this age flourished *Cyprian* Bishop of *Carthage*, certain of whose Epistles to *Lucius* Bishop of *Rome*, whom he calls his brother and colleague, are amongst divers others, yet extant: and many more of his to *Cornelius*, where amongst other matters, he complains of those, who being for their offenses being condemned by the Bishops of *Africa*, and degraded from the Priesthood, had appealed to *Rome*: for it is fit said he, that where the crime is committed, there the cause	Shifted the focus from "salvation in no other name [i.e. Jesus]" (Acts 4:12) to salvation in no other church! Acts 4:12, "Nor is there salvation in any other, for there is no other name under heaven given among men by which we must be saved." With several changes apply 1 Cor 7:17 to affirm apostolic authority in teaching to apply to all "churches"? 1 Cor 7:17 (NKJ), "But as God has distributed to each one, as the Lord has called each one, so let him walk. And so I ordain in all the churches." 1 Cor 7:17 (DRA), "But as the Lord hath distributed to every one, as God hath called every one, so let him walk: and so in all churches I teach. Two points here: (1) This text directly involves the Sacrament of Holy Orders in the RCC system of thought. In the Greek Orthodox Text as in the so-called Majority Text, it is God who distributes the marital status, and the Lord calls. In the revised Greek, it is the Lord/lord who distributes or divides out the allotment, whereas it is God who calls. Note which comes first. (2) Paul "ordains" in NKJ, whereas in Vulgate (as DRA), Paul "teaches" [Greek here is διατάσσω], so in RCC, this verse is used as a proof text the universal teaching office of the Pope to the all churches. Redefined the 35 NT plural uses of "church," hence "churches" (e.g. Acts 15:41; 16:5; Rom 16:4, 16; 1 Cor 7:17; 16:1, 19; Gal 1:2, 22; Rev 1:4; etc.), to refer to one "Church" hierarchical, (after Gregory I, the Latin-speaking Church was to be ruled from Rome by the Bishop of Rome): • Note, for example, the significance of John's letters to seven different churches in Asia Minor (Rev 1:20-3:22), each having its own issues or

---

[12]"She [the Church] offers to the Father, in Christ, the child of his grace, and she commits to the earth, in hope, the seed of the body that will rise to glory. This offering is fully celebrated in the Eucharistic sacrifice; the blessings before and after Mass sacramentals" (*Catechism*, §1683).

~Date	Prayer, Veneration, Sacraments and Other Doctrines	Ecclesiology/Politics	Rival Churches and Movements, Named by Their Antagonists	Biblical Assessment of Rome's Doctrines and Practices
		prescribed to the Waldenses)* *The full text reads: "We believe in our heart and confess with our mouth only one Church, not that of the heretics, but the Holy Roman Catholic [and] Apostolic Church, outside of which we believe that no one is saved" (DS 792). One cannot help but notice the language borrowed from Rom 10:9-10 in this section of the confession.	should be discussed. Since every Pastor has a certain portion of a flock committed to his charge, whereof he must render an account to the Lord: therefore the concord of Bishops is not to be abrogated, nor their decree to be annihilated, who had already given sentence in the cause, in *Africa*."[13]	problems; • Tyndale's translation of the Greek work ecclesia as "assembly" rather than "church" was one reason that he was burned at the stake—the term assembly (like convention) refers to a gathering of people rather than a permanent socio-political entity with a hierarchy based on government or military structure and leader • Abraham was called the father of many nations (Rom 4:18), which in the context of justification by faith cannot refer to different religions, or even Christian groups who do not believe in justification by faith; nor does nations apply to "all the families of the earth (Gen 12:3), the nations who are to be evangelized (Matt 28:19), or those from every nation who believe (Rev 5:9), but rather the nations must imply multiple individual gatherings, assemblies, or congregations As to the spiritual battle, Paul frequently refers to a spiritual battle (2 Cor 10:3-5; Eph 6:10-20), as is exemplified in the Book of Acts. The phrase "outside the Catholic Church there is no salvation" has been repeated throughout Rome's historical theology of the church. This phrase appears to be the logical extension of the centralization commanded in the OT Law, whereas Rome was-is considered the "New Jerusalem": • Deut 17:8, "If a matter arises which is too hard for you to judge, between degrees of guilt for bloodshed, between one judgment or another, or between one punishment or another, matters of controversy within your gates, then you shall arise and go up to the place which the LORD your God chooses" It must be clarified, that whereas Evangelicals believe that the Bible provides the necessary centralization as applied by the work of the Holy Spirit; thus truly allowing for the rulership of Christ in His church, Rome began to see, saw, and sees itself and its hierarchy as the necessary centralization, and that especially after Augustine (theologically) and after Gregory I (organizationally); for a further discussion of this thought see A.D. 401-417. The sentence, "Whosoever is separated from the Church is united to an adulteress," wherein "the Church" is considered to mean only the Church of Rome, goes way beyond the biblical basis for salvation. For example, the Bible states that those who are rightly united with Christ are those who are led by the Spirit of God: • Rom 8:14, "For as many as are led by the Spirit of God, these are sons of God"; • If it is believed that the Holy Spirit is received by grace alone, through faith alone in Christ alone, then [St] Cyprian has gone beyond Scripture in his

[13]Sleidan, 138-39.

~Date	Prayer, Veneration, Sacraments and Other Doctrines	Ecclesiology/Politics	Rival Churches and Movements, Named by Their Antagonists	Biblical Assessment of Rome's Doctrines and Practices

				letter;
				• However, if it is believed that the Holy Spirit is received only by the proper reception of the "signs and symbols" (sacraments) of the Church of Rome (cf. Augustine's *Contra Donatisten*), then Cyprian's quote is not an overstatement;
				• One must consider that the problem also comes with the equivocal use of the word "Church" by Cyprian, which word then is redefined to mean only the Church of Rome;
				• Notice that Paul used the words "as many as" (Rom 8:14), indicating more of a plurality rather than a narrowly defined group, such as said Cyprian.
				Further, to the use of parallel language from Rom 10:9 in the confession of Durand d'Osca approaches blasphemy, for it intimates that the Catholic Church is essentially identical to the "Lord Jesus":
				• "That if you confess with your mouth the Lord Jesus and believe in your heart that God has raised Him from the dead, you will be saved," Rom 10:9 (NKJ);
				• "We believe in our heart and confess with our mouth only one Church, not that of the heretics, but the Holy Roman Catholic [and] Apostolic Church, outside of which we believe that no one is saved" (DS 792).
				As to spiritual power only found in the Church of Rome, Paul wrote of those who have a form of godliness, but lack its power, 2 Tim 3:5; as Rome changed the un-confinable presence of the Holy Spirit (John 3:8) into a tangible presence in signs and symbols [water, the host, oil], they actually became the ones who had the form without the power!
				• Also consider Lev 10:9-11.
				Two verses in Hebrews are very interesting, as regards the phrase "outside the Catholic Church there is no salvation":
				• Heb 13:13, "Therefore let us go forth to Him, outside the camp, bearing His reproach":
				  ○ The need to "come out" and bear the reproach
				  ○ Being applied to leaving Judaism and suffering persecution, cf. John 12:42-43
				  ○ With the "New Law" of Rome: its "signs and symbols," its priests and ceremonies, its altar, sacrifices, and vestments;
				• Heb 13:14 (ASV), "For we have not here an abiding city, but we seek after *the city* which is to come":
				  ○ Has not the Church of Rome sought to establish an "abiding city"? Does it not consider itself the "New Jerusalem?
				John, in Revelation, wrote of Babylon, "come out from among her":
				• Rev 18:4, "And I heard another voice from heaven saying, "Come out of her, my people, lest you share in her sins, and lest you receive of her plagues."

~Date	Prayer, Veneration, Sacraments and Other Doctrines	Ecclesiology/Politics	Rival Churches and Movements, Named by Their Antagonists	Biblical Assessment of Rome's Doctrines and Practices
217-222	"Calistus I: Of fasting three times a year" (de Hainault, #8)	Bishop of Rome, Callistus, invoked Petrine authority		To the same one listed as, "The first, Simon," Matt 10:2, Jesus later said, "Get behind Me, Satan! You are a stumbling block to Me; for you are not setting your mind on God's interests, but man's," Matt 16:23 If one claims the first title, one ought also for consistency's sake, claim the second title! Very early, the Bishop of Rome appears to have considered his authority to handle disputes, much like "the place" of which spoke Deuteronomy, where difficult cases were to be brought, cf. Deut 17:8. "The place" eventually being Jerusalem. Thus, eventually, as in this day, Rome began to look on itself and its authority to render judgment as that of the chosen "New Jerusalem." One wonders if God knew that so many martyrs would ensue because of the use of the word "first" in Matt 10:2? Surely, He did, as we have in John 16:1-3: • Virtually Rome's entire theology of primacy, successionism, and apostolic authority hinges on the word "first" in Matt 10:2, with some rhetorical sophisms applied to Matt 16:18. Where it not for the word "first", the hierarchy, centralized authority, and primacy of the City of Rome topples as inconsequential. Building from Pius I (140-155) fasting at Easter, apparently Calistus I increased this requirement, further drifting from the simplicity of the New Testament pattern of worship.
222-230	"Urban I: Of fasting four times" (de Hainault, #9)			See Pius I (140-155) and Calistus I (217-222).
235-236	"Anterus: This one had the lives of the Martyrs written" (de Hainault, #10)			As a historian, I am grateful for the memory of some of the martyrs of the Early Church. However, I am also skeptical as to who was and who was not included and why they were or were not included.
236-250	"Fabian: Excommunicated those who were displeasing to priests" (de Hainault, #11)			**Church Government Two**: It appears that Fabian began to exercise the office of the Bishop of Rome in a hierarchical fashion, thereby usurping local church autonomy and rule. Moving church discipline to a hierarchy, other than passing rules and regulations to be followed, as noted above, appears to be another move to centralized hierarchical government, which is the most apparent market niche of the Church of Rome.
240		First known church building—since until it was an official religion Christianity was marginalized: "Unless claims for recent discoveries of early Christian meeting places are confirmed, the earliest building certainly		Church buildings were not able to be built until after the time of Constantine. It may be that this religion that had been so fiercely persecuted and yet remained and flourished impressed his administrative mind. After 312 churches were able to be build, and bishops and pastors were free to live and serve openly in and around these buildings. Of interest chronologically is that Bishop of Rome Felix was said to have "constituted the feasts for

~Date	Prayer, Veneration, Sacraments and Other Doctrines	Ecclesiology/Politics	Rival Churches and Movements, Named by Their Antagonists	Biblical Assessment of Rome's Doctrines and Practices
		devoted to Christian use is at Dura Europos on the Euphrates River in eastern Roman Syria. It was a house that came into Christian possession and was remodeled in the 240s. Two rooms were combined to form the assembly room, and another room became a baptistery—the only room decorated with pictures. Dura was destroyed by the Sassanian Persians in 256, so the house's use as a church was short-lived"[14]		the dedications of churches" (de Hainault, #13). He ruled from 269-274. Therefore there may be a slight discrepancy in dating. Nevertheless, it was at least 150-220 years after the time of the apostles that churches began to own their own buildings.
250-251				Another severe persecution of Christians took place under the rule or Roman Emperor Decius

251			Novatians: A schism within the Church of Rome came about when Cornelius was elected as Bishop of Rome after the assassination of [St.] Fabian;
			
			The issues surrounded the persecution under Roman Emperor Decius (250-251)
			
			Novatus did not accept second marriages [perhaps a divorce or 1 Tim 3 issue?], believed in a pure church [as in separation from the world?]; his opponents felt that he had not been properly baptized
				Issues:
				
				• Pure lifestyle and pure doctrine:
				  o Sacramentalism began to win out in the Roman Church over biblical orthodoxy:
				    ■ Col 2:8, "Beware lest anyone cheat you through philosophy and empty deceit, according to the tradition of men, according to the basic principles of the world, and not according to Christ"
				  o Eventually, especially after Augustine, the 1 Tim 3 and Titus 1 requirements for church leadership were philosophized away, making way for the unique magical nature of the sacraments—from the hands of rightfully ordained Catholic priests only
				• Church of the multitudes:
				  o As Sacramentalism took a hold on the Roman Church, Evangelicalism was squeezed to the periphery, later to be anathematized in various ways;
				  o A godly lifestyle eventually became secondary for Rome, whereas acceptance of Rome and its rituals and forms became primary;
				  o Perhaps the warning of 1 Cor 10:5 is appropriate here, where the Greek word *pleion* ("most") is used:
				    ■ 1 Cor 10:5, "But with most of them God was not well pleased, for *their bodies* were scattered in the wilderness."
				Problem in Rome becoming negative toward other Christians:
				
				• Negativity toward other Christians counters Paul's teaching in Philippians 1:
				  o Phil 1:15-18, "Some indeed preach Christ even from envy and strife, and some also from good

[14]Everett Ferguson, "Why and When Did Christians Start Constructing Special Buildings for Worship?"; available at: http://www.christianitytoday.com/ch/asktheexpert/ask_churchbuildings.html (online); uploaded: 12 Nov 2008; accessed: 25 Oct 2015; Internet.

~Date	Prayer, Veneration, Sacraments and Other Doctrines	Ecclesiology/Politics	Rival Churches and Movements, Named by Their Antagonists	Biblical Assessment of Rome's Doctrines and Practices
				will: The former preach Christ from selfish ambition, not sincerely, supposing to add affliction to my chains; but the latter out of love, knowing that I am appointed for the defense of the gospel. What then? Only *that* in every way, whether in pretense or in truth, Christ is preached; and in this I rejoice, yes, and will rejoice." • Making rules that make distinctions of dates and eating goes beyond NT freedom in Christ: ○ Rom 14:1-10, "Receive one who is weak in the faith, *but* not to disputes over doubtful things. For one believes he may eat all things, but he who is weak eats *only* vegetables. Let not him who eats despise him who does not eat, and let not him who does not eat judge him who eats; for God has received him. Who are you to judge another's servant? To his own master he stands or falls. Indeed, he will be made to stand, for God is able to make him stand. One person esteems *one* day above another; another esteems every day *alike*. Let each be fully convinced in his own mind. He who observes the day, observes *it* to the Lord; and he who does not observe the day, to the Lord he does not observe *it*. He who eats, eats to the Lord, for he gives God thanks; and he who does not eat, to the Lord he does not eat, and gives God thanks. For none of us lives to himself, and no one dies to himself. For if we live, we live to the Lord; and if we die, we die to the Lord. Therefore, whether we live or die, we are the Lord's. For to this end Christ died and rose and lived again, that He might be Lord of both the dead and the living. But why do you judge your brother? Or why do you show contempt for your brother? For we shall all stand before the judgment seat of Christ."
254-257		Rome's Stephen I, used "Chair of Peter" to describe his post		Gal 6:3, "For if anyone thinks he is something when he is nothing, he deceives himself" 1 Cor 12:24, "But God has *so* composed the body, giving more abundant honor to that *member* which lacked" Matt 20:16, "Thus the last shall be first, and the first last," cf. Matt 19:30. The title, "Chair of Peter," marks an early date when apostolic successionism and apostolic primacy was applied to the Bishopric of Rome. However, several problems emerge with the use of this title: • The link between "You are Peter and upon this rock I will build my church" (Matt 16:18) and Christ's deeding His entire saving purposes to the rightful successors of Peter ○ Are not the saving purposes of God through Christ lodged in the message of the gospel and not in a person or territorial church? People and churches change over time—the message of the Gospel as found in the Bible, the Word of God, never changes!

~Date	Prayer, Veneration, Sacraments and Other Doctrines	Ecclesiology/Politics	Rival Churches and Movements, Named by Their Antagonists	Biblical Assessment of Rome's Doctrines and Practices
				○ "Protestants also have a concept of unbroken continuity, but it refers to faithfulness to the 'apostolic teaching' of the Church rather than the transmission of the hierarchical outlook of the Church."[15] • The link between Peter in Caesarea Philippi and Peter in Rome: further, how does the seat of the church shift from Jerusalem to Rome? Was the original "seat" of the church ever Jerusalem in the first place (Matt 23:37-39; Acts 8:1)? Does not the Antioch Church have much stronger biblical support for (a) being the church on mission (Acts 11:26) and (b) first using the name "Christian"? • The link from one "bishop" to another "bishop" and the giving and receiving of the Holy Spirit via their hands one to another appears to be the primary error of Simon the Sorcerer in Acts 8:19 So, Apostolic succession seems to be highly questionable. Further affirming use of the primacy of Peter also seems questionable: • If the words of Christ are to be taken literally in Matt 16:18 and there obvious figurative nature is to be construed in with tunnel vision as to its meaning and application, even though it contradicts many other portions of Scripture • Then why not apply the words of Jesus in Matt 16:23 literally? They need no interpretation. Jesus called Peter "Satan," when He said, "Get behind Me, Satan!" ○ Was this use of "Satan" by Jesus foreshadowing that one calling himself in the "Seat of Peter" would eventually act as an antichrist or the antichrist? • BTW, another favorite text for the primacy of Peter, also found in Matthew, is the use of the word "first" in the narrative portion in Matt 10:2, "first, Simon, who is called Peter." This verse is the only place in the NT where the term "first" is applied to Peter: ○ In John 1:40 we have the conversion of Andrew, which takes place prior to that of Simon in John 1:41-42 ○ In Acts 1:13, Peter is listed first in a list of the Apostles, and he is the one who stands up among the eleven to seek a substitute for Judas Iscariot—appearing to show a propensity for successionism early on in his leadership ○ In Acts 1:14, Peter is the one who preaches the Pentecost sermon! ○ In Acts 3:1, we have the first of five uses of

[15]De Chirico, 6.

~Date	Prayer, Veneration, Sacraments and Other Doctrines	Ecclesiology/Politics	Rival Churches and Movements, Named by Their Antagonists	Biblical Assessment of Rome's Doctrines and Practices
				the pair of names, Peter and John ○ In Acts 9-11, we have the episode with Cornelius and his household, in which God removed the social restrictions of Jews dealing with Gentiles ○ In Acts 12, we have the murder of James, then we have the miraculous release of Peter from prison ○ Peter shows up again, speaking at the Jerusalem council in Acts 15:7-11 (an excellent passage) ○ Later in Acts, the focus of leadership of the Jerusalem church appears to be James, and the focus of the Book of Acts turns on the ministry of the Apostle Paul So biblically, there are several leaders that could be cited as figureheads: • Andrew; • Peter; • James, the brother of Christ; • Barnabas; • Paul. However, how does Scripture paint Peter? • As a bold disciple • As an important disciple in the history of salvation • But also as given to: ○ Concern with building spiritual sites, Matt 17:4; Mark 9:5; Luke 9:33; ○ Concern with being first [apostolic successionism?], Luke 22:24-32 (cf. Matt 20:20-21) ○ Concern with his financial well-being, Matt 19:27; Mark 10:28; Luke 18:28; ○ Picking up a sword, John 18:10-11; ○ Concern for his own physical well-being when faced with death, even denying Christ three times, Matt 26:33-35, 69-75 and parallels; ○ One whose attitude toward the crucifixion of Jesus typified that of Satan, Matt 16:21-23; Mark 8:32-33; **Church Government Three**: Using Peter as a precursor seeks to set up the prestige of the seat of the Bishop of Rome as superior to that of other Bishops, most notably Carthage in the Latin-speaking world, but also the four ancient patriarchates in the Greek-speaking Mediterranean world.
260-268	**"Dionysius: Divided up the Provinces and Parishes"** (de Hainault, #12)	[see 300 A.D below]		**Church Government Four**: Much like a government office, territory must be divided up for proper oversight by human overseers in proper relationship to the centralized seat of power.

~Date	Prayer, Veneration, Sacraments and Other Doctrines	Ecclesiology/Politics	Rival Churches and Movements, Named by Their Antagonists	Biblical Assessment of Rome's Doctrines and Practices
269-274	"Felix: Constituted the feasts for the dedications of churches" (de Hainault, #13)			Appears to be the beginning of dedicating churches: • Dedicating inanimate objects [stone buildings] as holy; • Dedicating churches in the name of departed Christians that are named as holy, or as saints.
284-303		Byzantine Empire was divided into four parts (a Tetrarchy) by Diocletian (Gaul, Italy, Illyricum, and Oriens); each Tetrarch appointed an Augustus to replace him; Constantine later replaced this system of government with a hereditary dynasty	This eventually led to the territorial division of: • East (Byzantine/Orthodox Church) versus • West (Rome/Roman Catholic Church)	Thus began the struggle between two subtly different territorial churches: • East [from Constantinople]: Its ecclesiastical power was diffused between the seven [or so] Orthodox Churches, with equally diverse theological variation • West [from Rome]: Its power gradually became very centralized [especially after Gregory I (590-604)] becoming completely autocratic over church and state by Gregory VII (1073-1085), Innocent III (1198-1215) and Boniface VIII (1294-1303)
300	"Prayers for the dead began about A.D. 300" (Boettner, #1)			Contra 1 Cor 15:29; cf. Deut 18:10-11; 26:14 Creeping into the early church is a type of ancestor worship that became: • A bondage to the Church of Rome because of supposed ancestral precedent in worshipping according to Rome's interpretation of the Christian faith • Silent, half-sung, or full-sung Masses paid for by relatives and sung by priests for various deceased grandparents and great-grandparents on predetermined days of the week • A pledge by Rome's leadership of ancestral relief from time spent in the fires of Purgatory based directly on the financial gifts and spiritual works of living relatives on behalf of their deceased ancestors[16]—all because the "Seat of Peter" is said to have the "keys of heaven and of earth" and in particular the keys of the treasury of merits in heaven
300	"Making the [Trinitarian] sign of the cross [established]" (Boettner, #2) Likewise, at some point, a distinctive niche of Roman Catholicism became prayer using the Trinitarian formula, rather than just prayer "in the name of Jesus" as taught in the NT.	Churches divided into parishes: (1) to aid in covering an area with churches; (2) to avoid competition; and (3) to allow for proper oversight of churches; (4) to more easily identify areas with problem teachers circulating problematic doctrines: "At what time the development [of parishes] was definitely completed cannot be stated; it took place at various times in various countries. The city of Rome had forty fully organized parish churches before the end of the third century. Parish organization	The misplaced early church emphasis on the Trinity rather than the death, resurrection, and unique mediatorial work of Christ gives pause as to the true theological context and motivations of the Trinitarian and Christological controversies. Questions arise as to the teachings and practices of those who were not a part of the political-territorial churches of Rome and Byzantium.	It appears that the sign of the cross became a type of spell or incantation with special powers. The Bible speaks against the use of special signs and signals (especially those that are demanded of others), Prov 10:10. Simultaneously, it appears that prayer began to be offered "in the name of the Father, and of the Son, and of the Holy Spirit," rather than "in the name of Jesus." Although this practice only appears to be a slight deviation from the New Testament teachings, it coincided with a growing concern for "proper" Trinitarian theology and a simultaneous lack of concern for the new birth, the Pauline gospel, the Substitutionary atonement, and justification by faith. Is this shift in emphasis not an example of a "zeal for God without knowledge" (Rom 10:3)? • Rom 10:3-4, "For they being ignorant of God's righteousness, and seeking to establish their own

---

[16]"Since the faithful departed now being purified are also members of the same communion of the saints, one way we can help them is to obtain indulgences for them, so that the temporal punishments due for their sins may be remitted" (*Catechism*, §1479).

~Date	Prayer, Veneration, Sacraments and Other Doctrines	Ecclesiology/Politics	Rival Churches and Movements, Named by Their Antagonists	Biblical Assessment of Rome's Doctrines and Practices
		is spoken of in France in the beginning of the fifth century. In England the first legislation on the subject is found in the laws of Edgar, about 970."[17] [See Dionysius, 260-268 A.D.] Once the church was politicized, the parish system became a parallel to any governmental authority. After Constantine accepted Christianity as his religion, every effort was made to subsume the authority of the state under the authority of the church of Rome. This amalgamation of church and state led to rivalry and war with Constantinople, and many skirmishes well into the modern era.		righteousness, have not submitted to the righteousness of God. For Christ *is* the end of the law for righteousness to everyone who believes." The New Testament only mandates baptism by use of the Trinitarian formula (Matt 28:19). It never mandates prayer by this formula. However, at some point in time, this formula was applied to prayer in the Roman Catholic Church. The NT makes it clear that the Christian ought to pray to God the Father in the name of Jesus: • John 14:13-14, "And whatever you ask in My name, that I will do, that the Father may be glorified in the Son. If you ask anything in My name, I will do *it*." • John 15:16, "You did not choose Me, but I chose you and appointed you that you should go and bear fruit, and *that* your fruit should remain, that whatever you ask the Father in My name He may give you" • John 16:23-24, "And in that day you will ask Me nothing. Most assuredly, I say to you, whatever you ask the Father in My name He will give you. Until now you have asked nothing in My name. Ask, and you will receive, that your joy may be full" It seems likely that the change in the prayer formula provides a methodological shift which coincided with a doctrinal drift in the territorial-political church. A proper analysis of this shift using extant documents is probably impossible,[18] because there has been systematic destruction of non-hagiographic literature about the church and its beliefs since at least 800 AD, if not all the way back to Gregory I or Leo I (on the destruction of the memory of the enemy see Deut 25:17-19).[19]
303-305				A number of restrictions on Christians were enacted by Diocletian leading to further widespread persecution
308-309		Marcellus, Bishop of Rome's decree: "*Marcellus* was then Bishop of *Rome*, whose decree is extant, prohibiting Bishops from calling a Synod, without the authority of the See of Rome, as also to condemn any Bishop who should appeal to *Rome*. But *Maxentius* the Emperor, persecuting him, his		Sleidan asked the interesting historiographic question, in that, if the Bishop of Rome was being sternly persecuted, he wondered if it was likely that he would have made such a universal decree, as to disallow other Bishops from meeting outside of his own authority.

---

[17]Schaff-Herzog; "Parish."

[18]"Here at last appears to be something tangible on which the historian would like to believe that he can lay his hand and begin to measure. Surely he can determine where Christians, because of their faith, have been a molding force in history. Yet he is warned that, since the Christian set of values is different from that of the rank and file of men, the record of the accomplishments of Christians may not be preserved in the documents on which he relies. 'The last shall be first and the first last.' The Kingdom of God, he is told, comes not by observation. Neither can men say about it 'lo here and lo there'" (Kenneth Scott Latourette, "The Christian Understanding of History"; available at: http://www.historians.org/info/aha_history/kslatourette.htm [online]; accessed: 11 Jan 2013; Internet).

[19]"Remember what Amalek did to you on the way as you were coming out of Egypt, how he met you on the way and attacked your rear ranks, all the stragglers at your rear, when you *were* tired and weary; and he did not fear God. Therefore it shall be, when the LORD your God has given you rest from your enemies all around, in the land which the LORD your God is giving you to possess *as* an inheritance, *that* you will blot out the remembrance of Amalek from under heaven. You shall not forget" (Deut 25:17-19).

~Date	Prayer, Veneration, Sacraments and Other Doctrines	Ecclesiology/Politics	Rival Churches and Movements, Named by Their Antagonists	Biblical Assessment of Rome's Doctrines and Practices
		estate as others before him, was both mean and miserable. Wherefore it may easily be conjectured, whether or not, he (in those perplexities and lurking corners) could take so much upon him, as to establish such manner of decrees."[20]		
309, 310	"Eusebius: This one instituted the feast for the invention of the cross" (de Hainault, #14)			An odd feast to invent. Sleidan considered how distant is this type of concept from the teachings of New Testament
311				Emperor of Rome, Galerius, gave a deathbed edict of toleration toward Christians
311-314	"Miltiades: That it was not proper to fast on Sunday" (de Hainault, #15)			
312		Constantine's so-called conversion (312) occasioned the debated "Donation of Constantine" to [Pope] Sylvester 1 (314-335), affirming Rome's ecclesial primacy and supremacy over and above all Christian churches. • As far as Constantine's true salvation, it must be remembered that he was not baptized until on his deathbed in A.D. 337, and that the baptism took place under the Arianizing bishop Eusebius of Nicomedia.[21] • Further, with Rome's current view, by way of Augustine of Hippo, that Baptism salvation and Baptism are inseparably mixed,[22] then all of Constantine's prior decisions, according to their system of thought, were made by a totally depraved man—including that of calling the Council of Nicaea in 325. • De Chirico explained the interrelationship that ensued: "The growing	This affirmation of Rome's primacy was politically convenient in dealing with the Donatists and Carthaginisan Empire (that of Carthage); When Constantine gave funds to the African churches, he gave none to the Donatists Later, [Pope] Gregory 1 (590-604), building on the precedent and example of Augustine, encouraged other repressive political and ecclesiastical measures against the Donatists. So Constantine's "acceptance" of Christianity led to: • The demise of the congregational church system or of local church rule: o Along with the demise of any type of pluriform church system • The demise of individual choice and freedom of conscience:	The so-called "Donation of Constantine" appears to parallel the language of God giving cities to the people of Israel, over which the king of Israel was then to give theological oversight: • Deut 17:2-5, "If there is found among you, within any of your gates **which the LORD your God gives you**, a man or a woman who has been wicked in the sight of the LORD your God, in transgressing His covenant, who has gone and served other gods and worshiped them, either the sun or moon or any of the host of heaven, which I have not commanded, and it is told you, and you hear *of it*, then you shall inquire diligently. And if *it is* indeed true *and* certain that such an abomination has been committed in Israel, then you shall bring out to your gates that man or woman who has committed that wicked thing, and shall stone to death that man or woman with stones" o The exact phrase, "which the Lord your God gives you," is found 6 times in Deuteronomy 13:12; 16:5, 18; 17:2; 20:14, 16. o The same idea of God giving a land is found throughout Deuteronomy 1:8, 20, 25, 35, 36, 39; 2:5, 9, 12, 19, 29, 31; 3:12, 13, 15, 16, 20; 4:1, 21, 38, 40; 5:16, 31; 6:10, 23; 7:13; 9:6; 10:11; 11:9, 14, 17, 21, 31; 12:1, 9, 10; 15:4; 16:20; 17:14; 18:9; 19:1, 2, 3, 8, 10, 14; 21:1, 23; 24:4; 25:15, 19; 26:1, 2, 3; 27:2, 3; 28:8, 11; 29:8; 30:20. o It was not long that the Bishop of Rome began to feel that all the land was his to control spiritually, as is taught in Deuteronomy. • This idea of God "giving" the land is often found linked to the need for spiritual discipline.

---

[20]Sleidan, 149-50.

[21]De Chirico, 32.

[22]De Chirico summarizing Joseph Cardinal Ratzinger, "For nearly half a century, the Church was split into two or three obediences that excommunicated one another, so that every Catholic lived under excommunication by one pope or another, and, in the last analysis, no one could say with certainty which of the contenders had right on his side. The Church no longer offered the certainty of salvation; she had become questionable in her whole objective form—the true Church, the true pledge of salvation, had to be sought outside the institution" (De Chirico, 40-41).

~Date	Prayer, Veneration, Sacraments and Other Doctrines	Ecclesiology/Politics	Rival Churches and Movements, Named by Their Antagonists	Biblical Assessment of Rome's Doctrines and Practices
		relationship between the church and the Empire caused their organizational differences to be less and less visible. A *do ut des* (i.e. exchange of favors) culture characterized the cooperation between the two."[23] Could the Emperor's appointment of Rome as the seat for the Roman Catholic church not: • Be linked to God choosing of Rome as the seat of the "New Jerusalem?" • And, by reverse logic, was it not the "divine right" of Roman emperors to rule and pass laws? • Therefore making the emperor's decree one from God Himself? • Further, since the emperor chose the Bishop of Rome, does not this same Bishop have the authority to pass on the divine right to other kings and queens? • But, then, why did Constantine ever move his capital to Byzantium in 330 A.D. if the city of Rome was so special? • Was this split dominance the reason that Rome did not start colonizing the world (A.D. 1455) until after the fall of Byzantium to the Turks (A.D. 1453)? May not also Constantine's conversion have been a wise power-grab to leverage the influence of the gospel for his political ends? Could not the following verse explain a political-apologetic reason for Constantine's reception of Christianity, seeking to garnish the cultural approval of all the peoples of the earth, followed by their submission to Rome's political control?	○ Along with freedom of speech and freedom of the press According to inquisitor Raynerius Saccho (d. 1259), the Waldenses taught that the Church of Rome began to slip into false teaching when Sylvester was "Pope": "Item. That the Church of Christ through the bishops and other leaders up until [Pope] Sylvester, and that it failed through him, up until they themselves restored it. But they say that there have always been some who feared God and will be saved."	**Church Government Five**: If and when the teaching on submission to government authority in Romans 13:1-2 was or is applied to the hierarchy of a church in a certain place or city, then the leadership of that church is falsely given a certain immunity of "divine origination." From that divine origination, then, it can call on a "divine authority." And from that divine authority, also divine authority to dispense its own judgment: • Rom 13:1-2, "Let every soul be subject to the governing authorities. For there is no authority except from God, and the authorities that exist are appointed by God. Therefore whoever resists the authority resists the ordinance of God, and those who resist will bring judgment on themselves." In this passage, the king or emperor receives his governing authority from God Himself. If this is applied to the authority of the Bishops of any given church, then, by deduction, their authority is also by appointment from God, and whoever resists this constituted authority brings judgment upon himself. As a rebuttal to this line of reasoning, 1 Peter 2:13 adds the line "for the Lord's sake," thereby bringing the entire enterprise under the highest authority of God, that being of the teaching of His Word, the Bible: • 1 Pet 2:13-14, "Therefore submit yourselves to every ordinance of man for the Lord's sake, whether to the king as supreme, or to governors, as to those who are sent by him for the punishment of evildoers and *for the* praise of those who do good." So the jump from Constantine giving primacy to the Bishop of Rome to God giving complete spiritual authority over all the earth to the Pope was a mere jump in logic, which jump can be readily noted in Gregory VII's 1073/1075 *Dictatus Papae*, the Pope being considered the rightfully elected "judge," in accordance with Deut 17:9: • Deut 17:9, "And you shall come to the priests, the Levites, and to the judge *there* in those days, and inquire *of them*; they shall pronounce upon you the sentence of judgment." • Hence, the ruling High Priest in the New Testament time, by whom Jesus and Paul were condemned, were merely filling their role of "the judge" as described by Deut 17:9. Further, the Episcopal system of church government was founded on a hierarchy as in Deut 1:13-15, later to become an Ecclesiocracy (political rule by the church), which was itself ruled by the absolute authority of the Bishop of Rome, the Pope. This Episcopal system followed the political precedent of the Roman Empire's rule by an Emperor, such as was the case with Emperor

[23]De Chirico, 32-33.

~Date	Prayer, Veneration, Sacraments and Other Doctrines	Ecclesiology/Politics	Rival Churches and Movements, Named by Their Antagonists	Biblical Assessment of Rome's Doctrines and Practices
		• Deut 4:6, "Therefore be careful to observe *them*; for this *is* your wisdom and your understanding in the sight of the peoples who will hear all these statutes, and say, 'Surely this great nation *is* a wise and understanding people.'" And is this not exactly what has taken place in Western Europe unto this very time, 1700 years later? The Latin language, its script, its derivative languages, and its religious systems still control the Western hemisphere, and via the West most of the world's populations.[24]		Constantine. The blending of political government with church (ecclesiastical) government created a major ongoing hermeneutical problem: passages dealing with intra- and inter-church relations were then often falsely applied to society-at-large. This lack of distinction between the righteous and the wicked yielded unfortunate results: ○ E.g. Lev 10:9-11, "Do not drink wine or intoxicating drink, you, nor your sons with you, when you go into the tabernacle of meeting, lest you die. *It shall be* a statute forever throughout your generations, that you may distinguish between holy and unholy, and between unclean and clean, and that you may teach the children of Israel all the statutes which the LORD has spoken to them by the hand of Moses" • For example, Christian-based Communism appears based on applying examples and teaching on inter-church relationships to society-at-large, often misunderstanding the following passages: ○ Acts 2:44-45, "Now all who believed were together, and had all things in common, and sold their possessions and goods, and divided them among all, as anyone had need" ○ Acts 4:32, "Now the multitude of those who believed were of one heart and one soul; neither did anyone say that any of the things he possessed was his own, but they had all things in common" ○ Acts 4:34-35, "Nor was there anyone among them who lacked; for all who were possessors of lands or houses sold them, and brought the proceeds of the things that were sold, and laid *them* at the apostles' feet; and they distributed to each as anyone had need" ○ 2 Cor 8:13-14, "For *I do* not *mean* that others should be eased and you burdened; but by an equality, *that* now at this time your abundance *may supply* their lack, that their abundance also may *supply* your lack-- that there may be equality" • Likewise, in a territorial church situation, biblical passages and guidelines for inter-church relationships are applied to those who are lost and to those who are saved: ○ As is the case with the 62 "one another" commands, 12 of which are "love one another"—these are whitewashed into a bland approach to "love your neighbor as yourself": ▪ Ignoring that Christ said "love one another" was a new command (John 13:34-35), as was inaugurated within the true church ▪ Mixing the needs of the world with the needs of those within the church, confusing benevolent giving and ministry priorities in general ▪ Resulting in the true love within the church becoming cold and indifferent

---

[24]Josef Cardinal Ratzinger [later Benedict XVI], *Dominus Iesus* (16 June 2000; 6 Aug 2000); available at: www.vatican.va; accessed: 1 Sept 2008; Internet.

~Date	Prayer, Veneration, Sacraments and Other Doctrines	Ecclesiology/Politics	Rival Churches and Movements, Named by Their Antagonists	Biblical Assessment of Rome's Doctrines and Practices
				○ Conversion was either watered down, neglected, or abandoned: ▪ This same problem was addressed by the Puritan Solomon Stoddard in his "Half-Way Covenant" in colonial America ○ Evangelism was and is negatively impacted, being obscured… ○ Ecumenism is encouraged, with doctrinal distinctions being largely ignored… ○ Inter-religious dialogue becomes openness to the Holy Spirit at work in and through all other religions and/or religious expressions • No matter how well-intentioned it may be, all state church models (overt or hidden) fall prey to this misunderstanding: ○ Furthermore they produce a naïve utopianism, which is abused by those with political motivations ○ This utopianism is not based on Millenarianism, with its focus on Christ's second coming and God's power to make changes, but based on the first coming of Christ and the church's full power to make the necessary cultural changes ○ Perhaps this utopian view of the ability of the church to usher in a Millenarian type of utopia is the reason why many State Church theologians are generally antagonistic: ▪ To Premillenialism and/or Dispensationalism, as well as ▪ To particular redemption; their thinking being generalist by their very nature (*sine qua non*) All this being said, it is under the state church model of the Anglican Church, as further expanded in the U.S. declaration of Independence and Bill of Rights, that this author can enjoy the freedom to write these notes: • It is with gratitude that this author appreciates the 1689 "Act of Toleration," passed under William of Orange, which provided for freedom of worship for nonconformists. This one act has protected many generations of English-speaking peoples all across the globe from religious tyranny and oppression. • Further, it was through the military conquests of Napoleon that this same freedom was partially provided for in many countries in Western Europe, which religious freedom these countries have enjoyed for over 200 years. • Further, were not these religious freedoms, given by political powers, bought by the blood of soldiers and God's sovereign hand acting over societies and peoples? I give God glory for His wisdom and design of which I am a beneficiary **Church Government Six**: Once church government was subsumed under state control, then the church's mission shifted from fulfilling the Great Commission (in a evangelistic and spiritual sense) to the transformation of culture or the Christianization of culture: • Conversion, subsumed into Infant baptism,

~Date	Prayer, Veneration, Sacraments and Other Doctrines	Ecclesiology/Politics	Rival Churches and Movements, Named by Their Antagonists	Biblical Assessment of Rome's Doctrines and Practices
				became a secondary matter; • Cultural transformation, cultural accommodation, and submission to cultural norms became the primary matter, or to say it in another way, the life of discipleship and discipline gained important over any kind of mere instantaneous conversion; • In this scenario it follows naturally that salvation became a matter of works; "faith" as a verb (to believe) was transformed into "the Faith" as a code of ethics.
312-313		Gonzalez explained the change that took place after Constantine's conversion, related to theological debate and the politics of the same: "After the conversion of Constantine, things changed. Now it was possible to invoke the authority of the state to settle a theological question. The empire had a vested interest in the unity of the church, which Constantine hoped would become the 'cement of the empire.' Thus, the state soon began to use its power to force theological agreement upon Christians. ... But their were many rulers who did not wish to see such prolonged and indecisive controversies in the church, and who therefore simply decided, on imperial authority, who was right and who should be silenced. As a result, many of those involved in controversy, rather than seeking to convince their opponents or the rest of the church, sought to convince the emperors. Eventually, theological debate was eclipsed by political intrigue."[25] Interestingly, it appears that Constantine's conversion has been made to parallel Paul's as described in Acts 9: • Acts 9:3, seeing a light in the heavens: ○ Constantine: "Seeing a cross in the sky"		Constantine apparently saw a cross in the heavens and heard "conquer with this", leading to his Christian baptism by Sylvester, Bishop of Rome, and to the reaffirmation of the edict of toleration of Galerius in the "Edict of Milan" Notice how important is conversion theology: • Was Constantine converted when he was baptized by Sylvester, Bishop of Rome? • Was He converted the moment he saw a cross in the sky? • Or if and when did Constantine ever show signs of repentance of sin and faith in the Lord Jesus Christ? In Rome's teaching, conversion and the reception of grace takes place the very moment that the Holy Water, made holy by the dedicatory prayer of the priest, drips onto the head of the baptismal candidate, normally a small infant. From this time on, the Roman spirit of conquering peoples appears to coalesce with the outward forms of the Christian faith. Leadership over the Christian religion from Rome eventually became an effective means for (1) "rule without borders" and (2) simultaneous oversight of multiple kings and nations.[26] Two verses may relate to Constantine's conversion experience. The first considers use of biblical Christianity as an apologetic for political control: • Deut 4:6-8 (DRA), "And you shall observe, and fulfill them in practice. For this is your wisdom, and understanding in the sight of nations, that hearing all these precepts, they may say: Behold a wise and understanding people, a great nation. Neither is there any other nation so great, that hath gods so nigh them, as our God is present to all our petitions. For what other nation is there so renowned that hath ceremonies, and just judgments, and all the law, which I will set forth this day before your eyes?" May the reader compare these verses with those in a Protestant translation. The second relates to the rule of "the Christ" [or

---

[25]Justo L. González, *The Story of Christianity*, revised and updated (New York: HarperCollins, 2010), 1:181-82.

[26]See 1000s below on Italy's resistance to the rule of Rome, from the diocese of Milan.

~Date	Prayer, Veneration, Sacraments and Other Doctrines	Ecclesiology/Politics	Rival Churches and Movements, Named by Their Antagonists	Biblical Assessment of Rome's Doctrines and Practices
		• Acts 9:4, hearing a voice say, "Saul, Saul…" ○ Constantine: "Conquer with this!" However, the statement more closely seems to resemble the first horseman of the Apocalypse, as first seal was opened by the Lamb: • Rev 6:2, "And I looked, and behold, a white horse. He who sat on it had a bow; and a crown was given to him, and he went out conquering and to conquer"		his vicar"] by a rod of iron: • Psa 2:9, "You shall break them with a rod of iron; You shall dash them to pieces like a potter's vessel" Perhaps the attitude of the Corinthian church toward Paul and his evangelism prefigured the motivation of Constantine and the attitude of Roman Bishops after hum: • 1 Cor 4:8, "You are already full! You are already rich! You have reigned as kings without us-- and indeed I could wish you did reign, that we also might reign with you!" One is reminded that the Lamb opened the seal in Revelation 6 as foreordained by God the Father. Therefore there is no need for wringing our hands at the outcome of events in Church History. God is in control and has always been in full control of all the events of Church History!
313		Donatists: Donatus was elected Bishop of Carthage by the people who opposed Felix, the Bishop designated by Rome, on the grounds that Felix had turned over Scriptures to be burned during the persecution under Diocletian	The Donatist church, with its own translation of the Scriptures and teachings, became the greatest rival to church rule from Rome in the West at that time; numerous political and ecclesial pressures were used to reincorporate Donatists into the Church of Rome, which appears to have come to fruition following the administrative prowess of Gregory I (590-604) noted in his correspondence to the Bishops of Numidia (Book 1, Letter 77 [Aug 591]): "And we, indeed, according to the tenour of your representation, allow your custom (so long as it clearly makes no claim to the prejudice of the catholic faith) to remain undisturbed, whether as to constituting primates or as to other points; save that with respect to those who attain to the episcopate from among the Donatists, we by all means forbid them to be advanced to the dignity of primacy, even though their standing should denote them for that	Issues: • Calling a group with which it does not agree by its presupposed founder: ○ So, the Novatians, Montanists, Donatists, Manicheans, Pelagians, Paulicians, Wycliffites, Hussites, Lutherans, Calvinists, Huguenots, Arminians, Wesleyans, etc. ○ Was not this same thing done by Sennacherib, King of Assyria, mouthpiece of Satan against the revival in the time of Hezekiah, when he wrote letters, as recorded in 2 Chron 32:17 ▪ "He also wrote letters to revile the LORD God of Israel, and to speak against Him, saying, 'As the gods of the nations of *other* lands have not delivered their people from my hand, so the God of Hezekiah will not deliver His people from my hand,'" 2 Chron 32:17 ○ He spurned the "God of Hezekiah," much like are spurned one supposed schismatic after another • The next step was to destroy all the original writings of the founder of a schismatic church, thereby destroying any ability for objectivity in understanding their position. • Upright leaders in the church, according to 1 Tim 3 and Titus 1 ○ Augustine countered that the sacraments are valid regardless of the spiritual falleness of the person administering it (see the A.D. 1208 Confession of former Waldensian leader Durand d'Osca)[27] ○ Desiring holiness in the priesthood was deemed heretical ○ Contra many Scriptures, including Heb 12:14

[27] "In the same way we do not reject in any way the sacraments that are celebrated in her [the Holy Roman Catholic Church], and through which the Holy Spirit cooperates by his inestimable and invisible virtue, even if they are administered by a sinning priest, as long as the Church recognizes him; nor do we despise the ecclesiastical acts and the benedictions accomplished by him, but we accept them with a grateful heart as if they came from the most holy of men, for the malicious [behavior] of a bishop or priest does not deny the baptism of a child, nor the consecration of the Eucharist, nor the other ecclesiastical duties celebrated for their subjects" (Heinrich Denzinger, Peter Hünermann (ed., original edition), and Joseph Hoffmann (ed., French edition), *Symboles et définitions de la foi catholique: Enchiridion Symbolorum* (aka. *Denzinger*, or DS), 38th ed. (37th ed., Freiburg: Herder, 1997; Paris: Cerf, 2005), DS 793; translation mine).

~Date	Prayer, Veneration, Sacraments and Other Doctrines	Ecclesiology/Politics	Rival Churches and Movements, Named by Their Antagonists	Biblical Assessment of Rome's Doctrines and Practices
			position. But let it suffice them to take care of the people committed to them, without aiming at the topmost place of the primacy in preference to those prelates whom the Catholic faith hath both taught and engendered in the bosom of the Church." In the second and third centuries, the political power of Carthage exceeded that of Rome, therefore, Carthage was a rival political power. When this rival political power was combined with a rival church, the problem for Rome was exacerbated. As both kingdoms used Latin as their unifying language, strategically speaking, Rome needed only to (1) delegitimize and undermine Carthage's ecclesiastical sovereignty, and (2) crush or subsume its political power. Several generations later, Augustine would provide the intellectual weight for both of these goals to be accomplished.	(ESV), "Strive for peace with everyone, and for the holiness without which no one will see the Lord." • Local church rule, Acts 6:3; 15:25: ○ The desire for local church rule was deemed a lack of submission to Rome, the seat of Peter, and to Christ Himself (eventually) ○ There is no salvation outside the [Roman] Catholic church (Cyprian and Ambrose) ○ Local church rule was considered Simony (based on Acts 8), paying for the right to give out the Sacraments, and was anathematized; ▪ Simony became a favorite accusation of Rome against any schismatic or so-called heretical group from then on • Schism (disagreement with the dictates of Rome or separation from its hierarchy) was positioned by Aquinas (in his *Summa* [1275]) as equal to or worse than any sin [murder, adultery] or heresy [blatant false teaching], as schism is sin against the charity of unity, and charity (love) being the highest virtue, the opposite of which is considered the greatest of all sins[28] As far as cooperation today: • Note the organizational cunning of Gregory I, in which he placed a glass ceiling on the advancement of Donatists, in which case they could not rise to a position of primacy (i.e. that of a Bishop), this gradually sequestered and squelched their ability to (1) self-rule; and (2) self-propagate in areas outside of their "parish" • Any today who doubt that Rome would put into place the exact same policy toward any churches that unite with them (Lutheran-Catholic talks, Methodist-Lutheran talks, Baptist-Lutheran talks, etc.) are likely misreading the historical record • Likewise, even today there seems to be a glass ceiling at educational institutions, in academic societies, on journal and publishing house editorial boards, and even in some Evangelical denominations against any who are not conciliatory toward Rome!
314	Council of Arles (314), Canon 9: "As concerns the Africans who follow a rule of their own, that of rebaptizing, it has been decided that if someone comes from heresy to the Church, he be questioned on the symbol, and if it is certain that he has been baptized		With this arrangement, as described in the Council of Arles, "Baptism in the name of Jesus only" Pentecostals would need to be rebaptized by Rome.	Notice in the current "Signs and Symbols" of the Catholic Church that there is no need to rebaptize "heretics", as long as they believe in the Trinity: • Notice that early on the concept of "heresy" had nothing to do with their Trinitarian belief (cf. 2 John, etc.), as "heresy" originally merely meant "schismatic" (cf. 1 Cor 11:19) • This teaching obviously applies to Protestants, Evangelicals, and Baptists, who believe in the Trinity (which is why it is included in today's

[28]Consider this interchange from the Anabaptist Martyrology titled, *Martyr's Mirror*: "First Jelis was brought forth, who, as he was going to death, said, among other things: 'Because I believe that Jesus is the Christ, the Son of the living God, born of the Virgin Mary, I must die.' Thereupon a monk, who walked at his side, instantly said, 'You lie.' Jelis further said, concluding his remark, 'And because I believe that the pope is the antichrist.' Finally, kneeling down, he said in a trembling voice: "O heavenly Father, into Thy hands I commit my spirit." A few moments more, and the executioner had dispatched him, and covered his dead body with wood, that the others who were to follow should not see it lie there" (Thieleman J. van Braght, *The Bloody Theater or Martyrs Mirror of the Defenseless Christians Who Baptized Only Upon the Confession of Faith, and Who Suffered and Died for the Testimony of Jesus, Their Savior, From the Time of Christ to the Year A.D. 1660*, trans from the Dutch by Joseph Sohm, 2nd English edition [1660; 1837; 1886; Scottdale, PA: Herald Press, 2007], 657).

~Date	Prayer, Veneration, Sacraments and Other Doctrines	Ecclesiology/Politics	Rival Churches and Movements, Named by Their Antagonists	Biblical Assessment of Rome's Doctrines and Practices

	in the name of the Father and of the Son and of the Holy Spirit, we need only to lay hands on him so that he receive the Holy Spirit. But if, being questioned, he does not answer by proclaiming this Trinity, he should be rebaptized" (DS123)			Denzinger), although Christology is still used as a club against other groups (e.g. Calvin against [ana]Baptists)
				• Gregory I applied this teaching on Baptism to the Visigoth "Arians", which means:
				  ○ That the "Arian" Visigoths did actually believe in the Trinity, or
				  ○ That [Pope] Gregory I applied this ruling to those who really did not believe in the Trinity!

314-335	**"Sylvester I: That cream was sacred only for Bishops; extreme unction is attributed to him"** (de Hainault, #16)			Apparently a "sacramental" benefit was added to the two ordinances of Christ.
320	**"[Use of] wax candles, about [A.D.] 320"** (Boettner, #3)			Compare with OT system, Lev 24:2

325		Council of Nicaea began to frame the main theological questions as Trinitarian issues; whereas the Trinity was and is a valid controversy, it was used as a launch-pad to attack other church groups; for example:
		• Evangelicals clearly have Docetic tendencies:
		  ○ Docetic=believing that Jesus was a ghost-like figure, that He was not fully human; and that because...
		  ○ Evangelicals believe that salvation is only and all of God by His Spirit in the soul through prayer, **without** the prerequisite use of a physical manifestation of an intermediary sign or symbol [sacrament]!
		  ○ Hence, believing that God acts directly upon he soul of man, through His word proclaimed, and that without any physical substance other than spoken or read words on a page, Evangelicals deny that salvation comes to individual "in the flesh," i.e. through a physical substance;
			While mainstreaming theology, during the time of Nicaea, each church was considered autonomous:
			"Amongst other, one decree was, that through *Egypt, Lybia*, and *Pentapolis*; the ancient custom should be maintained, that is all the Bishops there, should remain under superiority of the Bishop of *Alexandria*, notwithstanding the usurpation and withholding thereof by the Bishop of *Rome*: as also that the Church of *Antioch* and other Provinces and Churches should each one entirely retaine their peculiar privileges."[29]
			As the sacramental side of the Institutionalized Church gained control:
			• Christology was used as a club against rival churches
			• The two-natures of Christ, were leveraged to mean that there was a physical (sacramental) and spiritual side to salvation:
			  ○ Water and spirit, John 3:5; notice that "water" [physical?] is listed first
			• Those who did not hold
				Conversion and salvation are made secondary issues to philosophical theology: the doctrine of the Trinity; for example, Nicaea never explained why Christ was crucified; however, the two most disconcerting statements are:
				• "And [I believe] one Holy Catholic and Apostolic Church," a statement which provided the proof-text for which the "arch-heretic" (Heresiarch) John Huss was burned on a stake
				• "I acknowledge one Baptism for the remission of sins," which clearly teaches baptismal regeneration (remembering that in Rome's system infants are baptized)
				  ○ Baptism came to include washing from Original Sin (see Second Council of Orange [529]), which contradicts Eph 2:2-3, "among them too we all formerly walked"
				Remembering that when one acknowledges this Creed, they are confessing belief in the totality of its teaching.
				As for churches who regularly say this creed: the Nicene Creed is not necessarily "wrong", it just shades and frames the issues; most churches who say this creed on a regular basis also baptize infants, so the second statement is not a problem; and they sometimes include a footnote to point out that "catholic" really means "universal."
				Further, one wonders at what point one could ascertain that the creeds and many other decrees of the Mainstream Church began to supersede the command not to add or subtract from Scripture?
				Rev 22:18-19, "For I testify to everyone who hears the words of the prophecy of this book: If anyone adds to these things, God will add to him the plagues that are written in this book; and if anyone takes away from the words of the book of this prophecy, God shall take away his part from the Book of Life, from the holy city, and *from* the things which are written

---

[29]Sleidan, 156.

~Date	Prayer, Veneration, Sacraments and Other Doctrines	Ecclesiology/Politics	Rival Churches and Movements, Named by Their Antagonists	Biblical Assessment of Rome's Doctrines and Practices
		○ Therefore, the logic is extended, Evangelicals are framed to believe that Jesus did not come "in the flesh" either, but was just a ghost-like figure, a Docetic view, because they deny the need for the physical substance of water to bring incipient or ultimate regeneration to the soul.	to a saving agent active within the physical elements of the water of baptism and/or the bread [host] in the Lord's Supper [Eucharist] were deemed heretical, by virtue of a false understanding of Christology!	in this book." Could it not be said that the Three Symbols (Apostles Creed, Nicene Creed, and the Creed of Athanasius) as "Rules of Faith" began to take on an interpretive life of their own, becoming a prioritative hermeneutical grid by which Scripture was then viewed?
325		Council of Nicaea (325): González explained how Nicaea shaped the organizational structure of the Post-Nicene State Church: "They approved standard procedures for the readmission of the lapsed and for the election of presbyters and bishops, and for establishing the order of precedence of the various episcopal sees."[30]		A centralized form of church government was necessary for the church to be overseen and/or to relate to various levels of political power: emperors, kings, and governors. That being said, a centralized state-church model is not readily available in the New Testament. In light of this vacuum of teaching, the Book of Deuteronomy provides teachings related to religious centralization, such as: Deut 17:8-13, "If a matter arises which is too hard for you to judge, between degrees of guilt for bloodshed, between one judgment or another, or between one punishment or another, matters of controversy within your gates, then you shall arise and go up to the place which the LORD your God chooses. And you shall come to the priests, the Levites, and to the judge *there* in those days, and inquire *of them*; they shall pronounce upon you the sentence of judgment. You shall do according to the sentence which they pronounce upon you in that place which the LORD chooses. And you shall be careful to do according to all that they order you. According to the sentence of the law in which they instruct you, according to the judgment which they tell you, you shall do; you shall not turn aside *to the* right hand or *to* the left from the sentence which they pronounce upon you. Now the man who acts presumptuously and will not heed the priest who stands to minister there before the LORD your God, or the judge, that man shall die. So you shall put away the evil from Israel. And all the people shall hear and fear, and no longer act presumptuously." The esteemed reader will note the severity of these words related to a presumptuous person who has the audacity to disagree with the judge presiding over the religious body (in other words the schismatic or heterodox person).
326	Use of relics in worship in full force when Helen, mother of Constantine, pretended or presumed to find a piece of the real cross of Christ		Gregory I encouraged the Abbott Mellitus to place relics in the churches of the Angles [English], to assert Rome's theological niche on the churches that had at one time been Evangelical [e.g. the early	Jesus spoke out against the Jews who built the tombs of the prophets as part of their worship, Matt 23:29-32, although they did not worship God as declared by those same prophets, whom they sought to venerate by decorating their tombs. Likewise, notice that the making of so-called "holy objects" was part of the Old Covenant, e.g. Deut 10:1, "At that time the LORD said to me, 'Hew for

---

[30]González, *The Story of Christianity*, 1:187.

~Date	Prayer, Veneration, Sacraments and Other Doctrines	Ecclesiology/Politics	Rival Churches and Movements, Named by Their Antagonists	Biblical Assessment of Rome's Doctrines and Practices
			Celtic churches]	yourself two tablets of stone like the first, and come up to Me on the mountain and make yourself an ark of wood.'" Such making of "holy objects" or encapsulating of relics was never part of the teaching or example either of Jesus or of the teaching or example of Apostles under the New Covenant.
330			Constantine moved the Capital of the Roman Empire to Constantinople, beginning the Byzantine Empire, leading to the Orthodox Church (Greek-speaking) separate from the Catholic church (Latin-speaking); resulting in a multi-millennial rivalry between these two sacramental-territorial churches	Three territorial religions in the Mediterranean were in conflict (Orthodox, Catholic, and Jewish). After 600 A.D. there was the addition of a fourth into the mix, Islam, with its focus on militaristic conquest (Jihad) Two religious systems, while they have always had a presence, have not usually had a major political one, that being Jewish and Evangelical One possible benefit of this long-standing religious competition appears to be that the New Testament was saved from being totally reshaped over the years

330				Of the language issues:
				
				• When the capital of Rome was moved to Byzantium, two things happen:
				  o The political center of power was moved to Byzantium, apparently splitting the city of Rome from its prophetically assigned place as the fourth world kingdom in Dan 2, 7, and 9;
				  o The primary language of the empire was abruptly changed from Latin to Greek
				• That this was a very great ecclesiastical issue is seen on several fronts:
				  o Rome needed Latin to be the primary language to retain its political control over the entire church;
				  o The Greeks clearly had the upper hand in that the NT was written in Greek;
				  o Further, the Kingdom of Carthage was a threat to the South, that also used the Latin as its primary language;
				  o Further, the Kingdom of Carthage was overrun with Donatist "heretics" who did not submit to Rome's authority
				  o Something had to be done to remedy the situation
				• The apparent remedy:
				  o For the Greek Orthodox Church:
				    ■ Translate the Old and New Testaments into Latin, and proclaim that the only valid translation of the two covenants;
				    ■ Emphasize that the LXX is not that great a translation of the Hebrew, thus demeaning the OT and NT in Greek;
				  o For the Latin Carthaginian Church:

~Date	Prayer, Veneration, Sacraments and Other Doctrines	Ecclesiology/Politics	Rival Churches and Movements, Named by Their Antagonists	Biblical Assessment of Rome's Doctrines and Practices
				▪ Force the Donatists to use Jerome's edition, and destroy all the other Latin translations in existence at the time of Jerome; ▪ Subjugate the Donatist church under the authority of Rome by theology, politics, and ecclesiology ○ BTW: It appears that Rome is quite adept at absorbing various other churches, which it has been doing for quite some time!
336	"Marcus: Decreed that the Symbol be sung after the [reading of the] Gospel [passage]" (de Hainault, #17)			
366-383	"Damasus I: That the Psalms be sung, and the Gloria Patri at the end" (de Hainault, #18)			
375	"Veneration of angels and dead saints, and use of images" (Boettner, #4)			The Jews also worshipped the dead by building tombs to dead prophets, which worship Jesus denounced, Matt 23:29-32, also: • One who calls up the dead is considered detestable to the Lord, Deut 18:10-12; 26:14 • Contra worship of the dead, Psa 106:28 • Contra baptism for the dead, 1 Cor 15:29 • Contra the worship of angels, Heb 1 Basically, it appears that the Church of Rome accommodated to the "religions all around," condoning and seeking to sanctify the worship of all the religious personages of the pagan religions all around them. Eventually the worship of the saints became parallel to the worship of the "host of heaven" (Acts 7:42-43), with villages, cities, and countries having patron saints, saints being assigned various ailments to cure, saints being assigned to people in different professions or difficulties of life, chapels and mountains being named for saints, etc. • Interestingly, Jean de Hainault noted that the pre-Christian Romans worshipped the Emperors in a similar way, thereby poisoning religion, in essence, spitting in the face of God.[31] • Further, Erasmus noted that the worship of the

---

[31]"The Roman senate had this custom: to canonize as part of their pantheon of gods virtuous emperors, in order that this honor would serve as a spur to those who in the future would bear the scepter, in order to imitate their example. The goal was quite good, but this detestable means, if only to give certain spurs to the posterity, poisoned religion, profaned the altars, abused the people, and spit in the face of God. A more expedient means would have been, to hold in hand the lives of the virtuous emperors by the pens of some virtuous and eloquent pen of some historian. For their successors, seeing the rays of glory, these trumpet sounds of renown, these painting of the virtues of their predecessors, would have been better sharpened to imitate them, instead of by these flattering and false canonizations" (de Hainault, preface).

~Date	Prayer, Veneration, Sacraments and Other Doctrines	Ecclesiology/Politics	Rival Churches and Movements, Named by Their Antagonists	Biblical Assessment of Rome's Doctrines and Practices
				hosts of heaven closely paralleled the Pagan worship of the Greek or Roman Pantheons[32]—as well as that of the Native American Indians.
				• This misplaced worship was also defended and taught by Pope John XV (985-996).
				"When we revere and venerate the relics of the martyrs and confessors, it is those for whom they were martyred and confessors that we venerate; we honor the servants, so that the honor may overflow toward the Lord who said: 'He who receives you, receives Me' [Matt 10:40], and therefore we, who have no confidence in our own righteousness, by their prayers and their merits, we always have a help before the most gracious God" (DS 675).
				• Implying that its worship is built into the psyche and soul of fallen man, Rom 1:22-23, "Professing to be wise, they became fools, and changed the glory of the incorruptible God into an image made like corruptible man-- and birds and four-footed animals and creeping things."
				• Note: Col 2:18, "Let no one keep defrauding you of your prize by delighting in self-abasement and the worship of the angels, taking his stand on *visions* he has seen, inflated without cause by his fleshly mind."
				God in Deuteronomy repeatedly warns against going after other gods (using the phrase "other gods" 16 times):
				• Deut 6:14, "You shall not go after other gods, the gods of the peoples who *are* all around you"
				• Deut 7:4-5, "For they will turn your sons away from following Me, to serve other gods; so the anger of

---

[32]"Now there are not a few who are given over to the veneration of the saints, with elaborate ceremonies. Some, for example, have a great devotion to St. Christopher. Provided his statue is in sight, they pray to him almost every day. Why do they do this? It is because they wish to be preserved from a sudden and unprovided-for death that day. There are others who have a great devotion to St. Roch. Why? Because they believe that Roch can immunize them against certain physical ailments. Others mumble certain prayers to St. Barbara or St. George so they will not fall into the hands of the enemy. Still others fast in honor of St. Apollo so that they will not be troubled with toothaches. Others visit the image of holy Job to prevent boils. There are certain merchants who assign a portion of their profits to the poor so that they will not suffer a loss of merchandise in shipwreck. A candle s burned in honor of St. Jerome so that lost goods might be recovered. In short, for everything we fear or desire we set up a corresponding deity. This has gone to the extent that each nation has its own. Among the French St. Paul is esteemed, among us Germans St. Jerome has a special place. Certain areas hold St. James or St. John in lesser or greater esteem. This kind of piety, since it does not refer either our fears or our desires to Christ, is hardly a Christian practice. As a matter of fact, it is not a great deal different from the superstitions of the ancients. They pledged a tenth of their goods to Hercules that they might get rich, or a cock to Aesculapius to regain their health. A bull was sacrificed to Neptune to avoid mishap at sea. The names may have changed, but the purpose and intentions are the same.

"You pray that you may not be overtaken by a premature death. Would it not be more Christian to pray that you might be of such a virtuous mind that wherever death overtakes you, it will not find you unprepared? You have absolutely no intention of changing your way of life, and yet you ask God that you may not die. Certainly the only reason you pray is that you may continue your life of sin as long as possible. You pray for the material things of this world and have not the slightest idea of how to use divine things. Are you not actually praying for your own ruin? You pray for good health and yet you continue to abuse it. Is not this rather a dishonoring than an honoring of Almighty God?

"I am sure that these remarks will be disturbing to certain so-called saintly men who identify the worship of God with financial gain and who, with their sweet benedictions, deceive the minds of the innocent, serving their own bellies rather than Christ. They will protest that I am forbidding the veneration of the saints in whom God is also honored. I do not damn those who do these things with a simple and childish sort of superstition so much as I do those who, for their own advantage, magnify these practices completely out of proportion. They encourage these devotions, which of themselves are tolerable, for their own profit and thereby capitalize on the ignorance of the masses. What I utterly condemn is the fact that they esteem the indifferent in place of the highest, the nonessentials to the complete neglect of what is essential. What is of the smallest value spiritually they make the greatest. I will certainly praise them for seeking a healthy body from St. Roch, provided they consecrate their life to Christ. But I will praise them still more if they pray for nothing else than a love of virtue and of hatred for vice. As for dying or living, let them leave such matters in the hands of God, and let them say with Paul, 'Whether we live, we live unto the Lord; and whether we die, we die unto the Lord.' What would be ideal is that they desire to be dissolved from the body and be with Christ. It would be perfect if they, in disease and misfortune, make their real joy consist in this, that they have conformed their lives to Christ their Head. Accordingly, to practice these devotions is not so much to be condemned as is the danger inherent in them, namely, that of relying entirely or too much on them. I suffer from infirmity and weakness, but with St. Paul I show forth a more excellent way. Examine yourself in the light of these rules and you will not be content with these indifferent actions until all of them are referred to Christ; you will not stop midway but will continue so that all is aimed at serving and honoring God" (Erasmus, "Enchiridion" [aka. "The Handbook of the Militant Christian"], in John P. Dolan, *The Essential Erasmus* [New York: Mentor, 1964], 60-61).

~Date	Prayer, Veneration, Sacraments and Other Doctrines	Ecclesiology/Politics	Rival Churches and Movements, Named by Their Antagonists	Biblical Assessment of Rome's Doctrines and Practices
				the LORD will be aroused against you and destroy you suddenly. [5] "But thus you shall deal with them: you shall destroy their altars, and break down their *sacred* pillars, and cut down their wooden images, and burn their carved images with fire"
				• Deut 8:19-20, "Then it shall be, if you by any means forget the LORD your God, and follow other gods, and serve them and worship them, I testify against you this day that you shall surely perish. [20] "As the nations which the LORD destroys before you, so you shall perish, because you would not be obedient to the voice of the LORD your God"
				• Deut 11:26-28, "Behold, I set before you today a blessing and a curse: [27] "the blessing, if you obey the commandments of the LORD your God which I command you today; [28] "and the curse, if you do not obey the commandments of the LORD your God, but turn aside from the way which I command you today, to go after other gods which you have not known"
				• Deut 13:6-11, "If your brother, the son of your mother, your son or your daughter, the wife of your bosom, or your friend who is as your own soul, secretly entices you, saying, 'Let us go and serve other gods,' which you have not known, neither you nor your fathers, [7] of the gods of the people which *are* all around you, near to you or far off from you, from *one* end of the earth to the *other* end of the earth, [8] you shall not consent to him or listen to him, nor shall your eye pity him, nor shall you spare him or conceal him; [9] but you shall surely kill him; your hand shall be first against him to put him to death, and afterward the hand of all the people. [10] And you shall stone him with stones until he dies, because he sought to entice you away from the LORD your God, who brought you out of the land of Egypt, from the house of bondage. [11] So all Israel shall hear and fear, and not again do such wickedness as this among you."
				• Deut 17:2-5, "If there is found among you, within any of your gates which the LORD your God gives you, a man or a woman who has been wicked in the sight of the LORD your God, in transgressing His covenant, [3] "who has gone and served other gods and worshiped them, either the sun or moon or any of the host of heaven, which I have not commanded, [4] "and it is told you, and you hear *of it*, then you shall inquire diligently. And if *it is* indeed true *and* certain that such an abomination has been committed in Israel, [5] "then you shall bring out to your gates that man or woman who has committed that wicked thing, and shall stone to death that man or woman with stones"
				• See also Deut 11:16-17; 13:13; 18:20; 28:14, 36, 64; 29:26; 30:17; 31:18, 20.
				Turning to "other gods" parallels turning away from God, and visa versa; the worship of both cannot coexist together:
				• Deut 30:17, "But if your heart turns away so that you do not hear, and are drawn away, and worship other gods and serve them"
				• 1 Thess 1:9, "For they themselves declare concerning us what manner of entry we had to you,

~Date	Prayer, Veneration, Sacraments and Other Doctrines	Ecclesiology/Politics	Rival Churches and Movements, Named by Their Antagonists	Biblical Assessment of Rome's Doctrines and Practices
				and how you turned to God from idols to serve the living and true God" Furthermore, it would seem that the Bible lost its priority position in determining norms for worship: • Calvin rightly emphasized a "Regulative Principle" of worship = if a form of worship is not overtly taught in the Bible, it is invalid! Among other passages, Matt 15 discusses the possibility of forms of worship resulting from the traditions of men which contradict the clear teaching of the Word of God Furthermore, false approaches to worship, and the need to validate them from Scripture leads to the poor application of Scripture; for example, consider this passage as dealing with the Pantheon of Saints: • Col 1:3-4 (NAS), "We give thanks to God, the Father of our Lord Jesus Christ, praying always for you, since we heard of your faith in Christ Jesus and the love which you have for all the saints" • Col 1:3-4 (NAB [Roman Catholic]), "We always give thanks to God, the Father of our Lord Jesus Christ, when we pray for you, for we have heard of your faith in Christ Jesus and the love that you have for all the holy ones"
375	"Veneration of angels and dead saints, use of images [e.g. use of statues for meditation, prayer, and worship]" (Boettner, #4)	Notice how the Douai-Rheims Bible translated Deut 4:16, as compared to the 1560 English Geneva: • Deut 4:16 (DRA), "Lest perhaps being deceived you might make you a graven similitude, or image of male or female" • Deut 4:16 (Eng Gen), "That ye corrupt not your selves, & make you a graven image or representation of anie figure: whither it be the likeness of male or female," The Contemporary English Version below portrays the sophistry involved in the Catholic use of images in worship, by re-translating this verse to apply only to "idols"—not really "statues," "images," or the "representations" of individual saints and their unique virtues: • Deut 4:16 (CEV), "not to commit the sin of worshiping idols. Don't make idols to be worshiped, whether they are shaped like men, women,"		Contra the clear teaching of the Bible on the making and use of idols for worship: • Exod 20:4-6, "You shall not make for yourself an idol, or any likeness of what is in heaven above or on the earth beneath or in the water under the earth. You shall not worship them or serve them; for I, the LORD your God, am a jealous God, visiting the iniquity of the fathers on the children, on the third and the fourth generations of those who hate Me, but showing lovingkindness to thousands, to those who love Me and keep My commandments" • Deut 4:15-19, 23-24, "So watch yourselves carefully, since you did not see any form on the day the LORD spoke to you at Horeb from the midst of the fire, lest you act corruptly and make a graven image for yourselves in the form of any figure, the likeness of male or female, the likeness of any animal that is on the earth, the likeness of any winged bird that flies in the sky, the likeness of anything that creeps on the ground, the likeness of any fish that is in the water below the earth. And *beware*, lest you lift up your eyes to heaven and see the sun and the moon and the stars, all the host of heaven, and be drawn away and worship them and serve them, those which the LORD your God has allotted to all the peoples under the whole heaven. ... So watch yourselves, lest you forget the covenant of the LORD your God, which He made with you, and make for yourselves a graven image in the form of anything *against* which the LORD your God has commanded you. For the LORD your God is a consuming fire, a jealous God." • Deut 5:8-10, "You shall not make for yourself an idol, *or any likeness of* what is in heaven above or on the earth beneath or in the water under the earth. You shall not worship them or serve them; for I, the LORD your God, am a jealous God, visiting the

~Date	Prayer, Veneration, Sacraments and Other Doctrines	Ecclesiology/Politics	Rival Churches and Movements, Named by Their Antagonists	Biblical Assessment of Rome's Doctrines and Practices
		Moreover, this lesser sin can be forgiven for the higher cause of eliciting thoughts of worship among the unlearned faithful.[33]		iniquity of the fathers on the children, and on the third and the fourth *generations* of those who hate Me, but showing lovingkindness to thousands, to those who love Me and keep My commandments."

- Deut 7:5-6, "**But thus you shall deal with them: you shall destroy their altars, and break down their *sacred* pillars, and cut down their wooden images, and burn their carved images with fire**. For you are a holy people to the LORD your God; the LORD your God has chosen you to be a people for His own possession out of all the peoples who are on the face of the earth"

- Deut 7:25-26, "The graven images of their gods you are to burn with fire; you shall not covet the silver or the gold that is on them, nor take it for yourselves, lest you be snared by it, for it is an abomination to the LORD your God. **Nor shall you bring an abomination into your house, lest you be doomed to destruction like it. You shall utterly detest it and utterly abhor it, for it *is* an accursed thing.**"

- Deut 27:15, "'Cursed *is* the one who makes a carved or molded image, an abomination to the LORD, the work of the hands of the craftsman, and sets *it* up in secret.' And all the people shall answer and say, 'Amen!'"

- 1 Kings 11:4-10, " For it came about when Solomon was old, his wives turned his heart away after other gods; and his heart was not wholly devoted to the LORD his God, as the heart of David his father *had been*. For Solomon went after Ashtoreth the goddess of the Sidonians and after Milcom the detestable idol of the Ammonites. And Solomon did what was evil in the sight of the LORD, and did not follow the LORD fully, as David his father *had done*. Then Solomon built a high place for Chemosh the detestable idol of Moab, on the mountain which is east of Jerusalem, and for Molech the detestable idol of the sons of Ammon. Thus also he did for all his foreign wives, who burned incense and sacrificed to their gods. Now the LORD was angry with Solomon because his heart was turned away from the LORD, the God of Israel, who had appeared to him twice, and had commanded him concerning this thing, that he should not go after other gods; but he did not observe what the LORD had commanded."

- There are multiple other passages in the OT on the worship of idols, and in the NT the idolatry in Athens, the academic center of Greek Philosophy, greatly disturbed Paul causing him to evangelize all the more, Acts 17:16-17ff.

See also on the false worship of statues,

---

[33] "It was in this way that the Lord revealed Himself to the Israelite people in Egypt, permitting the sacrifices formerly offered to the Devil to be offered thenceforward to Himself instead. So He bade them sacrifice beasts to Him, so that, once they became enlightened, they might abandon one element of the sacrifice and retain another" (Gregory I, "Letter to the Abbot Mellitus"; in Bede, *A History of the English Church and People*, trans. L. Sherley-Price, rev. R. E. Latham [Harmondsworth, Middlesex, England: Penguin Books, 1979], 87).

"They will protest that I am forbidding the veneration of the saints in whom God is also honored. I do not damn those who do these things with a simple and childish sort of superstition so much as I do those who, for their own advantage, magnify these practices completely out of proportion. They encourage these devotions, which of themselves are tolerable, for their own profit and thereby capitalize on the ignorance of the masses. ... Accordingly, to practice these devotions is not so much to be condemned as is the danger inherent in them, namely, that of relying entirely or too much on them" (Erasmus, "Enchiridion" [aka. "The Handbook of the Militant Christian"], in John P. Dolan, *The Essential Erasmus* [New York: Mentor, 1964], 61).

~Date	Prayer, Veneration, Sacraments and Other Doctrines	Ecclesiology/Politics	Rival Churches and Movements, Named by Their Antagonists	Biblical Assessment of Rome's Doctrines and Practices
				1 Kings 19:18
				See on bowing and kissing, Hos 13:1-2
				Later, the so-called "Iconoclastic Controversy" between the Eastern and Western territorial churches revolved around the use of statues "in worship"—as an "aid" to the illiterate who could learn from the images to venerate their examples of piety (see Erasmus footnote above on the worship of the particular examples of "saints," accompanied with prayer for their aid, to receive from them the special graces and favors that they are said to bestow and exemplify). Eventually, while the Western Church kept their use of statues, the Eastern Church developed "Holy Icons," which were paintings of holy scenes, also giving them similar veneration.
				It appears that, rather than becoming "aids for worship and devotion," the use of statues and icons took on the power of a talisman, fetish, or charm. In a type of folk religion, these statues and other objects were worshipped and venerated, much as the host (or bread) of the Lord's Supper is worshipped. These practices were and are not discouraged by Rome, but actually encouraged and multiplied through relics, bestowing sainthood, pilgrimages with objects of veneration, and the blessing of Holy Water and numerous other items.

383	Bishop of Rome, Damasus, had his secretary, Jerome, translate (or compile) an official Latin text, to "unite" the many other Latin texts, likely to deemphasize contrary Donatist translations in North Africa:
	
	• Note Jerome's 69 uses of do "penance" for "repent," e.g. Matt 4:17:
	
	   ○ KJV, "From that time Jesus began to preach, and to say, Repent: for the kingdom of heaven is at hand"
	
	   ○ DRA (1899 Douay-Rheims), "From that time Jesus began to preach, and to say: Do penance, for the kingdom of heaven is at hand"
	
	• Note the nod to the concept later defined as transubstantiation (not fully defined until 851 A.D.) in the Lord's Prayer, Matt 6:11:
		Of Jerome's Vulgate (cont):
		
		• Note also Jerome's use of *decepti* as the translation of the Hebrew *shachath* ("act corruptly") in Deut 4:16:
		
		   ○ KJV, "Lest ye corrupt *yourselves*"
		
		   ○ DRA, "Lest perhaps being deceived"
		
		   ○ NAB (1991 New American Bible), "not to degrade yourselves"
		
		• Likewise note Jerome's theological downgrade in Rom 3:23:
		
		   ○ GEN, "for all haue sinned, and are depriued of the glorie of God"
		
		   ○ DRA, "For all have sinned, and do need the glory of God"
		
		• Jerome translated the Old Testament from the Greek LXX, as can be noted in the name for God being "God" (as in the LXX), instead of Rock (as in the Hebrew text) in Deut 32:31, for example:
		
		   ○ LXX, ὅτι οὐκ ἔστιν
			Jerome's Vulgate became a vehicle through which the sacramental system of salvation was imposed upon the Western Church, including infant baptism (translating Matt 28:19 as "teach") and the sacrament of penance (for "do penance").
			
			Was not Jerome's Vulgate the seedbed of a deeper issue? That being the following question:
			
			• When did the primacy of the Latin language become a divisive issue in the Early Church?
			
			In other words:
			
			• When did the Latin Church decide that in order to extent its primacy over all Christian Churches, Latin was to be the official language of the Bible, Christian scholarship, Christian dogma, and Christian jurisprudence?
			
			• Did not the Latin primacy provide a cultural primacy to Rome, completing
				Rome sought to take control of the Bible and of its translation and propagation, against freedom of conscience and freedom of interpretation (Rom 14:12; 1 Cor 2:12-16; 2 Pet 1:20-21; Acts 17:11).
				
				Later, whereas the Eastern churches encouraged the translation of the Bible into the language of the people, Rome would later decree that other language groups use only Latin in worship, and correspondingly use only the authorized translation of Jerome (one wonders what was found in the Donatist translations that must have been opposed by Rome).
				
				The Protestant use of Greek and Hebrew as foundational languages for translating became a threat to Rome's primary authority, wielded in part through its exclusive use of the Latin language.
				
				The number of theological and ecclesiastical glosses interspersed in Jerome's translation is quite significant.
				
				The existence of the various Greek-speaking and other Orthodox churches, as well as those faithful to Judaism allowed for the maintenance of original language texts apart from Rome's control. This competition yielded the fruit upon which textual criticism is founded. Yet Jerome's Vulgate held absolute sway only where Rome controlled both the ecclesial and political powers.
				
				Catholic antagonism to vernacular translation and its persecution of the Bible Societies in the 19th

~Date	Prayer, Veneration, Sacraments and Other Doctrines	Ecclesiology/Politics	Rival Churches and Movements, Named by Their Antagonists	Biblical Assessment of Rome's Doctrines and Practices
	○ KJV, "Give us this day our daily bread" ○ DRA (1899 Douay-Rheims), "Give us this day our supersubstantial bread" • Note Jerome's use of *caerimonias* instead of "statutes" in Deut 4:8, 14: ○ KJV, "And what nation *is there so* great, that hath statutes and judgments *so* righteous as all this law" ○ DRA, "For what other nation is there so renowned that hath ceremonies, and just judgments, and all the law" ○ KJV, "And the LORD commanded me at that time to teach you statutes and judgments, that ye might do them in the land whither ye go over to possess it" ○ DRA, "And he commanded me at that time that I should teach you the ceremonies and judgments which you shall do in the land, that you shall possess" ○ KJV uses "ceremonies" one time (Num 9:3); the DRA uses the word 65 times.	ὡς ὁ θεὸς ἡμῶν οἱ θεοὶ αὐτῶν· οἱ δὲ ἐχθροὶ ἡμῶν ἀνόητοι. ○ VUL, Non enim est Deus noster ut dii eorum: et inimici nostri sunt iudices. ○ DRA, "For our God is not as their gods: our enemies themselves are judges." ○ NKJ, "For their rock *is* not like our Rock, Even our enemies themselves *being* judges." For example, this translation discrepancy was changed in the version mandated by Vatican II (for the Psalms) and Paul VI, the "Nova Vulgata"—its final 1979 version was authorized by John Paul II in his Scripturarum Thesaurus (25 April 1979): ○ NOV, Non enim est petra eorum ut Petra nostra, et inimici nostri sunt iudices. • Jerome's Vulgate went from being considered a superior translation to being the only text allowed, and Latin became the only language of higher learning • Eventually, Jerome's translation of the Vulgate became considered to be "without error" • Non-use of Jerome's Vulgate eventually became a treasonable offense	what Constantine had only begun politically, then moving to Greek-speaking Byzantium? • [Gregory I (590-604) seems to have (1) codified Latin primacy (2) focused Western political power in Rome after the assassination of Emperor Maurice] If Greek is considered the language of the New Testament, as restored by the Protestant Reformation, then the authority of the Latin Church becomes subservient to the authority of the interpretations of Greek-speaking exegesis, and hence, the Greek-speaking Church. Similar to the destruction of Hebrew-speaking people (for a time), it would seem that the destruction of Greek speaking people would also be a priority to eliminate this competition! Note that Syriac-speaking Christians have been attacked in two ways: (1) by the injection of a Maronite church into the system; and (2) through the weapon of Islam.	Century seems to have been overlooked by Protestants and mainstream Evangelicals in the signing of the 1968 and 1987 "Guidelines for Interconfessional Cooperation in Translating the Bible" between the United Bible Society and Rome's Secretariat for Promoting Christian Union. It has also allowed Rome to influence original language texts both openly and secretly.[34]
384-399	**"Siricius: That the husbands of widows cannot be priests" (de Hainault, #19)**	Siricius was the first bishop of Rome to officially adopt the title "Pope"; Pope or Pape was derived from the Greek: *pappas* for father; the term was first used by Christians to describe their	The 13th Century Albigenses, originating in part from the 12th Century preaching of the Monk Henry, had only Bishops and Deacons, two titles actually found in the Bible;	The title pope is derived from the word for "father," and likewise finds alliteration with the title "pontifex," which is Latin for "high priest" (cf. Heb 5:1, 5, 10; pontifex is found 31 times in Latin Vulgate). Whereas, almost prophetically, Jesus said: "And do not call *anyone* on earth your father; for One

[34]"To find the most qualified persons to constitute the Working and Review Committees, it is necessary to use informal decision-making procedures. That is to say, an extensive investigation is made by some qualified individuals so as to assess the technical capacities of such persons and the probabilities of such persons being able to work together effectively in a committee. After determination, in consultation with church leaders, of the availability of such individuals in consultation with church leaders, they may be formally nominated by their respective churches and appointed by the Bible Societies. Without careful preliminary investigation unsuitable appointments have sometimes been made to the detriment of the whole project" ("Guiding Principles for Interconfessional Cooperation in Translating the Bible" [Pentecost, 1968], from Thomas F. Stransky, C.S.P., and John B. Sheerin, C.S.B., eds. *Doing the Truth in Charity: Statements of Pope Paul VI, Popes John Paul I, John Paul II, and the Secretariat for Promoting Christian Unity 1964-1980* [New York: Paulist, 1982], 165).

~Date	Prayer, Veneration, Sacraments and Other Doctrines	Ecclesiology/Politics	Rival Churches and Movements, Named by Their Antagonists	Biblical Assessment of Rome's Doctrines and Practices
			"priests" on the Eastern coast of the Mediterranean (Schaff-Herzog, "Pope")	although the Lombardian Inquisitor (and former Cathar) Raynerius Saccho stated (in 1250) that they also had "Sons" acting as under-Bishops or Bishops in training	is your Father, He who is in heaven," Matt 23:9 Use of pope as a title seems to be a first step in a move away from a New Testament church model, by adding a title and level of leadership not found in the NT, as well as directly contradicting the above Scripture! Hence, over time, Rome, through sophisticated sophistry legitimized its use of the word "Pope" while simultaneously delegitimizing the plain reading of the text of Scripture! Likewise note that in the Church of Rome, female spiritual leaders are called "Mother," such as "Mother Teresa," "Mother Angelica," etc. • Mark 3:32-35, "And a multitude was sitting around Him; and they said to Him, 'Look, Your mother and Your brothers[1] are outside seeking You.' [33] But He answered them, saying, 'Who is My mother, or My brothers?' [34] And He looked around in a circle at those who sat about Him, and said, 'Here are My mother and My brothers! [35] 'For whoever does the will of God is My brother and My sister and mother.'" It appears that Siricius is the first to encroach on liberty in the marriage of priests by this injunction (cf. 1 Cor 9:5). Eventually Rome will directly contradict 1 Tim 4:3, but it took an evolution of ideas and explanations for this contradiction to take hold.
385	Because of his being French, and because of his opposition to the Priscillian receiving the death penalty, Martin of Tours was made a Patron Saint of France (date uncertain). Sulpicius Severus wrote in the 4th Century the early life of "Saint Martin."		Priscillian, the so-called heretic and founder of the Priscillianists, was beheaded because of the legislative process against him initiated by Bishop Ithacius [Metropolitan bishop of Lusitania]; followers of Priscillian received the same fate.[35] **First Martyr for Matters of Religion:** Priscillian was beheaded for his teachings and beliefs, apparently the first time the "sword of the state" was used to fulfill an ecclesiastical condemnation for heresy.[36] If indeed Priscillian was the first Christian theologian to die for his beliefs at the hand of the territorial church of the time, this makes him a central figure for all future martyrdoms for	Of Freedom of Conscience versus Martyrdom: Following closely in the heels of the Council of Nicaea, the state was used to put heretics to death. Therefore, the Council of Nicaea was more than a mere declaration of doctrine, it was a state legislative document which took away freedom of conscience to those under its jurisdiction. Teaching at odds with Nicaea became a Capital crime. Along with other bishops of Hispania, Bishop Ithacius brought this doctrinal dispute before the secular Emperor Magnus Maximus for his judgment. He ruled against Priscillian. Of Assigning Patron Saints to Lands, etc.: Is not ascribing a "Patron Saint" for countries, cities, and days, leveraging human nature, and building on territorial rivalry against which Paul wrote in 1 Cor 1:12? • 1 Cor 1:12, "Now I say this, that each of you says, 'I am of Paul,' or 'I am of Apollos,' or 'I am of Cephas,' or 'I am of Christ.'" This practice of assigning saints seems to allow for "diversity with unity"—that is, unity under the religious system of submission to Rome—the downside of this practice is multiplied: • It leverages idolatrous practice as the means to

[35]"Martin of Tours"; available at: http://en.wikipedia.org/wiki/Martin_of_Tours (online); accessed: 7 May 2015; Internet.
[36]"Priscillian was condemned and, with six of his companions, executed in 385. Priscillian's execution is seen as the first example of secular justice intervening in an ecclesiastical matter" ("Priscillian"; available at: http://en.wikipedia.org/wiki/Priscillian [online]; accessed: 7 May 2015; Internet).

~Date	Prayer, Veneration, Sacraments and Other Doctrines	Ecclesiology/Politics	Rival Churches and Movements, Named by Their Antagonists	Biblical Assessment of Rome's Doctrines and Practices
			conscience: • Lack of freedom of conscience; • Death penalty for doctrinal disputes; • State church turning one condemned for doctrine to the secular arm; and • The secular arm applying the death penalty for doctrinal disputes among church members and leaders. Consider: At this time in his life, Augustine was a trained lawyer and skilled orator in Milan, Italy. He was "converted" to Roman-style Christianity in 386. Furthermore, it appears that dealing with those who erred from Roman doctrine and practice was an important part of Augustine's legacy; e.g. *Contra Donatisten* and *Contra Manichean*. One wonders the reason behind the fact that Augustine has been raised so highly in the minds of churchmen in these later years.	provide the end of diversity; • Opposers of this idolatrous practice are therefore considered in disunity with the Bishop of Rome and his judgments (Deut 17) and breadth of heart to accommodate the human spirit; • Opposers of this idolatrous practice are considered opponents of the Church of Rome, and therefore lacking in Charity, especially if they voice their opposition; and • Opposers are therefore targeted as enemy #1 of the Charity of the Church of Rome.
386	Consider the importance of Augustine to the Roman Catholic view of salvation and the Sacraments: "Scholastic Theologians of the Middle Ages have used St. Augustine's ideas as here set forth regarding the Beatitudes, the Gifts of the Holy Ghost and the petitions of the Lord's Prayer, to build up a complete system of Christian perfection which found its consummation in the writings of St. Bona-venture and St. Thomas Aquinas."[37]		Augustine converted to Roman-style Christianity	The *Sitz im Leben* of Augustine's life sheds light on the meaning and purpose of his writings, as well as how they have been leveraged into the future: • See especially Peter the Lombard's Four Books of Sentences and his use of Augustine for doctrinal matters, such as the Sacraments; • See secondarily Thomas Aquinas' use of Augustine on practical matters, such as dealing with heretics
394	**"The Mass [Eucharist, or 'giving of thanks'] as a daily celebration"** (Boettner, #5)			A daily Mass deemphasized worship on the first day of the week, Acts 20:7; 1 Cor 16:2: • Which day celebrates "Resurrection Day!" Matt 28:1; Mark 16:2, 9; Luke 24:1; John 20:1, 19

[37]St. Augustine, *The Lord's Sermon on the Mount*, trans. by John J. Jepson, S.S.; intro by Johannes Quasten and notes by Joseph C. Plumpe (Westminster, MD: Newman, 1948), 10.

~Date	Prayer, Veneration, Sacraments and Other Doctrines	Ecclesiology/Politics	Rival Churches and Movements, Named by Their Antagonists	Biblical Assessment of Rome's Doctrines and Practices
				Later the Host was worshiped as part of the Eucharist of the Mass (the Lord's Supper), contra Exod 20:3 (see A.D. 851) **Eucharist**—on the leveraging of a name: • How did Jesus give thanks? He "did the Eucharist," Matt 26:27; Mark 14:23; Luke 22:17, 19; 1 Cor 11:24: ○ Truly Jesus and Paul gave thanks to God in prayer, e.g. Matt 15:36; Mark 8:6; Luke 10:21-22; John 6:11, 23; 11:41-42; Acts 27:35 ○ As the Pharisee gave thanks in prayer, Luke 18:11 ○ As the healed Samaritan also gave thanks to Jesus, with no breaking of bread, Luke 17:16 • Paul stated in his epistles that he constantly "gave thanks" (Gk. Eucharisto), Col 1:3; 1 Thess 1:2; 2 Thess 1:3; 2:13 Thus, via the word "Eucharist" for the Lord's Supper, it was promoted to unlearned Christians that just as Jesus gave thanks by "doing the Eucharist," so Paul was constantly "doing the Eucharist"! Desperate to prove the Mass in the NT, the term for ministry was leveraged from interpreting Acts 13:1-2 as the "priests" of the Antioch Church worshipping God via the "Saying Mass" [or: the Eucharist] (see French 1646 revision of the Louvain Bible of [Father] François Véron, also found in the French 1643 *Bible de Corbin*): • Acts 13:2, "they [the priests] were saying Mass"[38] In Catholic theology, the Mass is a true and valid reenactment of the sacrifice of the very Christ, by which He is truly resacrificed as a pleasing sacrifice to God. However, the Bible states that Jesus died once and once only as a sacrifice: • Rom 6:10, "For *the death* that He died, He died to sin once for all; but *the life* that He lives, He lives to God" • Heb 9:27-28, "And as it is appointed for men to die once, but after this the judgment, so Christ was offered once to bear the sins of many. To those who eagerly wait for Him He will appear a second time, apart from sin, for salvation" • Heb 10:14, "For by one offering He has perfected forever those who are being sanctified" Note also that, to Rome, "doing the Eucharist" is said to be a true and valid proclamation of the

---

[38]"Ce dernier Nouveau Testament vaut la peine qu'on s'y arrête. Ces différentes Bibles firent souvent le tourment des polémistes catholiques. Ils ne pouvaient les récuser, et dans maints passages elles donnaient gain de cause à leurs adversaires. François Véron, prédicateur et lecteur du Roi (Louis XIV) pour les controverses, sentit vivement ce désavantage. Curé à Charenton, il avait de vives discussions à soutenir avec les ministres protestants, qui le battaient parfois par leurs citations bibliques. Impatienté, le P. Véron se décida à faire paraître, en 1646, une nouvelle traduction du Nouveau Testament, toujours sous le pavillon de Louvain. Il déclare qu'il a dû corriger plusieurs erreurs préjudiciables à la religion catholique. Il reprend ses prédécesseurs de ce qu'ils n'ont pas assez repurgé les traductions protestantes de leurs ordures. Veut-on savoir comment il «repurgeait» les traductions hérétiques de leurs «ordures»? Dans sa traduction, on lit à Actes 13, 2, au lieu de *pendant qu'ils servaient le Seigneur dans leur ministère* : EUX DONC DISANT LA MESSE (traduction qu'on trouve déjà dans la Bible de Corbin de 1643, dont nous aurons à reparler). Trois pages (in-4) de la préface sont consacrées à justifier cette traduction, que le traducteur déclare indiscutable, en rabrouant d'importance les contradicteurs. Dans un Nouveau Testament publié à Bordeaux en 1686, les mots *le sacrifice de la messe* se trouvent même dans le titre du chapitre (*)" (Samuel Lortsch, *Histoire de la Bible* [Paris: Société Biblique Britannique et Étrangère, 1910] (online); Part 3; available at : http://www.bibliquest.org/Lortsch/Lortsch-Histoire_Bible_France-3.htm; accessed: 2 Feb 2004; Internet).

~Date	Prayer, Veneration, Sacraments and Other Doctrines	Ecclesiology/Politics	Rival Churches and Movements, Named by Their Antagonists	Biblical Assessment of Rome's Doctrines and Practices
				Gospel (cf. 1 Cor 11:26). Thus are nullified the Great Commission passages as referring to the verbal proclamation of the Gospel, and thus were nullified the examples in the Book of Acts for the proclamation of the Gospel. Rather, Mark's Great Commission passage could read: • "Go into all the world and say the Mass among all nations."
395		Theodosius bequeathed the Roman Empire to his two sons, dividing the four praetorian prefectures: • Arcadius in the East (ruling from Constantinople) • Honorius in the West (ruling from Rome)		Again, this decision eventually led to a very long power struggle between two empires (only ended by the Muslim invasion forces of the Jihad, which crippled the Byzantine Empire): • Byzantine Empire, the Eastern Roman Empire, which was Greek-speaking, and • Roman Empire, the Western Roman Empire, ruled from Rome, and was Latin-speaking
397a	Augustine (353-430) began in earnest to write against the Donatist "sect" (Gk. αἵρεσις; Engl. heresy); likewise he admitted having been a "Manichean" for a time, which seems to be a code-word for an anti-sacramentalist (aka. anti-sacerdotalist; or Evangelical).[39] Consider the following quote of Augustine in Peter the Lombard (1160 A.D.), *Four Books of Sentences*, Book 1, Distinction 1, Paragraph 1, Sentence 1: "While considering the contents of the Old and New Law again and again by diligent chase [indagine], the prevenient grace of God has hinted to us, that a treatise on the Sacred Page is [versari] chiefly about things and/or signs. For as Augustine, the egregious Doctor, says in the book *on Christian Doctrine*:[1] 'Every doctrine is of things, and/or signs. But even things are learned through signs. But here (those) are properly named things, which are not	Date of the "Third synod of Carthage" (as by Denzinger) discussed, among other things, the canon of Scripture. Augustine was quoted by Aquinas (SS, Q[39], A[1]) as defining: a... "schismatic is one who holds the same faith, and practices the same worship, as others, and takes pleasure in the mere disunion of the community, whereas a heretic is one who holds another faith from that of the Catholic Church" [probably referring to a non-sacramental theology of conversion] (in *Contra Faust.* xx, 3) While the Donatists wanted priests (or clergy if you will) to adhere to a 1 Tim 3 lifestyle, Augustine argued against them, stating that the sacraments were valid *ex opere operato* (by virtue of the work) regardless of the piety of the clergy offering them (see also the letter of Anastasius II written in A.D. 496, DS356)	Could it be that later (590-604) Gregory I raised "Charity" (the unity of the church) above "Faith" (i.e. doctrinal purity)? Note this clever sophistry quoted in Peter the Lombard's *Sentences* (Book 4, Dist 13, Ch 2 (73), Part 3): 3. Gregory, *On Ezechiel*: "Someone who, in the exposition of the sacred word, fabricates something in order to please his listeners, speaks his own words, not God's. But anyone who, with regard to the Lord's words, understood them otherwise than he who spoke them, or even in another sense, and yet strives for the building up of charity, then the words which he speaks are the Lord's"[41] Manichean: A group against which Augustine wrote extensively, having spent some time among them. He framed their teaching as a blending of the Zoroastrian dualism of Mani with Christianity (because they framed life as a struggle of the saints of God against the Devil	Paul delineated a paradigm which applies to the Sacramental versus Evangelical issue in Gal 5:17, writing, "For the flesh sets its desire against the Spirit, and the Spirit against the flesh; for these are in opposition to one another." It is no wonder then that the flesh began persecuting the spirit, as in Gal 4:29, "But as at that time he who was born according to the flesh persecuted him *who was born* according to the Spirit, so it is now also" (cf. Gal 5:11). The last phrase of this verse seems to apply to almost the entirety of the history of the churches! Consider that in 1 Cor 1:22 Paul wrote, "the Jews ask for a sign"—likewise, Rome had its "signs and symbols" of the Sacraments. Paul continued, "and the Greeks seek wisdom." Rome gradually added its vices and virtues (by the time of Gregory I in 590-604 AD), very much parallel to Greek Stoicism: • The "signs and symbols" of Sacramentalism, as described above, have huge ramifications on exegesis, interpretation and Bible translation, as evidenced in Jerome's Vulgate; • The "Vices and Virtues" as part of spiritual, avoiding the vices and seeking the virtues, also have a strong influence on the human side of spiritual growth and development, as opposed to the divine side of the Holy Spirit's justifying and sanctifying power, and freedom in Christ. It appears that when the leadership of the Church of Rome fully adhered to "signs and symbols," as well as the "vices and virtues," that, according to 1 Corinthians 1:23, they were no longer preaching "Christ crucified," even though they had made the "sign of the cross" a symbol of the Blessed Trinity and made crucifixes into a type of fetish (an object

---

[39] By the way, B. B. Warfield rightly described the term "Evangelical" as applying to those who necessitate no intermediary between God and man, Christ Himself being the only Mediator (cf. Warfield, *The Plan of Salvation* [1918]). This mediation applies not only to a priest, but also to an object, such as a wafer, water, or oil. The caveat, however, according to the Great Commission, is the need for an evangelist to share the Gospel and the respondent to have a hearing of faith.

~Date	Prayer, Veneration, Sacraments and Other Doctrines	Ecclesiology/Politics	Rival Churches and Movements, Named by Their Antagonists	Biblical Assessment of Rome's Doctrines and Practices
	employed to signify anything; but signs, those whose use is in signifying.'"40 [Footnote 1: "Chapter 2, n. 2; here and in the next passage, but with many words omitted by Master (Peter) and not a few added or changed."] "Signs and Symbols" became a Central Interpretive Motif for Lombard, and he seems to base this emphasis on Augustine. Therefore, it appears, if understood contextually, Augustine may have been the most confounding apologist for the false teachings of the Church of Rome, as enumerated above, in the entire history if the church. He was so clever and equivocal that he is still used by "both sides," as it were, today. Did Augustine go too far, so that he was in actuality "fighting against God" (Acts 5:39)? By his subtle and coy use of logic and his twisting of heresies, was he not lacking a "fear of God" (Deut 25:18)? When does human logic and its use for self-serving ends become corrupted? Even Paul was careful to rejoice when others preached Jesus in a clearly schismatic way (Phil 1:15-18).		for the souls of men). Unfortunately, it is applied to Evangelical Christianity throughout the history of the churches, and can be applied to anyone who believes that we are in a spiritual battle, that there are saved people and lost people, and that holy objects are meaningless.	having spiritual power). • "For Jews request a sign, and Greeks seek after wisdom; but we preach Christ crucified, to the Jews a stumbling block and to the Greeks foolishness, but to those who are called, both Jews and Greeks, Christ the power of God and the wisdom of God" (1 Cor 1:22-24) When this shift actually took place is the quandary of these notes. Further, it appears that Augustine was asking Christians everywhere, especially in Carthage, to deed over their "freedom of conscience" to the Bishop of Rome: • Gradually ignoring, redefining, or removing all of these commands:42 ○ "Beware of false prophets," Matt 7:15; cf. Matt 24:5, 11, 24; Mark 13:22 ○ "Behold, I send you out as sheep in the midst of wolves. Therefore be wise as serpents and harmless as doves," Matt 10:16 ○ "Take heed and beware of the leaven of the Pharisees and the Sadducees ... to beware of the leaven of the Pharisees and Sadducees," Mat 16:6, 11 (Mark 8:15; Luke 12:1) ○ "And Jesus answered and said to them: 'Take heed that no one deceives you,'" Matt 24:4 ○ "See to it that no one misleads you," Mark 13:5 ○ "And then if anyone says to you, 'Behold, here is the Christ'; or, 'Behold, He is there'; do not believe him; for false Christs and false prophets will arise, and will show signs and wonders, in order, if possible, to lead the elect astray. But take heed; behold, I have told you everything in advance," Mark 13:21-23 (cf. Matt 24:23-24) ○ "Therefore, be on the alert-- for you do not know when the master of the house is coming, whether in the evening, at midnight, at cockcrowing, or in the morning--lest he come suddenly and find you asleep. And what I say to you I say to all, 'Be on the alert!'" Mark 13:35-37 ○ "See to it that you be not misled; for many will come in My name, saying, 'I am He" and, 'The time is at hand'; do not go after them," Luke 21:8 ○ "But take heed to yourselves, lest your hearts be weighed down with carousing, drunkenness, and cares of this life, and that Day come on you unexpectedly," Luke 21:34 ○ "Be on guard for yourselves and for all the flock," Acts 20:28 ○ "For such men are slaves, not of our Lord Christ but of their own appetites; and by their smooth and flattering speech they deceive the hearts of the unsuspecting," Rom 16:18

41Peter Lombard, The Sentences: Book 4: On the Doctrine of the Signs; trans by Guilio Silano (Toronto: Pontifical Institute of Mediaeval Studies, 2010), 69.
40Peter the Lombard, Four Books of Sentences, Book 1, "On the Unity and Trinity of God," Distinction 1, Chapter 1, "Every doctrine concerns things and/or signs"; available at: http://www.franciscan-archive.org/lombardus/opera/ls1-01.html (online); accessed: 16 May 2006; Internet.
42Unfortunately, but commonly, the easiest way to annul all these commands in one stroke is to argue based on the plural form of many of these commands, that the plurality refers to church leaders in concert and not individuals or schismatic groupings of individuals; therefore supposedly affirming the various state-controlled and approved symbols and councils, and their ensuing creedal formulations.

~Date	Prayer, Veneration, Sacraments and Other Doctrines	Ecclesiology/Politics	Rival Churches and Movements, Named by Their Antagonists	Biblical Assessment of Rome's Doctrines and Practices
				o "Do not be deceived," 1 Cor 6:9; 15:33; Gal 6:7
				o 1 Cor 11:28, "But let a man examine himself, and so let him eat of the bread and drink of the cup"
				▪ This text is clearly singular in form, and thus obviously individualistic
				o "Examine yourselves *as to* whether you are in the faith. Test yourselves. Do you not know yourselves, that Jesus Christ is in you?—unless indeed you are disqualified," 2 Cor 13:5 (NKJ)
				▪ Notice how this command assumes (1) soul competency, and also commands (2) individual discernment
				▪ Notice how the Nestle-Aland 27th ed removed the plural "is" in you, thereby removing a potentially "Manichean"-oriented concept of "Christ in you the hope of glory" (Col 1:27)!
				o "Let no one deceive you with empty words," Eph 5:6
				o "So then do not be foolish, but understand what the will of the Lord is," Eph 5:17
				o Eph 5:10 (KJV), "Proving what is acceptable unto the Lord."
				o Phil 1:10, "that you may approve the things that are excellent, that you may be sincere and without offense till the day of Christ"
				o "Beware of the dogs, beware of the evil workers, beware of the false circumcision," Phil 3:2
				o "See to it that no one takes you captive through philosophy and empty deception," Col 2:8
				o "Test all things; hold fast to what is good, Abstain from every form of evil," 1 Thess 5:21-22
				o "But the Spirit explicitly says that in later times some will fall away from the faith," 1 Tim 4:1
				o "But evil men and impostors will proceed *from bad* to worse, deceiving and being deceived," 2 Tim 3:13
				o "Let no one in any way deceive you," 2 Thess 2:3
				o "For there are many rebellious men, empty talkers and deceivors," Titus 1:10
				o "Do not be deceived, my beloved brethren," James 1:16
				o "Children, it is the last hour; and just as you heard that antichrist is coming, even now many antichrists have arisen; from this we know that it is the last hour," 1 John 2:18
				o "These things I have written to you concerning those who are trying to deceive you," 1 John 2:26
				o "Little children, let no one deceive you," 1 John 3:7
				o "Beloved, do not believe every spirit, but test the spirits, whether they are of God; because many false prophets have gone out into the world," 1 John 4:1
				o "For many deceivers have gone out into the world," 2 John 1:7

~Date	Prayer, Veneration, Sacraments and Other Doctrines	Ecclesiology/Politics	Rival Churches and Movements, Named by Their Antagonists	Biblical Assessment of Rome's Doctrines and Practices
				<ul><li>"Be on your guard lest, being carried away by the error of unprincipled men," 2 Pet 3:17</li><li>"Appealing that you contend earnestly for the faith which was once for all delivered to the saints," Jude 1:3</li></ul> Including commands related to comparing ministry: Gal 6:4, "But let each one examine his own work, and then he will have rejoicing in himself alone, and not in another" — This text is another singular in form, and therefore, due to plenary inspiration, affirms the need to individual watchfulness. Including, denying: The need for discernment, Phil 1:9-11 — Rome would have to argue that this is corporate language, and is not meant for individual Christians, but for the corporate church. Followed by the fact that Emperor Valentinian III stated in 445, that all difficult questions should be brought to the Holy See in Rome (or to [pope] Leo I at that time), even with the use of secular force as needed (see 445 below). Followed by the fact that individual discernment against the ruling of the Holy See is considered impertinence and high obstinacy (cf. the Reformation Martyrologies). The need to test the spirits, 1 John 4:1. In short, any verses that exhort the NT Christian to have [individual] discernment in any way, with the exception of individually discerning others who are contrary to or do not follow the teachings of Rome! Further, individual spiritual resolve is prophesied of Jesus, exemplified by Jesus, and exemplified in Ezekiel: Isa 50:5-7: "The Lord GOD has opened My ear; "And I was not disobedient "Nor did I turn back. "I gave My back to those who strike Me, "And My cheeks to those who pluck out the beard; "I did not cover My face from humiliation and spitting. "For the Lord GOD helps Me, "Therefore, I am not disgraced; "Therefore, I have set My face like a flint, "And I know that I shall not be ashamed" (Isa 50:5-7). Luke 9:51, "Now it came to pass, when the time had come for Him to be received up, that He steadfastly set His face to go to Jerusalem". Ezek 3:7-9, "But the house of Israel will not listen to you, because they will not listen to Me; for all the house of Israel are impudent and hardhearted. Behold, I have made your face strong against their faces, and your forehead strong against their foreheads. Like adamant stone, harder than flint, I have made your

~Date	Prayer, Veneration, Sacraments and Other Doctrines	Ecclesiology/Politics	Rival Churches and Movements, Named by Their Antagonists	Biblical Assessment of Rome's Doctrines and Practices

				forehead; do not be afraid of their looks, though they *are* a rebellious house."
				
				o Likewise Martin Luther said, "I cannot choose but adhere to the word of God, which has possession of my conscience; nor can I possibly, nor will I even make any recantation, since it is neither safe nor honest to act contrary to conscience! Here I stand; I cannot do otherwise, so help me God! Amen."
				
				• **Therefore, based upon and after Augustine, all individual theological assessment and discernment was effectively deeded to, bequeathed to, or turned over to Rome's hierarchy**:
				  o All with very meager NT support:
				    ▪ The false application of submission to church governing authorities as appointed by God in Rom 13:1
				    ▪ Rome's proof-text of and erroneous interpretation of the keys in Matt 16:19 and 18:18-19, giving its Hierarchy with its use of its Sacraments the autocratic monopoly to dispense God's grace
				    ▪ The need to obey spiritual leaders in Heb 13:17
				    ▪ The plural command forms (hence "corporate language") of some NT commands for discernment
				  o Thus, with their Traditions Rome obliterated clear teachings of the NT, cf. Matt 15:1-9, such as salvation by grace alone through faith alone in Christ's shed blood alone, outside of any works, as found written in Scriptures alone
				  o Hence, Mary's passive humility to God's will ("be it unto me according to thy word," Luke 1:38) became the model for the believer in the Church of Rome, who need not know beyond the necessary...
				  o Hence, Clement XIII wrote in his *In Dominico Agro* (1761), "The faithful should obey the apostolic advice not to know more than is necessary, but to know in moderation"
				
				• Hence, the major arguments against the Protestant Reformation were that it represents:
				  o "Humanism"—that individual humans can interpret Scripture equal to or better than Rome with its longstanding "Holy Tradition" going back to Jerome and Augustine, or
				  o "Rationalism"—that believing that individual man's rational being can be individually enlightened by the Holy Spirit outside of Rome's "signs and symbols" (its water, wafers, and oil)
				  o "Individualism"—is another catchphrase to seek to undermine personal conversion and the clear need for individual assessment, discernment, and conviction.
				
				Likewise as the command given to individuals to "take heed to yourself" (Deut 4:9; Acts 20:28) was turned into a corporate command, resulting in the eroding of so-called "individual interpretation"

~Date	Prayer, Veneration, Sacraments and Other Doctrines	Ecclesiology/Politics	Rival Churches and Movements, Named by Their Antagonists	Biblical Assessment of Rome's Doctrines and Practices
				probably even before the 4th Century:
				• Likewise any interpretation that effectively countered the arguments of Rome were neatly swept from the pages of history, leaving only one side of the story, which point objectively-oriented church historians have noted throughout the centuries
				Equally devastating was the removal of 1 Tim 3 and Titus 1 standards for church leaders [priests], which led to laxity in morals among priests and laity (perpetuated to this day), and was accompanied by a distain for those who did and do expect their leaders and laity to be "above reproach," calling them "cathars," "perfects," and "heretics" (again Gal 4:29 in action), or more recently Pietists and Puritans!
				If in fact, Augustine effectively required Donatists to bequeath their conscience to the Bishop of Rome, this went against quite a number of verses to the contrary!
397b	Augustine taught surprisingly lax moral principles on lifestyle issues, as quoted by Aquinas (SS, Q[10], A[11]): "If you do away with harlots, the world will be convulsed with lust" (in *De Ordine* ii, 4) Similarly, note that Ignatius Loyola appears to have taught that it is more meritorious to resist the same evil thought again and again, than to conquer it immediately.[43] Augustine also renumbered the Ten Commandments, so that the prohibition against making idols and worshipping them was subsumed as part of the First Commandment.[44]	This example shows part of the complexities of a territorial church seeking to provide laws for secular governance		As far as laxity in sexual immorality and temptation, the NT calls Christian to live holy lives, for example: • Rom 1:7, "To all who are in Rome, beloved of God, called *to be* saints..." • Titus 2:11-13, "For the grace of God that brings salvation has appeared to all men, teaching us that, denying ungodliness and worldly lusts, we should live soberly, righteously, and godly in the present age, looking for the blessed hope and glorious appearing of our great God and Savior Jesus Christ" • 1 Pet 1:15-16, "but as He who called you *is* holy, you also be holy in all *your* conduct, because it is written, 'Be holy, for I am holy.'" In the OT there are similar verses, e.g. Isa 55:6-7. Likewise, Paul made it clear that the Christian is to "flee immorality": • 1 Cor 6:18, "Flee sexual immorality. Every sin that a man does is outside the body, but he who commits sexual immorality sins against his own body" • 1 Cor 10:14, "Therefore, my beloved, flee from idolatry" • 1 Tim 6:11, "But you, O man of God, flee these things and pursue righteousness, godliness, faith,

[43]"*To help the exercitant purify himself and make better confessions.* I presuppose that I have three kinds of thoughts in my mind. The first is a thought which is my own and which comes solely from my own liberty and will; the other two come from without, the one from the good spirit and the other from the evil one.

"*Thoughts:* There are two ways of gaining merit from an evil thought which comes from without:

"1. The thought comes to me to commit a mortal sin; I resist the thought immediately and it is conquered.

"2. When the same evil thought comes to me and I resist it, and it returns again and again, but I continue to resist it until it is vanquished. This second way is much more meritorious than the first.

"One is guilty of venial sin if the same thought of committing mortal sin comes to him and he gives it some attention or takes some sensual pleasure in it, or when there some negligence in rejecting it" (Loyola, St. Ignatius. *The Spiritual Exercises of St. Ignatius.* Translated by Anthony Mottola. Imprimatur, Cardinal Spellman [Garden City, NY: Image Books, Doubleday, 1964], 50).

[44]"The present catechism follows the division of the Commandments established by St Augustine, which has become traditional in the Catholic Church. It is also that of the Lutheran Confessions. The Greek Fathers worked out a slightly different division, which is found in the Orthodox Churches and Reformed communities" (*Catechism*, §2066).

~Date	Prayer, Veneration, Sacraments and Other Doctrines	Ecclesiology/Politics	Rival Churches and Movements, Named by Their Antagonists	Biblical Assessment of Rome's Doctrines and Practices
	Augustine likewise made a distinction between "veneration" and "latria" in worship, which distinction was applied to allow a certain level of worship to Mary, the saints, and statues and relics. He likewise appeared to redefine religion to be a quest, rather than the Evangelical personal relationship with God wrought through the "new birth" experience, which experience was sullied as mystical and spiritistic.			love, patience, gentleness" • 2 Tim 2:22, "Flee also youthful lusts; but pursue righteousness, faith, love, peace with those who call on the Lord out of a pure heart" Likewise, the Christian is called to avoid sexual immorality: • 1 Thess 4:3-6, "For this is the will of God, your sanctification: that you should abstain from sexual immorality; that each of you should know how to possess his own vessel in sanctification and honor, not in passion of lust, like the Gentiles who do not know God; that no one should take advantage of and defraud his brother in this matter, because the Lord *is* the avenger of all such, as we also forewarned you and testified" Loyola's comments seem to be based on a non-plenary interpretation of wrestling with sin according to a French translation of James 1:2, which in old French translations may give the impression of "cherish" (remembering that he wrote his *Spiritual Exercises* near 1534 while in Paris): • James 1:2 (1522, 1530 Lefebvre), "Mes Freres, reputez estre toute joye quant cherrez diverses tentations."[45] • [My translation], "My brothers, judge to be all joy when you encounter [cherish] diverse temptations" Hence in English, note the NJB's use of the external "come upon": • James 1:2 (NJB), "My brothers, consider it a great joy when trials of many kinds come upon you" However, elsewhere in the Bible on cherishing sin: • Psalm 66:18-19 (ESV), "If I had cherished iniquity in my heart, the Lord would not have listened. But truly God has listened; he has attended to the voice of my prayer" Augustine's distinction between "veneration" and "latria" continues to this day in relation to the veneration of saints and Mary. Only the divine receives "latria" or worship. Saints receive "dulia" or veneration. The Blessed Virgin Mary, however, receives "hyperdulia," or special veneration reserved only for her. These distinctions were also made by Jerome (347-420 A.D.). Paul's reminder to the saints in the church of Corinth comes as a reminder against misplaced worship: • 1 Cor 1:13, "Is Christ divided? Was Paul crucified for you? Or were you baptized in the name of Paul?"

---

[45]The 1522 French LeFebvre "quant vous cherrez en diverses tentations" (when you cherish diverse temptations) is very difficult to translate, as the definition of "cherrez" is unclear even in Medieval and other old French dictionaries. It is phonetically closest to the modern French "cherir", which means "to cherish." The translation "cherrez"in James 1:2 was also used by 1534 Olivétan, the 1550 Louvain, the 1560 French Geneva, and the 1669 French Geneva. In 1707 David Martin changed French Protestant translation history by instead using the verb "exposés à" (exposed to). The 1744 Ostervald went further with the translation "vous arrivent" (arrive [upon] you). In 1859, Darby's French translated this verb with the colloquial phrase "quand vous serez en butte à" (are subjected to). In Greek, the word περιπίπτω can mean "to fall around, so as to embrace; to fall in with, fall into [hence] encounter" (Liddell-Scott). The Latin incideritis can mean "happen; fall into, fall in with, meet; fall upon, assail" (Lewis).

~Date	Prayer, Veneration, Sacraments and Other Doctrines	Ecclesiology/Politics	Rival Churches and Movements, Named by Their Antagonists	Biblical Assessment of Rome's Doctrines and Practices
				Is any Roman Catholic adherent baptized in the name of Mary? Was Mary crucified for anyone—now interestingly recent official Catholic writings Mary acting as Coredemptrix by her coparticipation in Christ when He was on the cross [by her proximity to His cross and His sacrifice as His Mother] (cf. John Paul II, *Redemptoris Mater* [25 Mar 1987]; see below A.D. 431).
399-401	"Anastasius I: That [people] must stand for the [reading of the] Gospel [passage]" (de Hainault, #20)			Again encroaching upon the liberty of the local congregation to decide its own worship style in submission to the Word of God
400s	It would seem that the sacramental side of the church gained control of the major positions of power, and began to undermine the proclamational (Evangelical) side of the church. This control included control over the copying (and the passing on to the next generation) of any writings affirming of or positive to the proclamational (Evangelical) side, while intentionally destroying any and all writings positive to or affirming of the proclamation of salvation by grace through faith. Remembering (1) that the Eastern churches were also predominantly sacramental (with their "Seven Mysteries", which are virtually identical to Rome's "Seven Sacraments") and (2) when any writings, old or new, are used to counter the historicity or practices of the Church of Rome, these go on a list of books, and soon in two or three generations, these books disappear from usage and history.[46] 			

It would seem that the sacramental side of the church gained control of the major positions of power, and began to undermine the proclamational (Evangelical) side of the church. This control included control over the copying (and the passing on to the next generation) of any writings affirming of or positive to the proclamational (Evangelical) side, while intentionally destroying any and all writings positive to or affirming of the proclamation of salvation by grace through faith. Remembering (1) that the Eastern churches were also predominantly sacramental (with their "Seven Mysteries", which are virtually identical to Rome's "Seven Sacraments") and (2) when any writings, old or new, are used to counter the historicity or practices of the Church of Rome, these go on a list of books, and soon in two or three generations, these books disappear from usage and history.[46]

Hence, there is currently a virtual vacuum of knowledge of the proclamational side of the Early Church, rendering any discussion of a proclamational side of the Early church from a positive point of view, an argument from silence. Thus the study of the extant Patristic writings is almost uniquely a study of the development of a sacramental system of salvation, from an affirmational point-of-view, with little if any positive mention of a proclamational side to the Church. Thus it is highly likely that a balanced and objective study of the true theology of the early Church (i.e. Patristics) is virtually impossible, which forces us to study the Bible for theology, rather than finding authority in what remains of Early Church theology.

Likewise code words are used in discussing early Church Evangelicals:

- These code words are related to the supposed "founders" of various movements (Donatists, Montanists, Novatians), to secondary philosophical schemes by which Evangelicals can be boxed in theoretically:
  - Manichean, or dualist: making a strong distinction between spiritual salvation and the non-spiritual aspects of matter [hence relics, statues, icons, and other symbols have no special spiritual powers]
  - Docetic, or not accepting the dual nature of Christ: hence of emphasizing a "merely spiritual" salvation, or a spiritual new birth, without the necessity for a sacramental sign or symbol
  - Gnostic, or adhering to a new or special knowledge: such as the need to be born again to properly understand the Scriptures
  - Cathars, or pure ones or holy ones (compare with Puritan and Pietist): for demanding a holy life of pastors.
- The irony is that some Evangelicals seem unaware of how they undermine themselves by using the above nomenclature, so some teach and propagate the same without understanding the potentially damaging nature of these teachings to their own doctrines.
- Eventually, as students and their teachers are more and more absorbed into the writings of the "Early Fathers of the Church" they may gradually change their views to adjust to the "ancient views" of the extant writings of the so-called Early Church "Fathers," hence succumbing to the question-framing handed to them in the remaining writings.

~Date	Prayer, Veneration, Sacraments and Other Doctrines	Ecclesiology/Politics	Rival Churches and Movements, Named by Their Antagonists	Biblical Assessment of Rome's Doctrines and Practices
402-412	"Innocent I: That the bread is given before Communion. Abstinence on Saturdays is attributed to him" (de Hainault, #21) Augustine strongly decried the Donatist practice of rebaptizing Catholics in his *Contra Donatisten*; to Augustine, this Donatist practice was like spitting in the face of Rome's unique place and authority and	Leo XIII quoted Augustine in his *Satis Cognitum* (1896): 9: "St. Augustine notes that other heresies may spring up, to a single one of which, should any one give his assent, he is by the very fact cut off from Catholic unity. 'No one who merely disbelieves in all (these heresies) can for that reason regard himself as a Catholic or call himself one. For there may be or may arise some	Augustine on the use of force and coercion to subdue and crush the Donatists and Manicheans: "CHAPTER 7.— 25. However, before those laws were sent into Africa by which men are compelled to come in to the sacred Supper, it seemed to certain of the brethren, of whom I was one, that although the madness of the Donatists was raging in	Augustine's counsel to go the secular powers to exact judgment on another Christian goes against 1 Cor 6:1-6: 1 Cor 6:1-6, "Dare any of you, having a matter against another, go to law before the unrighteous, and not before the saints? Do you not know that the saints will judge the world? And if the world will be judged by you, are you unworthy to judge the smallest matters? Do you not know that we shall judge angels? How much more, things that pertain to this life? If then you have judgments concerning things pertaining to this life, do you appoint those who are least esteemed by the church to judge? I say this to your shame. Is it so, that there is not a wise man among you, not even one, who will be able to judge

---

[46]Notice, for example, how hard it is to find James A. Wylie (1808-1890), *History of Protestantism* (London: Cassell, 1878), which went out of print in 1920, even in internet-based collections of 19th Century writings in English, or writings of the 17th Century Huguenot polemicist Pierre Jurieu, or those of French "desert church" preacher Claude Brousson (martyred 1698), who himself was accused of being a prolific writer!

~Date	Prayer, Veneration, Sacraments and Other Doctrines	Ecclesiology/Politics	Rival Churches and Movements, Named by Their Antagonists	Biblical Assessment of Rome's Doctrines and Practices
	the validity of its sacraments unto salvation; rather he explained the baptism of the heretic Donatists in this way: "For if men of the party of the devil, and therefore in no way belonging to the one dove, can yet receive, and have, and give baptism in all its holiness, in no way defiled by their waywardness, as we are taught by the letters of Cyprian himself, how are we ascribing to heretics what does not belong to them?" (Contra Don, Bk 4, Ch 10, §17) Of Rome's "sacrifice of the Mass" [the Lord's Supper], Augustine is quoted by Aquinas (TP, Q[82], A[7]) as saying: "there is no such thing as a true sacrifice outside the Catholic Church" (in Liber sentent. Prosperi xv)	other heresies, which are not set out in this work of ours, and, if any one holds to one single one of these he is not a Catholic' (S. Augustinus, De Haeresibus, n. 88)"; Likewise the Pope appears to have called himself "Innocent"; Likewise Augustine seems to have argued against the local church governance by elders Augustine argued for a state church in Mandatum Catholicorum (including the use of secular power to force heretics and schismatics to become Catholic) in Contra Donatisten	every direction, yet we should not ask of the emperors to ordain that heresy should absolutely cease to be, by sanctioning a punishment to be inflicted on all who wished to live in it; but that they should rather content themselves with ordaining that those who either preached the Catholic truth with their voice, or established it by their study, should no longer be exposed to the furious violence of the heretics. And this they thought might in some measure be effected, if they would take the law which Theodosius, of pious memory, enacted generally against heretics of all kinds, to the effect that any heretical bishop or clergyman, being found in any place, should be fined ten pounds of gold, and confirm it in more express terms against the Donatists, who denied that they were heretics. ... "26. But God in His great mercy, knowing how necessary was the terror inspired by these laws, and a kind of medicinal inconvenience for the cold and wicked hearts of many men, and for that hardness of heart which cannot be softened by words, but yet admits of softening through the agency of some little severity of discipline, brought it about that our envoys could not obtain what they had undertaken to ask."[47]	between his brethren? But brother goes to law against brother, and that before unbelievers! Further, Augustine's counsel to (1) exact fines and then (2) use physical coercion to force the Donatists to "return" to the Bishop of Rome sounds eerily like Satan in Job 1 and 2: Job 1:9-11, "So Satan answered the LORD and said, 'Does Job fear God for nothing? Have You not made a hedge around him, around his household, and around all that he has on every side? You have blessed the work of his hands, and his possessions have increased in the land. But now, stretch out Your hand and touch all that he has, and he will surely curse You to Your face!'" Job 2:4-5, "So Satan answered the LORD and said, 'Skin for skin! Yes, all that a man has he will give for his life. But stretch out Your hand now, and touch his bone and his flesh, and he will surely curse You to Your face!'" The unfortunate play out of these teachings of Augustine became the Medieval Inquisition (see starting in 1002). Of the kingdom or rulership of God, Jesus said, "My kingdom is not of this world," John 18:36; cf. Luke 17:20-21: John 18:36, "Jesus answered, 'My kingdom is not of this world. If My kingdom were of this world, My servants would fight, so that I should not be delivered to the Jews; but now My kingdom is not from here.'" Luke 17:20-21, "Now when He was asked by the Pharisees when the kingdom of God would come, He answered them and said, 'The kingdom of God does not come with observation; nor will they say, "See here!" or "See there!" For indeed, the kingdom of God is within you.'" Of the Bishop of Rome calling himself "Innocent": "There is none good but God," Matt 19:17; Mark 10:18; "For all have sinned," Rom 3:23; etc. Further, Augustine was against local church rule, or what we call "Congregational Church Rule," allowing local churches to make doctrinal, administrative, and financial decisions—the view of local church rule is known in the modern History of Missions as "Three-Self Churches": • Self-supporting; • Self-governing; and • Self-propagating. Rather Augustine appears to follow an OT paradigm for church government, in which God commanded a centralized form of religious life, focused on the eventual Temple in Jerusalem: • For example, Deut 12:5-6 commanded, "But you shall seek the place where the LORD your God chooses, out of all your tribes, to put His name for His dwelling place; and there you shall go. There

---

[47]Augustine, "A Treatise concerning the Correction of the Donatists" (Epistle CLXXXV); available from: http://www.ccel.org/ccel/schaff/npnf104.doc; accessed: 24 April 2007; Internet.

~Date	Prayer, Veneration, Sacraments and Other Doctrines	Ecclesiology/Politics	Rival Churches and Movements, Named by Their Antagonists	Biblical Assessment of Rome's Doctrines and Practices
				you shall take your burnt offerings, your sacrifices, your tithes, the heave offerings of your hand, your vowed offerings, your freewill offerings, and the firstborn of your herds and flocks" • Notice the centralized power and the anti-individualism of Deut 12:8-9, "You shall not at all do as we are doing here today—every man doing whatever *is* right in his own eyes—for as yet you have not come to the rest and the inheritance which the LORD your God is giving you" • See also Deut 17:8-13 (see below). This author recommends that the reader study the series of writings of Augustine combined under the title of *Contra Donatisten*. In these writings it is clear that Augustine argued for Rome's autocratic state-church interrelationship, and abused the interpretations of: • The parable of the wheat and the tares, most notably, "Let them grow together," Matt 13:24-30 • "Compel them come in," Luke 14:23 • And a number of other verses to justify the condemnation (particularly Deut 13; 17) of the Donatists, while simultaneously accepting their baptism and the fruit of their evangelism efforts!
401-417		Rome's "Innocent I" (affirmed by Augustine's writings) felt that all "greater causes" should be reserved for the apostolic see, adding that the pope's decisions affected "all the churches of the world"		Resulting not only in centralized church government, but also in the removal of freedom of conscience and freedom of biblical interpretation, including Rome deciding: • Right and wrong, • just and unjust, • holy and profane, Lev 10:10-11 Note what the High Priest said before they plotted Jesus' death: • John 11:51-52, "Now this he did not say on his own *authority*; but being high priest that year he prophesied that Jesus would die for the nation, and not for that nation only, but also that He would gather together in one the children of God who were scattered abroad" From these verses one can [falsely] deduce, based on the antagonists of Jesus: • That the high priest (Pontifex) can and ought to prophesy rightly • That He also, in the name of Jesus, is commissioned to gather together into one all the children of God. Note the Scriptural backing from Deuteronomy for Rome's judgments: • Deut 17:8-13, "If a matter arises which is too hard for you to judge, between degrees of guilt for bloodshed, between one judgment or another, or between one punishment or another, matters of controversy within your gates, then you shall arise and go up to the place which the LORD your God chooses. And you shall come to the priests, the Levites, and to the judge *there* in those days, and inquire *of them*; they shall pronounce upon you the sentence of judgment. You shall do according to

~Date	Prayer, Veneration, Sacraments and Other Doctrines	Ecclesiology/Politics	Rival Churches and Movements, Named by Their Antagonists	Biblical Assessment of Rome's Doctrines and Practices
				the sentence which they pronounce upon you in that place which the LORD chooses. And you shall be careful to do according to all that they order you. According to the sentence of the law in which they instruct you, according to the judgment which they tell you, you shall do; you shall not turn aside *to* the right hand or *to* the left from the sentence which they pronounce upon you. Now the man who acts presumptuously and will not heed the priest who stands to minister there before the LORD your God, or the judge, that man shall die. So you shall put away the evil from Israel. And all the people shall hear and fear, and no longer act presumptuously."

Notice several points from Deuteronomy:

- It deals with "a matter which is too hard for you to judge"
- Go to "the place which the Lord your God chooses"—Jerusalem's Temple must be reinterpreted as Rome
- "And to the judge *there* in those days" must be interpreted as the Bishop of Rome; cf. Deut 19:17
- Notice how they must strictly obey whatever this judge says
- Notice also the death penalty for not following the judgment of this judge!
- Note also the purpose to instill fear, thus affirming ruling by fear or terror

Furthermore, Deut 19:16-21 provides a parallel passage:

- "If a malicious witness rises up against a man to accuse him of wrongdoing, then both the men who have the dispute shall stand before the LORD, before the priests and the judges who will be *in office* in those days. And the judges shall investigate thoroughly; and if the witness is a false witness *and* he has accused his brother falsely, then you shall do to him just as he had intended to do to his brother. Thus you shall purge the evil from among you. And the rest will hear and be afraid, and will never again do such an evil thing among you. Thus you shall not show pity: life for life, eye for eye, tooth for tooth, hand for hand, foot for foot."

Please note:

- The centralized location (which, by the way, differentiated the Church of Rome from the Eastern Church)
- Notice one of the roles of this centralized ecclesiastical government is to study (Rome has perhaps for a millennia and a half maintained a focal brain-trust in terms of schools, libraries, and archives; not even Judaism has anything remotely similar to this centralized spiritual authority)
- Notice that they had to bring a judgment (Rome's many Bulls and Encyclicals, which it deems binding to all men in the entire world)
- Notice the purging of the evil from their midst (that being the duty of the Bishops of the various dioceses of the Church of Rome)
- Notice, again, the reign of terror, as well as the lack of pity upon the condemned |

~Date	Prayer, Veneration, Sacraments and Other Doctrines	Ecclesiology/Politics	Rival Churches and Movements, Named by Their Antagonists	Biblical Assessment of Rome's Doctrines and Practices
				• Notice, perhaps most importantly, that Jesus quoted, reinterpreted, and modified this command in Matt 5:38-42

In light of Deut 17 and 19, it is no surprise that Ignatius Loyola, founder of the Jesuits, actually stated in his *Spiritual Exercises* (1522-1523): "If we wish to be sure that we are right in all things, we should always be ready to accept this principle: I will believe that the white that I see is black if the hierarchical Church so defines it" (contrasting Isa 5:20)

Also see verses above regarding the self-exaltation of the Bishop of Rome to the Seat of Peter

Also notice how early was this self-aggrandizement in relation to the so-called "First Seven Ecumenical Councils" of the Territorial Churches (Nicaea I 325, Constantinople I 381, Ephesus 431, Chalcedon 451, Constantinople II 553, Constantinople III 680-681, Nicaea II 787) |
411		"The Conference of Carthage, held by the command of the Emperor Honorius in 411 with a view to terminating the Donatist schism, while not strictly a synod, was one of the most important assemblies in the history of the African sees, and of the whole Catholic Church. It was presided over by Marcellinus of Carthage who found in favour of the Catholic party, which led to the violent suppression of the Donatists"[48]	The Church of Rome used conferences, synods, and political decrees to suppress their competition in North Africa, the Donatist churches.	
412		Rome was sacked by the Goths under the leadership of Alaricus, being instigated to do so by Stilico Honorius (Sleidan)		
417-418	"Zosimus: The benediction of candles on the Saturday before Easter" (de Hainault, #22)			Hereby, it appears that Zosimus used Old Testament influences on the sanctification or purification of objects used in worship for New Testament worship (cf. Exod 29:36-37; 1 Chron 23:13; Matt 23:25)
418		Third and Fourth Council of Carthage:

"At this time flourished Augustine, who was present at the Third and Fourth Counsell [sic] of Carthage, where amongst others, those decrees passed, that | | The interest of this piece of information is as follows:

• A council was called to rule on the housing arrangements for Bishops (who at that time were allowed to be married);
• It appears that at that time, following NT church order, Bishops (as overseers of a |

---

[48]"Councils of Carthage"; available at: http://en.wikipedia.org/wiki/Synods_of_Carthage; accessed: 11 Aug 2013; Internet.

~Date	Prayer, Veneration, Sacraments and Other Doctrines	Ecclesiology/Politics	Rival Churches and Movements, Named by Their Antagonists	Biblical Assessment of Rome's Doctrines and Practices
		the Bishop should have a little mansion neer to his Church. "That his householdstuffe should be meane, and his table poore, and by his uprightnesse and integrity of life, should get himself authority. That he should vse the vtensils of the Church, as things committed to his charge, and not as his owne, "This *Innocent* the first writ also to Saint *Austine*, and to *Aurelius* Bishop of *Carthage*, where exhorting them to mutuall prayers, he cals them brothers, and fellow-priests" (Sleidan, 172-173).		number of churches) were seen as equal in rank. • BTW, Saint Austine is another name for Saint Augustin.
418-422		Boniface I stated that the Roman church stood to "the churches throughout the world as the head is to its members," though the bishops might hold "one and the same episcopal office," they should "recognize those to whom for the sake of ecclesiastical discipline they ought to be subject"		Centralized power given to one person, as a mirror of Rome's political organizational structure; "Ecclesiastical discipline" meant a system of works, which counters Rom 14:4, "Who are you to judge the servant of another? To his own master he stands or falls; and stand he will, for the Lord is able to make him stand" Often James is considered the first lawgiver among the leaders of the church, his giving four regulations in Acts 15:28-29, and repeated in 21:25, as proof-texts of this ungodly practice
422-432	"Celestin: They attribute to him the ordinance of the offertory" (de Hainault, #23)			Since when is an offering an ordinance? Paul said that the Corinthians should give voluntary and with cheer (2 Cor 9:7).
431	"Beginning of the exaltation of Mary, the term 'Mother of God' first applied to her by the council of Ephesus" (Boettner, #6)	Mary went from being the "Mother of Christ" (*Christotokos*) to the "Mother of God" (*Theotokos*), to the "Mother of the Church" (*Ecclesiotokos*): "We believe that the Most Holy Mother of God, the new Eve, the Mother of the Church, carries on in heaven her maternal role with regard to the members of Christ, cooperating in the birth and development of divine life in the souls of the redeemed" (from John Paul II, *Redemptoris Mater* [25 Mar 1987],§47, quoting Pope Paul VI, Solemn Profession of Faith [30 June, 1968], 15: AAS 60 [1968] 438 f.)		Beginning of idolatry with regard to Mary; see Jer 44:17-19 on the worship of the "Queen of Heaven" that seems to be a part of human nature and is therefore culturally acceptable. Talk about a "worship war"! This part of Rome's worship had three blunders: (1) It venerated a person, thereby disobeying God; (2) it diminished the role of Christ, sharing His unique mediatorial role with Mary [hence, Mary became Mediatrix of all the graces of God through Christ (contra 1 Tim 4:5; 1 John 2:1-2); and (3) it strangely deifies Mary by placing her as providing her essence in the ever-development of the Triune Godhead [talk about the Christological and Trinitarian controversies!]. Clearly, "a little bit of leaven leavens the whole lump of dough" Gal 5:9 As a result of the worship of Mary: • Roman Catholic homes became matriarchal, as regards spiritual things, with the mother being the spiritual guardian of the home • Feminism received a nod, as now a supreme

~Date	Prayer, Veneration, Sacraments and Other Doctrines	Ecclesiology/Politics	Rival Churches and Movements, Named by Their Antagonists	Biblical Assessment of Rome's Doctrines and Practices
				female deity was established
				Note, however, the comment of Jesus regarding the greatest person born of a woman:
				• Matt 11:11, "Assuredly, I say to you, among those born of women there has not risen one greater than John the Baptist; but he who is least in the kingdom of heaven is greater than he" (cf. Luke 7:28).
				Consider, however, as regards Christians rightfully worshiping Jesus:
				• 1 Cor 1:13, "Is Christ divided? Was Paul crucified for you? Or were you baptized in the name of Paul?"
				We are baptized in the name of Jesus, and Jesus was crucified for us. Further, in the book of Revelation, there is precedent as to the validity of worshipping solely in the name of Jesus:
				• Rev 5:11-12, "Then I looked, and I heard the voice of many angels around the throne, the living creatures, and the elders; and the number of them was ten thousand times ten thousand, and thousands of thousands, saying with a loud voice: 'Worthy is the Lamb who was slain 'To receive power and riches and wisdom, 'And strength and honor and glory and blessing!'"
				Hence we rightfully sing songs like: "Take the Name of Jesus with You," "There is a Name I Love to Hear," "Jesus Name above All Names," "His Name is Wonderful," etc.
				And all these songs rightfully worship the name and Person of Jesus apart from and outside of any Mediatorial work of Mary!
431-432			[St] Patrick (~378-460) was said to have begun his highly disputed ministry of evangelism in Ireland: some Evangelicals consider him a New Testament evangelist, some Roman Catholic scholars consider him to have been a syncretistic magician[49] (see below the exhortation to syncretism by Gregory I [590-604] in his letter to the Abbot Mellitus)	Of syncretism, the Bible is very clear, and clearly iconoclastic: • Deut 7:5-6, 25-26 (see quotations of these verses, 375 A.D.) • Deut 32:12, "So the LORD alone led him, And there was no foreign god with him" • Notice also God's disapproval of the syncretism of the proto-Samaritans who worshiped both God and the gods of their former lands, 2 Kings 17:24-41
435	Jerome taught penance ("Confession") to receive a priest's absolution from Daniel 4;[50] Jerome's		Jerome's Contra Luciferianos was quoted by Paul VI (Ecclesiam Suam [6 Aug 1964]—just	"Repent" (i.e. change of heart) changed to "do penance" (prescribed actions to gain absolution); leading to the gradual mocking of the concept of

[49]Listen to this quote by O'Donovan: "Patrick engrafted Christianity on the pagan superstitions with so much skill that he won the people over to the Christian religion before they understood the exact difference between the two systems of belief; and much of his half-pagan, half-Christian religion will be found, not only in the Irish stories of the Middle Ages, but in the superstitions of the peasantry of the present day" (O'Donovan cited in James Heron, The Celtic Church in Ireland [London: Service & Patton, 1898], 126).

[50]"It may be that God will forgive thy sins.' In view of the fact that the blessed Daniel, foreknowing the future as he did, had doubts concerning God's decision, it is very rash on the part of those who boldly promise pardon to sinners. And yet it should be recognized that indulgence was promised to

~Date	Prayer, Veneration, Sacraments and Other Doctrines	Ecclesiology/Politics	Rival Churches and Movements, Named by Their Antagonists	Biblical Assessment of Rome's Doctrines and Practices

	Vulgate was supposedly translated from the original languages, with all its sacramental glosses (e.g. "repent" as "do penance")
	
	For example, the word "penance" is found 67 times in the Douay-Rheims Bible (a literal translation of the Latin Vulgate into English in 1899), and the phrase "do penance" is found 29 times, "did penance" is found 5 times, and "done penance" is found 3 times (see A.D. 383 above).
			months before Vatican II's decree *Lumen Gentium* [21 Nov 1964]), when explaining the need for the papacy for unity:
			
			"As St. Jerome justly wrote: 'There would arise in the Church as many sects as there are priests'" [63: *Dial. Contra Luciferianos*, N.9.]
				"be diligent to be spotless" (2 Pet 3:14)
				
				Two problems with the Confessional (cf. A.D. 1054):
				
				• Confession became a one-way street: parishioner to the priest, rather than a two way street: to "one another":
				  ○ James 5:16, "confess your sins to **one another**, and pray for **one another**, so that you may be healed"
				  ○ Likewise omitting the second one another, "Pray for one another," again making the prayer of absolution a one-way street!
				
				• Rome usurped the role of Jesus as our only valid Confessor, inventing that title and giving it to men:
				  ○ 1 John 1:9-2:2, If we confess our sins, He is faithful and just to forgive us *our* sins and to cleanse us from all unrighteousness. If we say that we have not sinned, we make Him a liar, and His word is not in us. My little children, these things I write to you, so that you may not sin. And if anyone sins, we have an Advocate with the Father, Jesus Christ the righteous. And He Himself is the propitiation for our sins, and not for ours only but also for the whole world."
				
				Jerome also continued in the line of teachers who gave Rome's Bishop absolute spiritual authority: Cyprian, Augustine, Leo I

440-461	"Leo I: Litanies were instituted. Ordinance not to sing during Lent neither the Hallelujah nor the Gloria in excelsis" (de Hainault, #24)	Leo I called himself, "Peter prince of the apostles" who "rightly rules those who are ruled in the first instance by Christ"; the Bishop of Rome is the "representative of Peter"	Aquinas (TP, Q[82], A[7]) quoted Leo I as writing: "Elsewhere [i.e. other than in the Catholic Church which is Christ's body] there is neither valid priesthood nor true sacrifice [speaking of the sacrifice of the Mass]" (in Ep. lxxx; cf. Decretal i, q. 1)	Building on the writings of Callistus and Stephen I, and the fact that Rome was the capital of the Roman Empire; a false use of Petrine primacy, "you are Peter, and upon this rock I will build My church" (Matt 16:18; cf. Matt 10:2; Mark 8:29; Luke 9:20); in the very same chapter Jesus said to Peter, "Get behind Me, Satan! You are a stumbling block to Me; for you are not setting your mind on God's interests, but man's." (Matt 16:23), should not this name ["Satan"] also be applied to Peter? Is not the apparent descendent of Peter still setting his mind on man's interests? Moreover as to His kingdom, Jesus said, "My kingdom is not of this world. If My kingdom were of this world, then My servants would be fighting, that I might not be delivered up to the Jews; but as it is, My kingdom is not of this realm" (John 18:36), also of His kingdom He said, "The kingdom of God is not coming with signs to be observed; nor will they say, 'Look, here *it is*!' or, 'There *it is*!' For behold, the kingdom of God is in your midst." (Luke 17:20-21) Use of "the Great" after the name "Leo" is reminiscent of Simon the Sorcerer, who called himself "the great" in Acts 8:9-10, "But there was a certain man called Simon, who previously

---

Nebuchadnezzar in return, as long as he wrought good works" (*Jerome's Commentary on Daniel*, trans. by Gleason L. Archer, Jr. [Grand Rapids: Baker, 1958], 52).

~Date	Prayer, Veneration, Sacraments and Other Doctrines	Ecclesiology/Politics	Rival Churches and Movements, Named by Their Antagonists	Biblical Assessment of Rome's Doctrines and Practices
				practiced sorcery in the city and astonished the people of Samaria, claiming that he was someone great, to whom they all gave heed, from the least to the greatest, saying, 'This man is the great power of God.'"
445	Roman Emperor, Valentinian III decreed, "Whatsoever the authority of the apostolic see has sanctioned, or shall sanction, shall be the law for all"	Roman Emperor, Valentinian III decreed, "Whatsoever the authority of the apostolic see has sanctioned, or shall sanction, shall be the law for all"	Roman Emperor, Valentinian III decreed, "Whatsoever the authority of the apostolic see has sanctioned, or shall sanction, shall be the law for all"	Relegating theological authority to an office and thus to one man, the Pope: • Putting into place a hierarchical system in which the Bishop of Rome was to be the arbiter of all difficult cases, cf. Deut 17:8-13 • And as most theological matters concern the interpretation of Scripture, and as the Pope was made the final arbiter in determining the proper interpretation of Scripture, his position and ultimately his decisions placed him above Scripture, cf. 2 Pet 1:20-21 • It is only a short step to the sin of Jeroboam, 1 Kings 12:26-33 This statement is used as a proof-text to provide a legal basis for all the future theological and political excursions of Rome (including the "Two swords" of Boniface VIII in 1302)
445	Roman Emperor, Valentinian III decreed, "if any bishop summoned to trial before the bishop of Rome shall neglect to come" he was to be compelled by the secular powers	Roman Emperor, Valentinian III decreed, "if any bishop summoned to trial before the bishop of Rome shall neglect to come" he was to be compelled by the secular powers	Roman Emperor, Valentinian III decreed, "if any bishop summoned to trial before the bishop of Rome shall neglect to come" he was to be compelled by the secular powers	Further affirming the Bishop of Rome's a disobedience of 1 Cor 6:1-6; later leading to the false interpretation of Deut 13 and 17 as applied to the inquisition methodology of the church of Rome. Note for example the summons in Deut 17:4-5, "and it is told you, and you hear *of it*, then you shall inquire diligently. And if *it is* indeed true *and* certain that such an abomination has been committed in Israel, then you shall bring out to your gates that man or woman who has committed that wicked thing, and shall stone to death that man or woman with stones."
473	The Council of Arles in 473 resulted in a letter of submission by the Presbyter Lucidus, as concerns predestination, the free will of man, double-predestination, and the extent of the atonement[51] The letter was written by Bishop Fauste of Riez and was sent to the 30 synodal			This council appeared to take judgment against four of the five affirmations of TULIP, ascribed to the 1618-1619 Synod of Dort: • Total Depravity (man' freewill totally destroyed); • Unconditional Election (predestination); • Limited Atonement; • Irresistible Grace. Further, there was a statement in the letter of Lucidus (see footnote) which affirmed that baptism removes the sin nature from Adam, a tangential

[51]"Your correction is the salvation of all, and your decision [is] a remedy. This is why I esteem your sovereign remedy to exonerate myself by accusing my past errors and to return to innocence by a salutary confession. From now on, according to the recent statutes of the venerable council, I condemn with you this opinion:

"that says that the work of human obedience does not have to be united with divine grace;
"that says that after the fall of the first man the freedom of his will was totally destroyed;
"that says that Christ our Lord and Savior did not undergo death for the salvation of all;
"that says that the foreknowledge of God violently compels men unto death, or those that are lost are so by the will of God;
"that says that after having legitimately received baptism are dead in Adam whosoever sins;
"that says some are assigned to death, and others are predestined to life..." ("Council of Arles, 473: Letter of Submission of the Priest Lucidus"; DS330-335).

~Date	Prayer, Veneration, Sacraments and Other Doctrines	Ecclesiology/Politics	Rival Churches and Movements, Named by Their Antagonists	Biblical Assessment of Rome's Doctrines and Practices
	bishops of Gaul (France).			argument used to affirm baptismal regeneration (or that the grace of God is conferred through Holy [infant] Baptism), contra Rom 5:17-18: Rom 5:17-18, "For if by the one man's offense death reigned through the one, much more those who receive abundance of grace and of the gift of righteousness will reign in life through the One, Jesus Christ.) Therefore, as through one man's offense *judgment came* to all men, resulting in condemnation, even so through one Man's righteous act *the free gift came* to all men, resulting in justification of life"
476		The Fall of the [Western] Roman Empire		Rome's fall left the Bishop of Rome as the sole remaining institutional of Rome's era of the Caesars
492-496	**"Gelasius: Made it happen that the Canonical Books were adorned with the Apocryphal [Books]" (de Hainault, #25)**			The addition of the apocryphal books was quite early in the Church of Rome, long before the council of Trent (circa 1545)
496	Gelasius I, letter "Famuli vestrae pietatis" to the Emperor Anastasius I, 494: "This letter is the most celebrated document of the ancient church concerning the two powers: temporal and spiritual"[52]			Upholding and uplifting to power of the Pope over all and every other human power.
496-498	**"Anastasius II: Made the conclusion that the bad life of the minister did not diminish the dignity and virtue of the Sacrament" (de Hainault, #26)**			Was not this the conclusion of Augustine of Hippo, generations before Anastasius II?
500		**"Priests begin to dress differently from laymen" (Boettner, #7)**		Begin to make a distinction, contra Acts 15:9; Rom 3:22; 10:12; Col 3:11; James 2:4
517	On the origination of "stone altars" in Catholic churches, along with the reason behind kissing the stone altar several times during Mass. "...In 517, the provincial council of Epeaune in France decreed that altars should be made of stone to			Disclaimer: while the origination of the stone altar seems clear enough chronologically speaking, the origin of the when and the why of contemporary kissing of the altar is yet to be determined. This author was reminded that Judas betrayed the living Lord Jesus Christ with a kiss: Luke 22:47-48, "And while He was still speaking, behold, a multitude; and he who was called Judas,

---

[52]"(2) There are two principles by which the world is principally ruled: the sacred authority of the pontiffs and royal power; and among the two the charge of the priests is weightier as they must give an account to divine justice and those that even come from kings.

"You know it well, very gracious son: even though your dignity places you above human kind, you bow non-the-less, by a religious duty, the head to those who are charged with divine things and you wait [to hear] from them the means of salvation; and in order to receive the celestial mysteries and to dispense them as is convenient, you must, you are also aware, according to the rule of religion, submit yourself rather than lead. By consequence, in all that you depend upon their judgment, and you must not seek to diminish them according to your will. ...

"(3) It is there that piety acknowledges with evidence that never can anyone under any human pretext elevate themselves above the privileged voice that Christ Himself has placed over all, that the venerable Church has always understood and holds with devotion to be in first rank. They may hindered by human presumptions, the decisions of the divine judge, but overcome, they could not be by any power that there may be" (DS347).

~Date	Prayer, Veneration, Sacraments and Other Doctrines	Ecclesiology/Politics	Rival Churches and Movements, Named by Their Antagonists	Biblical Assessment of Rome's Doctrines and Practices
	signify "Christ Jesus himself being the cornerstone" of Catholicism. Venerated relics were conserved in cavities in the stone altars of newly built Basilicas, which were then placed directly above the tomb of a martyr... "An act of veneration, the holy kiss, or kiss of peace, occurs three times during the Mass, the first of which is at the altar. Like the cross on Calvary, where the Bible says that Jesus Christ sacrificed his life and was crucified, the altar is considered a place of sacrifice. In kissing the altar, the priest symbolizes the bond between Christ and his church; acknowledges the sacrifices of those martyrs (relics) who gave their life for the furtherance of the faith; and, when performed with the deacon, is an extension of peace to the community. The final kiss is also given at the altar to venerate the table as a symbol of Christ, as well as being the place where the faithful offer their bodies as a 'living sacrifice.' "The next holy kiss seals and venerates the Word after the liturgy of the Word at the Ambo. The Ambo is a lectern where the deacon carries the Gospel book. The Gospel is seen to have within it the power to transform the lives of the faithful. According to Catholicism, just as Christ became the living Word, so the faithful should seek to do the same."[53]			one of the twelve, went before them and drew near to Jesus to kiss Him. But Jesus said to him, 'Judas, are you betraying the Son of Man with a kiss?'" Therefore, the act of kissing need not necessarily imply true veneration. For, as in the case of Judas, the kiss actually symbolized betrayal of the living Christ.
526	"Extreme Unction [administered as a 'Sacrament' (means of holiness) to the dying]" (Boettner, #8)			Further leading Rome towards a mysticism; whereas the Bible has very little to say about funerals or last rites, Rome has used them as leverage by threatening the withholding of last rites and by disallowing "heretics" [Albigenses] from dealing with the dying. The Cathars, or so-called heretics, were especially appreciated for their ministry to the sick and dying.

---

[53]"The Catholic Tradition of a Priest Kissing the Altar"; available at: http://people.opposingviews.com/catholic-tradition-priest-kissing-altar-7418.html (online); accessed 10 Sept 2015; Internet.

~Date	Prayer, Veneration, Sacraments and Other Doctrines	Ecclesiology/Politics	Rival Churches and Movements, Named by Their Antagonists	Biblical Assessment of Rome's Doctrines and Practices
				Hence, Rome countered with its own special "sacrament" that only they could and can administer with divine power (according to their teaching).
527		Beginning of the rule of the Byzantine Roman Emperor Justinian (527-565), who re-gathered Italy and Carthage into the Eastern Roman Empire, whose laws were compiled by John the Cappadocian as *Corpus Juris Civilis*, or "Justinian's Code"; compiled as *Codex Justinianus* (529)	Some historians mock the "American Experiment" as a failure, believing that biblical laws were and are both insufficient and irrelevant to an evaluation of historical jurisprudence.	"Civilized" rule of law established by Byzantine Roman Empire Interestingly, Justinian laws on slavery contradict those in the Book of Deuteronomy:[54] Deut 23:15-16, "You shall not give back to his master the slave who has escaped from his master to you. He may dwell with you in your midst, in the place which he chooses within one of your gates, where it seems best to him; you shall not oppress him." In fact, it appears that these verses provide the foundation for a "free-worker" economy, which was foundational to the "American Dream" of "life, liberty, and property" (often ascribed to John Locke's "Letter on Toleration" [1689]). In the case of the verses of Scripture, a slave was treated differently from the ownership of an animal: Deut 22:1, "You shall not see your brother's ox or his sheep going astray, and hide yourself from them; you shall certainly bring them back to your brother."

529	In the [Second] Council of Orange (529), the Sacrament of [infant] Baptism taught as preveniently necessary prior to responding to the Gospel—in fact, it was considered a response to the Gospel! Individually responsibility to respond by faith and prayer was annulled as heretical			The heart and soul of New Testament evangelism was removed by the [Second] Council of Orange:
				
				• Removed were:
				  ○ The possibility of the unbaptized responding to the Gospel (because "total depravity" supposedly removes the ability of the Holy Spirit to impact the heart of unbaptized man through use of the Word of God as the gospel is proclaimed, contra Jer 23:29),
				  ○ The need for personal faith,
				  ○ Prayer as the appropriate response to the gospel, and
				  ○ Believer's baptism only.
				• Divine sovereignty was leveraged to promote the need for [the human work of] infant baptism as the only "means of grace" [sacrament] in order to be

[54]"VIII. Slaves.

"We now come to another division relative to the rights of persons; for some persons are independent, some are subject to the power of others. Of those, again, who are subject to others, some are in the power of parents, others in that of masters. Let us first treat of those who are subject to others; for, when we have ascertained who these are, we shall at the same time discover who are independent. And first let us consider those who are in the power of masters.

"1. Slaves are in the power of masters, a power derived from the law of nations: for among all nations it may be remarked that masters have the power of life and death over their slaves, and that everything acquired by the slave is acquired for the master.

"2. But at the present day none of our subjects may use unrestrained violence towards their slaves, except for a reason recognized by law. For, by a constitutio of the Emperor Antoninus Pius, he who without any reason kills his own slave is to be punished equally with one who has killed the slave of another. The excessive severity of masters is also restrained by another constitutio of the same emperor. For, when consulted by certain governors of provinces on the subject of slaves, who fly for sanctuary either to temples, or to the statues of the emperors, he decided that if the severity of masters should appear excessive, they might be compelled to make sale of their slaves upon equitable terms, so that the masters might receive the value; and this was a very wise decision, as it concerns the public good, that no one should misuse his own property. The following are the terms of this rescript of Antoninus, which was sent to Laelius Marcianus: The power of masters over their slaves ought to be preserved unimpaired, nor ought any man to be deprived of his just right. But it is for the interest of all masters themselves, that relief prayed on good grounds against cruelty, the denial of sustenance, or any other intolerable injury, should not be refused. Examine, therefore, into the complaints of the slaves who have fled from the house of Julius Sabinus, and taken refuge at the statue of the emperor; and, if you find that they have been too harshly treated, or wantonly disgraced, order them to be sold, so that they may not fall again under the power of their master; and, if Sabinus attempt to evade my constitutio, I would have him know, that I shall severely punish his disobedience" ("Medieval Sourcebook: The Institutes, 535 C.E." available at: http://www.fordham.edu/halsall/basis/535institutes.asp#VIII.%20Slaves; accessed: 7 Oct 2013; Internet).

~Date	Prayer, Veneration, Sacraments and Other Doctrines	Ecclesiology/Politics	Rival Churches and Movements, Named by Their Antagonists	Biblical Assessment of Rome's Doctrines and Practices
				born from above, born again, born of the Spirit, and to receive the "washing of regeneration" [to which they added the removal of original sin (see 473 above), giving the baptized all the necessary ability to respond to God's other means of grace, as defined by Rome, i.e. the other Sacraments of the Church of Rome] • All the items mentioned above (under bullet point 1) were removed in the name of removing the necessary grace of God, while the power of the Gospel and the sufficiency and efficacy of Word of God to prepare the heart was ignored; all items in bullet point 1 above, were framed by this Council as a form of semi-Pelagianism. • In a classic "tour de force" in the name of removing man from making efforts toward his own salvation, salvation was turned into a work of man via the 7 Sacraments, with a leadership that was even further enslaved to men by the Benedictine Vows, paradoxically, both in the same year (see below). **Both the Sacraments and the Vows contradict Paul who wrote:** 1 Cor 7:23, "You were bought at a price; do not become slaves of men."
529	Benedict of Nursia (480-543) formulated the Benedictine vows of poverty, abstinence, and, which became foundational vows in Western Monasticism	Gregory I was the first monk to become a Pope, having also founded six monasteries, eventually celibacy became a requirement for all clergy in the First Lateran Council of 1023 Vows of obedience to the hierarchy became codified as absolute (see also in chronology below): • Ignatius Loyola's "Rules for Thinking in the Church" (~1550); • "Obedience of the Jesuits" (~1560); • Pius IV's 1564 Bulle *Iniunctum nobis*; • Cardinal Lavigerie, "Spiritual Testament" (1884).	Therefore, the Church of Rome, in raising up the Benedictine Vows, returned to the Old Testament principle of vows and their fulfillment: • Deut 23:21-22 (NKJ), "When you make a vow to the LORD your God, you shall not delay to pay it; for the LORD your God will surely require it of you, and it would be sin to you. 22 "But if you abstain from vowing, it shall not be sin to you." Whereas, young men or women took vows to abstain from sex, God in this last verse said that it would not be sin to abstain from vowing! Notice that the Vulgate added the imputation of guilt in verse 21, which verb is neither in the Hebrew or Greek (thereby adding to Scripture, Deut 4:2; 12:32; Prov 30:6; Rev 22:18-19): • Deut 23:21-22 (DRA), "When thou hast made a vow to the Lord thy God,	The "monastic ideal" as it is sometimes called, with its Benedictine Vows, has a host of methodological and missiological problems. It appears that Wycliffe opposed the monastic vows. So follows an interchange contra Wycliffe from the 1415 Council of Constance. In it is elucidated the history of these vows, as well as the authorities upon which they are based: • The Article 21 of Wycliffe which was held against posthumously him at that council: "Art. XXI. Whoever enters into the Religious Orders, whether among the Begging Monks, renders himself less capable [not so fit] of obeying the commandments of God." • Discussion of the Council refuting this article: "This Proposition is reckon'd false, erroneous, contrary to Good Manners, and heretical. To prove it they quote a Passage in St. John, who says, that "all that is in the World is the Lust of the Flesh, and the Lust of the Eyes, and the Pride of Life"; for say they, the Monks, and especially the Begging Fryars, avoid the Lust of the Flesh by the Vow of Chastity, the Lust of the Eyes by the Vow of Poverty, and the Pride of Life by the Vow of Obedience. Nor are the other Scripture-Passages forgot, which enjoin all Christians to renounce the World; but above all, 'tis pretended, that the Advice Jesus Christ gave the young Man in the Gospel is the Foundation for a monastic Life. Finally, to confute this Article the Doctors assert, that they have no need of any other Argument, but that of the Authority of the Church of Rome, which approves of all these Religious Orders."[56] Notice how the three vows are juxtaposed (by way

[56]James Lenfant, *The History of the Council of Constance*. Translation of *Histoire du Concile de Constance*, new edition (Amsterdam: Pierre Humbert, 1727) by Stephen Whatley (London: A. Bettesworth, J. Batley, T. Cox, J. Clarke, R. Hette, T. Astley, S. Austen, J. Gray, and L. Gilliver, 1730), 1:224.

~Date	Prayer, Veneration, Sacraments and Other Doctrines	Ecclesiology/Politics	Rival Churches and Movements, Named by Their Antagonists	Biblical Assessment of Rome's Doctrines and Practices
			thou shalt not delay to pay it: because the Lord thy God will require it. And if thou delay, it shall be imputed to thee for a sin. 22 If thou wilt not promise, thou shalt be without sin." Further, notice that the Roman Catholic Douai-Rheims in verse 22 changed "vow" to "promise", thereby dividing the application of verses 21 and 22 under the same verb Not taking vows was one of the teachings of the so-called "Cathars" of the Middle Ages that differentiated them from the Catholics, making it the Shibboleth or *"Cause Célèbre"* by which Cathars could be caught, tried, and executed: "The prohibition against vowing brought many Waldenses to the stake."[55] The Waldenses, and their cousins, the Albigenses or Cathars, all chose to follow Jesus rather than the Church of Rome's application of Moses: • Matt 5:34-37, "But I say to you, do not swear at all: neither by heaven, for it is God's throne; nor by the earth, for it is His footstool; nor by Jerusalem, for it is the city of the great King. Nor shall you swear by your head, because you cannot make one hair white or black. But let your 'Yes' be 'Yes,' and your 'No,' 'No.' For whatever is more than these is from the evil one." Remembering also, that all the inquisitors had themselves taken the Benedictine Vows, and	of novel interpretation) to the three domains of sin in 1 John 2:16: • 1 John 2:16, "For all that *is* in the world-- the lust of the flesh, the lust of the eyes, and the pride of life-- is not of the Father but is of the world." Of human vows based on the philosophy of men, does not Paul call them the commandments and ordinances of men, the basic principles of men, which have no value against fleshly indulgence? • Col 2:18-23, "Let no one cheat you of your reward, taking delight in *false* humility and worship of angels, intruding into those things which he has not seen, vainly puffed up by his fleshly mind, and not holding fast to the Head, from whom all the body, nourished and knit together by joints and ligaments, grows with the increase *that is* from God. Therefore, if you died with Christ from the basic principles of the world, why, as *though* living in the world, do you subject yourselves to regulations— 'Do not touch, do not taste, do not handle,' which all concern things which perish with the using-- according to the commandments and doctrines of men? These things indeed have an appearance of wisdom in self-imposed religion, *false* humility, and neglect of the body, *but are* of no value against the indulgence of the flesh" Further, Paul made it clear that those who were justified by faith were no longer to walk according to the flesh, but according to the Spirit: • Rom 8:1, "*There is* therefore now no condemnation to those who are in Christ Jesus, who do not walk according to the flesh, but according to the Spirit." The perceptive reader will notice that the final two phrases in this verse have been removed from the critical edition Greek text. These phrases provide a weighty omission, given the historical-practical-theological importance of these two phrases and an understanding of the Great Commission. The three vows of Benedict, which follow, provide the methodological foundation for Western Monasticism, as well as the official requirements for all church leadership (being the Sacrament of Vocation). In turn, these three vows are foundational to understanding the Roman Catholic practice of spiritual disciplines and discipleship— hence their interpretation of what "making a disciple" meant in Matthew's Great Commission. On the taking of monastic vows, please consider the 1522 personal testimony of the strict Franciscan converted to Lutheranism, Francois Lambert of Avignon: "Hithertofore seduced and ignorant of what I was doing, I pronounced vows contrary to the Christian profession of faith. Oh well! I renounce to all these inventions of the *minorites* and recognize that the holy

---

[55]"L'interdiction de jurer a amené beaucoup de vaudois au bucher" (Jean Duvernoy, "Table Ronde"; in *Évangile et évangélisme [XIIe-XIIIe siècle]* ; Cahiers de Fanjeaux 34 [Toulouse : Privat, 1999], 235-36).

~Date	Prayer, Veneration, Sacraments and Other Doctrines	Ecclesiology/Politics	Rival Churches and Movements, Named by Their Antagonists	Biblical Assessment of Rome's Doctrines and Practices
			were therefore intellectually and emotionally tied to the superiority of Rome's view of taking vows—a by product of their pope taking the authority vested in the 1073/1075 *Dictatus Papae*. Disobeying the Bishop of Rome and the Church of Rome's canon law in their minds was disobeying the voice of	Gospel is my rule and should be that of all Christians."[57] **1. Of the vow of poverty:** • The term "Evangelical Poverty" appears to be a minimalistic approach to Christ sending out His disciples to preach the gospel in Matt 10; Mark 6; Luke 9, 10. Rather than emphasizing the command to preach, the vow of poverty focuses on a narrow lifestyle component, shifting that lifestyle choice to the central element of the evangelical call: ○ This same "evangelical poverty" is emphasized when considering the gospel preaching ministry of Peter Valdo and any other Reformer who seeks to follow the gospel passages where Jesus sent out

[57]"François Lambert, d'Avignon, useless servant of Jesus Christ, to the pious reader, may grace and peace be given to you in Jesus Christ.

"Received hithertofore into the minor orders [Observant Franciscans, a.k.a. O.F.M., *Ordo Fratrum Minorum*] who take the title of observing, I during several years, wearing the costume of their order, announced the Word of God in a number of counties. Lately I was forced to remove their habit and their society. It is therefore necessary that I make known the causes and that I give my reasons for my way of acting. If I would not do this, the simple would be scandalized, not understanding that I was able to do so in a Christian fashion. To this end I composed two tracts: in the first, it is this: I expose several of the reasons for my leaving the minor orders; in the second, I make know what are the rules of this order of monks, and how one ought to think of such. ...

"I had in my cell [small room] some very-evangelical books of the very illustrious doctor Martin Luther; they took these and placed them under lock and key. Then, without having examined them, the chapter condemned them and threw them in the fire. They should have at least read them before they cried out: they are heretical! They are heretical! This is how they act, condemning that which they do not know. I would say confidently, God knows that I am not lying, that there was in these books the truest theology of all the books of the monks of all time.

"Pardon me, good reader, to have taken so much time on the folly of these Pharisees.—Again however a few words to speak of the evil that these wicked men have done to me and to those like me who love the truth; wickedness so great that several volumes would not suffice to tell them all.

"Such are the men who proudly call themselves observant, when Jesus Christ, in the seventeenth chapter of Saint Luke [v 10], says: "When you have done all the things that are commanded you say, 'We are your useless servants!'" But these men, dear reader, in order that you might know it, despise the Holy Word even in the name that they carry [obervants]. They have placed in their rules, all the statutes of the other monks, in order to be able to, better than their brothers, call themselves observants,—but none do better than they wrong to the Church.—But how can men, who do not know their own rules nor do not want to understand them, how can they sincerely follow them?

"The glorious tomb of Jesus Christ was not yet open to me, and the rock of eternal wisdom under which was kept the loving truth of God, had not yet been rolled... How much I was mistaken!—Whom have they not seduced, these persistent enemies of the observance of the commands of God!—They persecute the one who announces to them the Holy Word and those among their brotherhood who push themselves to rigorously keep the rule. What would I have become among these godless men?

"Having received letters of commissioning from the general or vice-general of the order (I do not remember which), I went from France to Germany.—I seized the first favorable opportunity to remove my pharisaical costume, persuaded that the form and color of the habit are of little importance. I protested to God that I would never have left my order, if, by staying in my convent, I would have been able to freely announce the Gospel; but as that was impossible for me, I had to do what I did. If I had done otherwise, I would have sinned against the precept of the Apostle Paul, "You were purchased with a great price—do not become the slaves of men" [1 Cor 7:23]. Thus, those that attached themselves to the foolish constitutions of men, do they not make themselves slaves? Me therefore who, seduced, made myself the slave of men, how could I do anything else but to observe this other precept of Saint Paul, "If you can become free, do it." Separated from the assembly of the wicked, I arrived at the academy of Wittenberg, the first of the universe, and that leaves nothing to be desired as regards evangelical studies. I regret if I may say so of being mute and of not being able to announce with my own voice to the people the Word of God.—But I will wait the command of the Lord: I will place myself under His hand, and I will attempt with all that I can, by my writings, to exhort the world to receive the Gospel.

"I tell you only, dear reader, a few of the reasons that constrained me to leave the *minorites*... but it must suffice that I told you only summarily. In a few days, you will receive a commentary concerning the rule of their order, that will help you understand the totality. In the meantime, in order that all the world may know what to wait for as far as my resolutions and convictions, I will say these three things:

"1st Hithertofore seduced and ignorant of what I was doing, I pronounced vows contrary to the Christian profession of faith. Oh well! I renounce to all these inventions of the *minorites* and recognize that the holy Gospel is my rule and should be that of all Christians;

"2nd I retract what I have preached that does not conform to Christian truth. I pray all those who have heard me preach or who read my writings to reject all that is contrary to the Holy Books. I have confidence in Him who removed me from a captivity more difficult than that of Egypt, that I will repair with His divine help by my words and by my books my numerous errors;

"3rd As no one can come to the knowledge of the truth without being in disagreement with the Pope, I renounce him and all his decrees, and I no longer want to be a part of his reign of apostasy. I desire rather to be excommunicated by him, knowing that his reign is excommunicated and accursed of God...

"In another book, we will speak of these things in greater detail; we will do so for the name of Jesus Christ to whom be honor and glory."

To this testimony, the author of the text, Franck Puaux, added the following epilogue, "Henceforth speaks Francois Lambert: his simple words, but full of conviction, reveals in him one of those righteous souls thirsting to drink from the pure source of Christian truth. Such are almost all of the Fathers of Protestantism: theirs was a desire to know God and to be faithful to Him, we recognize all of them.

"The monk Lambert dated his letter from Wittenberg, where he arrived in 1523. That same year he was married. He was the first French monk who broke the vow of celibacy, and found in a virtuous and pious woman the help that God in his kindness has given to man.

"Lambert tried to come back to France to preach here the truths of salvation, but he could not. He established himself in Marburg [Germany], where he became a professor of theology and died there at the age of 43. Let us now return to the thread of our narrative interrupted for but a moment" (François Lambert d'Avignon, "Histoire du moine racontée par lui-même, traduite du latin" [story of a monk told by he himself, translated from Latin], in Franck Puaux, *Histoire de la Réformation Française* [1523; Paris: Michel Lévy Frères, 1859], 1:412-17; taken from Gerdesius, *Historia christianismi renovati*, vol IV; translation mine).

~Date	Prayer, Veneration, Sacraments and Other Doctrines	Ecclesiology/Politics	Rival Churches and Movements, Named by Their Antagonists	Biblical Assessment of Rome's Doctrines and Practices

			Christ Himself.	His disciples and the 70 others to preach
				
				• Two New Testament passages seem to contradict the vow of poverty:
				  ○ 2 Thess 3:10-12, "For even when we were with you, we commanded you this: If anyone will not work, neither shall he eat. For we hear that there are some who walk among you in a disorderly manner, not working at all, but are busybodies. Now those who are such we command and exhort through our Lord Jesus Christ that they work in quietness and eat their own bread."
				  ○ Eph 4:28, "Let him who stole steal no longer, but rather let him labor, working with *his* hands what is good, that he may have something to give him who has need"
				
				• In the Old Testament, the Levitical priest, when he left his hometown to go to Jerusalem, appeared to keep the earnings of his inheritance, according to Deut 18:8, rather than to give up his right to own possessions. The discerning reader will notice how this verse has led to variety in interpretation likely because of this very issue:
				  ○ Deut 18:8 (NKJ), "They shall have equal portions to eat, besides what comes from the sale of his inheritance"
				  ○ Deut 18:8 (NJB), "eating equal shares with them—what he has from the sale of his patrimony notwithstanding"
				
				• The vow of poverty may also be understood as a "**vow of community**," or a vow to live in a communal style of living (e.g. communism):
				  ○ Prov 1:14, "Cast in your lot among us, Let us all have one purse":
				    ▪ Consider the context of pillaging the homes of the righteous in light of the Inquisition, Prov 1:11-13;
				    ▪ Consider the biblical command or admonition not to join with them, Prov 1:15
				  ○ Further, all the vocational leaders in the Roman Catholic Church live in a communistic system of finances:
				    ▪ Pooling all their resources and thereby,
				    ▪ Working toward a common goal—the protection of and greater good of the whole (e.g. see Council of Constance's Articles against Wycliffe);[58]

---

[58]"Art. X. It is against the Holy Scriptures, that those holding Church office have goods of their own. The Article is judged erroneous, heretical, and seditious. They establish [their judgment] by diverse reasons pulled from Holy Scriptures the Right that Church Beneficiaries have to own goods. The Clergy in the Old Law possessed 48 cities with their villages, they enjoyed the tithe from all the people of Israel, and the first-fruits of wheat, of wine, of oil, etc., as well as all that was consecrated to God. Further, if it is necessary, according to St. Paul, that the Bishop should show hospitality, and if the Deacon ought to govern his own house, they must have had homes and the freedom. It appears by the Book of Acts that the faithful had possessions, and the Theologians of the Council pretend that among the faithful, their were Church Beneficiaries. Jesus Christ also had money, of which Judas was the Treasurer. God commanded Jeremiah to purchase a field or plot of land, which, according to a gloss, was owned by a Priest or a Levite, whom the Doctors of the Council call Ananias, and who is called Hanamiel in Scripture. To all these authorities they add that of St. Augustine, who says in a Letter to a Bishop named Boniface, that what he owns over-and-above what is necessary he should give to the poor, and finally they conclude this Article of Wycliffe is only proper to incite secular [folks] to seize the goods of Church Beneficiaries. In the "Great Sentence of Excommunication Explained" by Wycliffe, and his other Works, they summarize his opinions on this in this way, 1. That the Tithes are not a Divine Right, because they do not appear in the Gospels, that Jesus Christ paid them, nor that He ordained that they should be paid.

"2. In his complaints to the King, and to Parliament, he asks that the Tithes and Offerings be given, as in times past, to persons who are honest and able (2: This is an arrow against the Begging Monks that he does not so esteem), and that they not be extorted by force, nor by excommunication.

~Date	Prayer, Veneration, Sacraments and Other Doctrines	Ecclesiology/Politics	Rival Churches and Movements, Named by Their Antagonists	Biblical Assessment of Rome's Doctrines and Practices
				▪ This common lot is why, when one opposes the Church of Rome, one aligns oneself against all the past and living brainpower of that same Church! ○ Those then, who take the vow of poverty and still desire personal possessions, are accused of the sin of "luxury." Because of this sin therefore, the guilty must pay an indulgence—from what resources do they pay if they have nothing?[59] • Furthermore, "Voluntary Poverty" may feed an egotistical side, "I could be rich, but I have chosen to be poor[60] as an example and for your benefit" (a type of parallelism with the ministries of Paul and Jesus respectively, 2 Cor 6:10; 8:9) • Likewise "Voluntary Poverty" may appear to be pleasing men, and saying, "Look at me!" rather than saying "I am nothing, look at Him!" John 1:26-27; 3:30; 15:5 • Notice that Paul did not tell the rich to sell all that they had and give it to the poor (as was singularly the case for the Rich Young Ruler, Matt 19:21; Mark 10:21; Luke 12:33, where Jesus seemed to be answering him based on Deut 26:13); Paul rather instructed them as follows: ○ 1 Tim 6:17-19, "Command those who are rich in this present age not to be haughty, nor to trust in uncertain riches but in the living God, who gives us richly all things to enjoy. *Let them* do good, that they be rich in good works, ready to give, willing to share, storing up for themselves a good foundation for the time to come, that they may lay hold on eternal life" • Notice also that the poverty at the birth of Jesus was not voluntary on the part of Joseph and Mary, and the "no gold nor silver nor copper, nor bag, etc." (Matt 10:9-10; Luke 10:4) when Jesus sent His disciples was commanded (not voluntary), and both pragmatic and circumstantial, as was that of Paul, 1 Cor 4; 2 Cor 11; Phil 4: ○ The disciples were commanded not to bring anything, which assumes that they had something to bring in the first place ○ This command allowed the disciples to respond immediately (e.g. Matt 4:20, "The immediately left their nets and followed Him"; Mark 1:18); they didn't go to the bank, go back home to get another pair of shoes, or grab a sack lunch. • Likewise, when [St.] Dominic sent his followers to "beg food," this violated 2 Thess 3:12

"3. He disapproved that the Peoples were so oppressed, only to serve for the luxury of the Priest, that they could not maintain their families, nor give assistance to the poor.

"4. That as the People did not pay Tithes, but for being instructed in the Word of God, there are plenty of cases, wherein according to Divine and human Laws, that the people could refuse to pay them, and that the Parish Priests are more accursed of God, in refusing to teach by their preaching and by their example, the People, by their refusal of the Tithe, when they do not fulfill their duties. For the rest, he did not contest that it was reasonable, that a good Priest receive enough for honest support, and even over-and-above the necessary, and he blames the appropriations of Parish Churches to rich Monasteries, who take all the profit for themselves, placing in the church only some ignorant person, to whom they give precious little" (Jacques Lenfant, *Histoire du Concile de Constance*, rev. ed. (Amsterdam: Pierre Humbert, 1727): 1:210-11; translation mine.

[59]"A religious woman who has fallen several times in the sin of luxury [i.e. coveting things] will be absolved and will be reestablished in her order, even if she is the *abesse* [superior of a female abbey], comes to thirty-six *tournois*, nine *ducats*" (Puaux, *Histoire de la Réformation Française*, 1:407).

[60]Martin Luther saw on his trip to Rome that although the monks had made a "vow of poverty" they were richly fed, while the peasants around them were literally living in squalor.

~Date	Prayer, Veneration, Sacraments and Other Doctrines	Ecclesiology/Politics	Rival Churches and Movements, Named by Their Antagonists	Biblical Assessment of Rome's Doctrines and Practices
				• Rather, the so-called "Vow of Poverty" appears to be a self-determined choice to live the superior "contemplative life"[61] (hence rejecting the need of work to earn a living), while necessitating that the rest of human society pay for that choice of a contemplative lifestyle (either through the church receiving money from the state through taxes, or through the gifts of people): ○ This urge for the contemplative life appears to be based at least in part on the teaching of Aristotle[62] ○ This almost forces *ipso facto*, that the person taking the vow becomes greedy for gain, as he has no other choice for income (Prov 1:19) ○ True, when combined with the vow of celibacy, the complexity of supporting a wife and children is eliminated, but how about support of one's aging parents, as in the case of widows in 1 Tim 5:8? ▪ 1 Tim 5:8, "But if anyone does not provide for his own, and especially for those of his household, he has denied the faith and is worse than an unbeliever" ○ Further, it appears that this contemplative lifestyle is not earned through the rigors of years of teaching and publishing, but rather assumed by the individual and his ecclesiastical society at a very young age (15-16 years old), before the individual has shown intellectual propensity for such an honor. • Therefore, it appears that when Gregory I promoted Benedict and his lifestyle (690-604 A.D.), including his "vow of poverty," it came to be used as a Public Relations technique: ○ Luther explained the lavish lifestyle and meals of the monks when he traveled to Rome (who made come of their income by selling indulgences), comparing that to the languor of those outside the monasteries ○ Likewise, the people of Geneva chronicled the lavish lifestyle and meals of the monks in their city, once the monasteries were opened to the outside ○ While this is not to say that there are not some monks, nuns, and priests, who suffer great privation both voluntarily and involuntarily, the so-called "vow of voluntary poverty" taken by many leaders in the Catholic Church, combined with the secrecy of Rome and its properties, appears to have been used as an effective public relations technique ○ Could it be that the wealth gained by Protestants through capitalism has become a subject of envy? This author recommends to the reader a study of the history of capitalism in relationship

---

[61]As to "Whether the active life is more excellent than the contemplative?" Aquinas taught: "On the contrary, Our Lord said (Lk. 10:42): 'Mary hath chosen the best part, which shall not be taken away from her.' Now Mary figures the contemplative life. Therefore the contemplative life is more excellent than the active" (Thomas Aquinas, *Summa Theologica*, SS, Q[182], A[1], "Whether the active life is more excellent than the contemplative?").

[62]In his proof for dividing all of life into active and contemplative (Thomas Aquinas, *Summa Theologica*, SS, [Q]179, A[1], "Whether life is fittingly divided into active and contemplative?"), Aquinas quotes Aristotle five times (De Anima, ii. 4; iii. 10; ii. 4; Ethic, ix. 12; De Anima, iii. 7), Dionysius twice (both Div. Nom. iv), a homily by Gregory 1 once (Homily xiv, super Ezech.), and the Wisdom of Solomon 8:16.

~Date	Prayer, Veneration, Sacraments and Other Doctrines	Ecclesiology/Politics	Rival Churches and Movements, Named by Their Antagonists	Biblical Assessment of Rome's Doctrines and Practices

				to Reformation Geneva and the early Puritan United States of America.
				
				• When the Catholic "vow of poverty" is compared to the Protestant or Evangelical scenario where marriage is involved, then further issues emerge:
				
				  o What of the 60-75% of Protestants or Evangelicals who go to seminary and never "make it" in the ministry? How are these individuals figured into the lifelong "vow of poverty" scenario? Surely there are a percentage of persons in the Catholic model who take the vows and then "do not work out"; what happens to them?
				
				  o Whereas in the Protestant and Evangelical model, the normal pattern, which is not imposed, is that marriage occurs prior to, during, or after seminary, often children ensue, and thereupon a necessary period of 20-25 years occurs where the life of "contemplation" is impossible, due to raising children:
				
				    ▪ However, is that 20-25 year period in vain?
				    ▪ Are there not lessons in life, ministry, and theology gained in those years?
				    ▪ Furthermore, there is a built-in time of testing built-in prior to the minister entering into a period of the contemplative life.
				
				• The Vow of Poverty places a wedge between clergy and laity which may in fact unduly lift the office of the clergy while simultaneously decreasing the role of the laity in the church, thereby putting them "in their place":
				
				  o Putting the laity "in their place" keeps them from obeying 1 Tim 3 in both choosing and judging leaders in the church
				
				  o Putting the laity "in their place" keeps them from the "freedom of conscience" to judge all truth and live according to their own conscience, cf. Rom 14.
				
				## 2. Of the vow of abstinence (celibacy):
				
				• Consider the following biblical passages:
				
				  o Contra 1 Tim 4:1-4, [against those] "who forbid marriage"
				  o Gen 2:18, "It is not good for the man to be alone; I will make him a helper suitable for him."
				  o Prov 18:22, "He who finds a wife finds a good thing, And obtains favor from the LORD"
				  o Matt 19:12, "He who is able to accept this, let him accept it."
				
				• Paul specifically stated that he was not commanding some or any Christians to be single:
				
				  o 1 Cor 7:5-7, "Do not deprive one another except with consent for a time, that you may give yourselves to fasting and prayer; and come together again so that Satan does not tempt you because of your lack of self-control. But I say this as a concession, not as a commandment. For I wish that all men were even as I myself. But each one has his own gift from God, one in this manner and another in that."
				
				• So also, consider the example of the godly Enoch,

~Date	Prayer, Veneration, Sacraments and Other Doctrines	Ecclesiology/Politics	Rival Churches and Movements, Named by Their Antagonists	Biblical Assessment of Rome's Doctrines and Practices
				who begot sons and daughters while he walked with God: o Gen 5:21-24, "Enoch lived sixty-five years, and begot Methuselah. After he begot Methuselah, Enoch walked with God three hundred years, and had sons and daughters. So all the days of Enoch were three hundred and sixty-five years. And Enoch walked with God; and he *was* not, for God took him." • Consider also King David, a "man of God" (Neh 12:24, 26), who was also the father of many children. Consider also Zacharias, the father of John the Baptist, etc. Therefore, it is clear that the Bible does not teach or exemplify the need for celibacy to be a man of God. • From whence then did this teaching the need for celibacy come, in order to achieve some type of higher holiness? Was it not based on Stoicism, sex being considered part of the base human nature, and abstinence being considered a higher self-control? Is this self-imposed piety not vanity, vainglory, and grossly distorted? o Is this not strange in light of Rome's accusation that Evangelical leaders are Manichean (flesh is evil, spirit good), and yet Evangelicals allow sex within marriage? It appears that in this case it is Rome that is acting Manichean! o Note also teachings, such as Wisdom 4:1 (NJB), "Better to have no children yet to have virtue, since immortality perpetuates its memory; for God and human beings both recognise it" • Furthermore, this particular vow seems to have led to systemic sexual problems within Catholicism: o Note, for example, the problems of homosexuality as described in the 1054 A.D. letter of Pope Leo IX, *Ad splendidum nitentis* (DS 687-688), in which he responded to Pierre Damien's *Liber Gomorrhianus*, which called for greater severity in dealing with homosexual clerics (see A.D. 1054 below) o And yet, the problems associated with the Vow of Celibacy continue to our day, as mentioned in a BBC article: "A Church-commissioned report said more than 4,000 US priests had faced sexual abuse allegations since the early 1950s, in cases involving more than 10,000 children—mostly boys."[63] o Richard _ _ made the interesting point that celibacy is unnatural; o Similarly, it is unnatural for a woman to intentionally make herself ugly to others because of a vow of celibacy. • Does there not seem to be a problem of conflict of interests in those who have made a vow of abstinence seeking to convince others that such a vow is not only acceptable, but also commendable? • For the papal decree that all Roman clergy be

---

[63]"LA Cardinal Mahony 'stripped of duties' over sex abuse" (1 Feb 2013); available at: http://www.bbc.co.uk/news/world-us-canada-21289854 (online); accessed: 1 Feb 2013; Internet.

~Date	Prayer, Veneration, Sacraments and Other Doctrines	Ecclesiology/Politics	Rival Churches and Movements, Named by Their Antagonists	Biblical Assessment of Rome's Doctrines and Practices
				celibate, and for comments on the backlash against those who are married, see A.D. 1079.

3. Of the vow of obedience:

- Contra Rom 14:12; Col 2:16; see also Gal 4:21ff.
- The vow of absolute obedience is to be given to God alone (Deut 26:14)—see below in 1534 and 1884 to understand how far the vow of obedience was taken;
- The vow of obedience changes the giver of the rule or regulation from God to man, as well as what commandments are to be followed, clearly altering the forthright teaching of Scripture, for example:
  - "You shall not add to the word which I command you, nor take from it, that you may keep the commandments of the LORD your God which I command you" (Deut 4:2)
  - "You have commanded *us* To keep Your precepts diligently" (Psa 119:4)
- A vow of obedience runs counter to personal accountability:
  - To study, 2 Tim 2:15;
  - To diligently search the Scriptures, Acts 17:11;
  - To be on the alert, Acts 20:31; 1 Cor 16:13; etc.
- Even the NT command to obey one's parents has a caveat or disclaimer, "in the Lord":
  - "Children, obey your parents in the Lord, for this is right," Eph 6:1
- Therefore, it appears that the vow of obedience supersedes, and actually nullifies Scripture in various ways:
  - Confuses biblical readings having the word "Lord" as possibly or likely also pertaining to a human figure. For example, consider the following in light of taking vows of obedience:
    - "And this I say for your own profit, not that I may put a leash on you, but for what is proper, and that you may serve the Lord without distraction" (1 Cor 7:35)
  - Consider also, in the context of 1 Cor 7, that the vow of obedience is part of the Benedictine Vows to which one is to adhere as part of the Sacrament of Holy Orders, which is juxtaposed to the Sacrament of Holy Matrimony (or marriage)—further accentuating the level of commitment and obedience required to another person
- Further, because of its "top-down" hierarchical approach, the vow of obedience has several negative repercussions:
  - It reorganizes the gifts of the Spirit, putting it into a strict hierarchy, where the Bible places it in a collegiality:
    - "So we, *being* many, are one body in Christ, and individually members of one another" (Rom 12:5)
  - Strict hierarchy undermines mutual accountability ("any man," Gal 6:1) and the need for mutual repentance:
    - Basically, requiring a "Vow of Obedience"

~Date	Prayer, Veneration, Sacraments and Other Doctrines	Ecclesiology/Politics	Rival Churches and Movements, Named by Their Antagonists	Biblical Assessment of Rome's Doctrines and Practices
				nullifies the 62 "one another" commands in the New Testament (e.g. "submit to one another in the fear of God," Eph 5:21), making them into a one-way street!

o Strict hierarchy also nullifies innovation from the bottom-up, a hallmark of the economies of Evangelical societies.

Furthermore, the monastic vows in general:

- Seem to contradict: Isa 2:22; Jer 17:5-8; 1 Cor 3:21

- Cause the monk to be unable to obey the Great Commission of preaching the Gospel to all creation (as they live in solitude or in communal life sometimes or often completely isolated from the outside world), thereby disobeying the clear teaching of the New Testament:

  o 1 Cor 5:9-10, "I wrote to you in my epistle not to keep company with sexually immoral people. Yet I certainly *did* not *mean* with the sexually immoral people of this world, or with the covetous, or extortioners, or idolaters, since then you would need to go out of the world."

  o John 17:15, "I do not pray that You should take them out of the world, but that You should keep them from the evil one."

- It was not until the 13th Century that Rome produced the "preaching orders" (so-called) where monks had the vocation to preach outside the monasteries (Franciscans and Dominicans):

  o The purpose for these "preaching orders" was to counter the Matthew 10-type of evangelistic ministry of the so-called heretical Cathar denominations (16 of them) and the Waldenses (aka. Poor Men of Lyons)

  o As for the Dominicans, when they were founded by Bishop Diego, they were told to utilize the methods of "the enemy" of Rome to spread Rome's message

- Remember also that the reading and studying of Scripture in the vernacular tongue was forbidden even to clerics (by the 11th-12th Centuries), which means:

  o The monks had to learn Latin and rely on their Latin readings in Peter the Lombard for their spiritual development and discipleship

  o They likely did not have access to the Scriptures (even in Latin) that disallowed the particular vows they had made, until long into their "Holy Orders," at which time they were called upon to debate with so-called "Heretics" on these very issues

- Further in their striving for self-imposed Stoic self-perfectionism, Cenobitic monks (those living completely alone, like [St.] Benedict of Nursia) could not obey, and thus had to disobey, the 62 "one another" commandments in the NT given to guide the interrelationships of Christians within the local church.

- As regards the interpretation of Scripture:

  o While living in disobedience to the commands of Christ to "evangelize the lost" and to "love the brethren," these monks still presumably

~Date	Prayer, Veneration, Sacraments and Other Doctrines	Ecclesiology/Politics	Rival Churches and Movements, Named by Their Antagonists	Biblical Assessment of Rome's Doctrines and Practices
				memorized and chanted the Psalms and still handwrote portions of Scripture (for the communal monks), until the reading of Scripture was forbidden to them ○ The result of the disconnect of lifestyle from the clear teaching of Scripture was the reinterpretation of evangelistic passages and themes in the Bible, as is now codified in Lombard and Aquinas • One considers that it was in his masterful administrative prowess that Pope Gregory I (590-604) promoted Benedict and the Benedictine Vows. Consider the tragic impact of Gregory's choice of a hero down the corridors of time. The monastic movement, with its emphasis on "personal spiritual disciplines," its reinterpretation of the Great Commission as evangelizing, and its role in the [Holy] Inquisition, has resulted in a strongly negative influence on the ministry of the Gospel in the history of the churches It is interesting to note that while the living "above reproach" of the 1 Timothy 3 and Titus 1 regulations for church leadership were dropped as part of Augustine's quarrel against the Donatists, they were soon replaced by the three Benedictine Vows, thereby usurping those standards of the Bible for church leadership ("Nature abhors a vacuum")
530-532	**"Boniface II: Ordinance that Bishops do not choose their successors"** (de Hainault, #27)	"And in *Justinians* time, *Boniface* the second was Bishop of *Rome*, whose epistle is extant, wherein he sharply reprehends *Aurelius* Bishop of *Carthage* in the above-mentioned Councell, and saies, that he with his fellowes, did by the devils instigation resist the Church of *Rome*: as also, gives God thanks, that in his time, *Eulalius, Aurelius* his successor, was reconciled to the Church of *Rome*, and after that, rehearses the words of *Eulalius*, wherein he professes, that hee condemnes both his predecessors and successors whosoever they bee, that goe about to weaken the priviledges of the holy and Apostolic Church of *Rome*. (Sleidan, 201-202).		This enactment further increased the centralization of ecclesiastical power to the Bishop of Rome (e.g. Deut 17:8-13).
582-602		**"[Emperor] Maurice: They spoke at that time of the Turks; and of the establishment of the**	"At that time, *John* Bishop of *Constantinople*, stiled himself the vniversall Patriarch: but *Pelagius* the	Hence begins the early establishment of what later became the "Sacrifice of the Mass"—a bloodless reenactment of the sacrifice of Christ on the cross

~Date	Prayer, Veneration, Sacraments and Other Doctrines	Ecclesiology/Politics	Rival Churches and Movements, Named by Their Antagonists	Biblical Assessment of Rome's Doctrines and Practices
		Mass" (de Hainault, #61)	second, Bishop of Rome, vehemently resisted him, and pronounced his decrees void" (Sleidan, 205-206)	(perhaps wrongly using Gal 3:1 as a prooftext?)
590-604	When Gregory I chose to highlight the life [and ministry] of the hermit monk [St.] Benedict, by writing *Dialogues* on the life of [St] Benedict, he was consciously changing the missional emphasis of the Church of Rome	Likewise, Gregory spent his entire life writing a collection of thoughts on the Book of Job, titled *Moralia*—not the most evident portions of Scripture in which to find the Gospel, the Great Commission, and evangelization!		What is the Great Commission? What is the purpose of the church or the Church? Other than the lack of emphasis on the Great Commission in Augustine's *Confessions*, another shift in emphasis can be noted in Gregory I's choice to focus on the life of a celibate and cenobytic monk, by writing *Dialogues* on the life of [St] Benedict. By the way, Gregory I is arguably the "architect" of the Church of Rome as we see it in subsequent history and today. May the reader note the many citations to Gregory I above, as well as this section that follows. The following cites the Apostle Paul using words translated as "expert architect" in the French Geneva history: 1 Cor 3:10 (FGN), "J'ai posé selon la grâce de Dieu qui m'a été donnée, le fondement comme un architecte bien expert : & un autre édifie dessus : mais qu'un chacun regarde comment il édifie dessus." 1 Cor 3:10 (EGN), "According to the grace of God giuen to mee, as a skilfull master builder, I haue laide the foundation, and another buildeth thereon: but let euery man take heede how he buildeth vpon it."
590-604	Gregory I in his "Letter to the Abbott Mellitus" (on the affairs of the English) did not allow the destruction of the pagan Temples, but rather commanded: (1) "aspersing with holy water; (2) erecting altars, and (3) placing of relics of the saints in them.[64]	Gregory I reorganized the Church of Rome, with the hierarchy of the monastery, further centralizing Rome's place; he definitively moved Rome away from a New Testament church model Furthermore, Gregory I used the Church of Rome's funds to hire mercenary soldiers to wrestle political control of Rome from the	Ironically, while encouraging keeping whole the pagan places of worship, as part of the 13th Century Inquisition, Rome's Council of Beziers called for raising the houses of heretics to the ground!	The use of "holy water" to purify a location of pagan worship shows: (1) a disregard for the clear OT commands regarding the destruction of the same; and (2) the magical use of an object, in this case water, to perform a spiritual duty of cleansing from evil spirits: • As to the disregarding of the clear commands, some clear commands for destruction are found in Deut 7:4-5; 12:2-3 • Giving a physical object the designation of "holy", such as "holy water," and ascribing to that object some ability to cleanse from evil spirits disregards the examples and teachings of Scripture regarding

[64]"To our well loved son Abbot Mellitus: Gregory, servant of the servants of God.

"Since the departure of those of our fellowship who are bearing you company, we have been seriously anxious, because we have received no news of the success of your journey. Therefore, when by God's help you reached our most reverend brother, Bishop Augustine, we wish you to inform him that we have been giving careful thought to the affairs of the English, and have come to the conclusion that the temples of the idols among that people should on no account be destroyed, but the temples themselves are to be aspersed with holy water, altars set up in them, and relics deposited there. For if these temples are well-built, they must be purified from the worship of demons and dedicated to the service of the true God. In this way, we hope that the people, seeing that their temples are not destroyed, may abandon their error and, flocking more readily to their accustomed resorts, may come to know and adore the true God. And since they have a custom of sacrificing many oxen to demons, let some other solemnity be substituted in its place, such as a day of Dedication or the festivals of the holy martyrs whose relics are enshrined there. On such occasions they might well construct shelters of boughs for themselves around the churches that were once temples, and celebrate the solemnity with devout feasting. They are no longer to sacrifice beasts to the Devil, but they may kill them for food to the praise of God, and give thanks to the Giver of all gifts for the plenty they enjoy. If the people are allowed some worldly pleasures in this way, they will more readily come to desire they joys of the spirit. For it is certainly impossible to eradicate all errors from obstinate minds at one stroke, and whoever wishes to climb a mountain top climbs gradually step by step, and not in one leap. It was in this way that the Lord revealed Himself to the Israelite people in Egypt, permitting the sacrifices

~Date	Prayer, Veneration, Sacraments and Other Doctrines	Ecclesiology/Politics	Rival Churches and Movements, Named by Their Antagonists	Biblical Assessment of Rome's Doctrines and Practices
		Lombards and restore it to the Church of Rome's control.		the need for prayer and words to cast out demons. • It appears, rather, to be based on the proof-text of the miracles of Paul in Ephesus (descriptive or prescriptive?): Acts 19:11-12, "Now God worked unusual miracles by the hands of Paul, so that even handkerchiefs or aprons were brought from his body to the sick, and the diseases left them and the evil spirits went out of them" • More on "holy" objects below. Also, while Augustine argued that the sacraments administered by priests living in sin were still valid (thereby disregarding 1 Timothy 3 and Titus 1), while successive Pope's centralized their own authority in matters of faith and the interpretation of Scripture, Gregory combined its spiritual power with the temporal power, using money from the church's treasury to fight the invading Lombards. • .In the future, Lombardy was to become the haven of the Waldenses, for a time, and Lombardy was also the place where there was freedom of worship for the 12th and 13th Century Albigenses (or Cathars). In regard to dealing with the pagan religions, Rome appears to harbor a double-standard. When dealing with pagan religions, based on the precedent of Gregory I not allowing the destruction of their Temples (contra Deut 12:2-3). This pragmatic but compromising precedent has resulted in significant syncretism of Catholicism with pagan religions of various lands. Does this not follow the advice of the king of Assyria in 2 Kings 17:26-27? 2 Kings 17:26-27, "So they spoke to the king of Assyria, saying, 'The nations whom you have removed and placed in the cities of Samaria do not know the rituals of the God of the land; therefore He has sent lions among them, and indeed, they are killing them because they do not know the rituals of the God of the land.' Then the king of Assyria commanded, saying, 'Send there one of the priests whom you brought from there; let him go and dwell there, and let him teach them the rituals of the God of the land.'" Consider: • The syncretism of Catholicism with Voodoo in Haiti • The syncretism of Catholicism with Confucianism in China • And even to some degree, the syncretism of Catholicism with Puritanism in the U.S. However, when dealing with so-called "heretics"

formerly offered to the Devil to be offered thenceforward to Himself instead. So He bade them sacrifice beasts to Him, so that, once they became enlightened, they might abandon one element of the sacrifice and retain another. For, while they were to offer the same beasts as before, they were to offer to God instead of to idols, so that they would no longer be offering the same sacrifices. Of your kindness, you are to inform our brother Augustine of this policy, so that he may conduct consider how he may best implement it on the spot. God keep you safe, my very dear son.

"Dated the seventeenth of June, in the nineteenth year of the reign of our most pious Lord and Emperor Maurice Tiberius Augustus, and the eighteenth after his Consulship: the fourth indiction (Bede, *A History of the English Church and People*, trans. L. Sherley-Price, rev. R. E. Latham [Harmondsworth, Middlesex, England: Penguin Books, 1979], 86-87).

~Date	Prayer, Veneration, Sacraments and Other Doctrines	Ecclesiology/Politics	Rival Churches and Movements, Named by Their Antagonists	Biblical Assessment of Rome's Doctrines and Practices
				such as the Albigenses, Rome seemed to take an opposite or iconoclastic approach, when it had military and political prominence. For example, because the Albigenses worshipped in their homes, as part of the [Holy] Inquisition, Rome had their homes raised to the ground, as commanded in Deut 12:2-3

590-604	Gregory I reprimanded the Bishop of Marseille for destroying images, thereby affirming the veneration of what the images represent (DS 477)
	
	Sprinkling with "holy water" and depositing of relics of the saints in English churches encouraged in "Letter to the Abbott Mellitus," as well as the keeping of their habitual festival days[65]
		At the beginning of Gregory I's reign as Pope, the Bishop of Rome was one of the top five Patriarchates of the so-called "Early Church"; the name Patriarch was a title used to signify someone over the bishops of other cities, using an OT title and affirming their importance in the political hierarchy of their state church; these five Patriarchates were (listed biblically-chronologically):
		
		• **Jerusalem** (cultural seat of Judaism, and founding city of Christianity);
		
		• **Antioch** (considered the second capital of Christianity [after Jerusalem] and the third largest city of the Roman Empire in population, seat of the Antiochene Orthodox Church and Syriac Christianity);
		
		• **Rome** (capital of the Roman Empire until Constantine moved it from there in 334 A.D.);
		
		• **Alexandria** (founded in 332 B.C. by Alexander the Great, was directly under Rome's Emperor by 196 A.D., until conquered by the Arabs in 640 A.D.);
		
		• **Constantinople** (new capital of the Roman Empire under Constantine after 334 A.D.).
		
		Further, Gregory I standardized use of Latin language only (codified, and then decreed), as well as the Gallican [French] Missal, Gregorian Calendar, and Gregorian
			Arian church (of the Visigoths in present day Spain and the Lombards in present day Switzerland and northern Italy) was the big rival of Rome	As Rome more and more emphasized the worship of images (statues), it resulted in a misemphasis on the necessity of the physical element (statue, water, bread, candles, etc.) in worship:
				
				• 1 Tim 4:4 (NAS), "For everything created by God is good, and nothing is to be rejected, if it is received with gratitude.
				  o In other words, God does not place higher value on certain objects, "Everything created by God is good"
				  o Likewise, the tendency for man to place spiritual value on an object is dangerous, and is considered deception and part of "doctrines of demons" (1 Tim 4:1)
				• Rom 1:25, "For they exchanged the truth of God for a lie, and worshiped and served the creature rather than the Creator, who is blessed forever. Amen."
				  o As the emphasis is placed on the physical object (holy water, holy oil, holy host, statue, etc.), the worship is gradually misplaced from God to that object as a representation of some divine attribute or virtue
				  o This misemphasis represents the opposite of what 1 Thess 1:9-10 teaches:
				• 1 Thess 1:9-10, "For they themselves report about us what kind of a reception we had with you, and how you turned to God from idols to serve a living and true God, and to wait for His Son from heaven, whom He raised from the dead, *that is* Jesus, who delivers us from the wrath to come."
				
				Further, as Rome's authority became centralized:
				• Imposed a system of worship (the Gallican Missal), taking authority away from the Bible, requiring sacramental worship
				• Forming itself as the center of a hierarchy:
				  o Rome, using its inferior role under Byzantium and its unique place in the Western Empire, positioned itself from being one of five "Patriarchates" (as listed to the left) to headship over the entire Latin or Western Church
				  o It was only two years after the death of Gregory I until the Roman Emperor titled the Patriarch of Rome as the "Universal Bishop")
				    ▪ It appears that the title of "Universal Bishop" was given to Boniface III because the Emperor Phocas, ruling from Constantinople, did not appreciate that the Bishop of Constantinople disapproved of his murder of the Emperor Maurice to rise to power

[65]See footnote above, "To our well loved son Abbot Mellitus: Gregory, servant of the servants of God." (Bede, *A History of the English Church and People*, 86-87).

~Date	Prayer, Veneration, Sacraments and Other Doctrines	Ecclesiology/Politics	Rival Churches and Movements, Named by Their Antagonists	Biblical Assessment of Rome's Doctrines and Practices
		chants (originating in Eastern monasticism). These decrees of Gregory were exported to the Latin-speaking Donatists (North Africa), as well as the Celts (British Isles) and Visigoths (Spain). Gregory I also sent bishops to influence the Visigoth (Spain) and Lombard queens (Northern Italy).		▪ It also appears that the title of "Universal Bishop" gave the Patriarch of Rome precedence amongst the Five Patriarchates, but no formal authority over them • Notice the [un]intended impact of formalizing a "Missal" other than the variety of words used in the Bible: ○ The words of the Eucharist (Lord's Supper) became like an incantation; in order to achieve the proper result (eventually for effecting transubstantiation) ○ To truly transform the elements into the very body and blood of Jesus, the right people have to use the right words ○ Without these very words, no grace is communicated to the people, prayers for the dead become useless, etc. • Likewise, Gregory initiated the carnal political practice of "plowing with the heifer" (Judges 14:18): ○ He gained influence within the royal families of the Visigoths and the Lombards, by empowering and instructing a bishop to seek to convert the queen and her children ○ This same methodology became standard practice, not only with royal families of "heretical" or "enemy" groups, but also with all royal families and governments (hence now the Vatican has ambassadors) Later, the political power leveraged by the "conversion" of Constantine (which was removed to the Greek-speaking Byzantine empire), was enhanced via Bishops being "sent" to royal families by Gregory I, ended up as: • The practice of inciting good Catholic Kings to send their armies to gain physical territory for the Church of Rome—called "crusades" • Boniface VIII (1294-1303) stating that he alone, in his office of Pope, was supreme above all the political powers of the world
590-604	"**Gregory I: Decreed the introits in the Mass and nine kyrie-eleyson excepting the time of the Septuagisma [the third Sunday before Lent]**" (de Hainault, #28)	Gregory I is probably best known for "Gregorian Chants," the "Gregorian Calendar," and likely most importantly, the "Gregorian Sacramentary": • The Gregorian Chants codified earlier Greek and Latin chants into a Latin type of hymnal for communal monks	Likewise, in his first year as Pope, Gregory I urged Gennadius, Patrician and Exarch of Africa, to bravely fight ecclesiastical battles, using the sword to subdue the "men heretical in religion" who are "enemies of the Catholic church," naming in particular the need to Donatists[67]	Regarding the Gregorian Chants: • Gregory continued the movement of the Latin Church to a complete Latin model, including its prescribed singing, recognizing that the majority of monks had no knowledge of Latin upon entering their novitiate, and in the majority of lands in which the Church of Rome ministered the common people did not understand Latin • This elevated the distinction between the priesthood and the laity, and elevated the ceremonies and rituals of the monks and priests to

[67]"As the LORD hath made your Excellency to shine with the light of victories in the military wars of this life, so ought you to [op]pose the enemies of the Church with all activity of mind and body, to the end that from both kinds of triumph your reputation may shine forth more and more, when in forensic wars, too, you firmly resist the adversaries of the Catholic Church in behalf of the Christian people, and bravely fight ecclesiastical battles as warriors of the LORD. For it is known that men heretical in religion, if they have liberty allowed them to do harm (which GOD forbid), rise strenuously against the catholic faith, to the end that they may transfuse, if they can, the poison of their heresy to the corrupting of the members of the Christian body. For we have learnt that they are lifting up their necks against the Catholic Church, the LORD being opposed to the yoke of rectitude. But let your Eminence suppress their attempts, and subdue their proud necks to the ground of his standing, without regard to the merits of his life, since before GOD it is not the more distinguished rank, but the action of a better life, that is approved. But let the primate himself live, not, as is customary, here and there in the country, but in one city according to their selection, to the end that he

~Date	Prayer, Veneration, Sacraments and Other Doctrines	Ecclesiology/Politics	Rival Churches and Movements, Named by Their Antagonists	Biblical Assessment of Rome's Doctrines and Practices
		• The Gregorian Calendar guided which Saints were to be venerated on which days of the year • The Gregorian Sacramentary determined the legitimate form of rites and ceremonies in the Church of Rome, including the proper saying of the Mass and provided a calendar for readings and homilies In the formalizing of the liturgy of the church, Gregory I was said to have discipled at least 4 Centuries of the church, up until the time of Peter the Lombard's Four Books of Sentences. Those who did not submit to this rule, as long as they claimed allegiance to Rome and as long as they did not speak against Rome's liturgical methods, were allowed to maintain their own local liturgies.[66] It goes without saying that those who disagreed with Gregory's liturgy either on theological or methodological grounds were in serious disagreement with the Seat of Peter.		a druid type of mysterious importance • Further, this emphasis on Latin chants and the Latin Mass left the crowds ignorant of the teachings of the Word of God Regarding the Gregorian Calendar: • Eventually, the Gregorian calendar was full of days of saints and feast days, which captivated the attention of Catholic society, much like the signs of the zodiac does in Catholic countries today (e.g. the 12 signs of the zodiac are a part of the stone architecture at the entrance door of the Cathedral at Sainte-Anne de Beaupré outside of Quebec-city, Québec, Canada) Regarding the Gregorian Sacramentary (or Rule): • It has already been mentioned that the Latin worship separated the people from understanding the liturgy, but furthermore... • The enumeration of homilies and texts kept the priests from needing to prepare their sermons from their own study of the Word of God, as the approved homilies were already prepared for them (imagine preaching another pastor's sermons for a year, and then repeating the same sermons the next year, and so on) • Further, the choice of texts used in the liturgy included certain texts and therefore, by default, left out other texts; theological or pragmatic choices had to be made; the priests ability to preach the "whole council of God" (Acts 20:27) was blunted, and people were being fed the same spiritual meals year in and year out, much of the time in a language that they did not understand. It is clear that a New Testament form of worship was not being followed: • The Lord's Supper was not being taken as explained in 1 Cor 11 • The services were not being handled in accordance with 1 Cor 14:26-33, "How is it then, brethren? Whenever you come together, each of you has a psalm, has a teaching, has a tongue, has a revelation, has an interpretation. Let all things be done for edification. If anyone speaks in a tongue, *let there be* two or at the most three, *each* in turn, and let one interpret. But if there is no interpreter, let him keep silent in church, and let him speak to himself and to God. Let two or three prophets speak, and let the others judge. But if *anything* is

may be better able to bring to bear the influence of the dignity that has fallen to him in resisting the Donatists. Moreover, if any from the Council of Numidia should desire to come to the Apostolic See, permit them to do so; and stop any who may be disposed to bring charges against their character. Great increase of glory will accrue to your Excellency with the Creator, if through you the union of the divided churches could be restored. For when He beholds the gifts granted by Him given back to His glory, He bestows gifts so much the more abundantly as He sees the dignity of His religion to be thereby enlarged. Furthermore, bestowing on you, as is due, the affection of our paternal charity, we beseech the LORD to make your arm strong for subduing your enemies, and to sharpen your soul with zeal for the faith like the edge of a quivering sword" (Gregory I, "Epistle LXXIV: To Gennadius, Patrician and Exarch of Africa" [Book 1, Letter 74]; available at: http://www.ccel.org/ccel/schaff/npnf212.iii.v.i.xlix.html [online]; accessed: 25 Aug 2008; Internet).

[66]"Now you requested through Hilarus our chartulary from our predecessor of blessed memory that you might retain all the customs of past time, which, from the beginnings of the ordinances of the blessed Peter, Prince of the apostles, long antiquity has so far retained. And we, indeed, according to the tenour of your representation, allow your custom (so long as it clearly makes no claim to the prejudice of the catholic faith) to remain undisturbed, whether as to constituting primates or as to other points; save that with respect to those who attain to the episcopate from among the Donatists, we by all means forbid them to be advanced to the dignity of primacy, even though their standing should denote them for that position" (Gregory I, "Epistle LXXVII: To All the Bishops of Numidia" [Book 1, Letter 77; circa Aug 591]; available at: http://www.ccel.org/ccel/schaff/npnf212.iii.v.i.xlix.html [online]; accessed: 25 Aug 2008; Internet).

~Date	Prayer, Veneration, Sacraments and Other Doctrines	Ecclesiology/Politics	Rival Churches and Movements, Named by Their Antagonists	Biblical Assessment of Rome's Doctrines and Practices
				revealed to another who sits by, let the first keep silent. For you can all prophesy one by one, that all may learn and all may be encouraged. And the spirits of the prophets are subject to the prophets. For God is not *the author* of confusion but of peace, as in all the churches of the saints" • Much more could be stated here on NT forms of worship, which was the reason the Geneva Reformation sought a "Regulatory Principle" for worship from the pages of the Bible.
593	"The doctrine of Purgatory [as a temporary place for Christians to purge their mortal sins], established by Gregory I" (Boettner, #9)			Contra "once and for all" Christ died for all the sins of the world, with no need for repetition of the payment, nor need for additional payment in so-called "Purgatory": • Rom 6:10, "For *the death* that He died, He died to sin once for all; but *the life* that He lives, He lives to God." • Heb 7:26-27, "For such a High Priest was fitting for us, *who is* holy, harmless, undefiled, separate from sinners, and has become higher than the heavens; who does not need daily, as those high priests, to offer up sacrifices, first for His own sins and then for the people's, for this He did once for all when He offered up Himself." • Heb 9:11-12, "But Christ came *as* High Priest of the good things to come, with the greater and more perfect tabernacle not made with hands, that is, not of this creation. Not with the blood of goats and calves, but with His own blood He entered the Most Holy Place once for all, having obtained eternal redemption." • Heb 10:10-13, "By that will we have been sanctified through the offering of the body of Jesus Christ once *for all*. And every priest stands ministering daily and offering repeatedly the same sacrifices, which can never take away sins. But this Man, after He had offered one sacrifice for sins forever, sat down at the right hand of God, from that time waiting till His enemies are made His footstool." Likewise, purgatory contradicts: • Heb 9:27, "It is appointed for man to die once after that comes judgment" • Heb 5:9, "And having been perfected, He became the author of eternal salvation to all who obey Him" • 1 John 1:9, "If we confess our sins, He is faithful and just to forgive us *our* sins and to cleanse us from all unrighteousness" • Phil 1:21, "For to me, to live *is* Christ, and to die *is* gain" (purgatory is no gain!) • Phil 1:23, "For I am hard pressed between the two, having a desire to depart and be with Christ, *which is* far better" (rather than spend thousands of years purging mortal sins in purgatory) • 2 Cor 5:8, "We are confident, yes, well pleased rather to be absent from the body and to be present with the Lord" • Titus 2:11-14, For the grace of God that brings salvation has appeared to all men, teaching us that, denying ungodliness and worldly lusts, we should live soberly, righteously, and godly in the present

~Date	Prayer, Veneration, Sacraments and Other Doctrines	Ecclesiology/Politics	Rival Churches and Movements, Named by Their Antagonists	Biblical Assessment of Rome's Doctrines and Practices
				age, looking for the blessed hope and glorious appearing of our great God and Savior Jesus Christ, who gave Himself for us, that He might redeem us from every lawless deed and purify for Himself *His* own special people, zealous for good works" o Notice: "looking for the blessed hope" o Note also: "redeemed from every lawless deed"
600	"Latin language, used in prayer and worship, imposed by Gregory I" (Boettner, #10)	Imposition of Latin as the language for the educated class of people. Hence, important political and ecclesiastical information was communicated only in Latin—including access to the Holy Scriptures.		As far as teaching in the language of the people: • Paul spoke in the language of the people whom he was evangelizing in Acts 22:2 • In 1 Cor 14:11, Paul stated that speaking to someone in a foreign language has no significance to them • Even angels appeared to communicate to people in the Bible in a language that they understood (Greek, Hebrew, etc.), so much so that they could even entertain angels unawares (Heb 13:2)! The imposition of the Latin language in religion and education forced the cultural primacy, preeminence, and dominence of Rome ecclesiastically, linguistically, legally, and historically (i.e. historical memory). The Latin language has framed the question in the Western world since that time.
600	"Prayers directed to Mary, dead saints and angels, about A.D. 600" (Boettner, #11)			Prayer to Mary and in her name, not to speak of prayers to dead "saints" and angels, appears to be: • An affront to the unique mediatory place of Jesus, which is closely linked to His unique place in our redemption! o 1 Tim 2:5-6, "For *there is* one God and one Mediator between God and men, *the* Man Christ Jesus, who gave Himself a ransom for all, to be testified in due time" o Heb 2:17-18, "Therefore, in all things He had to be made like *His* brethren, that He might be a merciful and faithful High Priest in things *pertaining* to God, to make propitiation for the sins of the people. For in that He Himself has suffered, being tempted, He is able to aid those who are tempted" o 1 John2:1-2, "My little children, these things I write to you, so that you may not sin. And if anyone sins, we have an Advocate with the Father, Jesus Christ the righteous. And He Himself is the propitiation for our sins, and not for ours only but also for the whole world" o Jude 1:4, "For certain persons have crept in unnoticed, those who were long beforehand marked out for this condemnation, ungodly persons who turn the grace of our God into licentiousness and deny our **only** Master and Lord, Jesus Christ" ▪ The emphasis of the theological deviation is on the word "only"—"our only Master and Lord" • Likewise, His unique role as "only begotten of the Father," John 1:14; "the only begotten Son, who is

~Date	Prayer, Veneration, Sacraments and Other Doctrines	Ecclesiology/Politics	Rival Churches and Movements, Named by Their Antagonists	Biblical Assessment of Rome's Doctrines and Practices

				in the bosom of the father, John 1:18; "His only begotten son, John 3:16
				
				  o John 3:18, "He who believes in Him is not condemned; but he who does not believe is condemned already, because he has not believed in the name of the only begotten Son of God"
				
				• An affront to Christ's role as unique intercessor in heaven, Heb 4:15-16; 7:25, along with the Holy Spirit, Rom 8:26-27
				
				• The many commands to pray in His name (only):
				
				  o John 14:13-14, "And whatever you ask in My name, that I will do, that the Father may be glorified in the Son. If you ask anything in My name, I will do *it*."
				
				  o John 15:16, "You did not choose Me, but I chose you and appointed you that you should go and bear fruit, and *that* your fruit should remain, that whatever you ask the Father in My name He may give you"
				
				  o John 16:23-24, "And in that day you will ask Me nothing. Most assuredly, I say to you, whatever you ask the Father in My name He will give you. Until now you have asked nothing in My name. Ask, and you will receive, that your joy may be full"
				
				  o John 16:26-27, "In that day you will ask in My name, and I do not say to you that I shall pray the Father for you; for the Father Himself loves you, because you have loved Me, and have believed that I came forth from God"
				
				• As such, prayers to Mary and the saints is an affront to the doctrine of the deity of Christ:
				
				  o Heb 1:1-4, "God, who at various times and in various ways spoke in time past to the fathers by the prophets, has in these last days spoken to us by *His* Son, whom He has appointed heir of all things, through whom also He made the worlds; who being the brightness of *His* glory and the express image of His person, and upholding all things by the word of His power, when He had by Himself purged our sins, sat down at the right hand of the Majesty on high, having become **so much better** than the angels, as He has by inheritance obtained a more excellent name than they"
				
				    ▪ Emphasis here is on the "so much better" with the relational separation of its following context (co-equal Son versus servant ministers)
				
				  o 1 John 4:14-15, "And we have seen and testify that the Father has sent the Son *as* Savior of the world. Whoever confesses that Jesus is the Son of God, God abides in him, and he in God"
				
				  o 1 John 2:22-23, "Who is a liar but he who denies that Jesus is the Christ? He is antichrist who denies the Father and the Son. Whoever denies the Son does not have the Father either; he who acknowledges the Son has the Father also"
				
				  o Matt 24:5, "For many will come in My name, saying, 'I am the Christ,' and will deceive many"
				
				Therefore, the lack of the worship of the unique

~Date	Prayer, Veneration, Sacraments and Other Doctrines	Ecclesiology/Politics	Rival Churches and Movements, Named by Their Antagonists	Biblical Assessment of Rome's Doctrines and Practices
				and only role of Christ, shows that the Church of Rome became a false religion quite early: • 1 John 4:1-3, "Beloved, do not believe every spirit, but test the spirits, whether they are of God; because many false prophets have gone out into the world. By this you know the Spirit of God: Every spirit that confesses that Jesus Christ has come in the flesh is of God, and every spirit that does not confess that Jesus Christ has come in the flesh is not of God. And this is the *spirit* of the Antichrist, which you have heard was coming, and is now already in the world" • 1 John 3:23-24, "And this is His commandment: that we should believe on the name of His Son Jesus Christ and love one another, as He gave us commandment. Now he who keeps His commandments abides in Him, and He in him. And by this we know that He abides in us, by the Spirit whom He has given us" Likewise, the Bible speaks against offerings for the dead, Deut 26:14 And the Bible also decries the worship of angels: • As an affront to the salvific and mediatory roles of Jesus, Heb 1:4-14; 1 John 2:1-2 As the NT also decries man bowing to man or angels, Acts 10:25-26; Rev 19:10; 22:8-9 • And man taking the worship that belongs to God, Acts 12:22-23 • But not so of Jesus, e.g. Luke 7:37-38; John 9:38 All of these clear and consistent teachings of Scripture are philosophized away with complex sophistry, reminiscent of the false shepherds who taught the worship of God and the worship of Baal simultaneously in Jer 23
602-610	Encyclicals: It appears that after the assassination of Maurice, Gregory I became the *de facto* leader of the Western Roman Empire; from this point on in history papal writings gained the political authority of an Emperor. Hence, this historic event provides a marker whereby papal encyclicals gained a supra-territorial authority in the minds of those who would submit to the authority of the Western Roman Empire. Later, the addition of the role of a "Holy" [Germanic] Roman Emperor, with Charlemagne in 800 A.D. appears to be primarily a real authority as it relates	One of his generals, Phocas beheaded Emperor Maurice his wife and three children; Phocas then became the new Emperor.	Maurice favored the Patriarch of Constantinople, whereas Phocas favored the Bishop of Rome. Sleidan explained the reign of Phocas: "It is recorded that next after *Gregory, Boniface* the III obtained the primacy from *Phocas*, certaine Edicts and charters being published in that behalf. "In *Phocas* his raigne the *Persians* very grievously annoyed the Commonwealth: seizing vpon *Mesopotamia*, and *Assyria*, and marching on euen vnto the lesser of *Asia*, such was the negligence of this	The death of Maurice marks the official end of the Classical Era, or the Greek Era. Some encyclicals of the Mid-Middle Ages and Later Middle Ages seem to follow the same pattern as noted in the letter of Queen Jezebel in 1 Kings 21: 1 Kings 21:9-11, "She wrote in the letters, saying, 'Proclaim a fast, and seat Naboth with high honor among the people; and seat two men, scoundrels, before him to bear witness against him, saying, "You have blasphemed God and the king." Then take him out, and stone him, that he may die.' So the men of his city, the elders and nobles who were inhabitants of his city, did as Jezebel had sent to them, as it *was* written in the letters which she had sent to them." Hence, it seems like, when the Church of Rome began to condemn persons with differing views of Christianity, removing from the freedom of conscience, that it began to act like Queen Jezebel, and quite likely act as the Prophetess Jezebel in Rev 2:18-29. Likewise, Rome's condemnation of many condemned was two-fold:

~Date	Prayer, Veneration, Sacraments and Other Doctrines	Ecclesiology/Politics	Rival Churches and Movements, Named by Their Antagonists	Biblical Assessment of Rome's Doctrines and Practices
	to territorial and political acquisition of lands, but largely symbolic a authority with regard to the entire Western Empire, whose only true head, that is the Pope, also functioned as head over realms not directly controlled by the Holy Roman Emperor.		Prince. *Germany* also, together with *Gallia* and a great part of *Italy* reuolted. The *Saracens* wasted *Egypt:* and he himself being slain for his cruelty and neglect of the Common-wealth, *Heraclius* succeeded." (Sleidan, 206-207)	• They had to find a doctrinal basis for their disagreement with them: "You have blasphemed God"; • They likewise had a political motive for their disagreement, "You have blasphemed the king." Interestingly, the same two grounds were used when the Sanhedrin condemned Jesus, as well as when the Apostle Paul was condemned, that being, the political: speaking against Caesar and the religious: speaking against the Temple or the Law of Moses. It is noteworthy to consider that the two have to be kept together for this argument to stand. Hence there is a need for a State-run church, directly tied to the chief of state. So that any religious disagreement can be tied to blasphemy against the monarch, so that he can then bring swift judgment. The condemning of the righteous by Rome, for views that are not dissimilar from Protestant views of today, was clearly noted when are considered the condemnations of John Huss (d. 1415) and John Wycliffe (d. 1384). However, if one studies the beliefs of some (not all) of the Albigenses and Waldenses, the list of those condemned for their doctrinal views mounts significantly, and the calendar continues to be ratcheted back by quite a number of centuries. Many of these men were condemned on theological grounds because their "Christological" or "Trinitarian" views did not hold up to Rome's scrutiny on such matters. And many of the arguments used find their root form in the rhetorical skills of Augustin.

604	Gregory expounded: (1) the Seven Cardinal Sins (in contradistinction to the Greek Seven Cardinal Virtues): pride, envy, anger, dejection, avarice, gluttony and lust; (2) salvation through gradual enlightenment [rather than instantaneous conversion][68]	Gregory's lifelong passion was the study of the book of Job [*Moralia*], from which he seemed to derive a type of moral philosophy		Formalized a changed definition of sin:
				 • By the way, change to the definition of sin = change to the doctrine of the atonement, or why Christ died for sin!
				 • Sin was no longer seen as active rebellion against the Law of God (e.g. Ten Commandments)
				 • Sin became a type of antithesis to the Greek Cardinal Virtues:
				    o Humility > Pride
				    o Generosity > Avarice
				    o Selflessness > Envy
				    o Temperance > Wrath or Anger
				    o Self-control > Lust
				    o Moderation > Gluttony
				    o Diligence > Dejection, Sloth, or Acadia
				 • Hence, Catholic theology became modified toward and lulled into Greek Stoicism, exemplified in the

---

[68]"For it is certainly impossible to eradicate all errors from obstinate minds at one stroke, and whoever wishes to climb a mountain top climbs gradually step by step, and not in one leap. It was in this way that the Lord revealed Himself to the Israelite people in Egypt, permitting the sacrifices formerly offered to the Devil to be offered thenceforward to Himself instead. So He bade them sacrifice beasts to Him, so that, once they became enlightened, they might abandon one element of the sacrifice and retain another. For, while they were to offer the same beasts as before, they were to offer to God instead of to idols, so that they would no longer be offering the same sacrifices" (Bede, *A History*, 87).

~Date	Prayer, Veneration, Sacraments and Other Doctrines	Ecclesiology/Politics	Rival Churches and Movements, Named by Their Antagonists	Biblical Assessment of Rome's Doctrines and Practices
				Roman monastic movements in their quest for salvation
				• Notice that nowhere in the Bible do we find a list comparable to the "Seven Cardinal Sins." The closest is the fairly obscure passage in Ezekiel 16:
				○ Ezek 16:49, "Look, this was the iniquity of your sister Sodom: She and her daughter had pride, fullness of food, and abundance of idleness; neither did she strengthen the hand of the poor and needy"
				Notice in the OT, that the "pride" of an individual who disagrees with the teaching, decree, or directive of the sitting high priest (Pontifex) calls for the death penalty in Deut 17:8-13
604-606	"Sabinian: Decreed that the hours be distinguished as Prime, Tierce, Nonne. They put the beginning of bells at his time" (de Hainault, #29)			Herein is the beginning of what later became the "Hours of the Blessed Virgin" wherein the Rosary was eventually recited multiple times a day. The following were the times for the "Traditional Roman Breviary": • Matins (midnight); • Lauds (3 am); • Prime (6 am); • Terce (9 am); • Sext (noon); • None (3 pm); • Vespers (6 pm); • Compline (9 pm). Apparently, Paul VI shortened and adapted these hours to what is called the "Liturgy of Hours" (major and minor).[69] Herein the requirement is three times of prayer, possibly emulating Daniel, as found in Daniel 6:10: Dan 6:10, "Now when Daniel knew that the writing was signed, he went home. And in his upper room, with his windows open toward Jerusalem, he knelt down on his knees three times that day, and prayed and gave thanks before his God, as was his custom since early days."
607	"Boniface III: This Pope had declared by Emperor Phocas against the Patriarchs of Constantinople, that the Roman Church was the	"Title of Pope, or universal bishop, given to Boniface III by emperor Phocas" (Boettner, #12)		Contra Matt 23:9, "Do not call anyone father" (see above 384-399)

---

[69]Notice the hymn that is a part of the contemporary "Little Liturgy," recommended to be said on Sundays at Evening Prayer (backed by the following Church authorities: "The following version of the Little Office of the Blessed Virgin Mary is from the Liturgy of the Hours. It has a *Nihil Obstat* from Daniel V. Flynn, J.C.D., Censor Librarian; and an *Imprimatur* from Patrick J. Sheridan, Vicar General, Archdiocese of New York"):
"Mary the dawn, Christ the Perfect Day;
"Mary the gate, Christ the Heavenly Way!
"Mary the root, Christ the Mystic Vine;
"Mary the grape, Christ the Sacred Wine!
"Mary the wheat, Christ the Living Bread;
"Mary the stem, Christ the Rose blood-red!
"Mary the beacon, Christ the Haven's Rest;
"Mary the mirror, Christ the Vision Blest!
"Mary the mother, Christ the Mother's Son
"By all things blest while endless ages run. Amen" ("The Little Office of the Blessed Virgin Mary"; available at:
http://www.liturgies.net/Liturgies/Catholic/LittleOffice.htm [online]; accessed: 8 Dec 2014; Internet).

~Date	Prayer, Veneration, Sacraments and Other Doctrines	Ecclesiology/Politics	Rival Churches and Movements, Named by Their Antagonists	Biblical Assessment of Rome's Doctrines and Practices
	first of all" (de Hainault, #30)			
608-615	"Boniface IV: The Rotunda of Rome was dedicated to all the Saints" (de Hainault, #31)			Several things seem to collude in this decision: • The transfer of the worship of the Greek and Roman pantheon on all the saints; as well as • The collecting of the spiritual benefits of "all the Saints" to be wielded in and by Rome and its authority
619-625	"Boniface V: Commanded the exemption of churches from taxes" (de Hainault, #32)			The beginning or continuation of a contention in the history of churches in various lands
630			"Mohamed published his doctrine, it was 630" (de Hainault, #62)	
631-641	St. Romanus in 631-641 was said to have delivered the region of Rouen, France, from a monster named Gargoyle. When this monster was burned, his head and neck would not burn, so he was mounted to a newly built church to offer it protection. Following this usage, gargoyles came into common use in Medieval church architecture.			As to the church and its protection. When demonic figures are said to protect the church, through architecture, they serve an errant catechetic purpose. In the same time period that statues of the saints are said to be catechetic devises, so these figures of demons severely misrepresent who is protecting the true church of Jesus Christ. In the Bible Jesus said, "I will build My church, and the gates of Hades shall not prevail against it" (Matt 16:18). Then, along with Christ's protection of His own church, there is the Holy Spirit who is promised to guide His people into all truth, most clearly through God's Word: John 14:26, "But the Helper, the Holy Spirit, whom the Father will send in My name, He will teach you all things, and bring to your remembrance all things that I said to you." Further, to complete the thread of thought, God has promised that His word would be preserved: Psa 12:6-7, "The words of the LORD are pure words, Like silver tried in a furnace of earth, Purified seven times. You shall keep them, O LORD, You shall preserve them from this generation forever."
633	Of the Fourth Council of Toledo:[70] "In Heraclius his raigne, the fourthe council of Toledo was celebrated, where, because the Priests throughout Spain, did not euery day (but onely on that day which wee call Sunday) use the prayer which Christ himself taught vs: amongst other matters, a reformation therein was decreed, as also that the Apocalyps of S. John, as			Concerning "use" of the Lord's Prayer every day by priests: In Worship: the requirement of reading or not reading a passage, reminiscent of the State-Church mentality of sending out mandate after mandate. In Worship: forbidding the singing of the Hebrew "Hallelujah" during the 40 days of Lent:

[70]According to Wikipedia.com, there were eighteen "Councils of Toledo" from 400-702 A.D., being in 400, 527, 589, 633, 636, 638, 646, 653, 655, 656, 675, 681, 683, 684, 688, 693, 702 ("Councils of Toledo; available at: http://en.wikipedia.org/wiki/Council_of_Toledo; accessed 11 Aug 2013; Internet).

~Date	Prayer, Veneration, Sacraments and Other Doctrines	Ecclesiology/Politics	Rival Churches and Movements, Named by Their Antagonists	Biblical Assessment of Rome's Doctrines and Practices
	they say should bee read in the Church from Easter to Whitsontide. ...The singing of the Hebrew *Alleujah* in the Church, in the time of *Lent* was also forbidden, for that it was a time of sorrow and not of rejoicing" (Sleidan, 209-210).			
635-636			Arab Muslims conquered Lebanon, and began to conquer southern portions of what is now called Turkey	The Arab Muslims were doing the job of destroying the political and economic power and prestige of Rome's rivals, the Orthodox Churches of the Byzantine Empire; further enhancing Rome's maneuvering to be a spiritual primacy and monopoly: • The Antiochene Orthodox Church in Lebanon, with its Patriarch • The area of the "Cappadocian Fathers" in what is now called Southern Turkey
637			Arab Muslims conquered Iraq	
639-642			Arab Muslims conquered Egypt	• The Egyptian Coptic Church, with the Patriarch of Alexandria
640-642	"John IV: There was at this miserable time—in almost all the churches an Arian Bishop and a Catholic [one]" (de Hainault, #33)			May the esteemed reader consider the difference between the Arian and Catholic, while seeking to avoid the Trinitarian historiographic intrigue.
642			Arab Muslims conquered Iran	
642-643			Arab Muslims conquered Libya	• An area with churches of the rival Western Donatist Church
655-657	"Eugene I: Decreed that the Bishops have prisons to punish clerics: that monks cannot leave their cloister without cause" (de Hainault, #34)			Here is the beginning of bishops and others having prison cells in their houses (i.e. basement prison cells or dungeons). Later these were used for inquisition. Further, monks could not leave their cloister without cause. Herein the monastic ministry of preaching or evangelizing was curtailed, until the preaching of the Rosary and the Sacraments by the 13th Century preaching orders of the Franciscans and Dominicans.
663/664		The Synod of Whitby convened in England by King Owry. It pitted Rome's Bishop of Northumbria, Wilfrid, against the Iro-Scottish or Celtic [evangelical] Colman; the issue seems to have been tradition: • Colman argued for a tradition going back to [St]	Here is a case of the absorption of a loosely organized church (that of the Celts) into the well organized machinery of Rome's ecclesiology, along with its distinctive theological accoutrements	Somehow, Rome's spokesperson, Wilfrid, had managed to get a foothold into the Celtic church, according to the historian Montalembert: "Wilfrid appeared: by a fifty years' struggle, and at the cost of his peace, safety, and even his personal freedom, he first neutralised, and finally annihilated, the Celtic spirit, without at any time being guilty of persecution, coercion, or violence towards the vanquished. He did more than check the Celtic movement; he sent it back into chaos; he extirpated all the ritual and liturgic differences which served as a

~Date	Prayer, Veneration, Sacraments and Other Doctrines	Ecclesiology/Politics	Rival Churches and Movements, Named by Their Antagonists	Biblical Assessment of Rome's Doctrines and Practices
		Columba, the great evangelist-missionary • Wilfrid argued for a tradition going back to [St] Peter, as the founder of the Roman church Wilfrid prevailed, allowing Rome to firmly control the Church in England; Colman and his monks left the country and the Celtic evangelistic fervor, through which a large portion of Western Europe was evangelized, was drained from the Church of England		veil and pretext for the prejudices of race and opinion; he extirpated them not only in his immense diocese, the vast region of Northumbria, but throughout all of England; and not in England only, but, by the contagion of his example and influence, in Ireland, in Scotland, and finally in the very sanctuary of Celtic Christianity, at Iona."[71]
668-685		Of Constantine IV, ruler of Byzantium, the Bearded: "This Emperour, as it is recorded, was the first, that ordained, that whom the Clergy and people of *Rome* together with the souldiers, had created Bishop of that city, hee should obtaine full power: for till this time the dignity of Bishop of *Rome* depended vpon the confirmation either of the Emperour, or of his Deputy for *Italy*" (Sleidan, 213)		It appears that Constantine IV added, for the first time, that the choice of the Bishop of Rome should move from the Roman Emperor (residing in Byzantium), to the clergy, people, and soldiers of Rome.
680		A historiographic question about the Sixth Council of Constantinople: "The sicth Councell of Constantinople was held in his raign which consisted of 150. Bishops. Wherein, about the end thereof, mention is made (but in obscure words) of those Canons stiled the Apostles. But *Gratianus* reckons vp the contrary opinions, for he auerres, that they were compiled by heretiques, rejected by the Primitive Church, and accounted among the *Apocrypha's*. Yet it is written that *Zepherinus* B. of *Rome*, in order the sixteenth approued them: as also, after him, this Councell before mentioned, which (as they report) was ended in *Justine* the II. his time, *Constantine* the IIII. his sonne. In brief, all flotes vpon vncertain grounds, neither doe they agree in the		An interesting historiographic question as to the veracity and authenticity of the "Canons" of the Council of Constantinople, generally called the 3rd Council of Constantinople. These kind of historiographic issues render these councils "shaky ground" upon which to found one's faith (cf. Matt 7:24-27).

---

[71]Count of Montalembert, *Monks of the West from St. Benedict to St. Bernard* (London, England: William Blackwood and Sons, 1867), 4:116-117.

~Date	Prayer, Veneration, Sacraments and Other Doctrines	Ecclesiology/Politics	Rival Churches and Movements, Named by Their Antagonists	Biblical Assessment of Rome's Doctrines and Practices
		number of Canons, for some hold 50. others 60. others 84. in which number indeed are extant. Whereby it may easily be conjectured that more were added by degrees, and afterwards (though proceeding from many) comprehended vnder one title. Archbishop of *Ravenna*, subjected himself to the Bishop of *Rome*, who before that (but most especially after the translation tither of the Exarchy) would yield nothing at all to him" (Sleidan, 213-215).		
682-683	"Leo II: He allowed **Baptism every day [of the week]**" (de Hainault, #35)			
687-701	"Sergius I: Decreed that the **Agnus Dei** be sung three times" (de Hainault, #36)			
698			Arab Muslims conquered Carthage	• When the Arab Muslims conquered Carthage, they conquered the seat of Rome's rival Western church, the Donatist Church, with its locally-chosen Bishop of Carthage.
709		**"Kissing of Pope's foot began, Pope Constantine"** (Boettner, #13)		Kissing a person's foot requires bowing to man, contra Acts 10:25-26, etc. Kissing of the foot may seem to appear in several biblical passages: • Esther 4:17d (apocryphal; NJB), "Gladly would I have kissed the soles of his feet, had this assured the safety of Israel." • Psa 2:11-12 (NJB), "In fear be submissive to Yahweh; with trembling kiss his feet, lest he be angry and your way come to nothing" (cf. Luke 7:38, 45). Several texts are used to prove the acceptability of a man bowing or prostrating himself to a man: • 2 Sam 15:5 (NJB), "And whenever anyone came up to him to prostrate himself, he would stretch out his hand, draw him to him and kiss him." • Heb 11:21 (NJB), "By faith Jacob, when he was dying, blessed each of Joseph's sons, bowed in reverence, as he leant on his staff." Texts against man bowing to man: • Mordecai not bowing to Haman, Esther 3:2 • Cornelius stopped from bowing to Peter, Acts 10:25-26 Texts against man worshipping and/or bowing to angels: • Rev 19:10, "And I fell at his feet to worship him. But he said to me, "See *that you do* not *do that*! I am your fellow servant, and of your brethren who have

~Date	Prayer, Veneration, Sacraments and Other Doctrines	Ecclesiology/Politics	Rival Churches and Movements, Named by Their Antagonists	Biblical Assessment of Rome's Doctrines and Practices
				the testimony of Jesus. Worship God! For the testimony of Jesus is the spirit of prophecy." • Rev 22:8-9, "Now I, John, saw and heard these things. And when I heard and saw, I fell down to worship before the feet of the angel who showed me these things. Then he said to me, "See *that you do* not *do that*. For I am your fellow servant, and of your brethren the prophets, and of those who keep the words of this book. Worship God." Texts against man bowing to images: • Second Commandment, Exod 20:4-6; Deut 5:8-10 • Daniel's friends not bowing to an idol, Dan 3:12ff. Food for thought questions: • If it is acceptable for a man to bow showing respect to a political figure, then why should it also not be allowable for a man to bow before a religious leader? • Is there not a spiritual difference between a person bowing in honor before a political figure and a person bowing in honor before a religious leader or personality?
711-714			Arab Muslims conquered what is now Spain (kingdoms of Toledo and Seville)	The Arab Muslims attacked Spain, that had long been "Arian" in its persuasion under the control of Visigoth Kings: • Although 100 years before [pope] Gregory I had made some inroads into their conversion to "Orthodoxy" and to Roman oversight (by accepting the baptism of the Arians) • The breaking of their political and ecclesiastical power was probably not considered a bad thing • We know that later the Spanish Inquisition became famous for its brutality, to the point of torture by use of the "Iron Maiden," and the killing of 323,362 people burned alive over 330 years (1478-1808), and 17,659 burned in effigy (meaning also that their descendants lost all their rights to their houses or lands)![72]
717-741	"The emperor *Leo* throwes all statues & Images of Saints, out of Churches, and enjoynes the Pope also to doe the like: but he not onely disobeyes, but also denounces sharp punishment against him perseuering in his purpose" (Sleidan, 219-220).	Jean LeClerc of Meaux, France, was one of the first of many post-Reformation martyrs in France (1523): he broke some statues of saints the night before a solemn procession through the town of Metz, France; he was caught, branded, cut to pieces with pincers, and his remains were burned in Metz (Crespin).	"This *Leo* [of Byzantium] was a mortall enemy of Gregory II. Bishop of *Rome*: and charged his Vicar or Exarch in *Italy*, by all meanes to cut him off: but the Lombards defended the Pope, not for any loue that they bare him, but to the end, that by these dissensions, they might enlarge their owne Territories" (Sleidan, 219).	Herein the Iconoclastic Controversy (or anti-statue, anti-idol controversy) is in full swing, where the Church of Rome insisted on having statues, and the Church of Constantinople was against the same. Note the power and clarity of the Second Commandment: • Exod 20:4-6, "You shall not make for yourself a carved image, or any likeness *of anything* that *is* in heaven above, or that *is* in the earth beneath, or that *is* in the water under the earth; you shall not bow down to them nor serve them. For I, the LORD your God, *am* a jealous God, visiting the iniquity of the fathers on the children to the third and fourth *generations* of those who hate Me, but showing mercy to thousands, to those who love Me and keep My commandments." Note also that the Second of the Ten Commandments was subsumed as part of the

---

[72]Joseph F. Conley, *Drumbeats that Changed the World* (Pasadena: William Carey, 2000), 32.

~Date	Prayer, Veneration, Sacraments and Other Doctrines	Ecclesiology/Politics	Rival Churches and Movements, Named by Their Antagonists	Biblical Assessment of Rome's Doctrines and Practices
				First Commandment at least as early as Augustine of Hippo, the famous rhetorician of Milan, reordering them by dividing the Tenth Commandment into two in order to maintain the number "ten" in the Ten Commandments.
731-741	Gregory III moved Rome's celebration of "All Saints' Day" to November 1, possibly to coincide with the Druid "New Year's Day"?			Took the syncretism of Gregory I's "Letter to the Abbott Mellitus" to the next level? (cf. A.D. 590-604).
741-775	Of Leo III, Emperor of Byzantium (741-775): "He also, as his father *Leo* [of Byzantium], liued in discord with *Gregory* the III. Bishop of *Rome*, who forthwith sending his *Nuncio's*, excommunicates him: and they being cast in prison, hee [*Gregory*] made a decree in the Councell thereupon assembled: That, whosoever should demolish Images of the Saints, or contumeliously abuse them, should be vtterly excluded from the Communion of the Church: after this, with all diligence and endeavor he erected Images in diuers Churches, and as farre as he could, sumptuously adorned them" (Sleidan, 220-221).	Of Zachary, Bishop of Rome (741-752) and his dealings with a German Bishop, Boniface, and the French Emperor, Charlemagne: "After Gregory III. Zacharias succeeded. An Epistle of his is extant to one Boniface a Bishop in Germany; the same man, it appears whose help Gregory II used, as a little above mentioned. Zacharias satisfied his requests and permitted Bishopricks at Merburgh, Bamberg, and Erphord; and also gave him [Boniface] leaue to go to *Charlemaine, Charles Martel* his sonne, who was desirous to have a Councell held in some City of the French Kingdome: that he might diligently reforme the abuses of the Church, but most especially remoue adulterers, and those who had many wiues from the order of the Priesthood: for sithence after the vndertaking of the holy Ministery, they ought not to haue or touch as much as one wife, much lesse at one and the same time, they should haue more, for in *Paul's* words, that the Bishop should bee husband of one wife, is to bee vnderstood not of the time present, but past, to wit, that hee who desires to be admitted into the ministerial function, should haue no more wiues than one. To this Epistle *Charlemaines* Edict (who stiles himself Duke of the French) is annexed: wherein he ordaines that a Councell should be held euery year in		The "Iconoclastic Controversy" was in full swing, with Pope Zachary consolidating his state-church empire through Boniface, a German Bishop, and Charlemagne, the French Emperor and conquering military leader, who united much of Western Europe during his reign. The full extent of Charlemagne's (~742-814) empire by his death in 814 went from the Pyrenees mountains on the border of France and Spain all the way to the Baltic Sea in Northern Germany, from the coast of Brittany in France all the way to Southern Italy, and moving eastward into modern Hungary.

~Date	Prayer, Veneration, Sacraments and Other Doctrines	Ecclesiology/Politics	Rival Churches and Movements, Named by Their Antagonists	Biblical Assessment of Rome's Doctrines and Practices
		his presence: and commands that adulterous Priests, and whoremongers should be remoued out of their places: and likewise prohibits them from hunting and hawking, and charges them not to maintaine any whore at home: but concerning wiues not a word" (Sleidan, 221-223).		
732			Charles Martel (grandfather of Charlemagne) stopped advance of Arab Muslims at Poitiers, France	Arab Muslims were defeated in Southern France
741-752		**"Zachary: Commanded that Christians no longer be sold to infidels" (de Hainault, #37)**		Herein the Pope provides civil ordinances to acquiescent kings and princes.
750		**"Temporal power [political authority] of popes, given by Pepin, king of the Franks" (Boettner, #14)**[73]		Further giving political authority to Rome over those in the lands of Roman controlled emperors, kings, queens, or princes. The political oppression that Augustine used against the Donatists was now able to be leveraged against any schismatics in Roman controlled areas. Contra Matt 20:24ff., greatness by serving others, not by lording it over them, 1 Pet 5:3 "My kingdom is not of this world," John 18:36 "The kingdom of God does not come with observation; nor will they say, `See here!' or `See there!' For indeed, the kingdom of God is within you," Luke 17:20-21 Hence, today, the Vatican City is a political power, with all the vestiges of a political state, over which the Pope is the political ruler.
751		Pippin, who was the Mayor of the palace Neustria and Austrasia under King Childeric III, was made King of the Franks, after the Pope deposed Childeric III.[74]		Herein the papacy truly became a political power—the Pope became the kingmaker of the Western Europe of that time.[75]

---

[73]Interestingly, Sleidan spends several pages questioning the veracity of this claim, citing the writings of one Eginardus (Sleidan, 245-47).

[74]"Pippin III, also spelled Pepin, byname Pippin the Short, French Pépin le Bref, German Pippin der Kurze (born c. 714—died September 24, 768, Saint-Denis, Neustria [now in France]), the first king of the Frankish Carolingian dynasty and the father of Charlemagne. A son of Charles Martel, Pippin became sole de facto ruler of the Franks in 747 and then, on the deposition of Childeric III in 751, king of the Franks. He was the first Frankish king to be anointed—first by St. Boniface and later (754) by Pope Stephen II" ("Pippin III"; available at: http://www.britannica.com/EBchecked/topic/450778/Pippin-III (online]; accessed: 8 Dec 2014; Internet).

[75]"For as the writers of the French Annals deliuer it, the Kings there, for some yeers together, had nothing at all besides their title, the principalitie of gouernement belonging to the Gouerneur of the King's house. For those Kings degenerated from the worth of their Predecessors, and gaue themselues ouer to pleasure, reiecting the care of the Common-wealth: whereupon the Gouernour of the Pallace bore all sway, and by how much greater the king's negligence was, so much more hee augmented his authoritie. At length vpon this occasion, Pipin, who was Gouernour in Childricke's raigne, (when the cause, as they say, came to canuasing before Pope Zacharie) got the Kingdome. Hereof is mention made in that decree which they name Gratians, to wit, that it is lawfull for the Pope to depriue Kings of their principalitie: but the title and description of that place is false, seeing as there were two Anastatio's Emperours, and it cannot be referred to either of them; for the former raigned aboue 200. and the other, 37. years, before this happened: as also there was no Pope Gelasius in the later Emperours time.

~Date	Prayer, Veneration, Sacraments and Other Doctrines	Ecclesiology/Politics	Rival Churches and Movements, Named by Their Antagonists	Biblical Assessment of Rome's Doctrines and Practices
752		"Stephen II: Ravenna was placed in the hands of the Pope by Pepin, King of France, and the exarchs ousted from Italy" (de Hainault, #38) Of Pepin and the Pope: • Sleidan's political explanation;[76] and • The religious ramifications of that political change.[77]		
780-1180		Byzantine Arab Wars begun	Byzantine Arab Wars begun	These wars were the beginning of the slow downfall of the Byzantine Empire, much like the Holy Roman Empire never made gains into North Africa equal to the original Roman Empire of Julius Caesar: • Muslim attacks kept coming against the Byzantine Empire; and • It appears that Rome's Crusades to regain the Holy Land only festered and coalesced the Arabs to fight against the Eastern Roman Empire.
781		Charlemagne invited Alcuin [Alcoinus] from York (Great Britain) to establish biblical studies in Tours (France).[78] So also Charlemagne founded the "Academie of Paris."[79]		Thus began a new thrust of biblical knowledge among the French in the 9th and 10th Centuries.
782		"The year 782 marked one of the worst horrors of Charlemagne's reign, the reputed beheading of forty-five hundred Saxons who resisted the Frankish campaign of forced	Charlemagne compelled the Saxons "by force and with unexampled cruelty, to receive baptism" (Schaff-Herzog, 1:436)	The evangelism methodology of the first "Holy Roman Emperor", Charlemagne, appears to have been given to forced conversions!

"I thought to adde this for the Readers aduertizement, that they may wisely peruse the Papall records: for it is not one place alone which discovers this to be their prime practice, so to fasten an opinion of antiquitie vpon their laws, that they may carry the more weight and authority" (Sleidan, 238-40).

[76]"From this time Aistulphus King of the Lombards required a tribute from the Romans, sharply menacing them in case of non-payment Stephen the II, then Bishop of Rome, seeing hee could not stop his mouth neither with flatteries nor rewards sues to Constantine the Emperour for ayde, but no helpe coming from him, hee solicites Pipin, lately (as we below shall mention) made king of the French; to lend him his hand. He marching with an Army into Italy besieges Pauie, and compels Aistulphus to come to composition, but the Enemy, after Pipins return home, growne more kene, againe takes armes: whereupon Pipin, againe solicited, marches into Italy; then at length Aistulphus surrenders the Exarchie to Pipin in which Country those Cities are of chiefe account, Ravenna, Fauentia, Caesena, Forli, Forlimpopoli, Bologna, Reggio, Parma, and Placentia.

"It is written that Pipin deliuered all this Countrey into the Popes hands, though the Emperor first required him to restore them to him, as belonging to the Empire, not to the Church of Rome" (Sleidan, 223-24).

[77]"Pipin his Father committed the Exarchate, taken from the Lombards, into the Bishop of Romes hands, as above said, which indeed is so deliuered to memorie, and it is reported that hee directly gaue it to them, but that very many call into question" (Sleidan, 245).

[78]"En 781, Charlemagne avait rencontré à Parme le savant Alcuin, chef de l'école de la cathédrale d'York, et l'avait invité à s'établir auprès de lui, à Aix-la-Chapelle, pour l'aider à relever le clergé et la nation de leur ignorance. 'Ministre intellectuel de Charlemagne', comme a dit Guizot, jamais il ne mérita mieux ce titre que par ses travaux bibliques. En 796, l'année où il quitta Aix-la-Chapelle pour Saint-Martin-de-Tours, il demanda au roi l'autorisation et les moyens de faire venir d'York ses manuscrits des livres saints. Voici les dernières lignes de sa requête, tout empreintes d'enthousiasme et de poésie : Et qu'on rapporte ainsi en France ces fleurs de la Grande-Bretagne pour que ce jardin ne soit pas enfermé dans la seule ville d'York, mais que nous puissions avoir aussi à Tours ces jets du paradis et les fruits de ses arbres [S. BERGER, op. cit., p. 190, xv.]" (Samuel Lortsch, "Histoire de la Bible en France"; available at: http://www.bibliquest.org/Lortsch/Lortsch-Histoire_Bible_France-1.htm [online]; accessed: 4 Mar 2005; Internet).

[79]Sleidan, 248.

~Date	Prayer, Veneration, Sacraments and Other Doctrines	Ecclesiology/Politics	Rival Churches and Movements, Named by Their Antagonists	Biblical Assessment of Rome's Doctrines and Practices
		conversion to Christianity."[80]		

786	"Worship of the cross, images and relics, authorized in 786" (Boettner, #15)	What is authorized is not so innocent as it may seem. The "authorization of" is equivalent to the "requirement of" in worship.
		
		And opposition to is deemed opposition to the sitting judge (the Pope), as found in Deut 17:8-13:
		
		Deut 17:8-13, "If a matter arises which is too hard for you to judge, between degrees of guilt for bloodshed, between one judgment or another, or between one punishment or another, matters of controversy within your gates, then you shall arise and go up to the place which the LORD your God chooses. And you shall come to the priests, the Levites, and to the judge *there* in those days, and inquire *of them*; they shall pronounce upon you the sentence of judgment. You shall do according to the sentence which they pronounce upon you in that place which the LORD chooses. And you shall be careful to do according to all that they order you. According to the sentence of the law in which they instruct you, according to the judgment which they tell you, you shall do; you shall not turn aside *to* the right hand or *to* the left from the sentence which they pronounce upon you. Now the man who acts presumptuously and will not heed the priest who stands to minister there before the LORD your God, or the judge, that man shall die. So you shall put away the evil from Israel. And all the people shall hear and fear, and no longer act presumptuously."
			On the surface, this "little sin" or "small wink"[81] toward syncretism seems innocent enough. However, the backside of "authorizing" something like the worship of relics and images is as follows:
			
			Anyone who criticizes this teaching is going against the Church of Rome, and hence,
			
			Is deserving of some type of punishment!
			
			Furthermore, anyone who does not openly and actively participate in the worship via relics is deemed suspect of inwardly holding opposing views towards this "approved" practice, and hence,
			
			Is *de facto* guilty of holding opposing views until they prove themselves innocent by actively worshipping images and relics!
			
			A Lose-Lose scenario was thereby created for anyone opposing the worship of images or relics,
			
			Including a loss of their "freedom of conscience" on these matters (and any other issue upon which Rome made a determination).
				Contra Exod 20:4-6; et al. (see above); thus continues the "Idolatry Controversy" (a.k.a. "Iconoclastic Controversy")
				
				By the 12th Century, Henry of Lausanne protested Rome's veneration of the cross, as recorded in the third of five articles of Peter "the Venerable" of Cluny against Henry: "3. The cross is not an object of adoration; it is on the contrary a detestable object, as the instrument of the torture and suffering of Christ."
				
				Of the destruction of pagan idols and their temples (Deut 12:1-3): Deut 12:4 (KJV) states, "Ye shall not do so unto the LORD your God." One implication of this verse appears to be that, while the people of Israel were to destroy the pagan temples, they were not to do so with the worship of YHWH, that is destroy His temples and churches—herein is the historical non-sequetor:
				
				• The same church that would and will not destroy its own relics, images, and statues (idols)
				
				• Was eventually willing to destroy Jewish synagogues and burn their Torahs and to destroy Albigensian, Waldensian, Baptist, and Protestant churches and houses of prayer, and burn their Bibles and hymn books
				
				  ○ Notice how the persecution of the Jews goes against Rom 15:27, wherein the Macedonian churches were commended for giving a gift to their Jewish brethren:
				
				  ○ Rom 15:26-27, "For it pleased those from Macedonia and Achaia to make a certain contribution for the poor among the saints who are in Jerusalem. It pleased them indeed, and they are their debtors. For if the Gentiles have been partakers of their spiritual things, their duty is also to minister to them in material things."
				
				• Therefore, there was a strange but logical turning of the tables. As nature abhors a vacuum, so disobedience of one command (Exod 20:4; Deut 5:8), led to equal and opposite aggressiveness to those who did seek to obey that same command.

[80]Philip Jenkins, *The Lost History of Christianity: The Thousand Year Golden Age of the Church in the Middle East, Africa, and Asia—and How It Died* (New York: Harper-Collins, 2008), 16.

[81]Acts 17:30 (DRA), "And God indeed having winked at the times of this ignorance, now declareth unto men, that all should every where do penance."

~Date	Prayer, Veneration, Sacraments and Other Doctrines	Ecclesiology/Politics	Rival Churches and Movements, Named by Their Antagonists	Biblical Assessment of Rome's Doctrines and Practices
787		7th Ecumenical Council (Nicea II): emphasis is "Iconoclastic Controversy" between Rome and Constantinople: Rome allowed the veneration of statues in worship, Constantinople did not, but later established use of "Holy Icons" (paintings)		Statues in worship became a major dividing point between Constantinople (Orthodox or Eastern Church) and Rome (Catholic or Western Church), which will culminate in the East-West schism of 1054; notice the question-framing in the use of the term "iconoclastic", it should rather be "idolatry controversy"; the issue became are Rome's decrees above the Ten Commandments, to which Rome answered "Yes!"
789		Charlemagne made the following pronouncement concerning the education of children: "May schools be [established] where children are taught to read. May they be taught the Psalms, music [theory], hymns, arithmetic, grammar and the catholic books, from a version that is well maintained [corrected]. For often, while desiring to ask something of God, as is [only] proper, they ask wrongly, if they use books that are defective. And do not allow your children to alter that text, neither when they read, nor when they write it. And if you have need for copies of the Gospels, the Psalms, or the Missal, have them copied by a mature man, and may he be given over to this task with perfect care [or: great diligence]."[82]		It appears by this decree of Charlemagne, that he wanted elementary schools to be established to teach the Bible to children. Certainly, if this was the case, it is no wonder why we speak of the Carolingian Renaissance today! Could not this Carolingian emphasis on Bible reading have influenced the later growth and development of the Paulicians of the 9th-10th Centuries and the Cathars of the 11th-13th Centuries—predominantly in Southern France, according to what is currently known of them? Notice also that the 8th-9th Century Emperor was concerned with textual criticism, even as was Napoleon 900 years later!
795-816	"Leo III: The Romans plucked out his eyes and cut out his tongue" (de Hainault, #39)			In 799 Pope Leo III appears to have been attacked by certain members of the general populace of Rome, on suspicion of adultery and perjury. Charlemagne apparently sheltered the Pope and attempted judicial proceedings to clear up the matter. Later, in 800, Leo III would crown him Holy Roman Emperor. The farther one studies the soap-opera type of lives of some of the 9th and 10th Century popes, the more one wonders how "Papal Succession" could be argued to pass through some of these

[82]"Qu'il y ait des écoles où l'on fasse lire les enfants. Qu'on leur fasse apprendre les psaumes, le solfège, les cantiques, l'arithmétique, la grammaire et les livres catholiques, dans un texte bien corrigé, car souvent, tout en désirant demander quelque chose à Dieu comme il convient, ils le demandent mal, s'ils se servent de livres fautifs. Et ne laissez pas vos enfants altérer le texte, ni quand ils lisent, ni quand ils écrivent. Et si vous avez besoin de faire copier les Évangiles, le psautier, ou le missel, faites-les copier par des hommes d'âge mûr, qui s'acquittent de cette tâche avec un soin parfait [S. BERGER, Histoire de la Vulgate pendant les premiers siècles du moyen âge. Introduction, p. 185]" (Samuel Lortsch, op. cit.).

~Date	Prayer, Veneration, Sacraments and Other Doctrines	Ecclesiology/Politics	Rival Churches and Movements, Named by Their Antagonists	Biblical Assessment of Rome's Doctrines and Practices
				leaders—even if one accepts Augustine's argument that the sin of the priest is inconsequential to the effectiveness of the "Sacrament" that they offer!

800		[Pope] Leo III crowned Charlemagne [Western] Holy Roman Emperor, thereby:
		
		• Predisposing Rome's interest [or interference] in matters of State
		
		• Advancing Rome's supremacy over State affairs:
		  o On regulating the appointment of rulers;
		  o On determining the rule of law
		
		• Advancing Rome's claim to supremacy in the ongoing struggle, called the "Investiture Controversy"
		
		By his military exploits, Charlemagne reunited north-western Europe that Julius Caesar had conquered, and that was later divided between Constantine II and Constans I. After reigning 33 years, Charlemagne was crowned "Holy Roman Emperor."[83]
		
		Sleidan bemoaned the decay of Europe after Charlemagne, much like the earlier decay after Julius Caesar.[84]
				Jesus said, "Render to Caesar the things that are Caesar's" (Matt 22:21; Mark 12:17; Luke 20:25), versus "I [through My vicar on earth] will appoint and control future Caesars"?
				
				It's hard to ignore that the Fourth Monarchy of Daniel 2, 7, and 9, continues through the rulership of the Holy Roman Emperor, and is gradually transferred to the office of the Pope.

| ~800 | Portions of the so-called "Creed of Athanasius" are as follows:

1. Whosoever will be saved, before all things it is necessary that he hold the Catholic faith,
2. Which Faith except every one do keep whole and undefiled, without doubt he shall perish everlastingly.";
3. And the Catholic faith is this: that we worship one God in Trinity, and Trinity in Unity;
4. Neither confounding the Persons; nor dividing the Substance."
5. For there is one Person of the Father, another of the Son, and another of the Holy Ghost.
6. But the Godhead of the Father, of the Son, and of the Holy Ghost, is all one: the Glory Equal, the Majesty Coeternal.
7. Such as the Father is, such is the Son: and such is the Holy Ghost. | By the way, the "Creed of Athanasius" is read on Trinity Sunday in Anglican and other Protestant churches;

Hereby, the philosophical doctrines of the Trinity and Christology were made into the preeminent salvific doctrines in which to believe, rather than faith in the substitutionary atonement.

Beginning with a works salvation (as noted to the left), the Creed finally gets to the Atonement in Section 36, stating only, "Who suffered for our salvation":

36. Who suffered for our salvation: descended into hell, rose again the third day from the dead. |

---

[83]"Thus the Romane Empire in the West, rent almost into peece-meals, especially from the time of the Emperours made choice of Constantinople for their Court and seat (as appears out of that which we haue before mentioned:) was by Emperour Charles redintigrated, and as it were a new bodie, re-assumed beautie and feature, after so many and so great Prouinces were reduced to one man's principalitie" (Sleidan, 242).

[84]"And thus farre in Preface-wise touching the Germanes, and the Emperour Charles: henceforward ile briefly run ouer and shew, after what manner this part of the Romane Empire in the West, hard and sharpe restored and recollected by Charles: again decaied, which being diuided, fell into many mens dominions, who held the same, as their proper right, not acknowledging the fountaine from whence they flowed: Insomuch, as that Maiesticall and so much renowned sublimitie of the Romain Empire, is nothing else at this day, then a slender shadow of a great bodie, after it was shrunk from such a huge maste, to Germanie one onely particle of Europe. Last of all, ile briefly explaine, how Daniel foretold this interchangeable course of Monarchies, and the fall of the Romane Empire" (Sleidan, 248-49).

~Date	Prayer, Veneration, Sacraments and Other Doctrines	Ecclesiology/Politics	Rival Churches and Movements, Named by Their Antagonists	Biblical Assessment of Rome's Doctrines and Practices
	8. The Father uncreate, the Son uncreate: the Holy Ghost uncreate. 9. The Father is incomprehensible, the Son incomprehensible and the Holy Ghost incomprehensible. 10. The Father is eternal, the Son eternal: and the Holy Ghost eternal. 11. And yet they are not three Eternals: but one Eternal. 12. As there are not three uncreated, nor three incomprehensibles: but one uncreated and one incomprehensible. 13. So likewise the Father is Almighty, the Son Almighty: and the Holy Ghost Almighty. 14. And yet there are not three Almighties: but one Almighty. 19. For like as we are compelled by the Christian verity: to acknowledge every Person by himself to be God and Lord; So are we forbidden by the Catholic Religion: to say, There be three Gods, or three Lords. ... 27. Furthermore, it is necessary to Everlasting Salvation; that he also believe rightly the Incarnation of our Lord Jesus Christ. 28. For the right Faith is, that we believe and confess: that our Lord Jesus Christ, the Son of God, is God and Man; 29. God, of the Substance of the Father begotten before the worlds: and Man of the Substance of his mother, born in the world; 30. Perfect God, and perfect Man: of a reasonable soul and human flesh subsisting. 31. Equal to the Father, as touching his Godhead: and inferior to the Father, as touching his Manhood. [85]			37. He ascended into heaven; he sitteth on the right hand of the Father, God Almighty; from whence he shall come to judge the quick and the dead. **The creed then ended with a statement of works salvation (doing good versus doing evil):** 38. At whose coming all men shall rise again with their bodies: and shall give account for their own works. 39. And they that have done good shall go into life everlasting: and they that have done evil into everlasting fire. 40. This is the Catholic faith: which except a man believe faithfully, he cannot be saved. Therefore it seems that this Creed continued the trajectory of the Church of Rome towards the philosophical theology for which it would become famous with the later Medieval "Scholastics": Peter the Lombard, Thomas Aquinas, etc. They would develop a theological system with no need for the Pauline Gospel of justification by faith and its corresponding hearing to believe.
813		The 813 Council of Tours called by Charlemagne: [86] "But Charlemagne was also considering the people. Under his influence, the 813 Council of Tours decided that homilies for the people (including the text [of Scripture]) would be verbally translated into the vulgar tongue. 'This period,' said Mr. Trénel, 'marks the peak of the Vulgate [Bible] in France. One did not read another book. All the monasteries, in particular that of Saint-Martin-of-Tours, with its two hundred monks, or those of the north with Corbie as a center, were transformed into workshops where new		Could not these monasteries, fueled by the zeal of their Emperor, as well as by the Council of Tours, be the reason for the plethora of versions of the Bible published in the 9th-11th Centuries—often called "Majority Text" readings? Note also the interest in textual criticism of Theodulf of Tours, as explained in a footnote of Lortsch: "Theodulf worked with a different methodology than did Alcuin. Alcuin sought purely and simply to reestablish the text of the Vulgate in its [full] integrity. Theoldulf, for himself, sought to establish a critical text. He inserted in the margins all the variant readings that he could find. He did not hide the lessons derived from them [this work], but conserved them fro the purpose of information. 'His work,' said Mr. S. Berger, 'was not born in a suitable context in an Empire wherein unity was the law [of the land]. The reform of Alcuin, on the contrary, was inspired by the same spirit as that of reign of Charlemagne. Neither will those who have a historical inclination regret Theodulf's lack of success. His work was not for its time."[87]

---

[85]"Creed of Athanasius" available at: http://www.rca.org/aboutus/beliefs/athanasian.php; accessed 9/28/04; Internet.

[86]"Mais Charlemagne songeait aussi au peuple. Sous son influence, le concile de Tours (813) décida que les homélies au peuple (donc aussi le texte) seraient traduites oralement en langue vulgaire. «Cette époque, dit M. Trénel, marque l'apogée de la Vulgate en France. On ne lit pas d'autre livre. Tous les monastères, en particulier celui de Saint-Martin-de-Tours, avec ses deux cents moines, ou ceux du nord avec Corbie pour centre, se transforment en ateliers où se publient sans cesse de nouvelles éditions de l'Écriture».

"Parmi ces «ateliers» il faut aussi mentionner ceux que dirigeait un autre restaurateur des lettres, Théodulfe (S. BERGER, op. cit. xiii, xvii), originaire d'Espagne, évêque d'Orléans sous Charlemagne et sous Louis le Débonnaire. Deux des plus belles Bibles latines du temps de Charlemagne furent exécutées par ses soins et sont parvenues jusqu'à nous. Elles sont admirablement enluminées. Elles se trouvent, l'une dans le trésor de la cathédrale du Puy, l'autre à la Bibliothèque nationale (No 9380 des manuscrits latins)" (Lortsch, op. cit.).

[87]"Théodulfe travaillait d'après une autre méthode qu'Alcuin. Alcuin cherchait purement et simplement à rétablir le texte de la Vulgate dans son intégrité. Théodulfe, lui, visait à reconstituer un texte critique. Il insérait en marge toutes les variantes qu'il avait pu réunir. Il ne faisait pas disparaitre les leçons qu'il écartait, mais les conservait à titre de renseignement. «Son oeuvre, dit M. S. Berger, n'était pas née viable dans un empire dont l'unité était la loi. La réforme d'Alcuin, au contraire, était inspirée par l'esprit même du règne de Charlemagne. Ceux qui ont le sens de l'histoire n'en regretteront pas moins l'insuccès de la

~Date	Prayer, Veneration, Sacraments and Other Doctrines	Ecclesiology/Politics	Rival Churches and Movements, Named by Their Antagonists	Biblical Assessment of Rome's Doctrines and Practices
		editions of Scripture were unceasingly published.' "Among these 'workshops', one must also mention what was accomplished by another restorer of letters, Theodulf, native of Spain, Bishop of Orleans under Charlemagne and under Louis the Debonnaire. Two of the most beautiful Latin Bibles were carried out under his care, and have remained up to this day. They are beautifully illuminated. The are found, one in the treasury of the Cathedral of Puy, and the other in the National Library of France (Latin manuscript num. 9380)."		
826			Arab Muslims captured Crete	
827-844	**"Gregory IV: The feast of All-Saints received and celebrated in France" (de Hainault, #40)** "All Saints' Day" made a celebration of the "universal church" by Gregory IV			Based on the decrees of Gregory I and Gregory III, Gregory IV now paved the way for the celebration of all the saints on Nov 1, along with the syncretism involved in celebrating All Hallows Eve or Halloween; Interestingly this same day (Nov 1) became "Reformation Day" as Luther nailed the 95 Theses on the Cathedral Door in Wittenberg, Germany; it was probably not a coincidence, since the worship of the saints became the *"cause célèbre"* of Rome's Christian-based Druidism!
833		Sleidan wrote that the French Ecclesiastics stirred up a rebellion against Lewis [Louis I] in 833, led by his three sons, only to be reinstated 6 months later (Sleidan, 250-51).		
844-847	**"Sergius II: This one here changed his name after his election, because his name was Snout of a Pig (*Groin de pourceau*)" (de Hainault, #41)**			The Encyclopedia Britannica wrote of Sergius II: "Of noble birth, Sergius was made cardinal by Pope St. Paschal I and became an archpriest under Pope Gregory IV, whom he was elected to succeed by the Roman nobility against the wishes of the populace, which enthroned the deacon John as antipope. Although John momentarily occupied the Lateran Palace in Rome, he was soon imprisoned in a monastery by Sergius, who was consecrated in January 844 without waiting for the sanction of the Frankish emperor Lothar I. The emperor accordingly sent his son Louis II, later his successor, with an army to punish the breach of the Roman Constitution of

tentative de Théodulfe. Son oeuvre n'était pas de son temps» (S. BERGER, op. cit. xiii, xvii). Une telle tentative, à un tel moment, était remarquable, et il valait la peine de l'indiquer" (Lortsch, op. cit.; translation mine).

~Date	Prayer, Veneration, Sacraments and Other Doctrines	Ecclesiology/Politics	Rival Churches and Movements, Named by Their Antagonists	Biblical Assessment of Rome's Doctrines and Practices
				824, which had affirmed imperial sovereignty over the pope."[88] "Papal Succession"?
845		A gathering of forged manuscripts under the title of the "Decretals of Isidore," the writer was supposed to have lived in the 1st Century; this forgery is supposed to have established the basis for the Church's Canon Law[89]		Canon Law describes the rules and regulations that Rome has established over-and-above or alongside of the "law of Christ" (1 Cor 9:21). This so-called "law of Christ" is frequently called the "New Law" (Aquinas spins an amazing string of logic, equating the priest with Christ, then Christ as a teacher, that teaching being a new law, then the priest as a teacher of the new law): • "Reply to Objection 3: As stated above (Q[7], A[7], ad 1), other men have certain graces distributed among them: but Christ, as being the Head of all, has the perfection of all graces. Wherefore, as to others, one is a lawgiver, another is a priest, another is a king; but all these concur in Christ, as the fount of all grace. Hence it is written (Is. 33:22): 'The Lord is our Judge, the Lord is our law-giver, the Lord is our King: He will' come and 'save us.'", (Aquinas, *Summa*, III; Q22; A4, "Whether the effect of the priesthood of Christ pertained not only to others, but also to Himself?") • "I answer that, As was said above (FS, Q[3], AA[1],4), the gratuitous graces are ordained for the manifestation of faith and spiritual doctrine. For it behooves him who teaches to have the means of making his doctrine clear; otherwise his doctrine would be useless. Now Now Christ is the first and chief teacher of spiritual doctrine and faith, according to Heb. 2:3,4: 'Which having begun to be declared by the Lord was confirmed unto us by them that heard Him, God also bearing them witness by signs and wonders.' Hence it is clear that all the gratuitous graces were most excellently in Christ, as in the first and chief teacher of the faith" (Aquinas, *Summa*, III, Q7, A7) • "6. The difference between the Judaic dispensation and the Christian is this, that in the former God demanded flight from sin and a fulfillment of the Law by the sinner, leaving him in his own weakness; but in the latter. God gives the sinner what He commands, by purifying him with His grace. 7. What advantage was there for a man in the old covenant, in which God left him to his own weakness, by imposing on him His law? But what happiness is it not to be admitted to a covenant in which God gives us what He asks of us?" (Clement 11, *Unigenitus* [8 Sept 1713]). • "Christ is the source of all priesthood: the priest of the old law was a figure of Christ, and the priest of the new law acts in the person of Christ" (*Catechism*, §1548)

---

[88]"Sergius II""; available at: http://www.britannica.com/EBchecked/topic/535552/Sergius-II (online); accessed: 8 Dec 2014; Internet.

[89]"It became the foundation of the canon law, and continues to be so, although there is not now a Popish writer who does not acknowledge it to be a piece of imposture. 'Never,' says Father de Rignon, 'was there seen a forgery so audacious, so extensive, so solemn, so persevering' [*Etudes Religieuses* (November, 1866)]. Yet the discovery of the fraud has not shaken the system. The learned Dupin supposes that these decretals were fabricated by Benedict, a deacon of Mainz, who was the first to publish them, and that, to give them greater currency, he prefixed to them the name of Isidore, a bishop who flourished in Seville in the seventh century. 'Without the pseudo-Isidore,' says Janus, 'there could have been no Gregory VII. The Isidorian forgeries were the broad foundation which the Gregorians built upon' ["Janus," *The Pope and the Council* (London, 1869), 105]" (James A. Wylie, *The History of Protestantism* [London: Cassell, 1889], Vol 1, Book 1, Chap 3; available at: http://www.doctrine.org/history/HPv1b1.htm; accessed 10 Feb 2010; Internet).

~Date	Prayer, Veneration, Sacraments and Other Doctrines	Ecclesiology/Politics	Rival Churches and Movements, Named by Their Antagonists	Biblical Assessment of Rome's Doctrines and Practices
				Likewise, Luther in the preface of his New Testament (1522) accused Jerome (435) of making Christ into a second Moses, giving a "New Law"[90]
850	"Holy water, mixed with a pinch of salt and blessed by a priest" (Boettner, #16)	By 850 the Western Roman Empire was controlled by the Germanic Emperors, according to the German Protestant Reformation historian, Johannes Sleidan[91]		Further earmarks of Rome's Christianized Druidism; The Bible makes holiness a spiritual phenomenon, not a part of the physical world, when it says, "There is none good but God," Matt 19:17; Mark 10:18; One of the important marks of a godly teacher is the proper distinguishing between the holy and the profane, the just and the unjust: • Lev 10:8-11, "The LORD then spoke to Aaron, saying, 'Do not drink wine or strong drink, neither you nor your sons with you, when you come into the tent of meeting, so that you may not die—it is a perpetual statute throughout your generations—and so as to make a distinction between the holy and the profane, and between the unclean and the clean, and so as to teach the sons of Israel all the statutes which the LORD has spoken to them through Moses.'" A sign of a false teacher is the ascribing of spiritual value to veils and other such physical things, Ezek 13:17-23.[92] See also 105-115 A.D., de Hainault, #1.
851 [or 831]	Catholic French-born Monk, Paschasius Radbertus (785-865), described the Lord's			Changed the Lord's Supper into a ritual, conjured by several words, leading to worship of the bread, much like the people of Israel falsely worshipped the bronze serpent of Moses (2 Kings 18:4). See

[90]"Therefore, beware lest you make Christ into a Moses, and the gospel into a book of law or doctrine, as has been done before now, including some of Jerome's prefaces. In fact, however, the gospel demands no works to make us holy to redeem us. Indeed, it condemns such works, and demands only faith in Christ, because He has overcome sin, death and hell for us. Thus it is only by our own works, but by His work, His passion, and death, that He makes us righteous, and gives us life and salvation. This is in order that we might take to ourselves His death and victory as they were our own" (John Dillenberger, *Martin Luther: Selections...* [Garden City, NY: Doubleday, 1961], 18; taken from Bertram Lee Woolf, ed. and trans., *The Reformation Writings of Martin Luther*, vol 2, *The Spirit of the Protestant Reformation*, [London: Lutterworth Press, 1956], 278-83).

[91]"In the meane time whilest matters were thus tumultuously caryed at Constantinople, the name of Charles King of the French, grew famous. For he hauing finished the warre in Aquitania, at the request of Adrian Bishop of Rome, marches into Italy, and as his father Pipin repressed Aistulphus, King of the Lombards, as abovesaid: so he, after a long siege tooke Desiderius, Aistulphus his successor, a heavy foe to Italy, and Adrian the I. As also excluded his sonne Adalgisius out of the kingdome, and chased him quite out of Italy. For the Emperors of Rome, by reason of their farre remote absence (I meane at Constantinople) euer since Constantine the Great, and likewise hindered, not onely with forraigne wars, but also with ciuill & domesticall dissensions, in a manner neglected Italy, or at leastwise could not conveniently protect it, especially the Lombards raigning there: Furthermore, most of them also, being at deadly dissension with the Bishops of Rome, as we haue formerly specified, out of hatred towards them, were not moued at this prosperous estate of the Lombards. For this cause, the Popes prouided forraigne defence, and because no house was in those times, of more renowne and puissance, then that of the French Kings, in regard of the greatnesse of their noble exploits, to them they flie, as to a harbour in time of trouble. After this manner, Adrian dying, Leo the third, who succeeded him, hauing many aduersaries at Rome, sued to Charles, Pipins son: who, at his fourth accession to the Citie was by the Pope and all the people proclaimed Emperour, which happened at the same time, when nought but factious swarmed at Constantinople, insomuch as the very time it selfe, and state of the Common-wealth, seemed to administer the cause and occasion of this change.

"Thus therefore the Empire of the West, came to the Germanes: for without all doubt, Pipin and Charles were Germanes. This was in the eight hundred and first yeere after Christs birth." (Sleidan, 225-228).

[92]Ezek 13:17-23, "Likewise, son of man, set your face against the daughters of your people, who prophesy out of their own heart; prophesy against them, and say, 'Thus says the Lord GOD: "Woe to the *women* who sew *magic* charms on their sleeves and make veils for the heads of people of every height to hunt souls! Will you hunt the souls of My people, and keep yourselves alive? "And will you profane Me among My people for handfuls of barley and for pieces of bread, killing people who should not die, and keeping people alive who should not live, by your lying to My people who listen to lies?" 'Therefore thus says the Lord GOD: "Behold, I *am* against your *magic* charms by which you hunt souls there like birds. I will tear them from your arms, and let the souls go, the souls you hunt like birds. "I will also tear off your veils and deliver My people out of your hand, and they shall no longer be as prey in your hand. Then you shall know that I *am* the LORD. Because with lies you have made the heart of the righteous sad, whom I have not made sad; and you have strengthened the hands of the wicked, so that he does not turn from his wicked way to save his life. Therefore you shall no longer envision futility nor practice divination; for I will deliver My people out of your hand, and you shall know that I *am* the LORD.""'

~Date	Prayer, Veneration, Sacraments and Other Doctrines	Ecclesiology/Politics	Rival Churches and Movements, Named by Their Antagonists	Biblical Assessment of Rome's Doctrines and Practices
	Supper [the sacrifice of the Mass] as including the **transubstantiation** of the elements into the very body and blood of Christ			A.D. 394 on the "sacrifice of the mass" as part of the Eucharistic celebration. From this point on in the Roman church, rather than "Christ **in you** the hope of glory" (Col 1:27), it became Christ in, with, and by the Host—"Now you can receive Him not only into your heart, but also into your stomach to permeate every cell in your body!" • Contra Matt 15:17, "Do you not understand that everything that goes into the mouth passes into the stomach, and is eliminated" • Rather, "Do this in remembrance of Me," Luke 24:19; 1 Cor 11:24, 25 • Also "For you have not come to what may be touched," Heb 12:18 (ESV) However, for Rome, anyone who did not believe in transubstantiation was deemed a Christological heretic—not affirming that Christ literally came in the flesh! • Therefore, those who do not believe in transubstantiation were deemed to be Docetic, believing that Christ was only the ghost-like figure of a man • Leveraging the Christological controversy in this way, was also applied to U.S. Inerrantists in 1994, that because they do not believe that the Bible is tainted by human nature, that they misunderstand the incarnation[93] • Interesting, however, is the changing of one form of infallibility and holiness (that of the Bible, which repeatedly affirms its infallibility and holiness), to another form of infallibility (that of the Church and its Traditions, as well as its current Pope, who himself is called "His Holiness") and holiness (that of all the consecrated hosts, that of the Holy Water and the Holy Oil, and the special divine power in images and statues), all of which is presumably based on the

---

[93]"F. Fundamentalist Interpretation: ... Fundamentalist interpretation starts from the principle that the Bible, being the word of God, inspired and free from error, should be read and interpreted literally in all its details. But by "literal interpretation" it understands a naively literalist interpretation, one, that is to say, which excludes every effort at understanding the Bible that takes account of its historical origins and development. It is opposed, therefore, to the use of the historical-critical method, as indeed to the use of any other scientific method for the interpretation of Scripture.

"The fundamentalist interpretation had its origin at the time of the Reformation, arising out of a concern for fidelity to the literal meaning of Scripture. After the century of the Enlightenment it emerged in Protestantism as a bulwark against liberal exegesis.

"The actual term <fundamentalist> is connected directly with the American Biblical Congress held at Niagara, N.Y., in 1895. At this meeting, conservative Protestant exegetes defined 'five points of fundamentalism': the verbal inerrancy of Scripture, the divinity of Christ, his virginal birth, the doctrine of vicarious expiation and the bodily resurrection at the time of the second coming of Christ. As the fundamentalist way of reading the Bible spread to other parts of the world, it gave rise to other ways of interpretation, equally 'literalist,' in Europe, Asia, Africa and South America. As the 20th century comes to an end, this kind of interpretation is winning more and more adherents, in religious groups and sects, as also among Catholics.

"Fundamentalism is right to insist on the divine inspiration of the Bible, the inerrancy of the word of God and other biblical truths included in its five fundamental points. But its way of presenting these truths is rooted in an ideology which is not biblical, whatever the proponents of this approach might say. For it demands an unshakable adherence to rigid doctrinal points of view and imposes, as the only source of teaching for Christian life and salvation, a reading of the Bible which rejects all questioning and any kind of critical research.

"The basic problem with fundamentalist interpretation of this kind is that, refusing to take into account the historical character of biblical revelation, it makes itself incapable of accepting the full truth of the incarnation itself. As regards relationships with God, fundamentalism seeks to escape any closeness of the divine and the human. ...

"The fundamentalist approach is dangerous, for it is attractive to people who look to the Bible for ready answers to the problems of life. It can deceive these people, offering them interpretations that are pious but illusory, instead of telling them that the Bible does not necessarily contain an immediate answer to each and every problem. Without saying as much in so many words, fundamentalism actually invites people to a kind of intellectual suicide. It injects into life a false certitude, for it unwittingly confuses the divine substance of the biblical message with what are in fact its human limitations" (Pontifical Biblical Commission, "The Interpretation of the Bible in the Church"; available at: http://www.ewtn.com/library/CURIA/PBCINTER.htm; accessed: 17 Oct 2009; Internet).

~Date	Prayer, Veneration, Sacraments and Other Doctrines	Ecclesiology/Politics	Rival Churches and Movements, Named by Their Antagonists	Biblical Assessment of Rome's Doctrines and Practices
				Bible—which is not the infallible in and of itself, unless interpreted as it is defined by the current sitting Pope: o For example, notice the *Catechism's* linking of the corporeal nature of the Bible with that of the Eucharist: o "For this reason, the Church has always venerated the Scriptures as she venerates the Lord's Body. She never ceases to present to the faithful the bread of life; taken from the one table of God's Word and Christ's Body" (*Catechism*, §103). Is not the doctrine of transubstantiation, making the very person of Christ truly present in the very *accidens* of the elements of the Lord's Supper, upon the proper words prayed over them by a priest in proper subjection to the Bishop of Rome: • "Denying our only Master and Lord, Jesus Christ," Jude 4? • And also "Denying the Master who bought them," 2 Pet 2:1? o It follows, then, that the doctrine of transubstantiation is a Christological heresy o From which it then follows that it then falls under the judgment of all the NT passages that make pronouncements against Christological truth, which Evangelicals are wont to use against Mormons and Jehovah's Witnesses, and rightfully so, but often carefully avoid using against proponents of the Church of Rome's theology! • Likewise, is not the doctrine of transubstantiation bringing "Christ" down to earth in multiple places simultaneously, while in fact the Bible says that He is in heaven interceding before the Father, Heb 7:25? As far as worship and ministry goes, adding transubstantiation to the regular order of service made further changes: • The preaching of the Word of God took second place in the saying of the Mass • More and more the Catholic priests became masters of elaborate and mystical rituals and ceremonies, that they and only they had the power and authority to conjure up
858-867	"Nicolas I: Ordered that one ought not listen to the Mass of a cohabiting priest" (de Hainault, #43)			
867-872	"Adrian II: He declared that the confirmation of the Emperor was not necessary for Popes" (de Hainault, #44)			Further exacerbating the Investiture Controversy.
872-882	"John [or Jeanne] VIII: [A German woman, originally names Gilberte]: This Papesse			"Papal Succession"?

~Date	Prayer, Veneration, Sacraments and Other Doctrines	Ecclesiology/Politics	Rival Churches and Movements, Named by Their Antagonists	Biblical Assessment of Rome's Doctrines and Practices
	gave birth while going in [a public] procession [in Rome]" (de Hainault, #42)			
885-891	"Stephen VI [?]: This one had un-interred Formosus, and had his fingers thrown into the Tiber [river]" (de Hainault, #45)			"Papal Succession"?
890	"Worship of St. Joseph" (Boettner, #17)			Contra Exod 20:3; etc.
897	"Romanus: This one broke all the ordinances of Stephen his predecessor" (de Hainault, #46)			
904-911	"Sergius III: This one did more than Stephen, he had the rest of the body of Formosus cut up and thrown into the Tiber [river]" (de Hainault, #47)			
927		"College of Cardinals established" (Boettner, #18)		With the establishment of a "College of Cardinals," Rome no longer sought to follow the New Testament church organization nor offices, Eph 4:11; 1 Tim 3; Titus 1; etc., therefore, the Church of Rome could no longer be considered a New Testament church It must be noted that titles such as "Patriarch" and "Archbishop" are not New Testament offices either. This change in the organization of the Church of Rome was established by [Pope] Gregory I (590-604) as he reorganized the Roman church using a monastic hierarchical model.
963		Pope John XII deposed by Otto I "for his offences" (Sleidan, 263). Sleidan wrote: "A decree of his [Leo VIII] is extant incerted in the papall Law, where he says, that hee conferres on Otho the Emperor and to his successors for ever, the authority of choosing Popes, disposing of the See Apostolike, and confirming of Bishops: as also pronounces a most severe punishment against those, who (not expecting the Emperors approbation) consecrate Bishops" (Sleidan, 263-64).		Another turn in the "Investiture Controversy" over control of church appointments.
965	"Baptism of bells,			Wherein is the relationship of Baptism with

~Date	Prayer, Veneration, Sacraments and Other Doctrines	Ecclesiology/Politics	Rival Churches and Movements, Named by Their Antagonists	Biblical Assessment of Rome's Doctrines and Practices
	instituted by pope John XIII" (Boettner, #19)			conversion, if it is applied to inanimate objects, such as bells? Baptists and Evangelicals are called "Docetic" for not allowing that inanimate objects can be holy nor be made holy, or furthermore be baptized in the Holy Spirit and regenerated. Herein is leveraged an early church discussion of the two natures in Christ to allow for matter to have the spiritual nature of holiness: • Is not baptizing bells an example of confusing the holy and the unholy, the unclean and the clean, Lev 10:9-11? • Does not the baptizing of bells led to superstition and the worship of the created thing rather than the Creator, Rom 1:25 It appears that this Roman practice was gleaned from the pages of the Old Covenant: • Wherein the priests were to be clothed in "holy garments" Exod 28:2, 4; 31:10; 35:19, 21; 39:1, 41; 40:13; Lev 16:4, 32; • Wherein the objects of the Tabernacle were sprinkled with blood to be cleansed, Heb 9:21.
995	"Canonization of dead saints, first by pope John XV" (Boettner, #20)	Later the title "saint" was given to those particularly vehement for Rome's primacy and theology		God alone has the authority to decide who is and who is not a saint; likewise, all true believers are saints, Rom 1:7; 1 Cor 1:2, Eph 1:1; Phil 1:1; etc. Further, against offerings for the dead, Deut 26:14 Note also Jesus' chastising of Jerusalem's building lavish monuments to dead saints (Matt 23:29-31), showing their complicity in killing them. "Papal Succession"?
998	"Fasting on Fridays and during Lent" (Boettner, #21)	Debate as to which decrees are more important those in the Bible or those given by Rome...	...Ecclesiastical decrees continued to take precedence over New Testament decrees	Adding works to proper worship of God (i.e. salvation), Eph 2:8-9; and deciding what works are to be done by the entire church, contra Col 2:20-23: Col 2:16, "Therefore let no one act as your judge in regard to food or drink or in respect to a festival or a new moon or a Sabbath day" 1 Tim 4:1-5, "But the Spirit explicitly says that in later times some will fall away from the faith, paying attention to deceitful spirits and doctrines of demons, by means of the hypocrisy of liars seared in their own conscience as with a branding iron, *men* who forbid marriage *and advocate* abstaining from foods, which God has created to be gratefully shared in by those who believe and know the truth. For everything created by God is good, and nothing is to be rejected, if it is received with gratitude; for it is sanctified by means of the word of God and prayer."
999-1003	"Sylvester II: [apparently a practicing necromancer] This one gave all to the devil to become pope" (de Hainault, #48) "The Mass, developed gradually as a sacrifice, attendance made	Of resistance to the authority of Rome in Italy until the 11th Century: "It is an undoubted fact, though it may appear improbable to those who are unacquainted with ecclesiastical history, that the supremacy claimed by	"Attendance [at the Mass] made obligatory in the 11th Century" (Boettner, #22) Hence, non-attendance at Mass became a sign of atheism, non-belief (in Christianity or Catholicism), and/or	Whatever the case may be related to Pope Sylvester II's submitting to Satanic ritual, the year 1000 does seem to be a turning point in Rome's increased use of capital punishment against their antagonists. Regarding the Sacrifice of the Mass as a true reenactment and true repetition of the death of Christ on the cross:

~Date	Prayer, Veneration, Sacraments and Other Doctrines	Ecclesiology/Politics	Rival Churches and Movements, Named by Their Antagonists	Biblical Assessment of Rome's Doctrines and Practices
	obligatory in the 11ᵗʰ Century" (Boettner, #22) The Mass, the continuous bloodless reinactment of the crucifixion; including transubstantiation (Christ's true body and true blood) added an element of druidism or witchcraft to the Lord's Supper.	the bishops of Rome was resisted in Italy after it had been submitted to by the most remote churches of the west. The diocese of Italy, of which was the capital, remained long independent of Rome, and practiced a different liturgy, according to what is called the Ambrosian Liturgy. It was not till the eleventh century that the popes succeeded in establishing their authority in Milan, and prevailed over the bishops of that see to procure the archi-episcopal pall from Rome."⁹⁴	heresy, and was considered a treasonous offense.	Contra Rom 6:10, "For the death that He died, He died to sin, once for all" Contra Heb 9:28, "so Christ also, having been offered once to bear the sins of many" Contra 1 Pet 3:18, "For Christ also died for sins once for all"; The Mass turns the reception of grace into a work—attendance at an event and participation in a ritual. **Conundrum: when attendance at the "Sacrifice of the Mass" was made obligatory by the Roman Pontiff, his will could only be applied in those states where the crown adhered to his decrees.** Herein the close interrelationship of Rome with the Europe's royalty, begun with [Pope] Sylvester I (314-335) and Constantine, further exemplified in [Pope] Gregory I's (590-604) dealings with the Donatists, Lombards, Visigoths, and English, was now necessitated to establish Rome's ecclesiastical [and political] supremacy. Truly, it appears that somewhere along this timeline, Rome succumbed to the temptation which Jesus mastered in His earthly ministry—providing more proof that the Pope is not indeed the Vicar of Christ: • "Again, the devil took Him up on an exceedingly high mountain, and showed Him all the kingdoms of the world and their glory. And he said to Him, 'All these things I will give You if You will fall down and worship me.' Then Jesus said to him, 'Away with you, Satan! For it is written, "You shall worship the LORD your God, and Him only you shall serve."'" (Matt 4:8-10) If this author were to posit key 1ˢᵗ Millennium individuals along this timeline that advanced Satan's agenda of uniting all the kingdoms of the world in the name of Christ, here are some ideas: • Emperor Constantine (reign 306-337 A.D.) saw the potential in marrying Christianity with politics from the vantage point of political authority • Pope Gregory I (reign 590-604 A.D.), having been given political authority over earthly territory, leveraged his religious position as the only Patriarch over a Latin-speaking constituency to make a definitive break from Greek-speaking Byzantium • First Holy Roman Emperor Charlemagne (reign 800-814 A.D.), after being crowned as such by Pope Leo III, reinvigorated the unholy alliance between Rome and political power, focusing on his use of the sword to gain territories for church dominance: ○ Imagine the arguments that needed to be made at that time to legitimize the claim that Rome deserved to be the dominant church over all the territories conquered by Charlemagne! ○ In those arguments themselves, we have the

---

⁹⁴Thomas M'Crie, *History of the Progress and Suppression of the Reformation in Italy during the Sixteenth Century* (Edinburgh: William T. Blackwood, 1833; London: T. Cadell, 1833; Elibron Classics, 2004), 1.

~Date	Prayer, Veneration, Sacraments and Other Doctrines	Ecclesiology/Politics	Rival Churches and Movements, Named by Their Antagonists	Biblical Assessment of Rome's Doctrines and Practices
				common approach to teaching Church History One. The supremacy promised by the Devil in the temptation of Jesus was fully stated by [Pope] Boniface VIII (1294-1303), *Unum Sanctum*, and exemplified by [Pope] Innocent III (1198-1215). For the next Centuries Rome and Monarchs dealt craftily with one another: • It was not until the Protestant Reformation that Rome's monopoly was infringed upon in a minority of European states • It was not until Napoleon establishment of the Republican form of government after he conquered much of Western Europe in the early 1800s with the period of the Enlightenment that Rome's powerbase was severely depleted ○ A freedom that much of the Western World continues to enjoy to this day! Yet, in this unholy alliance, promised by the Devil in the temptation of Jesus, there appears to be the system by which the Antichrist will eventually rule the world, as noted in the Book of Revelation.
1000s	The RCC began to restrict freedom of conscience and individual interpretation of Scriptures, by initiating the torture and public executions of evangelistic or proclamational-side Christians who preached against the false doctrines of the RCC. The freedom of conscience was denied to all citizens who did not agree with the RCC, in lands ruled by RCC Bishops (1st Lateran Council of 1023); its enforcement was extended to the sword of the state where Catholic princes were called upon to enforce its multiplying anathemas, under pain of anathema (2nd Lateran Council, 1139); this encouraged use of the sword of the state against so-called "heretics" was reinforced and increased in the 3rd and 4th Lateran Councils (1179 and 1215 respectively). Schismatics, were those who believe rightly about theology (hence were sacramentalists), but did not submit to the supreme authority of the Bishop of Rome; they were considered even more dangerous than "heretics"!			
1002		10 "Cathars" executed in Orleans and Toulouse, France. The use of capital punishment was based on a reinterpretation of Romans 13 based on the state-church model, an interesting result of this model that seems to give any church leadership divine authority: Rom 13:1-2, "Let every soul be subject to the governing authorities. For there is no authority except from God, and the authorities that exist are appointed by God. Therefore whoever resists the authority resists the ordinance of God, and those who resist will bring judgment on themselves." From these verses comes the "divine right" of the	Rome definitively began using bloodshed against rival churches within territories that it "controlled" by political means. Consider John 15:1-16 in light of the bloodshed that began in 1002—needing only the Pope to be considered the "Vicar of Christ," or in the place of Christ on earth: • Every branch that does not "abide in Christ" (i.e. schismatics); • Every branch that does not abide is in Me ... t • hrown into the fire and they are burned (v. 6); • Every branch that does not "abide in my love" = not abiding in the Charity of the true Church or the Church of Rome = the Sacraments of the Church, and propoer	Contra: Matt 5:44 (NKJ), "But I say to you, love your enemies, bless those who curse you, do good to those who hate you, and pray for those who spitefully use you and persecute you" The perceptive reader will notice that the Critical Edition Greek text removes a significant part of this important verse, hence: Matt 5:44 (NAS), "But I say to you, love your enemies, and pray for those who persecute you" Luke 6:27-28, "But I say to you who hear: Love your enemies, do good to those who hate you, bless those who curse you, and pray for those who spitefully use you" In the Luke passage, the second and third command of Matthew's version were switched (it is a different sermon of Jesus); also, whereas the two verbs in the last command are subsumed into the one, Luke seems to have a progression of antagonism from the inner heart to the outward actions Rom 10:14-15, "How then shall they call on Him in whom they have not believed? And how shall they believe in Him of whom they have not heard? And how shall they hear without a preacher? And how shall they preach unless they are sent? As it is written: "How beautiful are the feet of those who preach the gospel of peace, Who bring glad tidings of

~Date	Prayer, Veneration, Sacraments and Other Doctrines	Ecclesiology/Politics	Rival Churches and Movements, Named by Their Antagonists	Biblical Assessment of Rome's Doctrines and Practices
		state-church authorities. Unfortunately for Rome, they choose to ignore: • The gospel of justification by faith alone as taught in Romans; and • They render corporate all the commands for individuals to remain watchful of false teachers and false teachings (see 397a), then they re-individualize them into the office of the papacy. From the "divine right" of the church, if one is to scour the NT for the precedent for an authoritative human leader, one eventually will find "the first" used of the disciple Peter in Matthew 10:2. Obviously, for Rome this must-needs be an Old Covenant administrative and authoritative "first." Thereby locking in the "divine right" of being first to Peter, and by stretching the Old Covenant priestly form of passing the anointing, Peter's "divine right" is passed to the successors of Peter by analogy. Jumping then, from the divine right of Peter to rule the church, anyone who dares to resist him, is in actually resisting God Himself, according to Rom 13:2. Now comes the application of capital punishment by the standing "judge" from the book of Deuteronomy: Deut 17:8-13, "If a matter arises which is too hard for you to judge, between degrees of guilt for bloodshed, between one judgment or another, or between one punishment or another, matters of controversy within your gates, then you shall arise and go up to the place which the LORD your God choose. And	submission to its Traditions and authority. Whereas the first Pope to officially use the title "Vicar of Christ" was Innocent III in a 1199 letter to Leo I, King of Armenia, use of this title is said to go back to Gelasius I in 495, and to be used of various bishops, especially after the 9th Century.	good things!" Notice that the reading "those who preach a gospel of peace" is contradicted both by the fires of inquisition and by the crusades. Therefore, it is convenient to blame the citation of both clauses of Isaiah 52:7 on dittography and remove the first line from the text as a scribal error, as was/is done through the Nestle-Aland Greek original text type. No longer did Rome need to be accused of preaching other than a "gospel of peace" during their centuries of crusade or during their centuries of Inquisition. Rom 12:18-21, "If it is possible, as much as depends on you, live peaceably with all men. Beloved, do not avenge yourselves, but *rather* give place to wrath; for it is written, '**Vengeance *is* Mine, I will repay**,' says the **Lord**.* Therefore 'If your enemy is hungry, feed him; If he is thirsty, give him a drink; For in so doing you will heap coals of fire on his head.' Do not be overcome by evil, but overcome evil with good" 　*Note that if the Pope is considered "Lord" and if a vow of obedience is made to him, the interpretation and application of this text is significantly altered. Rom 13:10, "Love does no harm to a neighbor; therefore love *is* the fulfillment of the law." Or, consider the question of Jesus, "Of what manner of spirit are you?" Luke 9:51-56, "Now it came to pass, when the time had come for Him to be received up, that He steadfastly set His face to go to Jerusalem, and sent messengers before His face. And as they went, they entered a village of the Samaritans, to prepare for Him. But they did not receive Him, because His face was *set* for the journey to Jerusalem. And when His disciples James and John saw *this*, they said, 'Lord, do You want us to command fire to come down from heaven and consume them, just as Elijah did?' But He turned and rebuked them, and said, 'You do not know what manner of spirit you are of. For the Son of Man did not come to destroy men's lives but to save *them*.' And they went to another village. This author is reminded of Bernard of Clairveaux, who cursed the Albigensian region in 1143 AD, prior to the first crusade against them under Papal Legate Henry of Clairveaux in 1181 A.D. Consider also: Rom 3:15-16, "Their feet *are* swift to shed blood; Destruction and misery *are* in their ways" (Paul here cites Isa 59:7) Deut 19:10, "lest innocent blood be shed in the midst of your land which the LORD your God is giving you *as* an inheritance, and *thus* guilt of bloodshed be upon you" Note the paradox here: Rome argued that the schismatics and heretics lacked love (Charity), therefore they separated themselves from Rome, the true Church. Therefore in their zeal to "bid them come in," Rome did the ultimate act of cruelty and barbarism by publicly burning people alive. Notice also the complexity of merely translating the Old Testament YHWH as "Lord," from the Greek Κύριος, rather than Jehovah, "Eternal One," etc. There are

~Date	Prayer, Veneration, Sacraments and Other Doctrines	Ecclesiology/Politics	Rival Churches and Movements, Named by Their Antagonists	Biblical Assessment of Rome's Doctrines and Practices
		you shall come to the priests, the Levites, and to the judge *there* in those days, and inquire *of them*; they shall pronounce upon you the sentence of judgment. You shall do according to the sentence which they pronounce upon you in that place which the LORD chooses. And you shall be careful to do according to all that they order you. According to the sentence of the law in which they instruct you, according to the judgment which they tell you, you shall do; you shall not turn aside *to* the right hand or *to* the left from the sentence which they pronounce upon you. Now the man who acts presumptuously and will not heed the priest who stands to minister there before the LORD your God, or the judge, that man shall die. So you shall put away the evil from Israel. And all the people shall hear and fear, and no longer act presumptuously." So herein we have the thread of logic of the inquisition, based on a lopsided view of Scripture. The astute reader will consider the role of Augustine in developing and providing a cogent defense for this logical progression.		numerous places both in the OT and NT where the Pope could and it appears does apply passages with "Lord" to himself. Furthermore, consider: 1 Thess 5:15, "See that no one renders evil for evil to anyone, but always pursue what is good both for yourselves and for all." Rather, was not the Church of Rome following Augustine's (see 402-412) counsel to (1) exact fines and then (2) use physical coercion to force the Donatists to "return" to the Bishop of Rome, sounding eerily like Satan in Job 1 and 2? Job 1:9-11, "So Satan answered the LORD and said, 'Does Job fear God for nothing? Have You not made a hedge around him, around his household, and around all that he has on every side? You have blessed the work of his hands, and his possessions have increased in the land. But now, stretch out Your hand and touch all that he has, and he will surely curse You to Your face!'" Job 2:4-5, "So Satan answered the LORD and said, 'Skin for skin! Yes, all that a man has he will give for his life. But stretch out Your hand now, and touch his bone and his flesh, and he will surely curse You to Your face!'" Remember the prophetic words of Jesus to Peter, "Put your sword back into its place" Matt 26:52! Could it be that Rome's 600 year worship of the Greek Pantheon, as noted by Erasmus [see footnote to A.D. 375], had escalated to the point of "burning one's sons and daughters" as found in Deut 12:31? Deut 12:29-31, "When the LORD your God cuts off from before you the nations which you go to dispossess, and you displace them and dwell in their land, take heed to yourself that you are not ensnared to follow them, after they are destroyed from before you, and that you do not inquire after their gods, saying, 'How did these nations serve their gods? I also will do likewise.' You shall not worship the LORD your God in that way; for every abomination to the LORD which He hates they have done to their gods; for they burn even their sons and daughters in the fire to their gods." Perhaps the advice of Gamaliel would have proved helpful to the Church of Rome before it began the practice of burning alive schismatic Christians, Jews, and others: Acts 5:34-40, "Then one in the council stood up, a Pharisee named Gamaliel, a teacher of the law held in respect by all the people, and commanded them to put the apostles outside for a little while. [35] And he said to them: 'Men of Israel, take heed to yourselves what you intend to do regarding these men. ... And now I say to you, keep away from these men and let them alone; for if this plan or this work is of men, it will come to nothing; but if it is of God, you cannot overthrow it-- lest you even be found to fight against God.' And they agreed with him...'" Rom 15:26-27, "For it pleased those from Macedonia and Achaia to make a certain contribution for the

~Date	Prayer, Veneration, Sacraments and Other Doctrines	Ecclesiology/Politics	Rival Churches and Movements, Named by Their Antagonists	Biblical Assessment of Rome's Doctrines and Practices
				poor among the saints who are in Jerusalem. It pleased them indeed, and they are their debtors. For if the Gentiles have been partakers of their spiritual things, their duty is also to minister to them in material things." (see A.D. 786) Might it be that, when Rome began to put to death possible, probable, or actual Christians, this act became the proof that it had itself become a false religion (cf. John 16:2-3)? Is there a chiliasm in Roman practice, wherein they thought that Rome was the New Jerusalem and that the Vicar of Christ was in fact Jesus returned among men, and that therefore they had the right and in fact the obligation to begin enacting the retributions and punishments of the eschatological age upon unrepentant antagonists: Psa 11:6, "Upon the wicked He will rain coals; Fire and brimstone and a burning wind *Shall be* the portion of their cup" Matt 3:10, "And even now the ax is laid to the root of the trees. Therefore every tree which does not bear good fruit is cut down and thrown into the fire" Matt 25:41, "Then He will also say to those on the left hand, 'Depart from Me, you cursed, into the everlasting fire prepared for the devil and his angels'" 2 Pet 2:12, "But these, like natural brute beasts made to be caught and destroyed, speak evil of the things they do not understand, and will utterly perish in their own corruption, ..." Rev 14:9-10, "Then a third angel followed them, saying with a loud voice, 'If anyone worships the beast and his image, and receives *his* mark on his forehead or on his hand, he himself shall also drink of the wine of the wrath of God, which is poured out full strength into the cup of His indignation. He shall be tormented with fire and brimstone in the presence of the holy angels and in the presence of the Lamb.'" etc. Further, Revelation 13 portrays a one world religion, in which the Beast from the Sea makes war with the saints, and overcome them: Rev 13:7, "It was granted to him to make war with the saints and to overcome them. And authority was given him over every tribe, tongue, and nation." The New Testament discussed the problem of false teachers, and in no case did it ever endorse the use of force either political or military. The unfortunate use of force comes from Augustine's writings called "Contra Donatisten" and Aquinas' Summa, *Secundum Secundae* [Second Part of the Second Part]. Note several NT admonitions on how to handle contrary teachers: 2 Thess 3:14-15, "And if anyone does not obey our word in this epistle, note that person and do not keep company with him, that he may be ashamed. Yet do not count *him* as an enemy, but admonish *him* as a brother" Phil 1:15-18, "Some indeed preach Christ even from envy and strife, and some also from good will: The

~Date	Prayer, Veneration, Sacraments and Other Doctrines	Ecclesiology/Politics	Rival Churches and Movements, Named by Their Antagonists	Biblical Assessment of Rome's Doctrines and Practices
				former preach Christ from selfish ambition, not sincerely, supposing to add affliction to my chains; but the latter out of love, knowing that I am appointed for the defense of the gospel. What then? Only *that* in every way, whether in pretense or in truth, Christ is preached; and in this I rejoice, yes, and will rejoice."
1022		14 persons burned alive in Orleans, France		[See A.D. 1002]
1023		1st Lateran Council: further centralized the Rome's preeminent power over the entire church; obligatory celibacy of the priesthood proclaimed, "We absolutely forbid priests, deacons or subdeacons to live with concubines and wives, and to cohabit with other women…"; Bishops made supreme protectors of the faith within their bounds; including the words "the sword of anathema"		Of obligatory celibacy, Rome who used the OT to prove much of its sacramental system, did not use the OT for celibacy of the priests, as OT priests were allowed [or even commanded] to marry (Lev 21:13-14, "And he shall take a wife in her virginity. A widow, or a divorced woman, or one who is profaned by harlotry, these he may not take; but rather he is to marry a virgin of his own people"), as was Zacharias, father of John the Baptist (Luke 1:5, 13), as is the case in 1 Tim 3:2

Likewise, Philip was married and had daughters, Acts 21:8-9; all the Apostles were married, excepting Paul, and so were the half-brothers of Jesus, 1 Cor 9:5

Furthermore, 1 Tim 4:3 states emphatically that "forbidding to marry" is a doctrine of demons!

Of Rome threatening use of the sword of anathema (the death penalty) Jesus told Peter, "Put your sword back into its place," Matt 26:52 |
1028		Synod of Charroux condemned "heretics"		[See A.D. 1002]
1032-1045	"Benedict IX: This one resigned as Pope; Platinus wrote that he sold it [that is, the papacy]" (de Hainault, #49)			
1045			Byzantine Empire was the most powerful state in the Mediterranean	
1049		Synod of Rheims discussed the "new" heresy in France		Synod against Evangelicals?
1049-1054	Leo IX appears to prohibit copulation by married Bishops, Priests, or Deacons in one of his epistles:

"A certain parcel of an epistle of his is extant, wherin he saies, it is not lawfull for a Bishop, Priest or Deacon, to forsake his wife for Religion sake, but it is fit that they should find her with such necessaries | | | Here Pope Leo IX provides the "inerrant" interpretation of 1 Cor 9:5 (according to Leo XIII's *Providentissimus Deus* [1893]). |

~Date	Prayer, Veneration, Sacraments and Other Doctrines	Ecclesiology/Politics	Rival Churches and Movements, Named by Their Antagonists	Biblical Assessment of Rome's Doctrines and Practices
	as belong to natural sustentation: notwithstanding, in case she vse carnall copulation, it is not lawfull: sithence Paul saies, "He had power aswell as the other Apostles, to lead about a wife"; which place he thus interprets. That the Apostles had their wiues always with them for this intent, that they should be maintained, together with them, by those, whom husbands instructed, in the Christian Religion and faith: and not that they should exercise the office of wedlock, or lye together: therefore Saint Paul thought fit to vse the word "lead about," and not "lye with" (Sleidan, 272-273).			
1052		Heretics hanged in Goslar, Germany		[See A.D. 1002]
1053		Henry IV becomes "King of the Romans" or "King of the Germans" at the age of 3 with his mother as vice-regent; at age 7 Henry was kidnapped and clergy took on the vice-regency; at 34 he was crowned Holy Roman Emperor; his rule was a major turning point in Rome's state-church relations		Another shift in the "Investiture Controversy"
1054		Mutual excommunication of Pope and Eastern Patriarch of Constantinople	Mutual anathema meant that all the ordinations, rites, ceremonies, sacraments, and teachings of the other church were NOT salvific, not providing the benefits of salvation to their adherents (likewise Leo XIII's 1896 *Apostolicae Curae*, in which he invalidated the rites of the Anglican Church)	Rome no longer had a monopoly on calling itself "The one true Church"; therefore, those who threatened its "unity in charity" and preeminent position became enemies of Rome (i.e. even English church [?] and later Southern France's so-called Bogomils or Cathar Church)
1054	Leo IX wrote *Ad splendidum nitentis* [DS 687-688] in response to Pierre Damien's *Liber Gomorrhianus* in which he called for greater severity in dealing with homosexual clerics. Leo			The result of this letter reveals the unimaginable disgust and the totally unnecessary complexity of assigning specific pardons to individual sins, as was/is done in confessionals as part of the said "Sacrament of Penance," outside of which [in Rome's theology] there is no forgiveness of sins. The "Sacrament of Penance" which involves going

~Date	Prayer, Veneration, Sacraments and Other Doctrines	Ecclesiology/Politics	Rival Churches and Movements, Named by Their Antagonists	Biblical Assessment of Rome's Doctrines and Practices
	IX responded of clerics within the "immaculate Church": "But because we act with a great humanity, we desire and we command, confident of divine mercy, that those who, … [the text then details three of four positions of homosexual deviancy], and who have not done it by long habit or with several, if they have refrained from their sexuality and if they have expiated their infamous acts by just penitence, be admitted to the same position in which they could not have remained forever had they remained in their misdeed" [DS 688]. Leo IX then went on to explain those who could not be readmitted to the same ecclesiastical rank were only those accused of performing the last of four types of homosexual acts.			to a Confessional, explaining individual sins in enough detail for the priest to assign appropriate penance, to then receive the spoken words of absolution from the priest or confessor (cf. A.D. 435). The whole process is an exaggeration and misrepresentation of James 5:16 (cf. Acts 19:18; Gal 6:2); Jesus being our only Confessor and Mediator, 1 John 1:8-2:2 (cf. 1 Tim 2:5); the mind of man is so corrupt (Gen 6:5; Jer 17:9) that many things need to be washed by the cleansing of the conscience by the Holy Spirit (Heb 10:19-22) and ought not be placed as seeds of thought into the minds of others. This sowing seeds of sin is likely why Paul discouraged the speaking about particular sins in Eph 5:3-4: Eph 5:3-4, "But fornication and all uncleanness or covetousness, let it not even be named among you, as is fitting for saints; 4 neither filthiness, nor foolish talking, nor coarse jesting, which are not fitting, but rather giving of thanks" Furthermore, this unfortunate letter shows the problems that threatened Rome due to their policy of vows of celibacy for the priesthood, as the letter was directed to explain who could remain priests and under what circumstances. Likewise the letter also shows why priests who are accused of certain sexual crimes, if they confess and do appropriate penance,[95] can be reinstated to their priesthood, at the same level in which they were prior to their confession. Yea, and because, in the Holy Traditions of Rome, their Canon Law is above the civil law of any given land, confessed priests can be moved from one location to another, as has been experienced in our day. And yet, the problems associated with the Vow of Celibacy continue to our day, as mentioned in a BBC article: "A Church-commissioned report said more than 4,000 US priests had faced sexual abuse allegations since the early 1950s, in cases involving more than 10,000 children—mostly boys."[96]
1059		Synod of Toulouse condemned "heretics"		Another synod against Evangelical Albigenses?
1066		William the Conqueror of France crossed the		Was the English church's independence, especially on doctrines regarding Mary, the Saints, and the

---

[95]"The absolution for all acts of impurity, of whatever nature they may be, committed by a [religious] clerk, be it with a nun, in the cloister or elsewhere, or with his/her parents or relatives, or with a spiritual daughter, or with another woman, whomever that may be; being that the absolution be requested not simply by the clerk, or by he himself or his concubines, with the exemption of being able to keep his orders [religious position] and of holding its benefits, and with no claim of forfeiture, costs only thirty-six *tournois* and nine *ducats*" (Endnote 4, page 17, "Old tariffs of indulgences and absolutions of the Roman Church," Franck Puaux, *Histoire de la Réformation Française* [*History of the French Reformation*] [Paris: Michel Lévy Frères, 1859], 1:406-07; quoting *Taxe des parties casuelles de la boutique du pape, en latin et en français, avec annotations précises des décrets, conciles et canons, vieux et modernes, pour la vérification de la discipline anciennement observée dans l'Eglise* ["tax of the casuistic parties of the Papal shop, in Latin and in French, with precise annotations of decrees, councils, and canons, ancient and modern, for the verification of the observance of the old discipline in the Church" [Lyon's 8th edition,1564]; translated by Thomas P. Johnston [August 2005]).

[96]"LA Cardinal Mahony 'stripped of duties' over sex abuse" (1 Feb 2013); available at: http://www.bbc.co.uk/news/world-us-canada-21289854 (online); accessed: 1 Feb 2013; Internet.

~Date	Prayer, Veneration, Sacraments and Other Doctrines	Ecclesiology/Politics	Rival Churches and Movements, Named by Their Antagonists	Biblical Assessment of Rome's Doctrines and Practices
		English channel and conquered the English crown, weakened by wars with the Danes; his was a "Holy Crusade"		sacraments a threat to Rome's dominance in that country?

For some reason, Pope Alexander II (two decades before Urban II), Papal Legate Hildebrand, and Abbott Lanfranc conspired with the French William the Conqueror to regain Ecclesiastical control over the English churches; which feat he accomplished. Thus William became the only known person to conquer the British Isles to date.

The crusade methodology represents a massive paradigm shift in an understanding of the Great Commission:

- From world evangelization
- To territorial-political-ecclesial acquisition.

Hence, the new Great Commission for the Church of Rome became verses like Deuteronomy 1:8 and 31:3:

> Deut 1:8, "See, I have placed the land before you; go in and possess the land which the LORD swore to give to your fathers, to Abraham, to Isaac, and to Jacob, to them and their descendants after them."

> Deut 31:3-5, "The LORD your God Himself crosses over before you; He will destroy these nations from before you, and you shall dispossess them. Joshua himself crosses over before you, just as the LORD has said. And the LORD will do to them as He did to Sihon and Og, the kings of the Amorites and their land, when He destroyed them. The LORD will give them over to you, that you may do to them according to every commandment which I have commanded you."

Notice the verbs: see, go in, possess in Deut 1:8 (cf. veni, vidi, vici—"I came, I saw, I conquered," Julius Caesar, 46 B.C.). Note also that the physical land rightfully belongs to those who are [or believe themselves to be] the rightful descendants of the reception of the promises of God. Further, the lands are to be inhabited by people who obey the commandments of the Lord, which was applied to the Inquisition of Southern France by the Third Lateran Council in 1215 A.D.

This misplaced Old Testament approach to the Great Commission fueled all of Rome's political-military exploits after that time, typically called "crusades" or "Holy Crusades."

This missiological refocus through territorial domination by the use of force continued well beyond the infamous Albigensian crusades (1181, 1209-1227, 1240-1255), to, during, and well after the Protestant Reformation:

- The anti-Hussite crusades in Bohemia (1420, 1421, 1424, 1426, 1433-1434, 1452);
- The anti-Radical crusades against Muenster and the Munsterites (1524, 1534, 1535);
- [The anti-Germanic peasant's crusade, pejoratively called a "Peasants Revolt" (1524-1526)—still needing further study];
- The anti-Anabaptist crusades against Waldshut (1524), in the Gusodein district (1529), the Tyrol and

~Date	Prayer, Veneration, Sacraments and Other Doctrines	Ecclesiology/Politics	Rival Churches and Movements, Named by Their Antagonists	Biblical Assessment of Rome's Doctrines and Practices
				Görz regions (1531), the Lowlands (1535), and in Steinborn (1539);
 • The anti-Zwinglian crusades in Switzerland (1529, 1531);
 • The anti-Waldensian crusade against Val Lucerna (1534);
 • The anti-Lutheran crusades in Germany (1546-1547, 1552);
 • The anti-Calvinist crusades in Merindol and Cabrières, France (1545), against the Huguenots (1559, 1562-1663, 1572).
  Not to mention the ongoing inquisitorial practices throughout these time periods, such as:
 • The anti-Anglican inquisition established by Queen Mary in England (1555-1558) in which 800 were put to death in her first two years.
  Note the following circular reasoning as related to crusades and their validity, based on Deut 20:14:
 "But the women, the little ones, the livestock, and all that is in the city, all its spoil, you shall plunder for yourself; and you shall eat the enemies' plunder which the LORD your God gives you."
 • Go to war to gain territory and force submission to Rome;
 • If and when the battle is won, it was God who gave the victory;
 • Therefore, because of the eventual victory, God Himself condoned the war, both in its purpose, methods, and outcome.
  For further details on William the Conqueror's crusade to regain control of England and its church, see "Inquisition and Martyrdom" chart.
  A text directly contradicted by the crusades is the fact that Christ sent his disciples out with a "gospel of peace." For example:
 Rom 10:14-15, "How then shall they call on Him in whom they have not believed? And how shall they believe in Him of whom they have not heard? And how shall they hear without a preacher? And how shall they preach unless they are sent? As it is written: 'How beautiful are the feet of those who preach the gospel of peace, Who bring glad tidings of good things!'"
  Notice that the reading "those who preach a gospel of peace" is contradicted both by the fires of inquisition and by the crusades. Therefore, it is convenient to blame the citation of both clauses of Isaiah 52:7 on dittography and remove the first line from the text as a scribal error, as was/is done through the Nestle-Aland Greek original text type. No longer did Rome need to be accused of preaching other than a "gospel of peace" during their centuries of crusade or during their centuries of Inquisition.
1067		"Heretics" executed in Sweden and Norway		As regards the executions, see A.D. 1002 for discussion.

~Date	Prayer, Veneration, Sacraments and Other Doctrines	Ecclesiology/Politics	Rival Churches and Movements, Named by Their Antagonists	Biblical Assessment of Rome's Doctrines and Practices
1073		Hildebrand elected as Pope Gregory VII without consent from the Emperor When Gregory called for a council in Germany, his request was denied: "The dispatching his Legates into Germanie to certaine Bishops, willed them to assemble in Councell: but they refused it, alledging, that it was contrary to the custome and priviledge of their Nation" (Sleidan, 279).		Another massive shift in the "Investiture Controversy" over control of bishoprics in a given country and the papal appointments of the same.
~1073		Pope Gregory VII (1073-1085), Hildebrand, took the title of "Vicar of St. Peter" [in the place of St. Peter], which within 125 years [1199] became "Vicar of Christ" (see below)		The "Vicar of [St] Peter" title further leveraged Rome's prominence in its struggle for supremacy over the Eastern church (and any other body [falsely] using the name "church"), through use of the adjective "first" in Matt 10:2 ("first, Simon, who is called Peter") to be the foundational pillar of truth for their entire doctrine of the church and all of its interpretation, teaching, and practice Among other things, Gregory VII deposed kings and queens, and forced the Germanic clergy to divorce their wives, and canonized transubstantiation. The so-called "Holy Inquisition" was established upon his policies.
1074	"Priests forbidden to marry" (Dreyer)[97] "This designe myscarying, He in some certaine Councels held in Italy, decrees, That Massing Priests shall have no wiues but shall dismisse them, or else leaue their places; sending this decree to the Bishops in Germanie, vrges earnestly, vnder penalty denounced, to haue it established: but the Clergy, as they call them, and whole stream of Massing Priests, stiffely reclaime calling him a heretike, that propounds such doctrine; sithence Christs words are, "That all should not receive this word." And Paul saith, "They that cannot containe let them marrie": But this Pope not regarding Christs word, and contemning Paul's authority, would constraine men, to reiect the vse of marriage, which		It appears that this action [see also 1079] led to forced divorce of priests, which was particularly felt in Germany. The so-called "Anti-Pope" Clement III was approved by the German court of Emperor Henry IV during this sad time.	Contra: • 1 Tim 4:1-3, "Now the Spirit expressly says that in latter times some will depart from the faith, giving heed to deceiving spirits and doctrines of demons, speaking lies in hypocrisy, having their own conscience seared with a hot iron, forbidding to marry, *and commanding* to abstain from foods which God created to be received with thanksgiving by those who believe and know the truth." For further notations on the Vow of Celibacy, see A.D. 529.

---

[97]F. C. H. Dreyer and E. Weller, *Roman Catholicism in Light of Scripture* (Chicago: Moody, 1960), 252.

~Date	Prayer, Veneration, Sacraments and Other Doctrines	Ecclesiology/Politics	Rival Churches and Movements, Named by Their Antagonists	Biblical Assessment of Rome's Doctrines and Practices
	is lawfull and ordained by God: and to burne in most filthy flames of lust, and rush into manifest lewdnesse, but they would rather leaue their Ministery then matrimony" (Sleidan, 279-280).			
1075		Pope Gregory VII's *Dictatus Papae* included 27 theses, some are as follows (from Henderson unless marked): 1. "That the Roman church was founded by God alone"; 2. "That the Roman pontiff alone can with right be called universal." 3. "That he alone can depose or reinstate bishops.." 4. "That, in a council his legate, even if a lower grade, is above all bishops, and can pass sentence of deposition against them." 5. "That the pope may depose the absent." 6. "That, among other things, we ought not to remain in the same house with those excommunicated by him." 7. "That for him alone is it lawful, according to the needs of the time, to make new laws, to assemble together new congregations, to make an abbey of a canonry; and, on the other hand, to divide a rich bishopric and unite the poor ones." 8. "That he alone may use the imperial insignia." 9. "That of the pope alone all princes shall kiss the feet." 10. "That his name alone shall be spoken in the churches." 11. "That this is the only name in the world" (Henderson); "The Pope's name is the chief name in the world."	Pope Gregory VII (1073-1085), formerly Hildebrand of Sovona, (1015/1028-1085) published, *Extra, De Haereticis, cap. Ad abolendam*: "Holding to the institutions of our holy predecessors, we, by our apostolic authority, absolve from their oath those who through loyalty or through the sacred bond of an oath owe allegiance to excommunicated persons: and we absolutely forbid them to continue their allegiance to such persons, until these shall have made amends" (quoted in Aquinas, *Summa*, SS, Q[12], A[2])	The idea of coming to the Holy City to appear "to see the face of the Lord your God" comes from Deut 31:11: • Deut 31:11 (FJB), "au moment où tout Israël se rend, pour voir la face de Yahvé ton Dieu, au lieu qu'il aura choisi, tu prononceras cette Loi aux oreilles de tout Israël." • Deut 31:11 (TOB), "quand tout Israël viendra voir la face du SEIGNEUR ton Dieu au lieu qu'il aura choisi, tu liras cette Loi en face de tout Israël, qui l'écoutera." • Deut 31:11 (BFC), "Vous la lirez à haute voix à tous les Israélites venus se présenter devant le Seigneur Dieu, dans le lieu qu'il aura choisi."[99] • Deut 31:11 (DRA), "When all Israel come together, to appear in the sight of the Lord thy God in the place which the Lord shall choose, thou shalt read the words of this law before all Israel, in their hearing." • Deut 31:11 (NJB), "when all Israel assembles in the presence of Yahweh your God in the place chosen by him, you must proclaim this Law in the hearing of all Israel." • Deut 31:11 (HCSB), "when all Israel assembles in the presence of the LORD your God at the place He chooses, you are to read this law aloud before all Israel." Therefore, substituting "the Person" for "the Place" in the OT, the "Judge" in the place (Deut 17:12), the chosen Judge becomes the representative head of the Lord Himself, before whom believing mankind is to appear. This type of reasoning explains the strong antagonism to a Dispensational approach to biblical interpretation, as church polity is largely based on the Centralized hierarchy as found in the Book of Deuteronomy. About the content of *Dictatus Papae*: Is not placing the name and authority of the Pope equal or in actuality over that of Jesus Christ: • Taking the name of the Lord our God in vain (Deut 5:11), by using God's name and His Holy Scripture to achieve carnal ends (Matt 16:23)? • Blasphemy against the name of Christ, e.g. Acts 18:5-6? Further, if the Pope is the Vicar of Christ (vicarious representation of Christ on earth), what happens to the actual promised present of the risen Christ among His people?

[99]Interestingly, the French "Bible en Français Courant" version in my BibleWorks did not search nor have this verse in it. I found this verse by doing a search at: http://www.interbible.org/interBible/ecritures/bu/ (online); accessed: 17 Feb 2014.

~Date	Prayer, Veneration, Sacraments and Other Doctrines	Ecclesiology/Politics	Rival Churches and Movements, Named by Their Antagonists	Biblical Assessment of Rome's Doctrines and Practices
		(Wylie). 12. "That it may be permitted to him to depose emperors" (Henderson); "It is lawful for him to depose emperors." (Wylie) 13. "That he may be permitted to transfer bishops if need be." 14. "That he has power to ordain a clerk of any church he may wish." 15. "That he who is ordained by him may preside over another church, but may not hold a subordinate position; and that such a one may not receive a higher grade from any bishop." 16. "That no synod shall be called a general one without his order" (Henderson); "That no council may be called 'general' without his commandment" (Pullan). 17. "That no chapter and no book shall be considered canonical without his authority." 18. "That a sentence passed by him may be retracted by no one; and that he himself, alone of all, may retract it" (Henderson); "His decision is to be withstood by none, but he alone may annul those of all men." (Wylie) 19. "That he himself may be judged by no one." 20. "That no one shall dare to condemn one who appeals to the apostolic chair." 21. "That to the latter should be referred the more important cases of every church." 22. "That the Roman church has never erred; nor will it err to all eternity, the Scripture bearing witness." 23. "That the Roman pontiff, if he have been canonically ordained, is undoubtedly made a saint by the merits of St.		• Matt 28:18-20, "And Jesus came and spoke to them, saying, "All authority has been given to Me in heaven and on earth. Go therefore and make disciples of all the nations, baptizing them in the name of the Father and of the Son and of the Holy Spirit, teaching them to observe all things that I have commanded you; and lo, I am with you always, *even to the end of the age*." Amen." In this case, if Christ's promised presence is usurped by a human representative, then it must be proof positive that (a) Christ's presence was not there in the decision-making of the pope at that time anyways, and (b) that if, in fact, His presence was there among some (Rev 3:4), it for sure was not after this decision. For God will not abide a counterfeit: • Deut 32:12, "So the LORD alone led him, And *there was* no foreign god with him." And of this very thing Jesus warned his disciples *maints* times, as in His first and second admonition in the Olivet Discourse: • Matt 24:4-5, "Take heed that no one deceives you. For many will come in My name, saying, 'I am the Christ,' and will deceive many." cf. Matt 24:11, 23-24. Note also that this problem is not only with Roman Catholicism; for example, the founder of the Baha'i Faith changed his name to Bahá'u'lláh, meaning "the glory of God," affirming that he himself was the incarnation of God the Father, an Islamic expectation in 19th Century Shi-ism. In Gregory VII's *Dictatus*, the concept of the Papacy, and loyalty to the same, combined teaching from the NT regarding the millennial rule of Christ (one reason that Rome strongly disagrees with the premillennial view, because it supposes that Rome's earthly kingdom was/is not the accomplishment of all or most of the millennial promises), with the OT Deuteronomic commands regarding the taking of the land and the spiritual and doctrinal rule of the same (see my notes under A.D. 312), and with the NT example of Paul appealing to Caesar for judgment in Acts 25: • Acts 25:11-12, "'For if I am an offender, or have committed anything deserving of death, I do not object to dying; but if there is nothing in these things of which these men accuse me, no one can deliver me to them. I appeal to Caesar.' Then Festus, when he had conferred with the council, answered, 'You have appealed to Caesar? To Caesar you shall go!'" Herein, absolute loyalty to the teachings and enactments of the Pope became the priority in being considered "orthodox"; anyone not agreeing with the rule of the Pope was considered heretical regardless of their doctrinal beliefs. Later, Aquinas called this a lack of love or charity. And because charity is considered the highest virtue, a lack of charity is considered the greatest sin, and it is therefore punishable by the death penalty,

~Date	Prayer, Veneration, Sacraments and Other Doctrines	Ecclesiology/Politics	Rival Churches and Movements, Named by Their Antagonists	Biblical Assessment of Rome's Doctrines and Practices
		Peter; St. Ennodius, bishop of Pavia, bearing witness, and many holy fathers agreeing with him. As is contained in the decrees of St. Symmachus the pope." 24. "That, by his command and consent, it may be lawful for subordinates to bring accusations." 25. "That he may depose and reinstate bishops without assembling a synod." 26. "That he who is not at peace with the Roman church shall not be considered catholic." 27. "That he may absolve subjects from their fealty to wicked men."[98]		"extirpation from the world through death." On Christ ruling over or exacting rulership over the whole world, please consider this brief sampling of verses on this topic: • 1 Cor 15:23-25, "But each one in his own order: Christ the firstfruits, afterward those *who are* Christ's at His coming. Then *comes* the end, when He delivers the kingdom to God the Father, when He puts an end to all rule and all authority and power. For He must reign till He has put all enemies under His feet." • Eph 1:20-23, "which He worked in Christ when He raised Him from the dead and seated *Him* at His right hand in the heavenly *places*, far above all principality and power and might and dominion, and every name that is named, not only in this age but also in that which is to come. And He put all *things* under His feet, and gave Him *to be* head over all *things* to the church, which is His body, the fullness of Him who fills all in all" • Rev 11:15, "Then the seventh angel sounded: And there were loud voices in heaven, saying, 'The kingdoms of this world have become *the kingdoms* of our Lord and of His Christ, and He shall reign forever and ever!'" • Etc. **On Breaking Fealty**: In *Dictatus*, we have the breaking of a vow of fealty or of allegiance to anyone who does not agree with the Pope. When applied to breaking submission a ruler, as it was used by Gregory VII, this teaching contradicted Romans 13:1: • Rom 13:1, "Let every soul be subject to the governing authorities. For there is no authority except from God, and the authorities that exist are appointed by God." This same breaking of fealty was also applied to dissolve and disallow the marriage of clergy during the rule of Gregory VII, and the concept of breaking fealty was and is much repeated afterward, as applied to all types of contractual agreements, including political, economic, marriage and family, etc. Does this not constitute the authorizing of lying, thereby contradicting many Scriptures on this issue, including the Ten Commandments? • "You shall not bear false witness against your neighbor, Exod 20:16 • "You shall not bear false witness against your neighbor," Deut 5:20 • "You shall not have in your bag differing weights, a

---

[98]Unless otherwise stated, citation comes from Ernest F. Henderson, *Select Historical Documents of the Middle Ages*, (London: George Bell and Sons, 1910), 366-367; other sources include James A. Wylie, *History of Protestantism*, Bk 1, Ch 4;; available at: http://www.doctrine.org/history/HPv1b1.htm (online); accessed: 10 Feb 2010; G. A. Loud. Unpublished translation. Translation of *Das Register Gregors VII.*, ed. E. Caspar (M.G.H. *Epistolae Selectae* 2, Berlin 1920-1923), 202-08; available at: http://faculty.cua.edu/pennington/churchhistory220/topicfive/DictatusPapae2.html (online); accessed: 4 July 2011; Internet; and Brian Pullan, *Sources for the History of Medieval Europe from the Mid-Eighth to the Mid-Thirteenth Century* (Oxford: Basil Blackwell, 1971), document no. III 9, translated from Gregory VII's *Register*, no. II 55a.; available at: http://faculty.cua.edu/pennington/churchhistory220/topicfive/DictatusPapaePullan.htm (online); accessed 4 July 2011; Internet.

~Date	Prayer, Veneration, Sacraments and Other Doctrines	Ecclesiology/Politics	Rival Churches and Movements, Named by Their Antagonists	Biblical Assessment of Rome's Doctrines and Practices
				heavy and a light. You shall not have in your house differing measures, a large and a small. You shall have a perfect and just weight, a perfect and just measure, that your days may be lengthened in the land which the LORD your God is giving you. For all who do such things, all who behave unrighteously, *are* an abomination to the LORD your God," Deut 25:13-16

- "But let your 'Yes' be 'Yes,' and your 'No,' 'No.' For whatever is more than these is from the evil one," Matt 5:37

- "But there shall by no means enter it anything that defiles, or causes an abomination or a lie, but only those who are written in the Lamb's Book of Life," Rev 21:27

On the Ongoing Application of Dictatus: Of the enactments of *Dictatus Papae*, it may the thoughtful reader ponder these enactments, each of which can easily be traced in the writings and actions of the Church of Rome up to the present day:

- There exists a "ruler of this world":
  - John 23:31, "Now is the judgment of this world; now the ruler of this world will be cast out"
  - John 14:30, "I will no longer talk much with you, for the ruler of this world is coming, and he has nothing in Me"
  - John 16:11, "of judgment, because the ruler of this world is judged"

- There exists a "prince of the power of the air":
  - Eph 2:2, "in which you once walked according to the course of this world, according to the prince of the power of the air, the spirit who now works in the sons of disobedience"

- Sometimes this person is called the "evil one":
  - Matt 6:13, "And do not lead us into temptation, But deliver us from the evil one. For Yours is the kingdom and the power and the glory forever. Amen"

- Others in history have made much about the "mystery of lawlessness" hither to fore restrained:
  - 2 Thess 2:7, "For the mystery of lawlessness is already at work; only He who now restrains *will do so* until He is taken out of the way"

Exactly when or how this evil personage is to be manifested on earth is a mystery. *Dictatus* appears to be a manifestation of one who sought to acquire the level of authority of "ruler of this age," and that in the name of Jesus!

By the way, when Jesus Christ no longer the rules an organization of men, it then ceases from being His church. For as only Christ in heaven is the head of His church (Eph 5:23), so the true church must have Christ for its head, and not allow a mere man to usurp that headship (Matt 24:5, 24-26). Christ supernaturally exerts His headship through His very words (Matt 24:35; John 6:68-69).

On the Church's Absolute Supremacy: When

~Date	Prayer, Veneration, Sacraments and Other Doctrines	Ecclesiology/Politics	Rival Churches and Movements, Named by Their Antagonists	Biblical Assessment of Rome's Doctrines and Practices
				enactments like *Dictatus Papae* are combined with certain teachings of Scripture there results a scenario in which all levels of society answer to and are subservient to Rome and her leaders. Consider the following: • Through use of the Latin language as the language of ecclesial education (590-604 A.D.), and because all education was ecclesial, Rome exercised its power over all the multiple language groups within the "Holy Roman Empire" (HRE), none of which speak Latin as their mother tongue • Through *Dictatus Papae* (1075 A.D.) Rome exerted its authority over every branch of government in all the states of the HRE • Through use of 1 Cor 6:1, Rome could call on its authority over all judicial proceedings in every state of the HRE: 1 Cor 6:1, "Dare any of you, having a matter against another, go to law before the unrighteous, and not before the saints?" Notice that "saints" is plural and not singular, hinting at a congregational form of church government. • Further, perhaps shocking to the reader, the implication is also that no state has the right or authority to judge Roman Catholic clergy, for they stand under their own system of jurisprudence: 1 Cor 6:6, "But brother goes to law against brother, and that before unbelievers!" For this reason the pedophiles among the Roman clergy are not often brought to judgment under the secular laws and judges of the states in which they reside, as they have their own Canon Law to deal with such issues (e.g. 1054 A.D.), which they deem to be superior to or above the laws of any nation-state. Rome's authority over every branch of society was complete by 1075 A.D.—None had the right or authority to disagree—any who did were deemed tainted with audacity against the centralized system instituted by God, Deut 17:12-13
1077		"Heretic" burned alive in Cambrai, Low lands	As Roman enactments were made, the redefinition of heretics continued. Since anyone who did not maintain Charity with Rome (i.e. gladly live under her enactments) was deemed a heretic.	[See A.D. 1002] It must be noted that those who did not agree with Gregory VII's *Dictatus* above were now also considered **heretics**! So the delineation and scope of who was or is considered a heretic was/is constantly in a state of flux. Further, not only were they considered heretics for their non-acceptance of Gregory VII's *Dictatus*, but simultaneously, they also needed to be condemned for a doctrinal motive—thereby following Jezebel's pattern of dual condemnation, "You have blasphemed God and the king": • 1 Kings 21:7-14, "Then Jezebel his wife said to him, 'You now exercise authority over Israel! Arise, eat food, and let your heart be cheerful; I will give you the vineyard of Naboth the Jezreelite.' And she wrote letters in Ahab's name, sealed *them* with his seal, and

~Date	Prayer, Veneration, Sacraments and Other Doctrines	Ecclesiology/Politics	Rival Churches and Movements, Named by Their Antagonists	Biblical Assessment of Rome's Doctrines and Practices
				sent the letters to the elders and the nobles who *were* dwelling in the city with Naboth. She wrote in the letters, saying, Proclaim a fast, and seat Naboth with high honor among the people; and seat two men, scoundrels, before him to bear witness against him, saying, 'You have blasphemed God and the king.' *Then* take him out, and stone him, that he may die. So the men of his city, the elders and nobles who were inhabitants of his city, did as Jezebel had sent to them, as it *was* written in the letters which she had sent to them. They proclaimed a fast, and seated Naboth with high honor among the people. And two men, scoundrels, came in and sat before him; and the scoundrels witnessed against him, against Naboth, in the presence of the people, saying, 'Naboth has blasphemed God and the king!' Then they took him outside the city and stoned him with stones, so that he died. Then they sent to Jezebel, saying, 'Naboth has been stoned and is dead.'" In the case of the Pope, he is considered the king of kings, thus equivalent to the head of state (i.e. blaspheming the king). So then a condemnation with respect to blaspheming God is needed. For this sordid work, scholastic rhetoricians often find for fuel the debates related to the early church's Trinitarian and/or Christological controversies.
1079	The Confession of Faith of Berengarius of Tours required of him by Gregory VII in 1079: "I Berengarius, believe in my heart and openly profess that the bread and wine which are placed upon the altar are, by the mystery of the sacred prayer and the words of the [our] Redeemer, substantially changed into the true and life-giving flesh and blood of Jesus Christ Our Lord, and that after the Consecration, there is present the true Body of Christ which was born of the Virgin and, offered up for the salvation of the world, hung on the Cross and now sits at the right hand of the Father, and that there is present the true Blood of Christ which flowed from His side. They are present not only by means of a sign and of the efficacy of the Sacrament, but also in the very reality and truth of their nature and substance. As contained in this brief exposition, as I have read	**"Celibacy of the priesthood, decreed by pope Gregory VII (Hildebrand)"** (Boettner, #23) 3rd Lateran council: obligatory celibacy of the priesthood reaffirmed (not just for monks taking the Benedictine vows). "Heretic" Bruno condemned, disappeared from history		Contra: • Gen 2:18, "And the LORD God said, '*It is* not good that man should be alone; I will make him a helper comparable to him'" • Prov 18:22, "*He who* finds a wife finds a good *thing*, And obtains favor from the LORD" • 1 Tim 4:1-4, "Now the Spirit expressly says that in latter times some will depart from the faith, giving heed to deceiving spirits and doctrines of demons, speaking lies in hypocrisy, having their own conscience seared with a hot iron, forbidding to marry, *and commanding* to abstain from foods which God created to be received with thanksgiving by those who believe and know the truth" Required celibacy also contains an unexpected backlash: • Those taking the vow of celibacy become strongly antagonistic to clergy who do not practice their vowed abstinence: ○ There is a jealousy against those who are married, which appears to lead to a violent hatred • This antagonism was noted in reactions to Luther's getting married, along with the names that he was called: ○ Similar responses can be found throughout much of the history of the churches for the same reason Sexual drive in man: • Could it be that jealousy in this one area, along with the exceedingly strong pent up sexual drive, perhaps more than any other reason, explains the almost inconceivable, unexplainable, and unbelievable acts

~Date	Prayer, Veneration, Sacraments and Other Doctrines	Ecclesiology/Politics	Rival Churches and Movements, Named by Their Antagonists	Biblical Assessment of Rome's Doctrines and Practices
	and as you understand, thus I believe and will no longer henceforth teach against this faith. May God come to my help and these holy gospels of God."[100] This Confession was partially quoted by Paul VI in *Mysterium fidei*, (3 Sept 1965) to reaffirm Rome's adherence to transubstantiation in light of the teachings of "transsignification" and "transfinalisation" that were being taught at that time (See Denzinger, Introduction to DS4410-4413).			of torture overseen by Roman clergy in the history of Holy Inquisition?[101] • For if we consider the history of the churches, it is during this time period that the atrocities committed by the Church of Rome "for the glory of God" seem to escalate significantly. For further notations on the Vow of Celibacy, see A.D. 529 and 1074.
1084-		Reign of the boy Emperor,		

---

[100]Gregory VII, "Profession of Faith given to Berengarius" (11 Feb 1079); DS700. Translation adapted from http://www.papalencyclicals.net/Paul06/p6myster.htm.

[101]James Wylie described the Chamber of Torture, and the instruments used in Inquisition gathered from around Bavaria, as well as the Max Tower, under which was the place where the final effort to extort a recantation was found, with horizontal and vertical torture rack and an Iron Maiden (or as he called it "iron image of the Virgin"). He noted, "The Author was conducted over the Inquisition at Nuremberg in September, 1871, and wrote the description given of it in the text immediately thereafter on the spot. Others must have seen it, but he knows of no one who has described it" (from J. A. Wylie, *The History of Protestantism* [London: Cassell, 1869], Vol 2, Book 15, Chap 11; available from: http://www.doctrine.org/history/HPv2b15.htm [online]; accessed: 10 Feb 2010; Internet).

"The 'Holy Offices' of Spain and Italy have been dismantled, and little now remains save the walls of the buildings in which the business of the Inquisition was carried on; but, strange to say, in Nuremberg, as we can testify from actual observation, the whole apparatus of torture is still shown in the subterranean chambers that were used by the agents of the 'Holy Office.' ...

"Turn we now to the town of Nuremberg, in Bavaria. The zeal with which Duke Albert, the sovereign of Bavaria, entered into the restoration of Roman Catholicism, we have already narrated. To further the movement, he provided every one of the chief towns of his dominions with a Holy Office, and the Inquisition of Nuremberg still remains—an anomalous and horrible monument in the midst of a city where the memorials of an exquisite art, and the creations of an unrivalled genius, meet one at every step. We shall first describe the Chamber of Torture.

"The house so called immediately adjoins the Imperial Castle, which from its lofty site looks down on the city, whose Gothic towers, sculptured fronts, and curiously ornamented gables are seen covering both banks of the Pegnitz, which rolls below. The house may have been the guard-room of the castle. It derives its name, the Torture-chamber, not from the fact that the torture was here inflicted, but because into this one chamber has been collected a complete set of the instruments of torture gleaned from the various Inquisitions that formerly existed in Bavaria. A glance suffices to show the whole dreadful apparatus by which the adherents of Rome sought to maintain her dogmas. Placed next to the door, and greeting the sight as one enters, is a collection of hideous masks. These represent creatures monstrous of shape, and malignant and fiendish of nature. It is in beholding them that we begin to perceive how subtle was the genius that devised this system of coercion, and that it took the mind as well as the body of the victim into account. In gazing on them, one feels as if he had suddenly come into polluting and debasing society, and had sunk to the same moral level with the creatures here figured before him. He suffers a conscious abatement of dignity and fortitude. The persecutor had calculated, doubtless, that the effect produced upon the mind of his victim by these dreadful apparitions, would be that he would be morally relaxed, and less able to sustain his cause. Unless of strong mind, indeed, the unfortunate prisoner, on entering such a place, and seeing himself encompassed with such unearthly and hideous shapes, must have felt as if he were the vile heretic which the persecutor styled him, and as if already the infernal den had opened its portals, and sent forth its venomous swarms to bid him welcome. Yourself accursed, with accursed beings are you henceforth to dwell–such was the silent language of these abhorred images. [Further: the inquisitors could hide their identity from their victim, perhaps covering up their unconscious shame for the pain and torture that they were about to inflict, as they were seeking a recantation from the heretic]

"We pass on into the chamber, where more dreadful sights meet our gaze. It is hung round and round with instruments of torture, so numerous that it would take a long while even to name them, and so diverse that it would take a much longer time to describe them. We must take them in groups, for it were hopeless to think of going over them one by one, and particularising the mode in which each operated, and the ingenuity and art with which all of them have been adapted to their horrible end. There were instruments for compressing the fingers till the bones should be squeezed to splinters. There were instruments for probing below the finger-nails till an exquisite pain, like a burning fire, would run along the nerves. There were instruments for tearing out the tongue, for scooping out the eyes, for grubbing-up the ears. There were bunches of iron cords, with a spiked circle at the end of every whip, for tearing the flesh from the back till bone and sinew were laid bare. There were iron cases for the legs, which were tightened upon the limb placed in them by means of a screw, till flesh and bone were reduced to a jelly. There were cradles set full of sharp spikes, in which victims were laid and rolled from side to side, the wretched occupant being pierced at each movement of the machine with innumerable sharp points. There were iron ladles with long handles, for holding molten lead or boiling pitch, to be poured down the throat of the victim, and convert his body into a burning cauldron. There were frames with holes to admit the hands and feet, so contrived that the person put into them had his body bent into unnatural and painful positions, and the agony grew greater and greater by moments, and yet the man did not die. There were chestfuls of small but most ingeniously constructed instruments for pinching, probing, or tearing the more sensitive parts of the body, and continuing the pain up to the very verge where reason or life gives way. On the floor and walls of the apartment were other and larger instruments for the same fearful end–lacerating, mangling, and agonizing living men; but these we shall meet in other dungeons we are yet to visit" ("Restoration of Inquisition," bk. 15, ch 11; ibid.).

~Date	Prayer, Veneration, Sacraments and Other Doctrines	Ecclesiology/Politics	Rival Churches and Movements, Named by Their Antagonists	Biblical Assessment of Rome's Doctrines and Practices
1105		Henry IV (1084-1105), wherein the government was at first rule by his mother, and then by clergy vice-regents; it appears that Henry grew licentious and lax in his morals and dealings		
1085		Death of Gregory VII who canonized transubstantiation		Contra: "In remembrance of Me," Luke 22:19; 1 Cor 11:24-25; "Then if anyone says to you, 'Behold, here is the Christ,' or 'There *He is,*' do not believe *him*" Matt 24:23
1088		[Pope] Urban II (1088-1099) was known for his preaching crusades [increasing the territory of the Church of Rome's monopoly]; after his preaching he invited candidates forward to receive a cross to be placed on their shirt as part of a vow to fight in the crusades		Contra, Matt 5:44 (NKJ), "But I say to you, love your enemies, bless those who curse you, do good to those who hate you, and pray for those who spitefully use you and persecute you" Contra: Rom 12:21 (NKJ), "Do not be overcome by evil, but overcome evil with good"; 1 Thess 5:15 (NKJ), "See that no one renders evil for evil to anyone, but always pursue what is good both for yourselves and for all." Contra Jesus' statement to Peter, "Put your sword back into its place" Matt 26:52; contra Jesus said, "My kingdom is not of this world" John 18:36; cf. Luke 17:20-21 The legitimizing of crusades portrayed a dramatic shift in the mission of the church, from fulfilling the Great Commission (a spiritual mandate) to accomplishing a ecclesiastical-territorial mission, based on Deuteronomic commands of Israel's conquest in taking of the land promised to Abraham, For example: • Deut 1:8, "'See, I have set the land before you; go in and possess the land which the LORD swore to your fathers—to Abraham, Isaac, and Jacob—to give to them and their descendants after them.'"; Deut 31:3, "The LORD your God Himself crosses over before you; He will destroy these nations from before you, and you shall dispossess them"; by the way this is an oft repeated concept in Deuteronomy: o In this case, the word "nations" is applied to other competing churches (Eastern Orthodox and Cathars), as well as other religious groupings (Muslims) o "Destroying" (Heb *shamad*; Gk ἐξολεθρεύω [in Deut 31:3]) refers to crushing by military power so that the other religious groupings have no power or control o "Take possession of" or "dispossess" or "possess" (Heb *yarash*; Gk κληρονομέω [in Deut 1:8] or κατακληρονομέω [in Deut 31:3]) meaning that church control is given over to Bishops appointed by Rome so that they may rule over them "in peace" under the rule of the High Priest (Pontifex) in Rome • There are many such commands in Deuteronomy which may be applied to military and territorial conquest or crusades (see especially Aquinas on this

~Date	Prayer, Veneration, Sacraments and Other Doctrines	Ecclesiology/Politics	Rival Churches and Movements, Named by Their Antagonists	Biblical Assessment of Rome's Doctrines and Practices
				subject) One must remember that the shift to territorial expansion and crusades as the primary mission of Rome necessitated a move away from the Great Commission as spiritual, for example: • Going (even in the midst of persecution) • Preaching the Gospel (the only power of God unto salvation) • Winning disciples (as converts to the Pauline Gospel are won to the Lord by His Spirit) • Teaching them to observe whatsoever the Jesus has commanded (which is a radical departure from the Deuteronomic conquest commanded to Israel for the promised land only) • All of these following the example of Christ and of Paul (1 Cor 11:1)
1088		Urban II was known for organizing crusades, strangely called "preaching the cross" Berengarius, deacon of Bruno, martyred on the day of Epiphany		Contra "My kingdom is not of this world," John 18:36; cf. Luke 17:20-21; contra all the Great Commission passages
1090	"The Rosary, mechanical praying with beads, invented by Peter the Hermit" (Boettner, #24)		Prayer to Mary and the Rosary became a "Market Niche" for the Church of Rome	Just like the false prophetesses in Ezekiel 13, physical trappings—prayer beads, were invented or borrowed from another religion, to assist in prayer. • Ezek 13:17-23, "Likewise, son of man, set your face against the daughters of your people, who prophesy out of their own heart; prophesy against them, [18] and say, 'Thus says the Lord GOD: "Woe to the *women* who sew *magic* charms on their sleeves and make veils for the heads of people of every height to hunt souls! Will you hunt the souls of My people, and keep yourselves alive? [19] And will you profane Me among My people for handfuls of barley and for pieces of bread, killing people who should not die, and keeping people alive who should not live, by your lying to My people who listen to lies?" [20] 'Therefore thus says the Lord GOD: "Behold, I *am* against your *magic* charms by which you hunt souls there like birds. I will tear them from your arms, and let the souls go, the souls you hunt like birds. [21] I will also tear off your veils and deliver My people out of your hand, and they shall no longer be as prey in your hand. Then you shall know that I *am* the LORD. [22] Because with lies you have made the heart of the righteous sad, whom I have not made sad; and you have strengthened the hands of the wicked, so that he does not turn from his wicked way to save his life. [23] Therefore you shall no longer envision futility nor practice divination; for I will deliver My people out of your hand, and you shall know that I *am* the LORD."'" Shifting the focus of prayer from communication with the Eternal One to the use of physical trappings. Whereas Romans 8:26 tells us that we do not know how to pray, but rather need the Holy Spirit's mediatory assistance in making proper request: • Rom 8:26, "Likewise the Spirit also helps in our weaknesses. For we do not know what we should

~Date	Prayer, Veneration, Sacraments and Other Doctrines	Ecclesiology/Politics	Rival Churches and Movements, Named by Their Antagonists	Biblical Assessment of Rome's Doctrines and Practices
				pray for as we ought, but the Spirit Himself makes intercession for us with groanings which cannot be uttered."
				Apparently, Rome does know how we ought to pray: "Pray the Rosary!"
				Whereas the NT makes it clear that the Christian ought to pray to God the father in the name of Jesus:
				• John 14:13-14, "And whatever you ask in My name, that I will do, that the Father may be glorified in the Son. If you ask anything in My name, I will do *it*."
				• John 15:16, "You did not choose Me, but I chose you and appointed you that you should go and bear fruit, and *that* your fruit should remain, that whatever you ask the Father in My name He may give you"
				• John 16:23-24, "And in that day you will ask Me nothing. Most assuredly, I say to you, whatever you ask the Father in My name He will give you. Until now you have asked nothing in My name. Ask, and you will receive, that your joy may be full"
				Any prayer outside of the norms set by Jesus, such as prayer to Mary or the saints, is blasphemy and idolatry
				On the public use of the Rosary, see A. D. 1214
1095-1101		Rome's "**First Crusade**" to recapture the Holy Land called by Urban II (see also recapture of England in 1066), at a council in Clermont-Ferrand, France on the 27th of November, 1095. His infallible words were "God wills it!"		Following the Old Covenant strategy for the capture of the promised land, as found in the book of Deuteronomy, Rome appears to have applied this teaching for their church territorial conquests:
		In its numbering and description of official "crusades," Rome has reduced the actual number by narrowing the definition of the term, as explained by Louis Bréhier:		Deut 20:10-15, "When you go near a city to fight against it, then proclaim an offer of peace to it. And it shall be that if they accept your offer of peace, and open to you, then all the people *who are* found in it shall be placed under tribute to you, and serve you. Now if *the city* will not make peace with you, but makes war against you, then you shall besiege it. And when the LORD your God delivers it into your hands, you shall strike every male in it with the edge of the sword. But the women, the little ones, the livestock, and all that is in the city, all its spoil, you shall plunder for yourself; and you shall eat the enemies' plunder which the LORD your God gives you. Thus you shall do to all the cities *which are* very far from you, which *are* not of the cities of these nations."
		"But modern literature has abused the word [crusade] by applying it to all wars of a religious character....		It appears that the state-church combination initiated at the time of Constantine and Sylvester reached its culmination in the crusades, wherein the Church of Rome became missionally-militaristic with its territorial expansion policies.
		"The idea of the crusade corresponds to a political conception which was realized in Christendom only from the eleventh to the fifteenth century; this supposes a union of all peoples and sovereigns under the direction of the popes. All crusades were announced by preaching. After pronouncing a solemn vow, each warrior received a cross from the		

~Date	Prayer, Veneration, Sacraments and Other Doctrines	Ecclesiology/Politics	Rival Churches and Movements, Named by Their Antagonists	Biblical Assessment of Rome's Doctrines and Practices
		hands of the pope or his legates, and was thenceforth considered a soldier of the Church. Crusaders were also granted indulgences and temporal privileges, such as exemption from civil jurisdiction, inviolability of persons or lands, etc. Of all these wars undertaken in the name of Christendom, the most important were the Eastern Crusades, which are the only ones treated in this article.[102]		
1123		Canon 1 of the First Lateran Council prohibits any clergy from receiving compensation, unless approved by Rome, calling it simony		This interpretation of Acts 8:18 is erroneous and plays into the hands of Rome's monopolistic behavior; in this way Rome can falsely accuse any competing church as being guilty of simony, which is a joke, as their priests are paid for saying Masses and forgiveness of sins (indulgences), which is clearly Acts 8 simony
1130-1143		Innocent II's letter, "Apostolicam Sedem," explained the "Baptism of Desire" [DS741] whereby a certain presbyter, who had never received baptism, through his faithfulness and obedience to the "faith of the Holy Mother Church" did in fact receive the benefits of baptism, being freedom from original sin, etc. (he cited Augustine and Ambrose)	This teaching was expanded to include as catechumens those who "are victims of invincible ignorance" (as applied to Billy Graham), see Pius XII, to the Archbishop of Boston [8 Aug 1949] (DS3866-3873)	Here, membership in the church of Rome was diminished to anyone who had positive feelings about Rome (Innocent II), or even who could be influenced to be non-negative toward the Church of Rome (Pius XII). It is amazing the political maneuvers of Rome to further its designs!
1134			Peter the Venerable (ninth Abbott of Cluny, 1122-1156) wrote a treatise highlighting five heretical propositions of Peter of Bruis, which were: 1. Refusal to baptize infants, under the pretext that it is faith that saves and that a young infant could not have sufficient conscience to believe. 2. Rejection of holy places; the Church of God does not consist of an assemblage of stones but of a spiritual reality, the communion of the faithful.	Let us treat the five heresies of "Peter of Bruys" one at a time: (1) Of infant baptism in a context describing the rebaptism of Christians: (2) Of the rejection of Holy Places: (3) Of the worship and adoration of the crucifix: (4) Of the continual re-sacrificing of Christ through the offering of the Eucharist: (5) Of refocusing worship for the benefit of the departed and dead:

[102]Louis Bréhier, "Crusades"; available at http://www.newadvent.org/cathen/04543c.htm (online); accessed: 2 Jul 2003; Internet.

~Date	Prayer, Veneration, Sacraments and Other Doctrines	Ecclesiology/Politics	Rival Churches and Movements, Named by Their Antagonists	Biblical Assessment of Rome's Doctrines and Practices
			3. The cross is not an object of adoration; it is on the contrary a detestable object, as the instrument of the torture and suffering of Christ. 4. 4. Priests and bishops dispense a lying teaching as to the matter of the Eucharist. The body of Christ was consumed only one time and only by the disciples, during the communion that preceded the Passion. All other later consumption is only vain fiction. 5. 5. The funeral liturgy in its whole (offerings, prayers, Masses, and alms) is useless; the dead can hope in nothing more than what they received when they were alive.[103] Here is how Iogna-Prat reported the context in which Peter the Venerable found the churches after Peter of Bruis' ministry: "In this introduction, Peter presents the circumstances that led him to inform himself about the "heretical poison" and to compose his work. It is in this place that he fournishes the only somewhat precise historical coordinates that we retain on Peter of Bruis. The Abbott of Cluny explains a reality that existed about 20 years, hence since 1119-1120. The faithful were then rebaptized, the churches were profaned, the altars knocked over, crucifixes turned over to the flames in large bonfires on Easter Sunday; meat was placed on these bonfires to cook and the faithful were invited to eat. Priests were whipped; and monks were locked up and delivered to women."[104]	

---

[103]Dominic Iogna-Prat, "L'argumentation défensive : de la polémique Grégorienne au 'Contra Petrobrusianos' de Pierre le Vénérable," in Monique Zerner, ed., *Inventer l'hérésie? Discours polémiques et pouvoirs avant l'inquisition* [Inventing heresy? Polemic discourses and powers before the inquisition], Collection du centre d'études médiévales de Nice, vol. 2 (Paris: C.I.D., 1998), 88.
[104]Ibid., 87.

~Date	Prayer, Veneration, Sacraments and Other Doctrines	Ecclesiology/Politics	Rival Churches and Movements, Named by Their Antagonists	Biblical Assessment of Rome's Doctrines and Practices
1139		The 2nd Lateran Council, Canon 23, decreed an anathema against all those who were non-sacramentalists; Also in this council, Rome claims its power over kings to dispense "justice": • 20. As is right, we do not deny to kings and princes the power to dispense justice, in consultation with the archbishops and bishops. The anathemas of the 2nd Lateran Council led to the systematic persecution and martyrdom of Henricians and Petrobusians in Southern France.	The 15th decree of the council protects inquisitors from those who would do them harm: • 15. In the same way we have decided to legislate that if anyone, at the instigation of the devil, incurs the guilt of the following sacrilege, that is, to lay violent hands on a cleric or a monk, he is to be subject to the bond of anathema; and let no bishop presume to absolve such a person unless he is in immediate danger of death, until he has been presented before the apostolic See and submits to its decision. We also prescribe that nobody dare to lay hands on those who flee to a church or cemetery. If anyone does this, let him be excommunicated	Contra, "Bless those who persecute you; bless and curse not," Rom 12:14; cf. James 3:9-10 Contra, Matt 5:44, "But I say to you, love your enemies, bless those who curse you, do good to those who hate you, and pray for those who spitefully use you and persecute you" Contra: Rom 12:21, "Do not be overcome by evil, but overcome evil with good"; 1 Thess 5:15, "See that no one renders evil for evil to anyone, but always pursue what is good both for yourselves and for all." See A.D. 1002 for further treatment in regards to martyrdom. The 1139 decision of the Second Lateran Council decreed protection for the "clerics or monks" from those who would lay hands on them. As inquisition became a major practice in the church, the office of Holy Inquisition (or the "Holy Office") had to be protected by the local political powers. People who dared to kill or harm an inquisitor were themselves anathema (see 1208 where the murder of inquisitor Peter de Castelnau led to the "Albigensian Crusade" against the peoples of Southern France, resulting in the annihilation of their language and civilization).
1143		[St] Bernard of Clairveaux preached against the Henricians in Southern France, pronouncing over them a curse: It appears that Rome's habit of pronouncing anathemas against critics or opponents goes back at least this far!		Thereby initiating what would become one of the greatest and most prolonged genocides in world history (all in the name of Jesus) This cursing of Bernard was against the clear teaching of Scripture: • Rom 12:14, "Bless those who persecute you; bless and do not curse"
1145-1147		Rome's "**Second Crusade**" preached by [St] Bernard of Clairvaux (1091-1153) and headed by Louis VII, to recapture the Holy Land.		[For preliminary analysis of Rome's crusades, see 1066, 1095-1101, and 1181]
1159-1181		"**Alexander III: This one placed his foot on the throat of the Emperor Frederick Barbarossa**" (de Hainault, #50)		Perhaps seeking to show that he was "King of kings and Lord of lords"? Being exalted to that role by the power and authority of the Church of Rome.
1164	Death of Peter the Lombard, author of the *Sentences*, which turned theology into a search for "signs and symbols" (spiritual graces [or powers] imputed into physical objects by certain prayers and ceremonies) rather than merely	The very beginning of Peter the Lombard's *Four Books of Sentences* (~1155-1160 A.D.), with the pivotal first quote of Augustine (Book 1, Distinction 1, Paragraph 1, Sentence 1): "While considering the contents of the Old and	Peter the Lombard's *Sentences* paved the way for the "Holy" inquisition and the murder of those who would not accept Rome's sacramental system	**From this point forward, "signs and symbols" became the Central Interpretive Motif or foundation of the church of Rome's theology— how to be saved and how to believe, and practice—how to worship and live (e.g. of theology adapting to practice). Master Peter used "sentences" from Augustine as proofs for this Central Interpretive Motif.** **Allegorical Interpretation**: When signs and wonders were made a Central Interpretive Motif,

~Date	Prayer, Veneration, Sacraments and Other Doctrines	Ecclesiology/Politics	Rival Churches and Movements, Named by Their Antagonists	Biblical Assessment of Rome's Doctrines and Practices
	"hearing and believing"	New Law again and again by diligent chase [indagine], the prevenient grace of God has hinted to us, that a treatise on the Sacred Page is [versari] chiefly about things and/or signs. For as Augustine, the egregious Doctor, says in the book *on Christian Doctrine*:[1] '**Every doctrine is of things, and/or signs**. But even things are learned through signs. But here (those) are properly named things, which are not employed to signify anything; but signs, those whose use is in signifying.'"[105] [Footnote 1: "Chapter 2, n. 2; here and in the next passage, but with many words omitted by Master (Peter) and not a few added or changed."]		this meant (1) that one had to look beyond a "literal" or "literalistic" view, to a more educated (2) figurative or allegorical view. Allegorical interpretation thus became the norm in the Church of Rome, except for those passages that were deemed beneficial to Rom's jurisprudence, such as "upon this rock I will build My church" (Matt 16:28). Quite contrary to "signs and symbols," Rom 10:17 makes faith a matter of hearing and believing God's Word alone, as do many other Bible portions, e.g. John 4:39-42; 5:24; Acts 15:7-11; Rom 3:21-26. Further, Romans 8 makes it clear that the Christian walk is a matter of the Spirit of God and not the reliance on the flesh: <ul><li>Rom 8:1-5 (Geneva), "Now then there is no condemnation to them that are in Christ Iesus, which walke not after the flesh, but after the Spirit. For the Lawe of the Spirite of life, which is in Christ Iesus, hath freed mee from the lawe of sinne and of death. For (that that was impossible to ye Lawe, in as much as it was weake, because of ye flesh) God sending his owne Sonne, in ye similitude of sinful flesh, and for sinne, condened sinne in the flesh, That that righteousnes of the Law might be fulfilled in vs, which walke not after ye flesh, but after the Spirit. For they that are after the flesh, sauour the things of the flesh: but they that are after the Spirit, the things of the Spirit."</li></ul> Rome's sacraments are a matter of "signs and symbols" (something physical, fleshly, or of the flesh) wherein the spiritual power lies intermingled in the water of Baptism, the wafer of the Lord's supper (called the Holy Host), the anointing oil (deemed "Holy Oil"), not to mention other Holy objects, such as the crucifix, statues, candles, etc. These objects are supposedly given spiritual power to avert evil or bring good by special prayers. The ceremonies originally instituted by Christ, with the addition of many others, were gradually converted into Druid-like rituals, akin to a type of white magic. The worship of objects is condemned in 2 Kings 18:3-4, and the giving of talismanic power to physical objects is condemned as "hunting for souls" in Ezek 13:17-23 Note also that the author of Hebrews made it very clear that it is not a matter of coming to signs and symbols which may be touched, as in the Old Covenant: <ul><li>Heb 12:18-21, "For you have not come to the mountain that may be touched and that burned with fire, and to blackness and darkness and tempest, and the sound of a trumpet and the voice of words, so that those who heard *it* begged that the word should not be spoken to them anymore. (For they could not</li></ul>

---

[105]Peter the Lombard, *Four Books of Sentences*, Book 1, "On the Unity and Trinity of God," Distinction 1, Chapter 1, "Every doctrine concerns things and/or signs"; available at: http://www.franciscan-archive.org/lombardus/opera/ls1-01.html (online); accessed: 16 May 2006; Internet.

~Date	Prayer, Veneration, Sacraments and Other Doctrines	Ecclesiology/Politics	Rival Churches and Movements, Named by Their Antagonists	Biblical Assessment of Rome's Doctrines and Practices
				endure what was commanded: 'And if so much as a beast touches the mountain, it shall be stoned or shot with an arrow.' And so terrifying was the sight *that* Moses said, 'I am exceedingly afraid and trembling.')"
1164b	An important part of Lombard's Four Books of Sentences was the formalizing of Rome's salvific sequence through the Seven Sacraments. Hence reports Encyclopedia Britannica: "In the 12th century the number of sacraments of the Western Christian church was narrowed by the theologian and bishop Peter Lombard to seven: baptism, confirmation, the Eucharist (the Lord's Supper), penance, holy orders, matrimony, and extreme unction. This enumeration was accepted by St. Thomas Aquinas, the Council of Florence (1439), and the Council of Trent (1545–63)."[106]			In the development of the Sacraments, the Sacrament of Holy Orders (ordination or priesthood) established a two-level Christianity. Gregory I used Moses going up Mount Sinai as the example that only a particular group were to ascend the hill and interpret and apply the Scriptures. This segmented two-tier Christianity goes against the concepts of soul-competency and the priesthood of all believers, and its resulting form of church government, congregational rule. Consider, for example, the second point Paul's statement in 1 Cor 8:1: 1 Cor 8:1, "Now concerning things offered to idols: We know that we all have knowledge. Knowledge puffs up, but love edifies."
1167		Bulgarian Bishop Nicétas arrived from Constantinople to the chateau Saint-Félix-de-Caraman° to ordain six bishops in four bishoprics for the independent church of Toulouse (Southern France). Information is preserved in the Charter of Niquinta (circa 1232)°2z2; these churches were later called "Albigensian" and "Cathar" and were considered Manichean (by using Augustine's *Contra Manichean*)	The Bulgarian Bishop Nicetas travelled to Southern France and ordained six Cathar or Albigensian Bishops; thereby organizing a rival church to that of Rome in Southern France. His ordinations were preserved in the "Charter of Ninquinta" (available at: http://www.couleur-lauragais.fr/pages/journau x/ 2005/cl69/histoire.html; accessed: 21 Sept 2007; Internet)	The ordination of so-called "Cathar"[107] Bishops by the Bulgarian Bishop Nicetas explains why the Cathars were later called "Bogomiles" (with derision). Their teaching on man's depravity and separation from the world made them perfect targets for the accusation of being Manichean, and their rejection of Infant Baptism and the Eucharist allowed the leveraging of the Christological controversy against them. Once accused of Manicheanism, then Augustine's writings, gathered under the title *Contra Manichean* [Against the Manicheans] could be used to prove that they were heretics. Eventually their "heresy" would result in a series of crusades against the Albigenses of Southern France (1181, 1209-1227, 1240-1255), followed by decades of Inquisition. These events led Jean Odol, a contemporary French historian, to call his region (Laurangais, France) the land of "blood and fire": • 1139, inquisition begun ◦ In 1143 in Southern France, when recruiting and raising funds for the crusade in the Holy Land, Bernard of Clairveaux "cursed the cities that refused him a hearing"[108]

---

[106]"Sacrament"; available at: http://www.britannica.com/topic/sacrament (online); accessed: 15 Feb 2016; Internet.

[107]The word "Cathar" means "pure one" or "clean one," not unrelated to the derogatory names used in modern times, such as Puritan, Pietist, Holiness movement, etc. (see the objection of Innocent III, Cum ex Iniuncto, in 1199 A.D.)

[108]Bede Jarrett, O.P., *Life of Saint Dominic* (London: Burns Oates and Washbourne, 1934), 23-24; cited from O'Leary, *Life and Times of St Dominic* (London, 1912), 45.

~Date	Prayer, Veneration, Sacraments and Other Doctrines	Ecclesiology/Politics	Rival Churches and Movements, Named by Their Antagonists	Biblical Assessment of Rome's Doctrines and Practices
				• 1159, inquisition rejuvenated by [Pope] Alexander III
				○ 1181, Papal Legate Henry of Clairveaux took up the cross of crusade against the Albigenses of Southern France; he and his knights captured Lavaur
				• 1184, [Pope] Lucius III's "Ad Adolendam" condemned Waldenses as heretics and excommunicated them (meaning "extirpation from the world through death")
				• 1198, Papal inquisition again established
				• 1208, inquisitor Peter of Castalnau was murdered and canonized
				• 1214-1215, The Dominican Order was established whose first mandate was to "extirpate heresy"
				• 1233, Itinerating inquisition established; Inquisitor Conrad of Marburg murdered; three Dominican inquisitors thrown into a well in Cordes, France
				• [For more details see the Inquisition and Martyrdom chart]
				The establishment of Orthodox [Byzantine] Bishops in Southern France seems to have been taken to be an act of war against the rule, authority, and land acquisitions of the Church of Rome, it led to skirmishes and finally to the Albigensian Crusade (1215-1255) followed by the ensuing Inquisition against them. The church of the Latins of Constantinople, the church of the Greeks, the Philadelphian church of Romania, and the Church of Bulgaria being listed as a heretical in Reinerius Sacchonius' 1250 book describing the 16 sects "of the Cathars and the Poor Men of Lyons."
1179		Third Lateran Council condemned Albigensian heretics by using the name of their region, "in Gascony and the regions of Albi and Toulouse [France]." Further, it appears that Pope Alexander III was instrumental in requiring all Roman Catholic Bishops to be involved in inquisition in their diocese: • Kidnapping those suspect of heresy; • Keeping them in church-run jails (in the basements of the homes of Bishops or Dominican houses); • Holding them without any time restraints; • And questioning them on religious matters, regarding themselves	Pope Alexander III wrote against the preaching of the Waldenses: "And because some, under an appearance of piety... protect their authority to preach... we bind them by the same bond of anathema all those who, even though they have been prohibited from doing so neither have they been sent, dare to preach either privately or publicly without having received the authorization of the Apostolic Seat or the Bishop of their locality..."[109]	Further appealing to the bigotry of the masses of people against Southern France, and inciting a crusading spirit among the Northern French (which were part of a different country at that time). Bernard of Clairveaux had cursed these cities in 1143, and 30 years later, in 1209, the crusade preacher Jacques de Vitry coined the term "Albigenses" as he called for a crusade against them. This move by Pope Alexander III basically put the Gospel on house arrest, and the house in which it was to be found had long been given over to ritualism. It wasn't long until the Bible was prohibited from unapproved clergy (cf. Augustine, Contra Donatisten), and then from the laity (1229). Hence, these popes went against 1 Cor 9:14: 1 Cor 9:14 (NAS), "So also the Lord directed those who proclaim the gospel to get their living from the gospel." At what point is inquisition "stealing a person"? Deut 24:7 (NKJ), "If a man is found kidnapping any of his brethren of the children of Israel, and mistreats him or sells him, then that kidnapper shall die; and you shall put away the evil from among you." The word for "kidnapping" in Hebrew is ganab, the same verb used in Exod 20:15 and Deut 5:19 for

---

[109]DS 760-761; translations mine.

~Date	Prayer, Veneration, Sacraments and Other Doctrines	Ecclesiology/Politics	Rival Churches and Movements, Named by Their Antagonists	Biblical Assessment of Rome's Doctrines and Practices
		and others, using all manner of torture.		"Thou shalt not steal." At what point was the office of "Holy Inquisition" multiplying those who kidnapped others and mistreated them (for the sake of the Holy Faith)? And at what point was this new approach to the mission of the church not condoning and multiplying larceny, both of humans and their lands and holdings, as well as multiplying those who inflicted pain and torment? Can any culture handle such religious leadership? May the reader consider how far removed Holy Inquisition is from the fulfilling of Christ's Great Commission, to go into all the world and preach the Gospel to all creation (Mark 16:15).
1181		**First Albigensian Crusade** (not considered an official "crusade" by Rome), led by Papal Legate, Henry, Abbott of Clairveaux, following in the footsteps of his predecessor, Bernard of Clairveaux		Contra, Matt 5:44, "But I say to you, love your enemies, bless those who curse you, do good to those who hate you, and pray for those who spitefully use you and persecute you" Contra: Rom 12:21, "Do not be overcome by evil, but overcome evil with good"; 1 Thess 5:15, "See that no one renders evil for evil to anyone, but always pursue what is good both for yourselves and for all." Contra "Put your sword back into its place" Matt 26:52.
1184	**"The Inquisition, instituted by the Council of Verona"** (Boettner, #25)	Pope Lucius III's *Ad Adolentam*, excommunicated heretics who "assumed the authority to preach" (e.g. Waldenses) Institution of organized searches for heretics, called "Inquisitions," to extirpate non-Catholics, Council of Verona	The Waldensians were deemed Heretics, after Peter Valdo was anathematized by the new Bishop of Lyons, France[110]	Falsely applying Deut 13 to the NT church, while ignoring Deut 12:29-31; due to the false view of the church as a political theocracy, soon to be considered having authority over the entire world; removal of the opportunity for lay people to obey the Great Commission to preach the Gospel to all nations as commanded by Christ (Mark 16:15)
1188-1192		Rome's **"Third Crusade"**; preached by Gregory VII, and conducted by Philip Augustus of France, Holy Roman Emperor, Frederick Barbarossa of Germany, and Richard the Lionhearted of England was to regain the Holy Land from Saladin, first Sultan of Egypt and Syria, founder of the Ayyubid dynasty		[For preliminary analysis of Rome's crusades, see 1066, 1095-1101, and 1181]
1190	**"Sale of indulgences**			Selling forgiveness of sins seems parallel to or to be

---

[110]"3. Finally, the history of Waldo in Lyons appears exemplary as regards the invention of the heresy and the establishment of the "Society of Persecution" that Robert Ian Moore described. Waldensianism as a heresy is not born in Lyon with Waldo, as the same, if my hypothesis is correct, collaborates with the Archbishop. It is outside of Lyon that it is born from the moment where this collaboration is rejected, and that Waldo and his followers have become not only useless but more so dangerous, and as a consequence they are condemned and chased out of Lyon" (Michel Rubellin, "Au temps où Valdès n'étais pas hérétique: hypothèses sure le rôle de Valdès à Lyon," in Monique Zerner, ed., *Inventer l'hérésie? Discours polémiques et pouvoirs avant l'inquisition*, Collection du centre d'études médiévales de Nice, vol. 2 [Paris: C.I.D., 1998], 217; translation mine).

~Date	Prayer, Veneration, Sacraments and Other Doctrines	Ecclesiology/Politics	Rival Churches and Movements, Named by Their Antagonists	Biblical Assessment of Rome's Doctrines and Practices
	[began]" (Boettner, #26)			worse than simony, Acts 8:19
				Offering spiritual services for money was likewise decried in Micah 3:5, 11 (cf. the sin of Balaam; 2 Cor 2:17; Jude 11; etc.)
				Notice that Esau sold his birthright for a mess of red pottage, not finding a place for repentance! Heb 12:16-17
				Indulgences for the living and for the dead, contra Deut 26:14 (see below in 1471)
1191		Urban II affirmed that the ordination of Clement III was based on Simony (DS 702); this was merely the application of the 1st Lateran Council's (1123) Canon 1		Herein, all ordinations not approved by Rome are considered "Simony" if the ordinand receives any financial assistance from those who ordained him (hence all Protestants are guilty of Simony—purchasing spiritual benefit, as well as stealing from what rightfully belongs to Rome). Consider again Paul's command in 1 Cor 9:14: 1 Cor 9:14 (NAS), "So also the Lord directed those who proclaim the gospel to get their living from the gospel." In the NAS translation, the onus of gaining his own support is made a responsibility of the preacher [plain rendering of the text], however, in the normal KJV translation history (based on the state-church model), the onus is placed on an unmentioned outside party: 1 Cor 9:14 (KJV), "Even so hath the Lord ordained that they which preach the gospel should live of the gospel." 1 Cor 9:14 (RSV), "In the same way, the Lord commanded that those who proclaim the gospel should get their living by the gospel." 1 Cor 9:14 (NKJ), "Even so the Lord has commanded that those who preach the gospel should live from the gospel."
1198		Innocent III on his supreme double power on earth, "Sicut universitatis" (30 Oct 1198) explained the power of the pope as the sun and the power of kings as the moon that gains its glory from the sun (DS767)		Contra "Great men exercise authority over them; it is not so among you," Matt 20:25-26; Mark 10:42-43; with voluntary oversight, 1 Pet 5:2
1198	"Innocent III: The *Decretals* were then made on the Trinity and the Catholic faith" (de Hainault, #51) The title "Vicar of Christ" solved several problems in Rome's theology: • Christ [alone] appointing leaders, Eph 4:11, hence anyone not appointed by the Pope through the sacrament of ordination, where not appointed by	Innocent III (1198-1216) took the title "Vicar of Christ" [in the place of Christ] (see citation in 1199] Therefore, the prophecy of Rev 11:15 was fulfilled in the Papacy: • "Then the seventh angel sounded: And there were loud voices in heaven, saying, 'The kingdoms of this world have become *the kingdoms* of our Lord	It is clear that rival churches did and do not see from the Scriptures that the "successor" of Peter, whoever that may be, and however that may or may not be determined, was the Bishop of Rome Therefore, the distinctive doctrine of the Bishop of Rome as the "Vicar of Christ" sets the Church of Rome apart from all other	Most Evangelicals and Baptists would think the doctrine of the Pope as actual "Vicar of Christ" as so ridiculous, that they can scarcely imagine or believe that it is truly upheld, much less do many understand the total impact of its teaching. • Using: "Christ is head of the church," Eph 5:23, for worldly benefit • Contra: "No one was found worthy," Rev 5:4; • Contra Jesus having all authority, Matt 28:18; taking the authority of Jesus for Himself, as head of the Church, Eph 1:22; • Rather: "many will come in My name saying, 'I am He', and will mislead many," Mark 13:6; Luke 21:8;

~Date	Prayer, Veneration, Sacraments and Other Doctrines	Ecclesiology/Politics	Rival Churches and Movements, Named by Their Antagonists	Biblical Assessment of Rome's Doctrines and Practices
	Christ, and did not have the authority to preach the Gospel or administer the "sacraments", and could therefore rightfully be anathematized and condemned to death by fire • Only God being able to forgive sins, Mark 2:17; Luke 5:21	and of His Christ, and He shall reign forever and ever!" Rev 11:15 Therefore, the Chiliast tendency alluded to at the turn of the 1st millennium (cf. 1000 A.D.) was doctrinally codified by Innocent III. For example, Leo XIII *Caritatis Studium* (1898) used this concept to quoted Luke 10:16 as applying to himself: • "But the supreme teaching authority was committed to one, on whom, as on its foundation, the Church must rest. For Christ when He gave the keys to Peter, gave him at the same time the power to govern those who were charged with the 'ministry of the word:' 'Confirm thy Brethren' (Luke xxii. 32). And since the faithful must learn from the 'magisterium' of the Church whatever pertains to the salvation of their souls, it follows that they must also learn from it the true meaning of Scripture" [Leo XIII *Caritatis Studium* (1898), §6].	Christian churches in modern history When the title "Vicar of Christ" is combined with the political power of the "Two Swords," then Psa 2 may be read as referring to the Pope: Psa 2:7-12, "I will declare the decree: The LORD has said to Me, 'You *are* My Son, Today I have begotten You. Ask of Me, and I will give *You* The nations *for* Your inheritance, And the ends of the earth *for* Your possession. You shall break them with a rod of iron; You shall dash them to pieces like a potter's vessel.' Now therefore, be wise, O kings; Be instructed, you judges of the earth. Serve the LORD with fear, And rejoice with trembling. Kiss the Son, lest He be angry, And you perish *in* the way, When His wrath is kindled but a little. Blessed *are* all those who put their trust in Him." Consider: 1. The clear Christological context, "You are My Son"; 2. The need to request for catholicity, "the nations"; 3. Ruling by a rod of iron, consider the iron crown given to the Holy Roman Emperor, Dan 2:33, 40; 7:7, 19; 4. The fealty of all the kings [political] and judges [jurisprudence] of the earth; 5. The need to fear this man, and to kiss him; 6. That the death penalty is allotted to him, "and you perish in the way."	"Then if anyone says to you, 'Behold, here is the Christ,' or 'There *He is*,' do not believe *him*," Matt 24:23; "Then if anyone says to you,`Look, here *is* the Christ!' or,`Look, *He is* there!' do not believe it," Mark 13:21. • Christ [alone] has been given a name above every name (Eph 1:21; Phil 2:9-10), and He will share His glory with no other (Isa 42:8; 48:11; cf. Matt 4:9-10; Luke 4:6-8). • Perhaps this is why the John used the term "only-begotten" when referring to Christ, emphasizing His uniqueness and separateness from all others (John 1:14, 18; 3:16, 18; 1 John 4:9; cf. Heb 11:17); note also that the author of Hebrews makes a clear distinction between Christ and all other beings, including angelic, in Hebrews 1 The theological impact of the Pope taking the title "Vicar of Christ" is **staggering** (see below: *Catechism*, §1547-1549), it makes the Pope the present incarnation of Christ on earth today!—by the way, could this not be the greatest blasphemy possible? For example, note the impact of reading Col 1:15-19 as referring to the Bishop of Rome: • The Bishop of Rome is the [vicarious] image of the God-man on earth, Col 1:15? • The Bishop of Rome is before all things, Col 1:16? • All things were created for the Bishop of Rome and by him, Col 1:16? • The Bishop of Rome is before all things and all things subsist by him, Col 1:17? • The Bishop of Rome is the head of the Church, Col 1:18? • In the Bishop of Rome God's fullness dwells, Col 1:19? Consider the impact of the following verses on the doctrine of the Pope as "Vicar of Christ": • God told Peter of Jesus at the Transfiguration, "listen to him" (Matt 17:5; Mark 9:7; Luke 9:35); • Luke 6:46, "And why do you call Me, 'Lord, Lord,' and do not do what I say?" • Matt 7:22-23, "Many will say to Me [Christ/the Pope] on that day, 'Lord, Lord, did we not prophesy in Your name [Christ], and in Your name [Christ] cast out demons, and in Your name [Christ] perform many miracles?' And then I will declare to them [non-Catholic 'Christians'], 'I [the Pope] never knew you; depart from Me, you who practice lawlessness.'" Furthermore, by way of false application: • All who do not bow the knee to and/or verbally confess the "Vicar of Christ," must therefore be refusing to bow the knee to and/or verbally confess Christ Himself, Phil 2:10-11! • All who oppose the Pope, must therefore oppose Christ Himself, Matt 12:30; Luke 11:23 (contra Mark 9:40; Luke 9:50) • All who deny this role for the Pope, must therefore deny Christ Himself, Matt 10:33; 26:34-35, 70-75 (and parallels); Luke 12:9; 1 Tim 5:8 (note Aquinas' use of

~Date	Prayer, Veneration, Sacraments and Other Doctrines	Ecclesiology/Politics	Rival Churches and Movements, Named by Their Antagonists	Biblical Assessment of Rome's Doctrines and Practices
				this verse); 2 Tim 2:12; 3:5; Titus 1:16; 2 Pet 2:1; 1 John 2:22-23; Jude 4

- All who don't believe that the Pope has this position, must therefore disbelieve in Christ Himself, therefore literally being "unbelievers", Matt 13:58; 17:17; Luke 12:45-46; Jude 5
- Those who do not preach this role for the Pope, are therefore stumbling blocks fit only to be cut off and burned, Matt 18:5-9

Now let's consider the impact of "Vicar of Christ" on eschatology (again, "a little leaven leavens the whole lump of dough, Gal 5:9):

- If Christ is on earth, through His incarnate "look-alike", the "Vicar of Christ," then we ought no longer expect Christ's Second Coming; the Second Coming of Christ becomes a mute point, or
- Believing in another Second Coming is actually a heretical concept (Millennarianism), being that it is not accepting the current [Millennial] reign of the Pope (the "Vicar of Christ") in Rome as legitimately fulfilling all the prophecies of the reign and rule of Christ, the kingdom of God, etc.
- The following are merely small steps that took place in the Early to Medieval Church of Rome:
  - From Rome being the only valid arbitrator of theological disagreements (Augustine);
  - To Rome ruling spiritually over the entire Christian church in all the world (Gregory VII's *Dictatus*);
  - To the [present and future] "Kingdom of God" being the here-an-now territorial reign of Christ from Rome;
  - To Rome being the "New Jerusalem come down from Heaven," Rev 21:2;
  - To Christ ruling over everything [church and state] through His Vicar on earth (Innocent III; cf. Eph 1:21-23):
    - Rev 1:5, "from Jesus Christ, the faithful witness, the first-born of the dead, and the ruler of the kings of the earth"
  - To military crusades against contrary organized states (both Muslim and heretical Christian groups), followed by colonization of barbarian regions, and that for territorial acquisition and aggrandizement of Rome's [rightful spiritual] holdings
  - Likewise it is another very small step to proclaim, announce, or confirm that the "official" pronouncements of the Pope are infallible (Vatican I; by the way, something that all Catholics knew already), and that was taught since the Pope was made the arbitrator of all theological debates during the time of Leo I (454)!

Similarly, a book on eschatology, relating a view negative to a premillennial return of Christ, may never mention that the reason for their view is that they believe the Pope to be the incarnation of Christ.

Furthermore, what does "Vicar of Christ" do to the doctrine of the Incarnation (Christology), so important for the Sacramental and anti-Evangelical "development" of theology in the Early Church? How

~Date	Prayer, Veneration, Sacraments and Other Doctrines	Ecclesiology/Politics	Rival Churches and Movements, Named by Their Antagonists	Biblical Assessment of Rome's Doctrines and Practices
				do the *Christotokos* and *Theotokos* debate influence the doctrine of the "Vicar of Christ"? Is that why Mary must be the "Mother of the Church" ever giving "birth" to one Pope after another as the "Vicar of Christ"? And how would a person considering himself the "Vicar of Christ" understand? • That Jesus was the "only-begotten" of the Father (John 1:), or • That God "did not spare His own Son" (Rom 8:32)
1198-1204		Rome's **"Fourth Crusade"** against Constantinople (therefore against a rival sacramental Christian state-church), preached by Innocent III, took and ransacked Constantinople; the purpose of the crusade was to render the Greeks in submission to Rome.[111]		Innocent III seems to have been following the dictum, "God helps those who help themselves," as it relates to the worldwide earthly rule of the Church of Rome. [For preliminary analysis of Rome's crusades, see 1066, 1095-1101, and 1181]
1199	How does the title "Vicar of Christ" impact Christology (e.g. the Creed of Chalcedon), which doctrine has been used since Augustine to denigrate any so-called "heretics"? Here is the impact of this doctrine as recorded in the 1994 *Catechism of the Catholic Church*, in the section on the "Sacrament of Holy Orders": "1547. The ministerial or hierarchical priesthood of bishops and priests, and the common priesthood of all the faithful participate, 'each in its own proper way, in the one priesthood of Christ.' ... "1548. In the ecclesial service of the ordained minister, it is Christ himself who is present to his Church as Head of his Body, Shepherd of his flock, high priest of the redemptive sacrifice, Teacher of Truth. This is what the Church means by saying that the priest, by virtue of the sacrament of Holy Orders, acts *in persona Christi Capitis*: "'It is the same priest, Jesus Christ, whose sacred person his minister truly represents. Now the minister, by reason of the sacerdotal consecration which he has received, is truly made like to the high priest and possesses the authority to act in the power and place of the person of Christ himself (*virtute ac persona ipsius Christi*) [citing Pius XII, Encyclical Letter: *Mediator Dei* (20 Nov 1947); AAS 39]. "'Christ is the source of all priesthood: the priest of the old law was a figure of Christ, and the priest of the new law acts in the person of Christ" [citing Aquinas, *Summa Theologica*, III; Q22; A4]. "1549. Through the ordained ministry, especially that of bishops and priests, the presence of Christ as head of the Church is made visible in the midst of the community of believers. In the beautiful expression of St. Ignatius of Antioch, the bishop is *typos tou Patros*: he is like the living image of God the Father [citing St. Ignatius of Antioch, *Ad Trall*. 3, 1: 2Ch 10, 112; cf. *Ad Magn*. 6, 1:SCh 10, 124]" (*Catechism*, §1547-1549).		This obvious false teaching did not sit unchanged, but evolved into further false teaching. Consider the fate of unbelievers in the doctrine of the Pope as Vicar of Christ, as applied to these verses: Jude 1:4-7, "For certain persons have crept in unnoticed, those who were long beforehand marked out for this condemnation, ungodly persons who turn the grace of our God into licentiousness and deny our only Master and Lord, Jesus Christ. Now I desire to remind you, though you know all things once for all, that the Lord, after saving a people out of the land of Egypt, subsequently destroyed those who did not believe. And angels who did not keep their own domain, but abandoned their proper abode, He has kept in eternal bonds under darkness for the judgment of the great day. Just as Sodom and Gomorrah and the cities around them, since they in the same way as these indulged in gross immorality and went after strange flesh, are exhibited as an example, in undergoing the punishment of eternal fire." Luke 12:45-46, "But if that slave says in his heart, 'My master will be a long time in coming,' and begins to beat the slaves, *both* men and women, and to eat and drink and get drunk; the master of that slave will come on a day when he does not expect *him*, and at an hour he does not know, and will cut him in pieces, and assign him a place with the unbelievers" [remembering that Luther was called a drunkard because he broke his monastic vows]
1199	Innocent III issued a Decretal on Heresy, *Vergentis in senium*	Episcopal inquisition established by Innocent III against those who studied		Against, Matt 5:44, "But I say to you, love your enemies, bless those who curse you, do good to those who hate you, and pray for those who

---

[111]"In his first Encyclicals he [Innocent III] summoned all Christians to join the crusade and even negotiated with Alexius III, the Byzantine emperor, trying to persuade him to re-enter the Roman communion and use his troops for the liberation of Palestine. ... At the news of these most extraordinary events, in which he had had no hand, Innocent III bowed as in submission to the designs of Providence and, in the interests of Christendom, determined to make the best of the new conquest. His chief aim was to suppress the Greek schism and to place the forces of the new Latin Empire at the service of the crusade" (Louis Bréhier, "Crusades"; available at http://www.newadvent.org/cathen/04543c.htm [online]; accessed: 2 Jul 2003; Internet).

~Date	Prayer, Veneration, Sacraments and Other Doctrines	Ecclesiology/Politics	Rival Churches and Movements, Named by Their Antagonists	Biblical Assessment of Rome's Doctrines and Practices
	(25 Mar 1199), written to the Papal in which he equates heresy to treason, applying Roman Law of 397 A.D. (*Quisquis*) to heresy against the Church of Rome, and tightening up the penalties.[112]	the Bible or owned a vulgar translation (DS770-771; see below).		spitefully use you and persecute you" Contra: Rom 12:21, "Do not be overcome by evil, but overcome evil with good"; 1 Thess 5:15, "See that no one renders evil for evil to anyone, but always pursue what is good both for yourselves and for all." Notice all the false Scriptural backing in Deut 13 and the passages cited above.
1199	Innocent III's *Cum ex Iniuncto* taught the necessity of the Magisterium of the church for proper biblical interpretation (DS770-771)	Innocent III's "Cum ex Iniuncto" To the inhabitants of Metz [12 July 1199] "Our venerable brother, the Bishop of Metz [Lorraine, France], We have come to know from his letter that in his diocese as well as in the town of Metz a rather important number of lay people and of women, drawn in some way by a desire for the Scriptures, made for themselves translations into the French language of the Gospels, the epistles of Paul, the Psalter, the Moralia of Job, and many other books; ... (with the result being) that in the secret gatherings lay people and woman dare to belch forth to each other and to mutually preach, and they equally despise the company of those who are not mixed up in such things ... Some of them also despise the simplicity of their priests, and when a word of salvation is proposed to these latter, they whisper in secret that they have better in their writings and that they are capable of express them more judiciously. "Even if a desire to understand the divine Scriptures and the care to exhort in conformity with them is not to blame but quite the opposite commendable, these people deserve nevertheless to be reprimanded that they hold secret conventicles, and that they usurp the office of preaching, that they scoff at the simplicity of the priests and that they distain the company of those that do not attach themselves to such practices. God in fact ... hates to this point the works of darkness that he commanded and said (to the apostles): "What I tell you in the dark, say it in the daylight; that which you hear in the deep of your ear proclaim it from the rooftops" (Matt 10:27); by this it is clearly manifest that the preaching of the Gospel ought to be proposed not in secret conventicles, as is done by the heretics, but publicly in the Church, in conformity with		False application of Jesus (hence, the Vicar of Christ) opening the minds of the disciples to understand the Scriptures, Luke 24:45 Based on the teachings of Augustine, here is the point at which the Pope became the final arbiter of all questions theological, practical, and political. Likewise, his decisions and/or teachings, which are considered to be a part of Holy Tradition, were and are considered infallible. Notice in Cum ex Iniuncto how Innocent III despised the private interpretation of the home Bible study movement in Metz, Lorraine, France. So also he did not appreciate their separation from the Church of Rome and its practices. Herein is a good example of the Pope shutting down the lay preaching of the gospel—therefore, lay people fulfilling the Great Commission.

---

[112]"Fifteen years later Innocent III felt that since, in spite of previous firm legislation, the cancer of heresy was continuing to spread, even more severe measures were called for. So, in 1199 he issued *Vergentis in senium*. This confirmed the previous measures, but it went a bit farther in that it drew a clear parallel between heresy and treason and stated that the same penalty should be inflicted for both these crimes; and it extended these penalties to the children of heretics whether they were orthodox Catholics or not. The severity of the penalties enjoined by this papal constitution was clearly derived from a harsh imperial measure of the late fourth century,--the constitution *Quisquis*—which had been an emergency measure to meet a particular crisis and which in fact does not seem to have been put into effect, though, of course, it was included in the *Codox*. That the sanctions were adopted from the Roman law is indicated by the wording of the papal decree:

[citing X. 5. 7. 10. (*Vergentis in senium*); cf. *Codex* 9. 8. 5. Quisquis].

"Innocent III does not stipulate the death penalty for heresy; '*Ecclestica districtione*' obviously refers to the penalty of excommunication. But on the matter of the disinheritance of the children the papal decree goes further than the imperial legislation, since it enjoins that not even orthodox Catholic children are allowed to inherit,—'*cuiusdam miserationis praetextu*'. Roman law, on the other hand, did permit the orthodox children of condemned heretics to succeed to their inheritance [cf. Cod. I. 5,19]. This contradiction between the Roman law and canon law led, as will be seen shortly, to a controversy among later canonists. *Vergentis in senium* also forbade lawyers to assist heretics in any way under pain of *infamia* and deprivation of office.

"All this very severe legislation was confirmed by the Fourth Lateran Council, but neither Innocent III nor the council had advocated the death penalty for heresy. Fines, confiscation of property, disinheritance of heirs, imprisonment and exile had all been permitted by the Church, but that was as far as it went. The last step was taken by the Emperor Frederick II when in 1224 he decreed that those convicted of heresy in certain of his territories were to be burnt alive. This later was accepted by Pope Gregory IX, and in 1231 he decreed that life imprisonment should be the penalty for repentant heretics..." (Clarence Gallagher, *Canon Law and the Christian Community: The Role of Law in the Church according to the Summa Aurea of Cardinal Hostiensis* [Roma: Universita Gregoriana, 1978], 190-92).

~Date	Prayer, Veneration, Sacraments and Other Doctrines	Ecclesiology/Politics	Rival Churches and Movements, Named by Their Antagonists	Biblical Assessment of Rome's Doctrines and Practices
		Catholic custom. … "Such is the depth of the holy Scriptures that not only simple and uncultivated people, but even those who are wise and learned are not able to scrutinize the meaning. This is why the Scripture says: "For many of those who sought failed in their search"(Psa 64:7). Also was it correct that it was established in the divine Law that if an animal touches the Mountain (of Sinai) he should be stoned (cf. Heb 12:20; Ex 19:12ff), in order that in fact no simple or uncultivated man should have the presumption to touch upon the sublimities of the holy Scripture or to preach it to others. It is written in fact: "Do not seek that which is too high for you" (Sir 3:22). This is why the apostle said: "Do not seek more than what is necessary to seek, but seek with sobriety" (Rom 12:3). "Similarly just as the body numbers many members, but not all the members have the same activity, likewise, the Church counts many levels, but not all have the same duty, for according to the Apostle "The Lord has given some as apostles, others as prophets, but others as doctors, etc." (Eph 4:11). Therefore the doctor is in some ways the principal in the church and this is why no one ought to usurp without deference the office of preacher" (DS 770-771)		
1202	The verb transubstantiated was used by Innocent III in his letter *Cum Marthae circa* (29 Nov 1202) to the Archbishop of Lyons: "You have asked in fact who, regarding the form of the words that Christ Himself expressed when He transubstantiated the bread and the wine into His body and His blood, added this word in the canon of the Mass utilized by the general Church, and that no evangelist expressed, as we can read. … In the canon of the Mass this word, being "mystery of the faith," finds itself in fact inserted into these words. … "Surely we find many things, words as well as actions of our Lord, that have been omitted by the evangelists and that, as we can read it, the apostles completed orally or expressed by their action" (DS782)			Herein, it is clear that there was push back from the Jean [de Bellesmains], Archbishop of Lyons, France, on the issue of portions of the ritual of the Mass not being from the words of the Bible. One also gets the idea that there was push back on the issue of transubstantiation, as can be documented in the preaching of Henry of Lausanne (whom Peter the Venerable wrote against in 1134-1135), the Second Lateran Council's condemnations (1139), as well as those of the Council of Verona (1184), and in the writings of Gerard de la Motte (1218). Notice that Innocent III answered by an appeal to unwritten oral and practiced tradition, whose establishment likely began with Gregory I (590-604), who promoted the Gallican Missal as the proper model, while allowing for some regional nuance. Archbishop Jean also asked the good question about the "transubstantiation" of the water into wine: when the form of the substance was in actually changed. This Innocent III answered in DS 784. "Equally, you have asked if the water at the same time as the wine is changed into blood. On this topic the opinions vary among the scholastics. Some in fact think that, since from the side of Christ flowed the two principal sacraments, that of redemption in the blood and that of regeneration in the water, the wine and water that are mixed in the chalice are changed in these two by divine virtue … Others on the other hand hold that the water is transubstantiated into blood with the wine, because mixed with wine it becomes wine … On the other hand it can be said that the water does not become wine, but that it remains encircled by the accidens of the exterior wine . … "But it is impious to think what some have had the presumption of thinking, that being that the wine is

~Date	Prayer, Veneration, Sacraments and Other Doctrines	Ecclesiology/Politics	Rival Churches and Movements, Named by Their Antagonists	Biblical Assessment of Rome's Doctrines and Practices
				changed into phlegm. ... "Nevertheless among the opinions mentioned above, the one is considered the most probable, that the water is changed into blood with the wine" (DS 784). For some rebuttal, see A.D. 851. Also, one writing asked, how can Christ be in heaven and on earth at the same time? (see "Placards Incident," 1534). Also, does it not say in Matthew, that if anyone says of Christ, "he is here," do not believe them (Matt 24:23)?
1204			Last Catholic-Cathar debate, included Bishop of Osma, Diego, and Durand d'Osca [de Huesca]	
1207			Durand d'Osca converts to Catholicism	
			Durand d'Osca founds the "Poor Catholics" the first in a string of "Lower Orders" founded to combat the spread of heresy: • 1208-1209, the Franciscans of [St] Francis; • 1210, the Poor Reconciled of the "first" Bernard; • 1215, the "Brothers Preachers" (Dominicans) of [St] Dominic	
1208		Waldsensian "leader" Durand d'Osca subscribed to a statement of faith reaffirming the distinctive theologies of the Church of Rome (DS 790-797) Note in particular this statement against the preaching (or evangelism) of the heretics: "We believe that preaching is very necessary and honorable, however we believe that it must be accomplished by virtue of the authority or with the permission of the sovereign pontiff or the prelates. But in all the places where manifest heretics live who deny and blaspheme God and the faith of the Roman Church, we believe that we must, according to the will of God, confound them	One item in the statement of faith of Durand d'Osca: "We do not condemn the saying of vows, even more, we believe from a sincere heart that it is permitted to swear according to the truth, judgment, and righteousness" (DS 795) Please consider the context as described in 1999 by French Medievalist Jean Duvernoy: "A second question upon which I would like to draw attention, is that it is absolutely necessary to separate the Waldenses from the Cathars. The Waldenses of the early period were not heretics, but schismatics, and not even that: they are simply disobedient. They wished	Rome seemed to widely disseminate this "statement of faith" of this traitor to the Waldenses, their evangelism efforts, and their cause, which statement is still used in Denzinger—Amazing! When the saying of vows became an issue is hard to determine; however, here is a timeline of issues: 15th Century B.C.: Moses specifically wrote of those who desisted from taking a vow, that it was not sin: Deut 23:22 (NKJ), "But if you abstain from vowing, it shall not be sin to you." 1st Century A.D.: Jesus spoke against the taking of special vows in Matthew 5: Matt 5:33-36 (NKJ), "Again you have heard that it was said to those of old, 'You shall not swear falsely, but shall perform your oaths to the Lord.' But I say to you, do not swear at all: neither by heaven, for it is God's throne; nor by the earth, for it is His footstool; nor by Jerusalem, for it is the city of the great King. Nor shall you swear by your head, because you cannot make one hair white or black." 475 A.D.: the Benedictine (and other monastic) vows became famous in Western Christianity, these same vows were preached against by Peter de Bruis and

~Date	Prayer, Veneration, Sacraments and Other Doctrines	Ecclesiology/Politics	Rival Churches and Movements, Named by Their Antagonists	Biblical Assessment of Rome's Doctrines and Practices
		through debate and exhortation, and oppose ourselves to them with the Word of the Lord, with heads held high and unto death, as against adversaries of Christ and of the Church" (DS 796).	to stay in the Church but they did not want to obey the prohibition to preach without authorization. For them, the rule was the evangelical example, the Sermon on the Mount, and, as said Valdès, it is to obey the counsels as also the precepts. The Waldensian has the obligation to obey the precepts: you shall not kill, you shall not take an oath ('Me I tell you not to swear at all'). He must equally conform himself to the *consilia*, as to the examples of the apostolic and evangelical lifestyle. The prohibition against vowing brought many Waldenses to the stake."[113]	Henry of Lausanne (in the 12th Century) 11th and 12th Centuries: Urban II (1088-1099) and Innocent III (1198-1216) or their legates preached in the open air to large crowds calling them to come forward for a public commitment to fight in the crusades, at which time they received a cloth cross which they were to sew to their garments until they had completed their crusade vow. 1522: Notice that the Lutheran Francois Lambert d'Avignon also opposed the unbiblical monastic vows that he had made when he entered a strict Franciscan monastery in Avignon, France (see 529 A.D.). 1527: Following both the teaching of Scripture and the historical precedent of the Albigenses and Waldenses, the 1527 Anabaptist Schleitheim Confession specifically forbade the taking of an oath.[114] Eventually, the inquisitors would ask their prisoners if they would make a vow. A negative response an almost sure indication that they were speaking to an Albigensian, Waldensian, or Anabaptist, depending on the location and the time period.[115]

[113]Jean Duvernoy, "Table Ronde," in *Évangile et évangélisme (XIIe-XIIIe siècle)* [*The Gospel and Evangelism (12th-13th Centuries)*], Cahiers de Fanjeaux, No 34 (Nice, France: Privat, 1999), 235-36.

[114]"VII. We are agreed as follows concerning the oath: The oath is a confirmation among those who are quarreling or making promises. In the Law it is commanded to be performed in God's Name, but only in truth, not falsely. Christ, who teaches the perfection of the Law, prohibits all swearing to His (followers), whether true or false - neither by heaven, nor by the earth, nor by Jerusalem, nor by our head - and that for the reason He shortly thereafter gives, For you are not able to make one hair white or black. So you see it is for this reason that all swearing is forbidden: we cannot fulfill that which we promise when we swear, for we cannot change (even) the very least thing on us. Now there are some who do not give credence to the simple command of God, but object with this question: Well now, did not God swear to Abraham by Himself (since He was God) when He promised him that He would be with him and that He would be his God if he would keep His commandments, - why then should I not also swear when I promise to someone? Answer: Hear what the Scripture says: God, since He wished more abundantly to show unto the heirs the immutability of His counsel, inserted an oath, that by two immutable things (in which it is impossible for God to lie) we might have a strong consolation. Observe the meaning of this Scripture: What God forbids you to do, He has power to do, for everything is possible for Him. God swore an oath to Abraham, says the Scripture, so that He might show that His counsel is immutable. That is, no one can withstand nor thwart His will; therefore He can keep His oath. But we can do nothing, as is said above by Christ, to keep or perform (our oaths): therefore we shall not swear at all (nichts schweren). Then others further say as follows: It is not forbidden of God to swear in the New Testament, when it is actually commanded in the Old, but it is forbidden only to swear by heaven, earth, Jerusalem and our head. Answer: Hear the Scripture, He who swears by heaven swears by God's throne and by Him who sitteth thereon. Observe: it is forbidden to swear by heaven, which is only the throne of God: how much more is it forbidden (to swear) by God Himself! Ye fools and blind, which is greater, the throne or Him that sitteth thereon? Further some say, Because evil is now (in the world, and) because man needs God for (the establishment of) the truth, so did the apostles Peter and Paul also swear. Answer: Peter and Paul only testify of that which God promised to Abraham with the oath. They themselves promise nothing, as the example indicates clearly. Testifying and swearing are two different things. For when a person swears he is in the first place promising future things, as Christ was promised to Abraham. Whom we a long time afterwards received. But when a person bears testimony he is testifying about the present, whether it is good or evil, as Simeon spoke to Mary about Christ and testified, Behold this (child) is set for the fall and rising of many in Israel, and for a sign which shall be spoken against.

Christ also taught us along the same line when He said, Let your communication be Yea, yea; Nay, nay; for whatsoever is more than these cometh of evil. He says, Your speech or word shall be yea and nay. (However) when one does not wish to understand, he remains closed to the meaning. Christ is simply Yea and Nay, and all those who seek Him simply will understand His Word. Amen" ("The Seven Articles of Schleitheim, Canton Schaffhausen, Switzerland [February 24, 1527]"; available at: http://www.anabaptists.org/history/schleith.html; accessed 28 Oct 2009; Internet).

[115]For example, here is an excerpt from the record of a famous Catholic inquisitor, Jacques Fournier, who later became Pope Benedict XII (1334-1342):

"Confession of Agnes, wife of the late Etienne Francou, a heretic or of the sect of the Poor of Lyons (diocese of Vienne).

"In the year of the Lord 1319, Thursday, the feast of St. Lawrence, Agnes, the wife of the late Etienne Francou of Vermela, in the diocese of Vienne, who was captured with Raymond de Costa, otherwise called 'of the Holy Faith', who was vehemently suspected of the heresy of the Waldensians or the Poor of Lyons, brought before the presence of the reverend father in Christ Lord Jacques, by the grace of God, bishop of Palmiers, having been sent for by this same bishop, who wished to question her concerning certain issues touching the Catholic faith, and especially concerning the Waldensian heresy and others who had been denounced and were strongly suspected of heresy, asked that she swear on the holy Gospels given to her, to tell the truth as much concerning herself as principal as concerning those others both alive and dead as witness.

"The above-said Agnes did not wish to swear an oath on the command of my said lord bishop, even though he gave her ample opportunity to do so, but said that she would never swear an oath concerning anything, even to save her life.

"-----Why? For what reason do you refuse to swear an oath? About a year ago, I was ill and I was anointed; I received extreme unction from a curate who was called, I believe, Etienne, who was the vicar of the church in that place. After the anointing and confession that I made to him, he ordered me never, for any reason or in any circumstances, to swear or take a personal oath, nor to walk barefoot. He added that our Lord Jesus Christ had not lied out of fear of death, and

~Date	Prayer, Veneration, Sacraments and Other Doctrines	Ecclesiology/Politics	Rival Churches and Movements, Named by Their Antagonists	Biblical Assessment of Rome's Doctrines and Practices
				As explained by Medievalist, Jean Duvernoy, the deeper issue seems to be one of biblical interpretation: Is the Christian going to interpret the Bible in a straight-forward-common sense way, or is the person going to interpret the Bible according to the interpretive scheme

that I ought never to lie out of fear of death, but to tell the truth, without oath in response to questions that anyone posed to me. I promised him I would not take an oath for any reason.

"-----Do you believe that swearing in order to tell the truth is a sin? Yes, after what this curate told me.

"-----Were you instructed by anyone else besides this Etienne never to take an oath to tell the truth? No.

"-----Have you said to anyone or any others not to take oaths? No.

"-----Have you ever taken an oath? No. ...

"January 18. She was once again asked by my said lord bishop to swear to tell the truth concerning herself as well as others, both living and dead, concerning the faith, each time being presented frequently a book containing the Gospels. She would not take an oath at all, but turned her face from the Gospel book which was presented to her, bringing forth the same reason for not taking an oath as above.

"-----Do you believe that taking an oath to tell the truth is a sin? Since I have promised not to take oaths, as a result, if I were to take one, I believe I would sin.

"-----If my lord the bishop released you from this promise, would you believe yourself released? Yes.

"-----Well then, if you believe it, and if he released you, would you take an oath? I do not wish to take an oath at all, even to save my life.

"-----Do you believe that swearing to tell the truth is a sin? I do not know; I do not even know what to believe concerning this subject.

"-----Would you be prepared to swear that you are now before my lord the bishop, if in doing so you would be liberated from prison? I will not take any oath at all. ...

"After this, the same year as above, on January 21st, the said Agnes appeared for questioning in the château of Allemans before my said lord bishop, assisted by the said Brother Gaillard de Pomiès.

"The bishop told her once again to swear to tell the truth. She replied that she would not take an oath at all, no matter what. But she asked and begged my said lord bishop not to speak to her anymore concerning taking oaths, because she would not take one ever, just as she stated above.

"After this, the same year as above, on January 23rd, the said Agnes appeared for questioning in the château of Allemans before my said lord bishop, assisted by the said Brother Gaillard de Pomiès.

"-----Do you wish to take an oath? No.

"-----Do you believe it to be a sin? I believe that it is evil to swear by God, by one's faith or by one's belief.

"-----But do you believe that swearing is the same evil as the evil of sin? I believe that it is evil because it is a sin.

"-----Do you believe in Purgatory? Yes.

"The 25th of April 1320, the above said Agnes, appearing for questioning at the chateau of Allemans before my said lord bishop, assisted by the venerable and religious person my lord Brother Jean de Beaune, inquisitor of the heretical depravity in the kingdom of France, commissioned by the Apostolic See, was once again requested by them to swear to tell the truth, and he told her that she was compelled by law to swear when she was judicially requested to do so, and by not doing so, she sinned mortally and that if she persisted obstinately in refusing to swear to tell the truth, as required by law in the case of faith, she could and would be condemned as a heretic.

"Although she was frequently requested and counseled, she replied that she would not take an oath for any reason.

"-----Why? Because God has forbidden all swearing.

"-----If you were to swear to tell the truth, do you believe you would sin mortally? If I myself were to take an oath, I believe I would sin mortally.

"-----You say that you do not know how to read. Who taught you that taking an oath is a sin and against the teaching of the Lord, and specifically swearing to tell the truth? It was Raymond de la Côte, with whom I was arrested, who taught me never to take an oath of any sort, even to tell the truth.

"-----For how long have you believed that taking an oath, even to tell the truth, is a mortal sin? I have believed this for about 20 years.

"The above-named woman was admonished, begged and ordered by our said lords bishop and inquisitor once, twice, and three times for charity to leave and abandon the said errors and heresies which she avowed to have held and still to hold, during many requests and court appearances before my lord the bishop, and now before my said lord inquisitor, to abjure the Waldensian heresy, and the sect of the Poor of Lyons, and to denounce all her companions, accompliced and believers, and return to the faith and unity of the Roman church. She replied that she would not take an oath.

"Our said lords bishop and inquisitor protested that unless she wished to take an oath and abandon her errors, proceedings would begin against her as against a heretic, according to canonical sanctions and the forms of law. Present were my lord Germain de Castelnau, archdeacon of the church of Pamiers, Brother Gaillard de Pomiès, Brother Arnaud du Carla, of the order of the Preachers of the convent of Pamiers, Brother Jean Estère of the same order, companions of my lord the inquisitor, and master Barthelemy Adalbert, notary of the Inquisition. And master Guillaume Peyre-Barthe, notary of my lord the bishop, who wrote and received all of the above said by order of my lords bishop and inquisitor.

"On Wednesday, the 30th of April 1320, I, master Guillaume Peyre-Barthe, notary of my lord the bishop of Pamiers, came in person to the chateau of Allemans and presented myself by the order of my lords the bishop and the inquisitor to the said Agnes, to ask that she appear before them in person the following day before the church of Allemans, to hear the sentence passed on her above confessions. The said Agnes accepted this day purely and simply.

"In the presence of master Marc Rivel, notary of the terre du paréage (terre pariagi), Raymond Gasc of Allemans and Garnot, sargeant of the said terre du paréage, etc.

"The sentence in this case was given thus the 1st of May and is inscribed in the Book of sentences of the Inquisition [note: Agnes was burned along with Raymond.]

"And I, Rainaud Jabbaud, cleric of Toulouse, sworn to the service of the Inquisition, have faithfully corrected this deposition against the original on the order of my lord the bishop above-named." ("Confession of Agnes Francou," translated by Nancy P. Stork; available at: http://www.sjsu.edu/depts/english/Fournier/afrancou.htm; accessed 5 Dec 2006; Internet; the Latin version is known as "Le Registre d'inquisition de Jacques Fournier, évêque de Pamiers : Manuscrit Vat. latin n 4030 de la Bibliothèque vaticane (Bibliothèque méridionale)"; English translation cross-checked with the French translation of Jean Duvernoy, *Le Registre d'Inquisition de Jacques Fournier*, vol 1 (Paris: Bibliothèque des Introuvables, 2006), 123-27.

~Date	Prayer, Veneration, Sacraments and Other Doctrines	Ecclesiology/Politics	Rival Churches and Movements, Named by Their Antagonists	Biblical Assessment of Rome's Doctrines and Practices
				and dictates of Rome?
				One touchstone for a difference in interpretation is the relatively "mild" issue of the saying of vows, which is more of an issue in light of monastic vows and vows for participation in the physical expansion of territory through "Holy Crusades" (billed as "the work of God")
1209-1215		**Second Albigensian Crusade** to capture the Albigensian territories in Southern France, preached and led by [St] Dominic, founder of the Dominicans, and Simon of Montfort		[For preliminary analysis of Rome's crusades, see 1066, 1095-1101, and 1181]
1214	The Virgin Mary was supposed to have appeared to [St] Dominic, presenting him the rosary as "the greatest weapon for conversion"; first public use of Rosary, as Dominic gave it as a weapon to his army the night before battle to encourage them in God's name to massacre Albigensian men, women, and children	In 1214, Dominic, Simon de Montfort, and their armies were ransacking Albigensian territories in the Battle of Bouvines, the capture of the fortresses of Domes and Montfort		In the case of this event, [St] Dominic became a false teacher (according to Gal 1:8-9; 1 John 4:1; etc.) because of an extra- and contra-biblical apparition, which was likely demonic in its origin; their battle against the competing Albigensian church negates "love your enemies" and fulfills the prophecy of Jesus that a day was coming when those killing disciples would think that they were offering a service to God (John 16:2-3) Likewise, the Rosary has become a repetitious chanting of some biblical and non-biblical portions, contra Matt 6:7, "And when you are praying, do not use meaningless repetition, as the Gentiles do, for they suppose that they will be heard for their many words" Repeating the 150 Hail Mary's is supposed to replace the chanting of the 150 Psalms in the Psalter. See above on prayer to the Father only in the name of Jesus, see 1090.

1215	**"Auricular [verbal] confession of sins to a priest instead of to God, instituted by pope Innocent III, in the Lateran Council"** (Boettner, #28)	**"Transubstantiation, proclaimed by pope Innocent III"** (Boettner, #27)
		
		4th Lateran council: princes required to execute convicted heretics under penalty of excommunication (which meant deposing and executing them!). Further, their lands were deeded over:
		
		"We excommunicate and anathematize every heresy raising itself up against this holy, orthodox and catholic faith which we have expounded above. We condemn all heretics, whatever names they may go under. They have different faces indeed but their tails are tied together
			Fourth Lateran Council condemned suspected heretics to the sword; encouraged Second Albigensian crusade	Against heretics:
				• "Let those condemned be handed over to the secular authorities present, or to their bailiffs, for due punishment" (4th Lateran Council)
				• Rome encouraged and taught the use of the secular arm to punish heretics after they had been tried by the Church, much like the Jews asked the Romans to crucify Christ (an interesting precedent)
				Against the Catholic practice of using confessionals:
				• James 5:16, "Confess *your* trespasses to one another, and pray for one another, that you may be healed"
				  ○ The astute reader will notice that both commands to confess and pray include the prepositional phrase "to one another." In the case of Rome's confessionals it is a one way street, removing that important element of the command.
				• Gal 6:2, "Bear one another's burdens, and so fulfill the law of Christ"
				  ○ Again, the all important "one another" providing a level playing field from a discipleship point-of-view

~Date	Prayer, Veneration, Sacraments and Other Doctrines	Ecclesiology/Politics	Rival Churches and Movements, Named by Their Antagonists	Biblical Assessment of Rome's Doctrines and Practices
		inasmuch as they are alike in their pride. Let those condemned be handed over to the secular authorities present, or to their bailiffs, for due punishment. Clerics are first to be degraded from their orders … to make the land available for occupation by Catholics so that these may, after they have expelled the heretics, possess it unopposed and preserve it in the purity of the faith."116 Thereby setting a precedent for Catholic superiority or sovereignty over all lands where this end was achievable. The French King could not hold himself back from this motive to invade the rich land of the Cathar "Hereticks"117		Against transubstantiation: • "In remembrance of Me," Luke 22:19; 1 Cor 11:24-25 • "Then if anyone says to you, 'Behold, here is the Christ,' or 'There *He is*,' do not believe *him*" Matt 24:23 Commanding citizens of a given country to rebel against their prince, on the basis of the fact that he or she is not a good Catholic, goes against the teaching of the Apostle Paul in Titus 3:1: • Titus 3:1, "Remind them to be subject to rulers and authorities, to obey, to be ready for every good work" In calling for crusade against their rival church of the Albigenses of Languedoc in Southern France, the Pope was falsely applying Deut 13:12-18 to his far-reaching political theocracy: • Deut 13:15-16 (DRA), "Thou shalt forthwith kill the inhabitants of that city with the edge of the sword, and shalt destroy it and all things that are in it, even the cattle. And all the household goods that are there, thou shalt gather together in the midst of the streets thereof, and shalt burn them with the city itself, so as to consume all for the Lord thy God, and that it be a heap for ever: it shall be built no more." Through use of the language of Deut 13, he called for the extermination of whole cities and regions of these that he deemed to be heretical peoples. Meanwhile, the Pope gave indulgences [remission of sins] for those who participated in these Holy Crusades against the heretics. The promise of remission of sins was repeated in council after council related to the funding of or participation in Holy Crusades: • Fourth Lateran Council (1215), Section 3, "On Heretics": "Catholics who take the cross and gird themselves up for the expulsion of heretics shall enjoy the same indulgence, and be strengthened by the same holy privilege, as is granted to those who go to the aid of the holy Land" • First Council of Lyons (1245), Section 3, "Admonitions...": "Therefore we earnestly beg all of you, commanding you in our lord Jesus Christ, that by your pious admonitions you should persuade the faithful committed to your care, in your sermons or when you Impose a penance upon them, granting a special indulgence, as you see it to be expedient, that in their wills, in return for the remission of their sins, they should leave something for the help of the holy Land or the eastern empire"

116"If however a temporal lord, required and instructed by the church, neglects to cleanse his territory of this heretical filth, he shall be bound with the bond of excommunication by the metropolitan and other bishops of the province. If he refuses to give satisfaction within a year, this shall be reported to the supreme pontiff so that he may then declare his vassals absolved from their fealty to him and make the land available for occupation by Catholics so that these may, after they have expelled the heretics, possess it unopposed and preserve it in the purity of the faith—saving the right of the suzerain provided that he makes no difficulty in the matter and puts no impediment in the way. The same law is to be observed no less as regards those who do not have a suzerain" (Fourth Lateran Council [1215]; available at: : http://www.dailycatholic.org/history/12ecume1.htm; accessed: 23 June 2003).

117"It had to be that the country tempting the appetite of the *Capétien* become heretical in order to be conquered. 'Albigensian' became synonymous to heretical and a crusade followed, legitimizing the conquest. Today the preferred nomenclature for this country is 'Country of the Cathars,' which is nothing more than the latent but zealous echo of the propaganda for crusade. Thus the identity constructs itself by looking at the other" (Jacques Dalarun, "Conclusion," in *Évangile et évangélisme (XIIe-XIIIe siècle)*, Cahiers de Fanjeaux 34 [Toulouse, France: Éditions Privat, 1999], 336).

~Date	Prayer, Veneration, Sacraments and Other Doctrines	Ecclesiology/Politics	Rival Churches and Movements, Named by Their Antagonists	Biblical Assessment of Rome's Doctrines and Practices
				• Second Council of Lyons (1274), Constitution 1, "The fines prescribed in this constitution are to be exacted in full through the authorities of the place where blasphemy is committed, and through others who exercise temporal jurisdiction there. Coercive measures, if necessary, are to be taken through diocesan and other local ordinaries. The money is to be assigned to the collectors for the subsidy. Moreover, we strictly command confessors who hear confessions by ordinary jurisdiction or by privilege to prompt and enjoin on their penitents to give the said money to the holy Land in full satisfaction for their sins; and they should persuade those making wills to leave, in proportion to their means, some of their goods for aid to the holy Land. We direct also that in each church there should be placed a box fitted with three keys, the first to be kept in the possession of the bishop, the second in that of the priest of the church, the third in that of some conscientious lay person. The faithful are to be instructed to place their alms, as the Lord inspires them, in this box for the remission of their sins. Mass is to be sung publicly in the churches once a week, on a certain day to be announced by the priest, for the remission of such sins and especially of those offering alms. ... To those who do not go there in person but send suitable men at their own expense, according to their means and status, and likewise to those who go in person but at others' expense, we grant full pardon for their sins" • Council of Vienna (1311), Section 5, Help for the Holy Land: "We grant the same power to your delegates, in each city or diocese for which they have been delegated.... This power may also be used to constrain any opponents and rebels. In addition, we grant full and unrestricted power to you to absolve in your cities and dioceses.... In order that you and your delegates may have a reward for the labours undertaken, we enjoin on you the above things in remission of your sins"
1215		The Dominican Order, under the leadership of [St] Dominic is established by Bishop Diego: "By an official document, which is still extant, Bishop Foulques constituted Brother Dominic and his companions preachers in the diocese of Toulouse. They were to [1] extirpate heresy, [2] combat vice, [3] teach the faith, and [4] train men in good morals."[118]	The founding of the Dominicans, and the establishment of the Albigensian crusade did not bode well for these separatist churches in Southern France	Thus the first point in the commissioning for the Dominican Order (designated by the letters O.F.P. for *Ord Fratrum Praedicatorum*,.or O.P. for *Ordo Praedicatorum*) was borrowed from the OT language of extermination, which was communicated at several levels. The verb "extirpate" was used in Sirach 47:8 and 1 Maccabees 3:35. Sirach says of King David: • Sir 47:7-8 (DRA), "So in ten thousand did he glorify him, and praised him in the blessings of the Lord, in offering to him a crown of glory: For he destroyed the enemies on every side, and extirpated the Philistines the adversaries unto this day: he broke their horn for ever" Of King Antiochus seeking to extirpate the memory of the Jews from Jerusalem: • 1 Macc 3:35 (DRA), "And that he should send an army against them, to destroy and root out [Vulgate: *extirpandam*] the strength of Israel,

[118]Pierre Mandonnet, O.P., *St. Dominic and His Work,* trans by Mary Benedicta Larkin, O.P. (St. Louis: B. Herder, 1948), 27.

~Date	Prayer, Veneration, Sacraments and Other Doctrines	Ecclesiology/Politics	Rival Churches and Movements, Named by Their Antagonists	Biblical Assessment of Rome's Doctrines and Practices
				and the remnant of Jerusalem, and to take away the memory of them from that place"
				The concept of "extirpate" parallels the language of Deuteronomy concerning the complete removal of the Canaanite nations and their memory from what was to become Israel:
				• Deut 12:29-31 (NKJ), "When the LORD your God cuts off from before you the nations which you go to dispossess, and you displace them and dwell in their land, take heed to yourself that you are not ensnared to follow them, after they are destroyed from before you, and that you do not inquire after their gods, saying, 'How did these nations serve their gods? I also will do likewise.' You shall not worship the LORD your God in that way; for every abomination to the LORD which He hates they have done to their gods; for they burn even their sons and daughters in the fire to their gods"
				More importantly to this study, it is the language used to deal with false teachers and false prophets that are seeking converts from among the people:
				• Deut 13:5 (DRA), "And that prophet or forger of dreams shall be slain: because he spoke to draw you away from the Lord your God, who brought you out of the land of Egypt, and redeemed you from the house of bondage: to make thee go out of the way, which the Lord thy God commanded thee: and thou shalt take away the evil out of the midst of thee [Vulgate: *et auferes malum de medio tui*]" (cf. Deut 13:11, 17)
				• Deut 17:12 (DRA), "But he that will be proud, and refuse to obey the commandment of the priest, who ministereth at that time to the Lord thy God, and the decree of the judge, that man shall die, and thou shalt take away the evil from Israel"
				These commands against the false teachers in the Book of Deuteronomy became the primary Great Commission for the founding of the Dominican Order, counter-intuitively called an order of "preachers."
1215		On June 15, 1215 in Runnymede, English barons pressured King John of England to sign the *Magna Carta*, ensuring the individual liberties of the English people, as described by Lord Denning: The Magna Carta was, "The greatest constitutional document of all time, the foundation of the freedom of the individual against the		

~Date	Prayer, Veneration, Sacraments and Other Doctrines	Ecclesiology/Politics	Rival Churches and Movements, Named by Their Antagonists	Biblical Assessment of Rome's Doctrines and Practices
		arbitrary authority of the despot."[119] This document provided for rule by a document, rather than mere rule by the unfettered whims of a monarch.		
1215-1227		**Third Albigensian Crusade**, fueled by the Third Lateran Council, Simon of Montfort (d. 1218)[120] and Prince undertook the task of territorial war against the Albigenses; Toulouse finally fell into the hands of the king of France through marriage alliances		[For preliminary analysis of Rome's crusades, see 1066, 1095-1101, and 1181]
1217		Rome's "**Fifth Crusade**" included the capture of Damietta on Egypt's Nile delta		[For preliminary analysis of Rome's crusades, see 1066, 1095-1101, and 1181]
1220	**"Adoration of the wafer (Host), decreed by pope Honorius III"** (Boettner, #29) The wafer (or Host) was/is called "the Lamb of God", and Mass was the "Eucharistic sacrifice," or the duplication (or multiplication) of the sacrifice of Christ on the cross for sins			Blatant idolatry, contra Exod 20:4-6 (and very many other Scriptures)
1221			"The heretics lurk in this region [Bosnia] from their dens," wrote [Pope] Honorius III in 1221, "but, after the example of the vampire that breastfeeds its young with naked breast, they dogmatize in public and openly preach their depraved errors."[121]	
1224		Holy Roman Emperor Frederick II "decreed that those convicted of heresy		

---

[119]Daniel Hannan, "Magna Carta: Eight Centuries of Liberty," The Saturday Essay, *Wall Street Journal* (30 May 2015).

[120]The memory of Simon of Montfort was sung as follows: ""Si, pour tuer des hommes et répandre le sang, pour perdre des âmes, pour consentir à des meurtres, pour croire des conseils pervers, pour allumer des incendies, pour détruire des barons, pour honnir Parage [détruire l'honneur], pour prendre des terres par violence, pour faire triompher orgueil, pour attiser le mal et éteindre le bien, pour tuer des femmes, égorger des enfants, on peut en ce monde conquérir Jésus-Christ, il doit porter couronne et resplendir dans le ciel !" (Simon IV de Montfort; available at: http://fr.wikipedia.org/wiki/Simon_IV_de_Montfort (online); accessed 2 Feb 2013; Internet).

[121]Christine Thouzellier, *Un traité cathare inédit du debut du XIIIe siècle d'après le Liber Contra Manicheos de Durand de Huesca* (Louvain: Publications Universitaires, 1961), 38; citing Potthast 6725; T. Smičiklas, *Codex...*, III, p. 196 (171), 3 déc. 1221; - Potthast 6749; *Codex...*, p. 198 (174), 5 déc. 1221: "*in partibus Bosnie ... heretici receptati ... dogmatizando palam sue pravitatis errores*"; translation from the French mine.

~Date	Prayer, Veneration, Sacraments and Other Doctrines	Ecclesiology/Politics	Rival Churches and Movements, Named by Their Antagonists	Biblical Assessment of Rome's Doctrines and Practices
		in certain of his territories were to be burnt alive. This was later accepted by Pope Gregory IX"[122]		
1228-1229		Rome's "Sixth Crusade" was largely diplomatic on the part of Frederick II, in which certain temporary alliances expanded German holdings in the Holy Land		[For preliminary analysis of Rome's crusades, see 1066, 1095-1101, and 1181]
1229		**"Bible forbidden to laymen, placed on the index of Forbidden Books by the Council of Toulouse"** (Boettner, #30) "*Lay people shall not have books of Scripture, except the psalter and the divine office: and they shall not have these books in the vulgar tongue.* Moreover we prohibit that lay people should be permitted to have books of the Old or New Testament, except perchance any should wish from devotion to have a psalter, or a breviary for the divine office, or hours of the blessed Virgin: but we most strictly prohibit their having even the aforesaid books translated into the vulgar tongue"[123] Without a Bible to study for spiritual growth and discipleship, Roman Catholic lay people were left to read approved theological books, such as Peter the Lombard's *Sentences*, if they could read Latin. Nor were they allowed to speak to anyone about spiritual things outside of a Roman Catholic church building, hearing it only from approved clergy in the church (see 1179).		Contra admonitions to read the Bible: Col 4:16 "Now when this epistle is read among you, see that it is read also in the church of the Laodiceans, and that you likewise read the *epistle* from Laodicea" 1 Thess 5:27, "I charge you by the Lord that this epistle be read to all the holy brethren" 1 Tim 4:13, "Till I come, give attention to reading, to exhortation, to doctrine" Contra admonitions and examples to study Scripture: Josh 1:8, "This Book of the Law shall not depart from your mouth, but you shall meditate in it day and night, that you may observe to do according to all that is written in it. For then you will make your way prosperous, and then you will have good success" Acts 17:11, "These were more fair-minded than those in Thessalonica, in that they received the word with all readiness, and searched the Scriptures daily *to find out* whether these things were so" 2 Tim 2:15, "Be diligent to present yourself approved to God, a worker who does not need to be ashamed, rightly dividing the word of truth" Contra the admonition to handwrite the Bible: Deut 17:18, "Also it shall be, when he sits on the throne of his kingdom, that he shall write for himself a copy of this law in a book, from *the one* before the priests, the Levites" Contra admonitions regarding the importance of the Bible: Acts 20:32, "So now, brethren, I commend you to God and to the word of His grace, which is able to build you up and give you an inheritance among all those who are sanctified" Cf. 2 Tim 3:16-17; 2 Pet 1:20-21; etc. Contra further biblical teachings: Note how often Jesus questioned: "Have you not read," Matt 12:3, 5; 19:4; 22:31; Mark 2:25; 12:26 "Have you never read," Matt 21:16, 42 "Have you not even read," Mark 12:10; Luke 6:3 Note the comment, "whoever reads, let him

---

[122]Clarence Gallagher, *Canon Law and the Christian Community: The Role of Law in the Church according to the Summa Aurea of Cardinal Hostiensis* (Roma: Universita Gregoriana, 1978), 192.

[123]Margaret Deanesly, *The Lollard Bible and Other Medieval Biblical Versions* (Cambridge University Press, 1920; Eugene, OR: Wipf and Stock, 2002), 36-37.

~Date	Prayer, Veneration, Sacraments and Other Doctrines	Ecclesiology/Politics	Rival Churches and Movements, Named by Their Antagonists	Biblical Assessment of Rome's Doctrines and Practices
				understand," Matt 24:15
				Notice how the Ethiopian Eunuch was made open to spiritual things by reading, Acts 8:28-32
				Note that Paul assumed that those to whom he wrote would read his letter: Eph 3:3-5, ""how that by revelation He made known to me the mystery (as I have briefly written already, by which, when you read, you may understand my knowledge in the mystery of Christ), which in other ages was not made known to the sons of men, as it has now been revealed by the Spirit to His holy apostles and prophets"
				The blessing available to those who read the Bible: Rev 1:3, "Blessed *is* he who reads and those who hear the words of this prophecy, and keep those things which are written in it; for the time *is* near"
1231		"Pope Gregory IX in *Excommunicamus* decreed life imprisonment for repentant heretics,— '*damnatio vero per ecclesiam saeculari iudicio relinquantur, animadversione debita puniendi, clericis prius a suis ordinibus gradatis*'. In 1231, however, it was quite clear that the *debita animadversion* meant burning at the stake. By appointing special envoys to ensure that his anti-heretical legislation was carried out in various parts of the Church, Gregory IX also established the Inquisition, empowering judges delegated by himself to search out and condemn heretics."[124]		
1240-1241		**Fourth Albigensian Crusade**, in which Carcassonne was beseiged		[For preliminary analysis of Rome's crusades, see 1066, 1095-1101, and 1181]
1243 [1246]		The Council of Beziers, Canon 36 stated: "You will fully watch, according to all that is right and legal, that theological books not be possessed, even in Latin, by lay people, nor in the vulgar language by clerics."[125]		Herein, the prohibition against owning, and therefore reading and studying the Bible was enlarged, to the detriment of Christian discipleship and the spiritual maturity of true believers. True Christians, who were commanded by God to crave the pure milk of the Word (1 Pet 2:2) were being spiritually starved by enactments from a so-called church!
1243-1244		**Fifth Albigensian Crusade**, when Montségur		[For preliminary analysis of Rome's crusades, see 1066, 1095-1101, and 1181]

---

[124]Gallagher, *Canon Law and the Christian Community* (Roma: Universita Gregoriana, 1978), 192-193.
[125]*Histoire du Livre Saint en France*.

~Date	Prayer, Veneration, Sacraments and Other Doctrines	Ecclesiology/Politics	Rival Churches and Movements, Named by Their Antagonists	Biblical Assessment of Rome's Doctrines and Practices
		was taken		
1243-1254	"**Innocent IV: The red caps of the Cardinals were then invented. Several orders and the immunity of monks**" (de Hainault, #52)			
1245		Pope Innocent IV proclaimed a crusade to regain Jerusalem from the Muslim, which did not appear to amount to anything		[For preliminary analysis of Rome's crusades, see 1066, 1095-1101, and 1181]
1249-1252		Rome's "**Seventh Crusade**" in which Louis IX (St. Louis) of France sent two Dominicans with Genghis Khan and gained control of the Island of Cyprus		[For preliminary analysis of Rome's crusades, see 1066, 1095-1101, and 1181]
1250			Dominican Inquisitor Raynerius Sacchoni wrote *Summa de Catharis et Leonistis*, which named and described the 16 denominational churches of the so-called Cathars, as well as that of the Poor Men of Lyons (Waldenses), mostly found in Northern Italy and Southern France	The much copied and cited work of Raynerius provides historical interest regarding the churches and beliefs of the 16 denominations of Cathar churches, who were seen to be "Manichean," much like this charge was laid on the Donatists of the time of Augustine
1251	"**The Scapular*, invented by Simon Stock, an English Monk**" (Boettner, #31) *The Scapular was the wearing of a devotional artifact, said to be of spiritual benefit to the wearer			Contra Ezek 13:17-23
1252		"The process [of Inquisition legislation] was completed by Pope Innocent IV who, in 1252, made the imperial constitutions [of Frederick II in 1224, etc.] applicable throughout the Church, and by the bull, *Ad extirpanda*, he allowed civil authorities to force heretics under torture to		On the "loss of life and limb." The author Gallagher sought to explain the drastic measures to which Inquisition was taken by adding: "Most of the legislation that has just been discussed was certainly intended to frighten the faithful against the danger of being led into heresy and also to compel the heretics to come to their senses and repent."[127]

---

[127]Gallagher, 193.

~Date	Prayer, Veneration, Sacraments and Other Doctrines	Ecclesiology/Politics	Rival Churches and Movements, Named by Their Antagonists	Biblical Assessment of Rome's Doctrines and Practices
	confess their error and denounce their accomplices,—although he did not stipulate that there should be no loss of limb or danger of death in the torture used."[126]			
1255		**Sixth Albigensian Crusade**, in which the last Albigensian stronghold, Quéribus, was taken		[For preliminary analysis of Rome's crusades, see 1066, 1095-1101, and 1181]
1261-1264	**"Urban IV: They place the institution of the Feast of God in his time"** (de Hainault, #53)			
1270		Rome's "**Eighth Crusade**," preached by Humbert de Roman, in which Louis IX (St. Louis) and his three sons took the sign of the cross, with the design of capturing the city of Carthage in Tunisia		[For preliminary analysis of Rome's crusades, see 1066, 1095-1101, and 1181]
1274	The 2nd Council of Lyons required celibacy of the priesthood: "Putting an end to an old debate by the present declaration, we declare that bigamists are deprived of any clerical privilege and are to be handed over to the control of the secular law, any contrary custom notwithstanding. We also forbid bigamists under pain of anathema to wear the tonsure or clerical dress" (Article 16)			The 2nd Council of Lyons answered an "old debate", that of married clergy, calling it an old debate (being that it is so contrary to the Scriptures [see above, 1023]) and calling married clergy "bigamists" as male clergy were presumably married to the church [illustrated as Mary the Holy Mother of the Church] and female clergy were married to Christ, thus those men who were married in an earthly way were considered "bigamists"—married to two women! Interesting is that Rome attacked the Albigenses for not accepting Rome's marriages, as they were deemed (1) a sacrament [means of obtaining grace], and thus only properly conferred by Rome's clergy (meaning any marriage from any schismatic or "heretical" clergy was deemed invalid and adultery), and (2) it was solemnized by the sacrifice of the Mass, which was repugnant to the Albigenses
1275	Thomas Aquinas' *Summa Theologica* defended and promoted the extirpation of heretics by death (SS, Q[11], A[3], "Whether heretics ought to be tolerated?" "I answer that"): "I answer that, With regard to heretics two points must be observed: one, on their own side; the other, on the	Where Catholics are not in power, they should avoid making Rome appear offensive, even participating in the rites of heretics or pagans: "On the other hand, the rites of other unbelievers, which are neither truthful nor profitable are by no means to be tolerated, except perchance in order to avoid an evil, e.g. the	Schismatic evangelism is considered the absolute worst kind of sin: "Nevertheless of all sins committed by man against his neighbor, the sin of schism would seem to be the greatest, because it is opposed to the spiritual good of the multitude" (SS, Q[39], A[2]; cf. SS, Q[6], A[6]; SS, Q[94], A[3]; etc.) Therefore,	Contra Paul's exclamation in Phil 1:15-18, "…Christ is proclaimed; and in this I rejoice, yes, and I will rejoice."

---

[126]Gallagher, *Canon Law and the Christian Community* (Roma: Universita Gregoriana, 1978), 192-193.

~Date	Prayer, Veneration, Sacraments and Other Doctrines	Ecclesiology/Politics	Rival Churches and Movements, Named by Their Antagonists	Biblical Assessment of Rome's Doctrines and Practices
	side of the Church. On their own side there is the sin, whereby they deserve not only to be separated from the Church by excommunication, but also to be severed from the world by death. ... much more reason is there for heretics, as soon as they are convicted of heresy, to be not only excommunicated but even put to death. On the part of the Church, however, there is mercy which looks to the conversion of the wanderer, wherefore she condemns not at once, but 'after the first and second admonition,' as the Apostle directs: after that, if he is yet stubborn, the Church no longer hoping for his conversion, looks to the salvation of others, by excommunicating him and separating him from the Church, and furthermore delivers him to the secular tribunal to be exterminated thereby from the world by death."	scandal or disturbance that might ensue, or some hindrance to the salvation of those who if they were unmolested might gradually be converted to the faith. For this reason the Church, at times, has tolerated the rites even of heretics and pagans, when unbelievers were very numerous" (SS, Q[10], A[11]), as is the case in the United States	excommunication (extirpation from the world by death) is necessary (SS, Q[39], A[4], "Whether it is right that schismatics should be punished with excommunication?": "Now a schismatic, as shown above (A[1]), commits a twofold sin: first by separating himself from communion with the members of the Church, and in this respect the fitting punishment for schismatics is that they be excommunicated. Secondly, they refuse submission to the head of the Church, wherefore, since they are unwilling to be controlled by the Church's spiritual power, it is just that they should be compelled by the secular power."	
1275			Reply to Objection 1: "It is not lawful to receive Baptism from a schismatic, save in a case of necessity, since it is better for a man to quit this life, marked with the sign of Christ, no matter from whom he may receive it, whether from a Jew or a pagan, than deprived of that mark, which is bestowed in Baptism." Reply to Objection 2: "Excommunication does not forbid the intercourse whereby a person by salutary admonitions leads back to the unity of the Church those who are separated from her. Indeed this very separation brings them back somewhat, because through confusion at their separation, they are sometimes led to do penance" Reply to Objection 3: "The punishments of the present life are medicinal,	SS, Q[39], A[4]. Reply to Objection 2 shows why Roman Catholics can lawfully infiltrate "schismatic" communions to seek to bring back schismatics from separation from Rome. This involvement of families and children in the churches of the heretics provides an entry point for Rome into the society and culture of the heretical churches: • Children of Catholics brought up in heretical churches speak like them and sound like them, which makes them good future political candidates (cf. Janissaries) • The devout Catholic parent, through the confessional, can report back to the local priest about what he/she sees and hears • Confusion of beliefs can be promoted as members of the so-called heretical church do not want to say anything objectionable in the presence of the Catholic parents, who can likewise make false claims about the real teachings of Rome, primarily speaking from ignorance • Intermarriage can be encouraged, thereby weakening the theological principles of further families in the so-called heretical community • Then, in the case of major appointments to positions of ecclesial control (societies, seminaries, etc.), a one issue measuring stick can be applied, neutrality toward the Church of Rome. Roman Catholics appear to have accomplished these ends quite effectively in the past 30-50 years

~Date	Prayer, Veneration, Sacraments and Other Doctrines	Ecclesiology/Politics	Rival Churches and Movements, Named by Their Antagonists	Biblical Assessment of Rome's Doctrines and Practices
			and therefore when one punishment does not suffice to compel a man, another is added: just as physicians employ several body medicines when one has no effect. In like manner the Church, when excommunication does not sufficiently restrain certain men, employs the compulsion of the secular arm. If, however, one punishment suffices, another should not be employed."	among U.S. Evangelicals. The result has been to gradually bring the fruit of 200 years of worldwide Evangelical missions to work in partnership with Rome (especially through the Bible Societies); this section coincides with Aquinas' SS, Q[10], A[11], as noted above.
1294	"Celestin V: This one was duped by his successor, Boniface, who caused him to resign the papacy, crying out to him by night with much racket that God wanted it this way; afterwards he put him in prison" (de Hainault, #54)			
1294-1303	"Boniface VIII: They place the first Jubilee in his time. He told a Ghibelline [member of a German political party] *Memento homo*, and threw ashes in his eyes" (de Hainault, #55)	Boniface VIII, "Unum Sanctum" (18 Nov 1302) reaffirmed the "two suns" of Innocent III by calling them two swords, the spiritual and the secular, the latter "must be exercised for the Church" (DS 873)		Jesus said to Peter, "Put your sword back into its place" Matt 26:52; also against Matt 13:29-30, "Let them both grow together" This teaching appears to follow the following logic: • The Pope as the "Vicar of Christ" (much like Jesus was the "Vicar of God" on earth, Heb 1:3) • Christ being over all things (Eph 1:21-22) • The Pope being over all things (spiritual, governmental, scientific, economic, etc.). Basically, the world is the commune (or monastery), and the Pope is the ruler (or Abbott) of the world commune (almost like Dan 6:7) • [Where Mary, the Mother of the Church and the Queen of Heaven and of Earth, fits into this paradigm of power, with her effervescent spiritual presence, is part of this mystery] An unexpected impact of the "two swords" is that Rome can be made to feel that it is above the law of any particular sovereign nation, as it laws that are universal, supra-national, and supra-governmental: • This supra-governmental authority is taken as a divine right, moreso even than the divine right of kings to reign over their territories; • The communication and recognition of this authority is closely monitored and guarded, so as to appeal to all forms of governments and ecclesiology in any given age ○ In democratic governments, a quiet infiltration approach is more convenient (including through higher education, see Pius VI's *Inscrutabile* [25 Dec 1775])

~Date	Prayer, Veneration, Sacraments and Other Doctrines	Ecclesiology/Politics	Rival Churches and Movements, Named by Their Antagonists	Biblical Assessment of Rome's Doctrines and Practices
				○ When dealing with totalitarian governments, a more bold and aggressive approach can be utilized, while being hidden and denied for the sake of stability in democratic environments
1300	"On February 22, 1300, Boniface VIII published the Bull *Antiquorum fida relatio*, in which, appealing vaguely to the precedent of past ages, he declares that he grants afresh and renews certain 'great remissions and indulgences for sins' which are to be obtained 'by visiting the city of Rome and the venerable basilica of the Prince of the Apostles'. The long trajectory of the practice of indulgences that eventually led to the sixteenth century Protestant Reformation started here."[128]	Ottoman gains control of Turkey[129]		While agreeing with De Chirico on his statement regarding the importance of indulgences in triggering the Protestant Reformation, indulgences for sins were also granted for fighting heretics and for participation in Holy Crusades.
1304-1374		Here is an excerpt from the confidential letters of Petrarch (1304-1374): "I am at present in the western Babylon, than which the sun never beheld any thing more hideous, and besides the fierce Rhone, where the successors of the poor fishermen now live as kings. Here the credulous crowd of Christians are caught in the name of Jesus, but by the arts of Belial; and being stripped of their scales, are fried to fill the belly of gluttons. Go to India, or wherever you choose, but avoid Babylon, if you do not wish to go down alive to hell. Whatever you have heard or read of as perfidy or fraud, pride, incontinence and unbridled lust, impiety and wickedness of every kind, you will find here collected and heaped together. Rejoice, and glory in this, O Babylon, situated on the Rhone, and thou that art the enemy of the		Ascribing to the Church of Rome the likeness of the Woman dressed in scarlet in Revelation 17 is perhaps one of the most difficult exegetical positions to hold. It brings with it ire unlike most other positions. Unearthed are the hidden powers of "nihil obstat" held in secret by publishers and academicians in every denomination and at all levels. It is interesting that the pre-Reformation Petrarch, all the Protestant Reformers, most Puritans and Reformed scholars, and most English Protestant scholars held this position until the mid to late 1900s. In 1888, J. A. Wylie wrote a short book titled, *The Papacy*. In this book he persuasively argued that in all of world history since the birth of Christ, only the Bishop of Rome can rightly be considered the "man of sin" of 2 Thessalonians. As in my case, the many Inquisitions of the Church of Rome (that continued even beyond Napoleon's era) clarified its role as the "Mother of Harlots," as it did to Petrarch.

---

[128]De Chirico, 37.

[129]"Now, after Nicephorus, the Emperors of the East were tossed with continuall warres; for the first, the Bulgars often incountred them, then the Sarazens issuing out of Africa, tooke the Ile of Candie, as afterwards Sicilie, and made hauocke in Asia farre and wide: and last of all the Turks, a people of Scythia.

"The Emperours of Greece, from Nicephorus to Constantine Palaelogus the last, are reckoned as to 50, some whereof were women: but most of those were sloathfull. And in Constantine Monomachus his raign, the Turks from a base originall, by degrees getting ground more and more, began to wast Asia, and daily increase their power, at length made vp a Monarchie, but no new or fifth one, but sprouted out of that part of the Romane Empire lying in the East. Of which Monarchie, Ottoman was the head, about the year 1300" (Sleidan, 228-229).

~Date	Prayer, Veneration, Sacraments and Other Doctrines	Ecclesiology/Politics	Rival Churches and Movements, Named by Their Antagonists	Biblical Assessment of Rome's Doctrines and Practices
		good, the friend of the bad, the asylum of wild beasts, the whore that has committed fornication with the kings of the earth! Thou art she whom the inspired evangelist saw in the spirit; yes, thee, and none but thee, he saw, 'sitting upon many waters.' See thy dress,—'A woman clothed in purple and scarlet.' Dost thou know thyself, Babylon? Certainly what follows agrees to thee and none else—'Mother of fornications and abominations of the earth.' But hear the rest—'I saw,' says the evangelist, 'a woman drunk with the blood of the saints, and the blood of the martyrs of Jesus.' Point out to whom this is applicable but thee."[130]		
1305		The Roman Pontif, Clement V, left Rome and moved to Southern France, beginning the "Avignon Papacy" This move to the "front lines" of the Inquisition against the so-called Albigensian heretics, provided the Pope with greater control of the very lucrative Inquisition with its massive territorial and financial acquisitions.	The so-called "Albigenses" were crushed first by crusade, and then by door-to-door Inquisition under the watchful eye of Clement V and his successors Success in Southern France, as well as prior successes in the territorial expansion of Rome's control became patterns for Rome's future efforts in territorial expansion.	Consider 1 John 2:15-17
1309-1311		Boniface VIII wrote *Romano Pontifici*, where the Latin "pontifex" means "high priest"		Contra Heb 5:1-6 where Christ is the only High Priest, called of God However, note also that Heb 5:1-3 provides Rome a New Testament "precedent" for their entire system of the priesthood: Heb 5:1-3 (Catholic NJB), "Every high priest is taken from among human beings and is appointed to act on their behalf in relationships with God, to offer gifts and sacrifices for sins; 2 he can sympathise with those who are ignorant or who have gone astray, because he too is subject to the limitations of weakness. 3 That is why he has to make sin offerings for himself as well as for the people." (Heb 5:1 NAS), "For every high priest taken from among men is appointed on behalf of men in things pertaining to God, in order to offer both gifts and sacrifices for sins; 2 he can deal gently with the ignorant and misguided, since he himself also is beset

---

[130]Thomas M'Crie, *History of the Progress and Suppression of the Reformation in Italy during the Sixteenth Century* (Edinburgh: William T. Blackwood, 1833; London: T. Cadell, 1833; Elibron Classics, 2004), 22-23.

~Date	Prayer, Veneration, Sacraments and Other Doctrines	Ecclesiology/Politics	Rival Churches and Movements, Named by Their Antagonists	Biblical Assessment of Rome's Doctrines and Practices
				with weakness; [3] and because of it he is obligated to offer *sacrifices* for sins, as for the people, so also for himself."
1311		Regarding relapsed sinners (in the case of the 1311 Council of Vienna, those of the Knights Templar), "With regard to those who are impenitent and have relapsed, if any—which God forbid—be found among them, justice and canonical censure are to be observed"		Whereas, relapse led Rome to censure through excommunication and extirpation in many cases, the Bible tells its readers: • To forgive seventy times seven (Matt 18:22) • To keep no account of wrongs (1 Cor 13:5) Also stating that God: • Removes our sin as far as the East is from the West (Psa 103:12) • Casts our sins behind his back (Isa 38:17) • Remembers our sin no more (Isa 43:25) Surely the church of God should do the same.
1343	Clement VI, in his *Unigenitus Dei Filius* (27 Jan 1343), developed for the first time (acc to Denzinger) the concept of a "Bank of Merits" in heaven, whose merits are distributed by the [Roman Catholic] "Church" (cf. DS1025-1027)			Herein the monopoly of Rome's spiritual authority was again emphasized. Rome, and only Rome, had the authority (via the statement in Matt 16:19), to dispense the merits (or the blessings of their virtues) of Jesus, Mary, and the saints upon the faithful. Those merits were dispensed during the sacrament of penance, whereby absolution was pronounced for confessed sin, and particular acts of penance were required according to the demands of the priest or confessor.
1362-1367		**Roman Crusade** to regain losses in the Holy Land, pillaged and ransacked various eastern Mediterranean cities		[For preliminary analysis of Rome's crusades, see 1066, 1095-1101, and 1181]
1378-1389	"Urban VI: There was another Pope in France, and they excommunicated each one the other" (de Hainault, #56)			
1380s		Wycliffite doctrines considered a threat to Rome and the English church, comes under severe repression under the guise of being a "Peasant Revolt"	So-called "Peasant Revolt" under Wycliffe in England is smothered by the church and the crown.	Rome used the term "Peasant revolt" to crush a revival of Evangelical Christianity in the case of Wycliffe, Hus, the Anabaptist movement, and Luther, and to maintain dominance in the Western church; these so-called "Peasants Revolts" appear to be the desire of populations for freedom of conscience from Rome's oppressive practices These peasants' revolts, as they were called, should rather be called "Revivals of True Spirituality" and "Peaceful Movements for Freedom of Conscience." It was the local bishops and priests that called in the armies of Catholic princes backed by Rome to crush the revival movements and force their adherents to return to Confession, Mass, and the baptizing of their babies in the Church of Rome Rome's proof-texts to deny freedom of conscience and to validate military action seem to be verses like:

~Date	Prayer, Veneration, Sacraments and Other Doctrines	Ecclesiology/Politics	Rival Churches and Movements, Named by Their Antagonists	Biblical Assessment of Rome's Doctrines and Practices
				• Rom 13:1-2, "Let every soul be subject to the governing authorities. For there is no authority except from God, and the authorities that exist are appointed by God. Therefore whoever resists the authority resists the ordinance of God, and those who resist will bring judgment on themselves." • 1 Tim 6:1, "Let all who are under the yoke as slaves regard their own masters as worthy of all honor so that the name of God and *our* doctrine may not be spoken against" It is a stretch for these verses to be used to validate armed military action, especially in light of verses like: • Matt 5:44-45, "But I say to you, love your enemies, bless those who curse you, do good to those who hate you, and pray for those who spitefully use you and persecute you, that you may be sons of your Father in heaven; for He makes His sun rise on the evil and on the good, and sends rain on the just and on the unjust" (cf. Luke 6:27-37) God's Word, however, does make it clear that He does not favor armed military action against the constituted rule of law, for the people by the people (Deut 1). Note that Rome's interference in foreign political processes has been a problem since the time of Augustine's writings against the Donatists (408-412). Its discussion is sometimes called the "Investiture Controversy."
1389-1404	**"Boniface IX: This one found the Annals, and as said Platinus, made a good market of pardons"** (de Hainault, #57)			
1409-1410	**"Alexander V: The Council of Pisa elected Alexander V"** (de Hainault, #58), thereby initiating the Pisan Papacy that lasted until the Council of Constance in 1415			
1414		**"Cup forbidden to the people in communion by Council of Constance"** (Boettner, #32)	This issue addressed a criticism of John Hus, and it led to the Ultraquists (referring to taking communion in both kinds), which issue ultimately divided the Hussites weakening them so that they could ultimately be conquered through a Holy Crusade in the fifth attempt in 1434	Contra, "drink **ye** all of it" [Byz: Πίετε ἐξ αὐτοῦ πάντες], Matt 26:27 [both the verb and the "all" are in the masculine plural form, which is less readily apparent in the English language, due to similar forms of the verb in the second person singular and plural] Furthermore, because the priests drink the cup on behalf of the people, this injunction causes them to disobey the injunction of Moses to the sons of Levi in Leviticus 10: Lev 10:9-11, "Do not drink wine or intoxicating drink, you, nor your sons with you, when you go into the tabernacle of meeting, lest you die. *It shall be* a statute forever throughout your generations, that you may distinguish between holy and unholy, and between

~Date	Prayer, Veneration, Sacraments and Other Doctrines	Ecclesiology/Politics	Rival Churches and Movements, Named by Their Antagonists	Biblical Assessment of Rome's Doctrines and Practices
				unclean and clean, and that you may teach the children of Israel all the statutes which the LORD has spoken to them by the hand of Moses."
1415	"Jean XXIIII (sic): Was deposed by the Council of Constance, with Benedict XIII and Gregory" (de Hainault, #59)			
1420		**First Anti-Hussite Crusade**, Rome defeated		[For preliminary analysis of Rome's crusades, see 1066, 1095-1101, and 1181]
1421		**Second Anti-Hussite Crusade**, Rome defeated		[For preliminary analysis of Rome's crusades, see 1066, 1095-1101, and 1181]
1424		**Third Anti-Hussite Crusade**, Rome defeated		[For preliminary analysis of Rome's crusades, see 1066, 1095-1101, and 1181]
1426		**Fourth Anti-Hussite Crusade**, Rome defeated		[For preliminary analysis of Rome's crusades, see 1066, 1095-1101, and 1181]
1431-1449	**Eugenius IV: Was deposed by the Council of Basel, and Aime Duke of Savoy was elected in his place"** (de Hainault, #60)	The Council of Basel was called by Martin V, who died before the council started. It was dissolved by Eugene IV, but refused to be dissolved, eventually electing Felix, Duke of Savoy as Felix V (in 1439)		
1433		**Fifth Anti-Hussite Crusade**, Rome defeated		[For preliminary analysis of Rome's crusades, see 1066, 1095-1101, and 1181]
1434			Hussite civil war between the Taborites and the Ultraquists (who believed that the Lord's Supper should be taken in both kinds)	
1436		Peace agreement was accepted by Hussites and the Church of Rome		
1437-1439		Eugene IV moved the powers of the Council of Basel to Ferrera to consider reunion with the Greeks. The council was moved to Florence in 1439		
1439	"Purgatory proclaimed as dogma by the Council of Florence (Boettner, #33)	"The doctrine of the Seven Sacraments* affirmed" (Boettner, #34) *These are: • Baptism • Confirmation • Eucharist (Mass) • Penance • Extreme Unction		Purgatory taught contra 2 Cor 5:8; Phil 1:23 The seven "Sacraments" [or means to holiness, or means of grace] taught in opposition to Acts 15:7-11; Gal 3:1-5; Heb 4:2, wherein grace is received through a hearing of faith, and not through the receiving of a physical sign or symbol Rome places the word "Holy" in front of each of their Sacraments to teach that they consider these Sacraments as means of achieving holiness; they are considered primary examples of the words of Jesus in Matt 28:20, "teaching them to observe all

~Date	Prayer, Veneration, Sacraments and Other Doctrines	Ecclesiology/Politics	Rival Churches and Movements, Named by Their Antagonists	Biblical Assessment of Rome's Doctrines and Practices
	• Marriage • Orders (Boettner, 189)			that I have commanded you," a lifetime of observation of which leads to eternal salvation [by works], after the penalty of any mortal sins are purified in the fires of Purgatory By the way, in the eyes of Rome, because they believe that they own the "keys" to heaven (Matt 16:19), they believe that they are the only ones who have the right to decide who can and who can't give the Sacraments, as well as who does or who does not rightly bestow their graces
1439-1446		**Roman Crusaders** gathered to capture Servia, Bulgaria; then continued on to Constantinople		[For preliminary analysis of Rome's crusades, see 1066, 1095-1101, and 1181]

1453		Fall of Byzantium described by Sleidan.[131]
		Could Rome not say today when looking at the Western world and its colonies, "Look what my hands have done" (cf. Dan 4:30)? Looking with satisfaction and the pity of a father!?
			Arab Muslims captured Constantinople and conquered the Byzantine empire:
			"The conquest of Constantinople, in 1453, had scattered learned Greek professors all over the continent of Europe."[132]
				Rome's long time rival, the Eastern Empire, and the seat of the Eastern Patriarch of Constantinople, weakened by the Roman crusaders, was finally defeated by the hand of Arab Muslims. A similar fate at the hand of Islamic Jihad had destroyed the Carthanagian empire, seat of the Donatist churches of North Africa, in the 7th Century.
				
				While the Eastern Churches still remained, fragmented, the Bishop of Rome's stature as unique and unrivaled head over world affairs was confirmed by this feat in history.
				
				Further, whether intentional or unintentional, it appears that this fate of Constantinople "gave permission" to or removed an obstacle for Rome to act on its claim of "catholicity" or "universality":
				
				• 579 A.D.: Gregory, to become Pope Gregory I in 590, was sent to Constantinople as an envoy to monitor relations between these two historic State-Church Patriarchates;
				
				• 800 A.D., Pope Leo III decided that there needed to be a Western Empire, and so he crowned Frankish king Charlemagne emperor of the "Holy Roman Empire" or "Holy Roman Empire of the Germanic Nation."
				
				  o It seems that Leo III followed the precedent of the prophet Ahijah in 1 Kings 11, who anointed Jeroboam as King over Israel, thus dividing the kingdom of Israel into Israel and Judah;
				
				  o Leo III was likewise intentionally dividing the Roman Empire into two states:
				
				    ▪ One under the authority of the Bishop of

---

[131]"Afterwards, Mahomet of that name the second, great Grandfather to Solyman, who now swaies the Empire, taking Constantinople, & putting Constantine Palaeologus the Emperour before mentioned, together with his whole family, to the sword, vtterly extinguished the name, and succession of Emperours of our Religion, in those parts. And the Turks to this day hold Asia, Syria, Egypt, Mesopotamia, Indea, the Rhodes, all Greece, Thracia, Bulgaria, Macedonia, Illyricum, both the Mysia's, and of late, almost the other part of Hungary, and some part of Africa.

"In former times, the Churches of Ierusalem, Antioch, Constantinople, and Rome, contended amongst themselves for primacie, but especially the two last, as wee formerly shewed: but the Turks ended that controuersie, and set such a constitution in those three places, that there is not a tract remaining of a Church or Christian Congregation: and the matter it selfe shewes, of what colour the face, and what the state of that Church now remaining, which now (those riuals or eye-sores before remoued) alone triumphs." (Sleidan, 229-230).

[132]M. F. Cusack, *The Black Pope: A History of the Jesuits* (London: Marshall, Russell, & Co., 1886), 21.

~Date	Prayer, Veneration, Sacraments and Other Doctrines	Ecclesiology/Politics	Rival Churches and Movements, Named by Their Antagonists	Biblical Assessment of Rome's Doctrines and Practices
				Rome or Pope (as the person who placed the crown) and the other under the divine right of the Emperor, under the tutelage of the Patriarch of Constantinople; ▪ One called "Holy Roman Empire"; and by implication, the other the "Secular Roman Empire." • 806-810 A.D., the newly crowned Charlemagne, Frankish Emperor of the Germanic Roman Empire went to war with Byzantium over rulership of Venice, a disputed territory in debates over the boundaries between the now two Roman Empires, as discussed in the Pax Nicephori. ○ It appears that Roman Emperor Nikopheros I did not consider Charlemagne a rightful emperor, not accepting "Pope" Leo III as having the authority to crown an emperor over his empire; • 1054 A.D.: The mutual anathema [curse] gave Rome the spiritual authority to act on its own, without deference to the Patriarch of Constantinople, as he no longer had any spiritual authority, either in matters of salvation or in matters of world politics; • 1167 A.D.: With Rome's view of state-church inter-relations, the fact that a bishop from Constantinople, the Bulgarian Bishop Nicetas, had the audacity to travel to France and anoint four bishops of the "Cathar Churches" was seen as an act of war, eventually leading to the multiple Albigensian crusades in Southern France. • 1453 A.D.: With the fall of Constantinople to Muslims, Rome's historic rival was out of the way; it could now set up its one "kingdom of God on earth." ○ Not as a strange two-headed monster, or worse yet, a multiple-headed monster (as is discussed in a number of papal encyclicals and writings) In 1455, Rome then began to colonize the world (establishing earthly political realms under its triple authority): • Its authority to sanction explorers and partition the world into States, dividing them between committed rulers of Catholic states; • Its authority to send missionaries to these states to establish either by conversion or by force the Catholic Church as the State Church over those colonies; • Its ongoing authority to monitor and oversee the theology and politics of the states that it allowed and encouraged to be set up. This included the colonization of:

~Date	Prayer, Veneration, Sacraments and Other Doctrines	Ecclesiology/Politics	Rival Churches and Movements, Named by Their Antagonists	Biblical Assessment of Rome's Doctrines and Practices
				• Central and South America, beginning in the 15th-16th Centuries; • North America in the 17th Century; • Africa in the 19th Century.
1455		**JOHANNES GUTENBERG BIBLE** (aka. Gutenberg Press, Mainz, Germany): The development of offset printing by offset printing with movable type. This invention led to a information and educational revolution in the Western World		Movable type led to a revolution of in the dissemination of information: • 15th Century: Bibles, prayer books, and indulgence books; • 16th Century: Gospel tracts, billets, and [wanted] posters, along with Protestant and Catholic Bibles, along with a revolution of Bibles, theological, and polemical literature; • 18th Century: Magazines and newspapers; • 19th Century: Encyclopedias Notice that this invention came in the Western World, the Latin [or authorized] Bible bring the first item printed: • While Hubmaier noted in 1524 that most of the Catholic priests and pastors in his area did not have access to a Bible, lack of availability of the Bible would soon change; • The "Book Society for Promoting Religious Knowledge among the Poor" was formed in 1750; it was reformulated as the "Religious Tract Society" in 1799; then in 1802 out of its board room came the "British and Foreign Bible Society" (BFBS) • In 1820 the BFBS could report that it had formed 265 Auxiliaries and 364 Branch Societies, totaling 629 groups; • By London 1888, the Bible and significant Bible portions had been translated by Protestant missionaries into 300 languages • After World War II the BFBS joined a number of other Bible societies to form the United Bible Society in 1948

1455	In the Bull "Romanus Pontifex," [Pope] Nicholas V divided the new lands discovered (in West Africa) between the kingdoms of Portugal and Castille; This Papal Bull became precedent for the colonization of South America and later Africa In 1493, [Pope] Alexander VI amended the decision of his predecessor in a Bull titled "Inter Caetera," because of the discovery of the Western hemisphere; in which the region which is now Brazil was deeded to the kingdom of Portugal. The only kings who had authority from the Pope to colonize were "Very Christian Kings" (or princes) who had sworn and exemplified their allegiance to the Pope; others who explored lands and territories, and established trade routes, were not recognized by Rome (e.g. David Livingstone): "We bestow suitable favors and special graces on those Catholic kings and princes, who, like athletes and intrepid champions of the Christian faith, as we know by the evidence of facts, not only restrain the savage excesses of the Saracens and of other infidels, enemies of the Christian name, but also for the defense and increase of the faith vanquish them and their kingdoms and habitations" (Nicholas V, *Romanus Pontifex* [1455]) The policy for colonization was related "especially of the rise and spread of the Catholic faith":	Moses was said to have divided the land East of the Jordan between the tribes; hence in Deut 3:19 and 20 he wrote of the land "which I have given you," as also Moses divided up the land and personally "gave" it to the various tribes, see Deut 3:12, 13, 15, 16. The phrase, "land which the Lord your God gives you" is found about 25 times in Deuteronomy. This example was then leveraged to apply to the Vicar of Christ, giving the Pope the authority to give land and to take it away (as part of the "keys" of Matt 16:19). Further, as God divided the boundaries of the people (Deut 32:8), so now the Vicar of Christ has the authority to set the territorial boundaries of the peoples. So, in Rome's system, Christ being the Second lawgiver, or the Second Moses, and the Pope being the Vicar of Christ, it is the Pope who has the authority to decide questions of land grants and

~Date	Prayer, Veneration, Sacraments and Other Doctrines	Ecclesiology/Politics	Rival Churches and Movements, Named by Their Antagonists	Biblical Assessment of Rome's Doctrines and Practices
	"Wherefore, as becomes Catholic kings and princes, after earnest consideration of all matters, especially of the rise and spread of the Catholic faith, as was the fashion of your ancestors, kings of renowned memory, you have purposed with the favor of divine clemency to bring under your sway the said mainlands and islands with their residents and inhabitants and to bring them to the Catholic faith" (Alexander VI, Inter Caetera [1493])			colonization This being the case, the title ascribed to Jesus in Revelation, "King of Kings and Lord of Lords," was/is ascribed to Popes who are above all the kings of the earth.
1466		The Pope promulgated a decree as to how shoes ought to be made: "A Papal decree in 1466 decreed that: 'No cordwainer [shoemaker] shall make any pikes (the pointed toe ornaments) more than 2 inches long, or sell shoes on Sunday, or even fit a shoe upon a man's foot on Sunday, on pain of excommunication. Neither shall any cordwainer attend any fair on Sundays, under the same penalty,' The Bull was approved by the King's Council and also confirmed by Act of Parliament, and a proclamation was made at St. Paul's Cross to that effect."[133]		Politics: It is very strange that the Pope should be writing laws to be enacted in the states under his influence. Such are that actions of a Federal Head of individual states. Fashion: It is interesting to note the nature of the laws which the Pope decreed to those willing to listen to him: all the way to the style of shoes that they were or were not to wear. In this way he was a policing fashion and dress. It is fascinating for a church leader in Rome, Italy, to be policing fashion in London, England.[134] It makes one wonder who were merchants who benefitted from the Pope's decisions, and who were the losers in the shoe business due to the Pope's decisions. Or to ask the question: who profited and who was hurt financially by the economic decrees of the Pope? For example, consider how import and export laws appear to have hurt predominantly Catholic-led African colonies, as opposed to those colonized by England (compare the economic prosperity of the countries of Togo and Ghana—both were one country, Togoland, being colonized by Germany before being partitioned after WW1; or consider the Portuguese colonies of Angola and Mozambique in comparison with any of their English neighboring countries; or compare any African French speaking country with any African English speaking country). Blue Laws: Notice also what kind of businesses were allowed to sell goods and services on Sunday and which were not, for example, were saloons allowed to sell alcohol at fairs on Sundays, but not shoe salesmen were not allowed to do so?
1471	Under Sixtus IV (in the first year of his pontificate) Rome began multiplying its sales of indulgences as a new and powerful source of revenue,[135] as:		The sale of indulgences, long being a burden for righteous souls, eventually sparked the German Reformation (1517)	A Win-Win for Rome: • Prior to Indulgences, a "Taxation without Borders," Rome's revenues appeared to come from three main sources: o Voluntary offerings (as stated in the New

---

[133]Susan Cunnington, *The Story of William Caxton* [London: Harrap, 1917], 66-67.

[134]BTW, in my American upbringing, when we set the table for supper, my mother said that we should ask the question, "How does the Queen of England set her table?" Hence, the rule for propriety in our American home for my mother was the fashion or style of the sitting Queen of England.

[135]"On the subject of indulgences, we have chosen to respond to the authors of *l'Univers* [The Universe], this great placater of falsehoods, the same who becomes indignant when we attribute to the papacy the medallion commemorating the Saint Bartholomew [day massacre], having heretofore (on 23 May 1854) *treated as a Protestant invention* the Catholic tariff of penitences, or absolutions for each crime, whatever it be, was valued in terms of cash payment. We do not think it unuseful herein to consider certain details.

"The Protestant invention as claimed by *l'Univers*, is the book entitled: *"Taxe des parties casuelles de la boutique du pape, en latin et en français, avec annotations précises des décrets, conciles et canons, vieux et modernes, pour la vérification de la discipline anciennement observée dans l'Eglise"* ["tax of the

~Date	Prayer, Veneration, Sacraments and Other Doctrines	Ecclesiology/Politics	Rival Churches and Movements, Named by Their Antagonists	Biblical Assessment of Rome's Doctrines and Practices

casuistic parties of the Papal shop, in Latin and in French, with precise annotations of decrees, councils, and canons, ancient and modern, for the verification of the observance of the old discipline in the Church"] (Lyon's 8th edition,1564).

"That this work was published by a Protestant, this is unconscionable. It is the conscientious author, Antoine du Pinet, sieur de Nauroy, who edited it, after having embraced the Reformed religion. But it is not a question of playing with words. This edition of the Roman tax was it unique? Was it without precedent? Du Pinet was he the author of the origination of this work? Did he invent it, in the end? For that is the question. Thus here is the answer:

"The Catholics, says *France Protestante* (4:44), wanted to deny the authenticity of this hideous tax, and pretended that it had never been sanctioned by the Roman court. But we responded to them that if the Popes disapproved and condemned this horrible tariff, as they claim, there would not have been any printed after 1471, date of the first edition published in Rome, with so many successive reprints, not only in Cologne (in 1515 and 1522), in Paris (en 1520, 4th ed., 1531, 1533, 1545, 16th ed.), in Venice (in 1532 and 1584), but also in Rome itself (1486, 1492, 1503, 1508, 1509, 1512, 1514), without speaking of the two editions without date, published between 1472 and 1486, under the eyes of Sixtus IV, Innocent VIII, Alexander VI, Pius III, Julius II, and Leo X. There is nothing more authentic than this tax that rates absolution for murder, incest, theft, abominable crimes, at nearly the same price as the transgression of ecclesiastical law on fasting and abstinence of meats, in-other-words several *écus* [1 *écu* (crown) equals approximately 3 pounds].

"One must add that du Pinet, far from exaggerating, did not even reproduce all the abominations contained in the original Latin of which diverse critics criticize him, thinking that he was doing a favor to omit the most despicable portions. But Bayle conjectures that in all probability he followed the edition that the Protestant princes had inserted into the *Centum gravamina*.

"Is it now time to explain how and why *l'Univers*, having to choose from so many original texts that are poking out their eyes, decides to take a translation that it considers a Protestant invention?

"One sees, by this new example that one cannot believe the word of *l'Univers* and their cohorts when they award French Protestantism with the certificate of invention and others. But they keep therefore what belongs to them alone and that they are so effective in exploiting, not without the guarantee of to whom it belongs (*Bulletin de l'Histoire du protestantism*, year 1854, page 210) (Ibid., 15-17).

"We have traced the portrait of the papacy following natural [means], in-other-words following the sure principles of history; but we have omitted one fact that characterizes it. This fact brings to light the too celebrated book of *Taxe de la chancellerie Romaine* [Tax of the Roman Ministry (Cabinet or Authority)]. This book all by itself accuses Rome more than all the writings of the Protestants. Therein, every sin had its price, every crime its rate.

"Far from us in the mean time the idea of rendering guilty all the Church for the depravity in the Roman court. However interrelated in her shame, not everyone participated in all her iniquities. By the grace of God, in these times of ignorance and of spiritual slumber, there were simple and pious souls who did not walk with the multitude. In those days of moral decadence, there were the Elijah's and the Elisha's and the Shunnamite who afflicted their righteous souls, like Lot afflicted his in the guilty towns on the plain. On occasion fervent women like Thérèse, holy men like Gerson, raised their voices against the ruling godlessness. But, alas! their voices were little heard; but when pious preachers were able to make themselves heard, the masses pressed in around their pulpits. Rome then alarmed itself and attacked the Protestants of this period with sticks and the burning stake. Thanks to its violent methods, she made silence around her and was able to hurl into the world around her the too celebrated book of *Taxes of the Roman Ministry*.

"The papacy repudiates today this book that she would not now be able to use, but she published it. It came from her presses, and is nothing more than the consequence of her being, and is the action by which she maximized [proved] her works.

"Here are several extracts of this work. We will cite only several appetizers. Leaving by the wayside the big sins: our ears would not easily accept their reading.

'Absolution for the one who reveals the confession of any penitent is taxed at seven *carlins* [The *carlin* is an Italian currency of varying value (*Larousse*)].

'Absolution for the one who abuses a young girl is taxed at six *carlins*.

'Absolution for a priest who lives with a concubine is taxed at seven *carlins*.

'Absolution for a lay person guilty of the same is taxed at eight *carlins*.

'Absolution for the one who has killed his father, his mother, his brother, his sister, his wife, or any other relative or associate, being a lay person, is taxed at five *carlins*.

'Absolution for a current lay person who has killed an Abbot or another ecclesiastic inferior to a Bishop, is taxed at seven, eight, or nine *carlins*.

'Absolution for a husband who strikes his wife in such a way that she has an abortion or a pre-term delivery, is taxed at eight *carlins*.

'Absolution for a woman who takes any remedy to cause her to have an abortion, or who does anything else with the design of causing the fetus to perish, is taxed at five *carlins*.

'The father, the mother, or whatever other relative who suffocates a child, will pay for each murder four *tournois* [The *tournois* is a currency minted in Tours, France, up to the 13th Century, followed by a French currency minted after the same model (*Larousse*)], one *ducat* [The *ducat* is a gold coin first minted in Venice in the 13th Century (*Larousse*)], eight *carlins*.

'The one who has committed anyone of these crimes (blasphemies [lit. *sacrilèges*], thefts, arsons, perjury, or other similar) is fully absolved, and his honor reestablished in every form and without forfeiture, comes to thirty-six *tournois* and nine *ducats*.

'The absolution for all acts of impurity, of whatever nature they may be, committed by a [religious] clerk, be it with a nun, in the cloister or elsewhere, or with his/her parents or relatives, or with a spiritual daughter, or with another woman, whomever that may be; being that the absolution be requested not simply by the clerk, or by he himself or his concubines, with the exemption of being able to keep his orders [religious position] and of holding its benefits, and with no claim of forfeiture, costs only thirty-six *tournois* and nine *ducats*.

'Absolution for a lay person for the crime of adultery given for the inner heart of his conscience, costs four *tournois*.

'A religious woman who has fallen several times in the sin of luxury [i.e. coveting things] will be absolved and will be reestablished in her order, even if she is the *abesse* [superior of a female abbey], comes to thirty-six *tournois*, nine *ducats*.

'Absolution for a priest who keeps a concubine, with the exemption to keep his orders and to hold its benefits, costs twenty-one *tournois*, five *ducats*, six *carlins*.

'If there is adultery and incest one the part of lay people, they will need to pay for each head six *tournois*.

'Permission to eat milk products when it is forbidden [prohibited] costs, for only one person, six *tournois*.'

"In reading this shameful taxation, we think that we are dreaming, and we ask ourselves how the church of Rome, so pure and beautiful at its start, was able to degenerate to that extent. Like Thyatira and Laodicea, she had, alas!" (Endnote 4, page 17, "Old tariffs of indulgences and absolutions of the Roman Church," Franck Puaux, *Histoire de la Réformation Française* [Paris: Michel Lévy Frères, 1859], 1:406-07; translated by Thomas P. Johnston [August 2005]).

~Date	Prayer, Veneration, Sacraments and Other Doctrines	Ecclesiology/Politics	Rival Churches and Movements, Named by Their Antagonists	Biblical Assessment of Rome's Doctrines and Practices

	• All have sinned
	• Only Rome has the keys (in their thinking) to the bank of merits in heaven—thus, organizationally-speaking, they have the monopoly on forgiveness of sins!
	• Indulgences were a new method for:
	  ○ Re-tapping old sources of revenue
	  ○ A "taxation without borders" (as the church operated in many city-states)
	  ○ Getting out into the streets
	  ○ Using the services of the less-needed inquisitors
	  ○ Public relations with the communities
	  ○ And it went [at least a percentage] to "a good cause," i.e. the building St. Peter's Basilica
	  ○ Meanwhile, kings and princes could not stop them from financially raping their people (much like they could not prohibit inquisition and still remain in power); further the church was tax-free and considered itself above the law of any city-state!
				Testament),
				  ○ Payment for services: weddings, funerals, Masses, Penance enactments, etc., and
				  ○ The massive income source from the confiscation of the properties of heretics and schismatics (which income dried up in the 15th Century)
				• With indulgences, a new type of "Taxation without Borders":
				  ○ Penance enactments were taken "to the streets" as it were; it provided a way to bring the "Sacrament of Penance" out of the private confessionals to where the people were—in the marketplaces!
				  ○ Because "all have sinned" (Rom 3:23), Indulgences were a fail-safe unending source of income for Rome;
				  ○ Meanwhile, good Catholic kings and princes could not disallow this new level of taxation (because of submission to the enactments of Rome, as ably argued by Augustine), further impoverishing their people, as the new Dominican tax gatherers sold indulgences from town to town;
				  ○ Meanwhile this provided a new missional purpose and activity to Inquisitors who had all but eradicated any non-Catholic faith from their areas.
				Unfortunately, while it was a financial Win-Win for Rome, it was neither biblical, nor was it theologically sound.
				Why the indulgence system was not new:
				• "Suffranges for the dead" go back to prior to the time of Henry of Lausanne and Peter de Bruis (1116-1118);
				• The 3rd Lateran Council (1179) promised indulgence to those involved in the extirpation of heretics;
				• 1190, the sale of indulgences was apparently established (under Urban II [1088-1099], the pope known for being a crusade preacher).
				However, it was based on new delivery systems:
				• In the marketplaces and in the streets;
				• Printed on paper, using the newly created [1455] printing presses (remembering that in the early days the printed page was a novelty to the largely illiterate peasantry).
				[As to the competition between indulgence providers ["My Indulgence is better than your indulgence"], see the interesting letter written to Thomas Muntzer (letter #4) while he was at St. Martin's School in Brunswick)][136]

[136]"Letter 4. The Rector of St. Martin's School in Brunswick to Müntzer (Brunswick, 1518[?]). [letter was originally written in Latin]

"To his reverence Master Thomas M., Master of Arts and most learned of men, at present a guest of Hans Pelt.

"As the person now in charge of the academy of St. Martin's School, Brunswick, but as a disciple to his master, I write to his reverence Master Thomas Müntzer, master of arts, most learned of men, glad to put my mind at his disposal (a rude and very darkened one indeed, but one ready to be instructed and illuminated by sounder information). And I ask Master Thomas to be good enough formally to communicate and graciously share with him his esteemed judgments about the queries set out in this sheet of paper, as is pleasing to him.

~Date	Prayer, Veneration, Sacraments and Other Doctrines	Ecclesiology/Politics	Rival Churches and Movements, Named by Their Antagonists	Biblical Assessment of Rome's Doctrines and Practices
1475	Alan de la Roche founded Confraternity of the Rosary			For the blasphemy of prayer to Mary, see above (431 AD); as to prayers to a dead person, see 1 Cor 15:29; cf. Deut 18:10-11; 26:14
1502	Salvation for Erasmus in his *Enchiridion* began with the Greek maxim, "Know Thyself." He then provided a system of thought in which the Christian can overcome the flesh through the use of various weapons (*Enchiridion*) provided to him. For Erasmus, the end result using these spiritual weapons provided was putting to death the vices and enhancing the virtues, resulting in a perfect life, Christlikeness, and salvation.	Erasmus wrote his *Enchiridion*, which discussed the need to interpret Scripture in light of the ancients (Plato and Aristotle),[137] reminiscent of the Medieval methods of Lombard and Aquinas		Notice that Erasmus' approach to salvation was not too distant from that expressed by Pascal (see 1653 below). Erasmus' proposed style of interpretation leads to the placing of another rubric over the interpretation of Scripture, specifically an allegorical one, in which points of agreement are sought with the ancient Greek authors, to the scorn of the plain reading of the text. Consider what the Bible says about man's knowledge and ability to understand: • Isa 55:9, "For *as* the heavens are higher than the earth, So are My ways higher than your ways, And My thoughts than your thoughts." • 1 Cor 1:18-25, "For the message of the cross is foolishness to those who are perishing, but to us who are being saved it is the power of God. For it is written: 'I will destroy the wisdom of the wise, And bring to nothing the understanding of the prudent.' Where *is* the wise? Where *is* the scribe? Where *is* the disputer of this age? Has not God made foolish the wisdom of this world? For since, in the wisdom of God, the world through wisdom did not know God, it pleased God through the foolishness of the message preached to save those who believe. For Jews request a sign, and Greeks seek after wisdom; but we preach Christ crucified, to the Jews a stumbling block and to the Greeks foolishness, but to those who are called, both Jews and Greeks, Christ the power of God and the wisdom of God. Because the foolishness of God is wiser than men, and the weakness of God is stronger than men." Also, consider the great danger of placing a human

"First and foremost, Master Thomas, your aforesaid disciple and pupil does not know what meaning to attach to that clause in the apostolic letters of indulgence from penalty and guilt affirming that guilt is remitted in the sacramental absolution.

"Again, what meaning is of can be attached to the firm statement that man cannot absolve a sin which has been perpetrated against God; since the prelates are only men and yet, so we are told, this plenary power has been entrusted to them.

"Again, whether or not all that our lord, the pope, intends or desires in this church matter, or is credibly attested in authentic letters as desiring or intending, has in fact been done by him or at his behest in the sight of God.

"Again, whether we should put our faith in the letters which are authentic.

"Again, whether or not the ordinary layman should put his faith in apostolic letters which are not suspect and are immune from any erroneous falsification, after they have been scrutinised, examined, and received, and publicly examined and promulgated by the prelates; whether, I say, they should take them as gospel, as is said, so that, as such letters argue, he can further his soul's salvation.

"Again, whether or not the treasure of the church (which is the passion of Christ) is in any way augmented by the merits of the saints (as is preached to us).

"Again, with nothing but good will in his heart and no trace of evil intent, he asks Master Thomas to explain in as brief a compass as possible, what his own view is of the indulgences which of late the friars of the Order of Preachers [Dominicans] have been promulgating amongst us, despite the fierce and well-known opposition of the prelates.

"Likewise, whether or not the indulgences in Königslutter which were proclaimed many years ago have now been revoked, as some claim.

"Thomas, my father, do not be affected by the usual weariness at teaching the unlearned and informing the unlettered, since an aureola of the third kind awaits you. Bear in mind that these are not idle queries but have a bearing on our salvation" (*The Collected Works of Thomas Müntzer*, Trans. and ed., Peter Matheson [Edinburgh: T. & T. Clark, 1988], 9-12).

[137]"Literature shapes and invigorates the youthful character and prepares one marvelously well for understanding Holy Scripture, to pounce upon which with unscrubbed hands and feet is something akin to sacrilege. ...

"However, just as divine Scripture bears no great fruit if you persist in clinging only to the literal sense, so the great poetry of Homer and Vergil is of no small benefit if you remember that this is all allegorical, a fact that no one who has but touched his lips with the wisdom of the ancients will deny. . . . I would prefer, too, that you follow the Platonists among the philosophers, because in most of their ideas and in their very manner of speaking they come nearest to the beauty of the prophets and the gospels" (Raymond Himelick, *The Enchiridion of Erasmus* [Gloucester, MA: Peter Smith, 1970], 51).

~Date	Prayer, Veneration, Sacraments and Other Doctrines	Ecclesiology/Politics	Rival Churches and Movements, Named by Their Antagonists	Biblical Assessment of Rome's Doctrines and Practices
				interpretive rubric over Scripture: • Psa 19:11-13, "Moreover, by them Thy servant is warned; In keeping them there is great reward. Who can discern *his* errors? Acquit me of hidden *faults*. Also keep back Thy servant from presumptuous *sins*; Let them not rule over me; Then I shall be blameless, And I shall be acquitted of great transgression."
1508	"The 'Ave Maria' (part of the last half was completed 50 years later and approved by Sixtus V at the end of the 16th Century)" (Boettner, #35)			For the blasphemy of prayers to Mary, see 431 AD.
1516			Sir Thomas More's *Utopia* mocked urgent evangelism. In a way, he appeared to be mocking the Lollards of his day, i.e. descendants of Wycliffe[138]	The man who was soon to become the Lord Chancellor of England mocked New Testament evangelizing and fulfilling of the Great Commission according to the Book of Acts. Sad!
1517			Luther nailed his 95 Theses on the Wittenberg Door, thereby initiating what Protestants call the Reformation era; this era gave birth to many rival churches to Rome, and was followed by wars [Holy Crusades] to bring various territories back under Rome's dominion	It is interesting to note that the wars initiated by Rome to recapture lands lost to revival or Reformation were called "Peasants Revolts", as those who participated in the revivals were deemed mere uneducated peasants who were rebelling against the religion of their Catholic kings, queens, or princes.
1518	Valid versus invalid indulgences questioned by an unknown author in a letter to Thomas Muntzer[139]			

---

[138]"By degrees all the Utopians are coming to forsake their own superstitions and to agree upon this one religion that seems to excel the others in reason. . . .

"We told them of the name, doctrine, manner of life, and miracles of Christ, and of the wonderful constancy of the many who willingly sacrificed their blood in order to bring so many nations far and wide to Christianity. . . . Whatever the reason, many came over to our religion and were baptized. . . .

"Those among them that have not yet accepted the Christian religion do not restrain others from it or abuse the converts to it. While I was there, only one man among the Christians was punished. This newly baptized convert, in spite of all our advice, was preaching in public on the Christian worship more zealously than wisely. He grew so heated that he not only put our worship before all others, but condemned all other rites as profane and loudly denounced their celebrants as wicked and impious men fit for hell fire. After he had been preaching these things for a long time, they seized him. They convicted him not on a charge of disparaging their religion, but of arousing public disorder among the people, and sentenced him to exile" (Thomas More, *Utopia* [1516; Arlington Heights, IL: AHM Publishing, 1949], 70-71).

[139]"To his reverence Master Thomas M., Master of Arts and most learned of men, at present a guest of Hans Pelt.

"As the person now in charge of the academy of St. Martin's School, Brunswick, but as a disciple to his master, I write to his reverence Master Thomas Müntzer, master of arts, most learned of men, glad to put my mind at his disposal (a rude and very darkened one indeed, but one ready to be instructed and illuminated by sounder information). And I ask Master Thomas to be good enough formally to communicate and graciously share with him his esteemed judgments about the queries set out in this sheet of paper, as is pleasing to him.

"First and foremost, Master Thomas, your aforesaid disciple and pupil does not know what meaning to attach to that clause in the apostolic letters of indulgence from penalty and guilt affirming that guilt is remitted in the sacramental absolution.

"Again, what meaning is of can be attached to the firm statement that man cannot absolve a sin which has been perpetrated against God; since the prelates are only men and yet, so we are told, this plenary power has been entrusted to them.

"Again, whether or not all that our lord, the pope, intends or desires in this church matter, or is credibly attested in authentic letters as desiring or intending, has in fact been done by him or at his behest in the sight of God.

"Again, whether we should put our faith in the letters which are authentic.

~Date	Prayer, Veneration, Sacraments and Other Doctrines	Ecclesiology/Politics	Rival Churches and Movements, Named by Their Antagonists	Biblical Assessment of Rome's Doctrines and Practices
1522-1529	Statues and images of the saints were burned in Wittenberg under Luther. This marked a clear break from the doctrinal foundation ascribed to Augustine by Peter the Lombard,[140] along with the Inquisitorial instructions of Thomas Aquinas	When the political leaders were controlled by Rome, then it used inquisition to ferret out heresy. When they did not have political control, they used crusade to gain political control, often accusing the population who had experienced an Evangelical Revival of a "Peasant's Revolt." The first wave of martyrs among the non-Catholic churches of Europe; it appears that the persecution of Antiochus in 2 Macc 7:1-23 became a guideline for how inquisitions and martyrdoms were accomplished.	From H. Sypphen in 1522 in Bavaria to H. Koch and L Meister in Augsburg in 1523, to J. Vallière in Paris and J. Leclerk in Meaux, France, those burned at the stake for not following the religion of Rome multiplied across Europe, the armies were sent out against Anabaptist and Lutheran strongholds as Rome unleashed another wave of Holy Crusades.	It is amazing that Rome appeared to use the brutality associated with Antiochus in 2 Macc 7:1-23 against French Huguenots and Dutch and German Anabaptists. Antiochus was an antithetical figure in Maccabees and never appears to have been given as an example to be followed. Here is an excerpt for those not familiar with this passage: 2 Macc 7:1-5 (Brenton), "It came to pass also, that seven brethren with their mother were taken, and compelled by the king against the law to taste swine's flesh, and were tormented with scourges and whips. 2 But one of them that spake first said thus, What wouldest thou ask or learn of us? we are ready to die, rather than to transgress the laws of our fathers. 3 Then the king, being in a rage, commanded pans and caldrons to be made hot: 4 Which forthwith being heated, he commanded to cut out the tongue of him that spake first, and to cut off the utmost parts of his body, the rest of his brethren and his mother looking on. 5 Now when he was thus maimed in all his members, he commanded him being yet alive to be brought to the fire, and to be fried in the pan: and as the vapour of the pan was for a good space dispersed, they exhorted one another with the mother to die manfully…" Consideration of several biblical injunctions may be in order here: 3 John 11, "Beloved, do not imitate what is evil, but what is good. He who does good is of God, but he who does evil has not seen God." Rom 12:21, "Do not be overcome by evil, but overcome evil with good."
1525		Diet of Spier affirmed **"Whose region, his religion"**		Built upon an Old Covenant view of the church, the territorial church idea, with boundaries formed by land conquered by war, follows the pattern of Deut 20:11: Deut 20:10-11, "When you go near a city to fight against it, then proclaim an offer of peace to it. And it shall be that if they accept your offer of peace, and open to you, then all the people who are found in it shall be placed under tribute to you, and serve you" This same concept is also applied to tithes and offerings from any region. If you combine these

"Again, whether or not the ordinary layman should put his faith in apostolic letters which are not suspect and are immune from any erroneous falsification, after they have been scrutinised, examined, and received, and publicly examined and promulgated by the prelates; whether, I say, they should take them as gospel, as is said, so that, as such letters argue, he can further his soul's salvation.

"Again, whether or not the treasure of the church (which is the passion of Christ) is in any way augmented by the merits of the saints (as is preached to us).

"Again, with nothing but good will in his heart and no trace of evil intent, he asks Master Thomas to explain in as brief a compass as possible, what his own view is of the indulgences which of late the friars of the Order of Preachers [Dominicans] have been promulgating amongst us, despite the fierce and well-known opposition of the prelates.

"Likewise, whether or not the indulgences in Königslutter which were proclaimed many years ago have now been revoked, as some claim.

"Thomas, my father, do not be affected by the usual weariness at teaching the unlearned and informing the unlettered, since an aureola of the third kind awaits you. Bear in mind that these are not idle queries but have a bearing on our salvation" (Letter 4. "The Rector of St. Martin's School in Brunswick to Müntzer [Brunswick, 1518(?)]; *Collected Works of Thomas Müntzer*, Trans. and ed., Peter Matheson [Edinburgh: T. & T. Clark, 1988], 9-12).

[140]"While considering the contents of the Old and New Law again and again by diligent chase [indagine], the prevenient grace of God has hinted to us, that a treatise on the Sacred Page is [versari] chiefly about things and/or signs. For as Augustine, the egregious Doctor, says in the book *on Christian Doctrine*: 'Every doctrine is of things, and/or signs. But even things are learned through signs. But here (those) are properly named things, which are not employed to signify anything; but signs, those whose use is in signifying'" (Peter the Lombard, *Four Books of Sentences*, Book 1, "On the Unity and Trinity of God," Distinction 1, Chapter 1, "Every doctrine concerns things and/or signs"; available at: http://www.franciscan-archive.org/lombardus/opera/ls1-01.html [online]; accessed: 16 May 2006; Internet).

~Date	Prayer, Veneration, Sacraments and Other Doctrines	Ecclesiology/Politics	Rival Churches and Movements, Named by Their Antagonists	Biblical Assessment of Rome's Doctrines and Practices
				ideas with the fact that the Pope sees himself as the universal pastor and teacher, then all peoples should bring tribute to him.
1534		"Jesuit* order founded by [Ignatius] Loyola" (Boettner, #36); *Jesuits were also called "The Church of Christ Millitant"		As noted below, the Jesuit order was/is a particularly lucid example of the excesses applied to the third Benedictine Vow, "The Vow of Obedience."

1534	Ignatius Loyola's *Spiritual Exercises*, "Rules for Thinking within the Church": "13. If we wish to be sure that we are right in all things, we should always be ready to accept this principle: I will believe that the white that I see is black if the hierarchical Church so defines it._For, I believe that between the Bridegroom, Christ our Lord, and the Bride, His Church, there is but one spirit, which governs and directs us for the salvation of our souls, for the same Spirit and Lord, who gave us the Ten Commandments, guides and governs our Holy Mother Church."[141]			Note how Psalm 139:12 can be misinterpreted in light of Statement 13: • Psa 139:12, "Indeed, the darkness shall not hide from You, But the night shines as the day; The darkness and the light *are* both alike *to You*." Note also the woe of Isaiah 5:20: • Isa 5:20, "Woe to those who call evil good, and good evil; Who put darkness for light, and light for darkness; Who put bitter for sweet, and sweet for bitter!"
~1534	From "The Obedience of the Jesuits": "Let us with the utmost pains strain every nerve of our strength to exhbit this virtue of obedience, firstly to the Highest Pontiff, then to the Superiors of the Society; so that in all things, to which obedience can be extended with charity, we may be most ready to obey his voice, just as if it had been issued from Jesus Christ our Lord..., leaving nay work, even a letter, that we have begun and have not yet finished; by directing to this goal all our strength and intention in the Lord, that holy obedience may be made perfect in us in every respect, in performance, in will, in intellect; by submitting to whatever may be enjoined on us with reainess, with spiritual joy and perseverance; by persuading ourselves that all things [commanded] are just; by rejecting with a kind of blind obedience all opposing opinion or judgement of our own; and that in all things which are ordained by the Superior where it cannot be clearly held [*definiri*] that any kind of sin intervenes. And let each one persuade himself that they that live under obedience ought to allow themselves to be borne and ruled by divine providence working through their Superiors exactly as if they were a corpse which suffers itself to be borne and handled in any way whatsoever; or just as an old man's stick which serves him who holds it in his hand wherever and for whatever purpose he wish use it...."[142] See also Jesuits axioms, promulgated in Cologne (1560)			Similar to comments on the Benedictine vow of obedience above, notice how far Loyola took this "vow of obedience"; it is interesting that men were willing to follow this "Rule" Could this fanatical obedience be based on a misreading or misapplication of Phil 2:14, which is translated variously? [GNV] "Do all things without murmuring and reasonings," [KJV] "Do all things without murmurings and disputings:" [ETH] "Do every thing without murmuring and without division;" [MRD] "Do all things without murmuring, and without altercation;" [ERV] "Do all things without murmurings and disputings;" [DRA] "And do ye all things without murmurings and hesitations;" [ASV] "Do all things without murmurings and questionings:"
1540		As far as the change in the Ten Commandments, combining two as part of one, and even omitting the section on the making and worship of images[143]		In the *Catechism of the Catholic Church*, the same combination of the first two of the Ten Commandments was done, with the division of the tenth into two in order to make up the complete number. This 1994 arrangement of the Ten Commandments is presumably said to have been established by

[141]St. Ignatius Loyola, *The Spiritual Exercises of St. Ignatius*, translated by Anthony Mottola, S.J., imprimatur, Cardinal Spellman (Garden City, NY: Image Books, Doubleday and Company, 1964), 140-41.

[142]"Obedience of the Jesuits," in Henry Bettenson, *Documents of the Christian Church* (London: Oxford University Press, 1963), 261.

[143]"In 1540, Robert [Estienne] was brought into special jeopardy through an impression of the Decalogue executed in large characters and printed in the form of a hanging map for placing in schoolrooms. Such an undertaking seems to our present understanding innocent enough, whether considered from a Romanist or a Protestant point of view, but in this publication of the Ten Commandments, the divines discovered little less mischief than in the heresies of Luther. The censors caused to be put in print a counter-impression of the Decalogue in which the first two commandments were combined into one, with the omission of the prohibition of making and worshipping images, while the tenth commandment was divided into two in order to make up the complete number" (George Haven Putnam, *The Censorship of the Church of Rome* [New York: Putnam's, 1906], 2:16).

~Date	Prayer, Veneration, Sacraments and Other Doctrines	Ecclesiology/Politics	Rival Churches and Movements, Named by Their Antagonists	Biblical Assessment of Rome's Doctrines and Practices
				Augustine (353-430): "The present catechism follows the division of the Commandments established by St Augustine, which has become traditional in the Catholic Church. It is also that of the Lutheran Confessions. The Greek Fathers worked out a slightly different division, which is found in the Orthodox Churches and Reformed communities" (*Catechism*, §2066).
				Furthermore, in order to get around the regular and continual prohibition against the setting up of images, the Church of Rome said the following (from 1994 *Catechism*):
				• "2130 Nevertheless, already in the Old Testament, God ordained or permitted the making of images that pointed symbolically toward salvation by the incarnate Word: so it was with the bronze serpent, the ark of the covenant and the cherubim [cf. Num 21:4-9; Wis 16:5-14; John 3:14-15; Exod 25:10-22; 1 Kings 6:23-28; 7:23-26].
				• "2131 Basing itself on the mystery of the incarnate Word the seventh ecumenical Council, at Nicaea (787), justified against the iconoclasts the venerations of icons–of Christ, but also of the Mother of God, the angels, and all the saints. By becoming incarnate, the Son of God introduced a new 'economy' of images.
				• "2132 The Christian veneration of images is not contrary to the first commandment, which proscribes idols. Indeed, 'the honour rendered to an image passes to its prototype', and 'whoever venerates an image venerates the person portrayed in it.' [St. Basil, *De Spiritu Sancto* 18, 45; PG 32, 149C; Council of Nicaea II: DS 601; cf. Council of Trent
				• : DS 1821-1825; Vatican Council II: *SC* 126; *LG* 67]. The honour paid to sacred images is a 'respectful veneration', not the adoration due to God alone:
				o "Religious worship is not directed to the images themselves, considered as mere things, but under their distinctive aspect as images leading us on to God incarnate. The movement towards the image does not terminate in it as image, but tends toward that who image it is [St Thomas Aquinas, *STh* II-II, 81, 3, ad 3]."
				For some preliminary verses against the worship of statues and images, see A.D. 375 above.
1545	"Tradition declared equal authority with the Bible by the Council of Trent" (Boettner, #37)			Therefore, Holy Tradition interprets the Holy Scriptures rather than the Holy Scriptures interpreting Holy Tradition.
				Note also the words of Jesus in Matt 15:6, "And *thus* you invalidated the word of God for the sake of your tradition"
				Note also Paul's discussions of the regulations of men in Col 2:20-23
1546	"Apocryphal books [definitively] added to the Bible by the Council of Trent" (Boettner, #38)			The reader of the Bible is specifically commanded not to add or subtract to its words: Deut 4:2; 12:32; Prov 30:6; Rev 22:18-19
				Notice at least one erroneous doctrine (indulgences, giving money for the forgiveness of sins) taught in the apocryphal books, along with

~Date	Prayer, Veneration, Sacraments and Other Doctrines	Ecclesiology/Politics	Rival Churches and Movements, Named by Their Antagonists	Biblical Assessment of Rome's Doctrines and Practices
				many other erroneous doctrines of Rome: • Tobith 4:10 (NJB), "For almsgiving delivers from death and saves people from passing down to darkness." • Tobith 12:9 (The American Bible), "for almsgiving saves one from death and expiates every sin. Those who regularly give alms shall enjoy a full life."
1547	In the Council of Trent's "Canons on Justification," Justification by faith is anathematized, faith is redefined, etc.: • Canon 9. If anyone says that the sinner is justified by faith alone,[114] meaning that nothing else is required to cooperate in order to obtain the grace of justification, and that it is not in any way necessary that he be prepared and disposed by the action of his own will, let him be anathema. • Canon 11. If anyone says that men are justified either by the sole imputation of the justice of Christ or by the sole remission of sins, to the exclusion of the grace and the charity which is poured forth in their hearts by the Holy Ghost,[116] and remains in them, or also that the grace by which we are justified • Canon 12. If anyone says that justifying faith is nothing else than confidence in divine mercy,[117] which remits sins for Christ's sake, or that it is this confidence alone that justifies us, let him be anathema. • Canon 13. If anyone says that in order to obtain the remission of sins it is necessary for every man to believe with certainty and without any hesitation arising from his own weakness and indisposition that his sins are forgiven him, let him be anathema. • Canon 14. If anyone says that man is absolved from his sins and justified because he firmly believes that he is absolved and justified,[118] or that no one is truly justified except him who believes himself justified, and that by this faith alone absolution and justification are effected, let him be anathema.		The three pillars in Luther's view of salvation were: • Grace alone [not because water was sprinkled on the head of a baby] • Faith alone [not human actions in cooperation with the signs and symbols of any particular church] • Scriptures alone [God's Word is the agent of salvation, not signs and symbols, not tradition, not any sacraments or ordinances] To these could be added: • Christ alone [the bloods of Christ and His merits alone; not the addition of any merits of the Virgin Mary or the Saints]	These Canons attack the heart of the Protestant Reformation and "Justification by Faith," and undermine the Bible's teaching of salvation by grace alone through faith alone: • Gen 15:4, 6, "And behold, the word of the LORD came to him, saying, 'This one shall not be your heir, but one who will come from your own body shall be your heir.' Then He brought him outside and said, 'Look now toward heaven, and count the stars if you are able to number them.' And He said to him, 'So shall your descendants be.' And he believed in the LORD, and He accounted it to him for righteousness." • Acts 15:7, "And when there had been much dispute, Peter rose up and said to them: 'Men and brethren, you know that a good while ago God chose among us, that by my mouth the Gentiles should hear the word of the gospel and believe. So God, who knows the heart, acknowledged them by giving them the Holy Spirit, just as He did to us, and made no distinction between us and them, purifying their hearts by faith. Now therefore, why do you test God by putting a yoke on the neck of the disciples which neither our fathers nor we were able to bear? But we believe that through the grace of the Lord Jesus Christ we shall be saved in the same manner as they.'" • Heb 11:1, "Now faith is the substance of things hoped for, the evidence of things not seen." Of the many anathemas (canons) in the Council of Trent: • Rom 12:14, "Bless those who persecute you; bless and do not curse"
1547-1559		Under Henry II, King of France (1547-1559), was instituted a special courtroom to prosecute with heretics, "La Chambre Ardente" (1547-1559), as a result 600 Huguenots were arrested from 1547-1550 No official records were kept of those tried, sentenced, or martyred as a result of the 12 years of decisions of these special tribunals that were set up in 10 or 12 of the larger cities of France!		Hence, question 3 in Rome's 1215 Inquisition methodology: "Does any one know of your imprisonment?" (van Braght, 311), of which a negative response led to complete ignorance of his/her arrest, followed by history's ignorance of how many actually died from Rome's Inquisitorial practices! An ignorance that is ignored and undermined even today. These steps allowed Rome to practice its inquisition under a cloak of secrecy, see: John 3:19-20, "And this is the condemnation, that the light has come into the world, and men loved darkness rather than light, because their deeds were evil. For everyone practicing evil hates the light and does not come to the light, lest his deeds should be exposed." Also: John 16:1-4, "These things I have spoken to you, that

~Date	Prayer, Veneration, Sacraments and Other Doctrines	Ecclesiology/Politics	Rival Churches and Movements, Named by Their Antagonists	Biblical Assessment of Rome's Doctrines and Practices
				you should not be made to stumble. They will put you out of the synagogues; yes, the time is coming that whoever kills you will think that he offers God service. And these things they will do to you because they have not known the Father nor Me. But these things I have told you, that when the time comes, you may remember that I told you of them. And these things I did not say to you at the beginning, because I was with you. Neither did this practice follow the example of Jesus: John 18:20-21, "Jesus answered him, 'I spoke openly to the world. I always taught in synagogues and in the temple, where the Jews always meet, and in secret I have said nothing. 21 'Why do you ask Me? Ask those who have heard Me what I said to them. Indeed they know what I said"
1553-1558		Queen [Bloody] Mary I Tudor took the throne, Crespin wrote "during the first two years of her reign 800 Protestants were put to death"		The only reason that we know some of the extent of Queen Mary's executions is that John Foxe was given a copy of the official court records, which release was deemed treasonous by Rome, and is therefore vehemently decried, followed by a denial of its veracity along with cries of exaggeration and excessively emotive language
1560	**"Creed of Pius IV imposed as the official creed" (Boettner, #39)** The absolute authority of the Pope is expressed via this decree, which is likely regarding the giving of communion in two kinds to the laity. The papal response was as follows: "Desiring now to be able to for the greater salvation of those for whom this request was made, the council decreed that the entire affair be deferred to our very Holy Father, as he defers it by the present decree, according to his singular prudence, he himself will decide what he judges to be [both] useful for the Christian States and salvific for those who request the use of the chalice" (DS 1760)			The Church of Rome gave a window of leeway to the Hussites regarding the use of the cup in the Lord's Supper, in order to quiet their antagonism, and act as if they made changes to conform to Scriptures Only to take it back several years later, several generations after the issue had died down, probably using the method of Gregory I, "To the Bishops of Numidia," in which those who practice such (use of both kinds) do not advance to primacy (or teaching authority) By the way, in 1575 two thirds of the Czech (Bohemian Brethren) joined the Lutheran Reformation by accepting a confession of faith inspired by the 1530 Augsburg Confession. In the 1560 Creed of Pius IV, he sounded more like a politician, and less like a humble servant of God who is obliged to say "thus says the Lord" and no more or no less; compare with: • Micaiah in 1 Kings 22:14 • What God said to Jeremiah in Jer 26:1-2 • See also Acts 20:20, 27 For another person who went according to what was in his heart, see: • Jeroboam 1 in 1 Kings 12:26, 33
1560	From the Jesuits axioms, promulgated in Cologne (1560): I. That the traditions of the Church, although not all can be proved by Scripture, nevertheless have the same authority, and must be received with the same faith as what is found by the express testimonies of Scripture. That after so many Councils, one must no longer call into question the traditions, and notably that of Trent, whereby it was decreed that which such reverence and affection one must receive the said traditions, as the Gospel in writing. II. That the continual succession of Roman Pontiffs is a manifest indicator of the			Notice also, in the "axioms": No. 1, that one's view of Tradition informs the interpretation of Scripture, and thus impacts all of theology, especially the theology of salvation, "You must be born again!" (John 3:7) Notice as regards No. 3: • "Bloody" Mary I of England was an example of blind

~Date	Prayer, Veneration, Sacraments and Other Doctrines	Ecclesiology/Politics	Rival Churches and Movements, Named by Their Antagonists	Biblical Assessment of Rome's Doctrines and Practices

	catholic Church and the Apostolic faith.
	
	III. That it is not-at-all for the political Magistrates to mix themselves with or gain knowledge of the doctrine that is proposed to the people: but that this solicitude is delegated to the priests. That upon issues of religion, the only duty of the Magistrates is, to execute the rebellious and contradictory of the Roman seat.
	
	IV. In conferring the doctrine of the Church with the rules of the word of God, whoever finds them in discord, contradicts those of the Pope, ought to be exterminated from the midst of men, either by sword or by fire, so that peace and tranquility may be conserved. If so had occurred 40 years ago in the location of Luther and his sectarians, it would have been seen for a long time that there would have been a restitution of Ecclesiastical repose so desired.[144]
				obedience to this unfortunate axiom
				
				• The admonition in Deut 17:18-20 for the king to write for himself with his own hand a copy of the Book of Deuteronomy in a scroll shows from the Old Testament:
				
				  o That God did not segment the knowledge of or interpretation of His Word only to priests and their hierarchies, but rather
				
				  o That God wanted the person who had the highest political office to read, write, and interpret the biblical books for himself, for example:
				
				    ▪ Note Moses' use of personal pronouns directed to the reader, Deut 1:20; 2:30, 37; 5:1-6; 7:19; 11:4, 7
				
				    ▪ Note Moses' use of "today," Deut 4:4, 39; 5:3; 29:14-15
				
				    ▪ The implication of political leaders handwriting the Book of Deuteronomy on their interpretation and of politics is immense
				
				Notice in No. 4: the regret that Rome was not more attentive to the threat caused by Luther, to exterminate him immediately!

1562		France's "Edict of January" included the stipulation that Protestant churches could not meet within the city walls of any town; later, these churches, expulsed from towns and cities, became known as the "desert church"		Laws wherein the Reformed Huguenots had to meet outside of the city were analogous to those with leprosy being quarantined "outside the camp," based on the fact that the teaching of the Huguenot was infectious; consider the following: • False teaching as an infectious disease, 1 Tim 6:4 • Laws on infectious diseases in Leviticus, esp. skin diseases, to be determined by the "priest," Lev 13 • False teachers, and their churches, therefore, to be quarantined outside the city: o Lev 13:45-46, "Now the leper on whom the sore *is*, his clothes shall be torn and his head bare; and he shall cover his mustache, and cry, 'Unclean! Unclean!' "He shall be unclean. All the days he has the sore he shall be unclean. He *is* unclean, and he shall dwell alone; his dwelling *shall be* outside the camp"
1564		Findings of the Council of Trent rendered binding on all humanity Because the Pope felt/feels that he was/is over state and church, and because he felt/feels that he is the universal pastor, his judgments are binding upon all Christians.	Hence all who dared to disagree with Rome faced the fires of Inquisition, using the Council of Trent as the measuring stick, see Pius IV, *Iniunctum nobis* (13 Nov 1564; DS 1862-1870), stated in the form of professions or propositions to be acknowledged by all people For example, on the issue of obedience:	Most conciliating Protestants and Evangelicals seem completely ignorant of the role of the historical doctrines of Rome in its contemporary theology The fact that both Vatican II and the 1994 *Catechism of the Catholic Church* cite portions such as that found in DS 1863, confirms what John Paul II stated, that Vatican II did not change the Old Church (see below) How could any true Evangelical sign the 1994 "Evangelicals and Catholics Together Statement"? Giving these Evangelicals the benefit of the doubt, one must assume that they do not have a thorough understanding of pre-Reformation, Reformation, or

[144]Jean Crespin's *Histoire des vrais tesmoins de la verite de l'evangile, qui de leur sang l'ont signée, depuis Jean Hus iusques autemps present* [*History of the True Witnesses to the Truth of the Gospel, Who with Their Blood Signed, from John Hus to the Present Time*] (Geneva: Crespin, 1570; Liège: Centre nationale de recherches d'histoire religieuse, 1964), 635.

~Date	Prayer, Veneration, Sacraments and Other Doctrines	Ecclesiology/Politics	Rival Churches and Movements, Named by Their Antagonists	Biblical Assessment of Rome's Doctrines and Practices
			"I accept and I embrace very firmly the apostolic traditions and those of the Church, and all the other observances and constitutions of this same Church. In the same way I accept the Holy Scriptures, following the interpretation that has held and holds our Mother Church, to whom it belongs to judge the true meaning and interpretation of the Holy Scriptures. I will not accept and nor will I ever interpret the Scripture except according to the unanimous consensus of the Fathers" (DS 1863; *Catechism of the Catholic Church*, §192; n.10)	post-Reformation Church History
1571	Superior Moslem fleet destroyed at Lepanto in the midst of a Rosary 'crusade' for victory			This event shows Rome's superstitious devotion to and affirmation of the use of prayer beads and repetitious prayers
1572			St. Bartholomew massacre in Paris, approximately 100,000 Huguenots killed by Roman Catholics; Cardinal Richelieu was first to stab the Huguenot head of the French army, Admiral Coligny [Pope] Gregory XIII minted a medallion to honor of the 24 Aug 1572 massacre of Huguenots	Herein is an example of a post-Reformation massacre so devastating that its very reality is almost surreal; how could anyone even imagine the execution or genocide of 100,000 people in the name of the New Testament, Jesus Christ, and His Church? General American ignorance of this event, which is so well-known in France that a secular movie was made of its horror in 1999, displays that: • The Saint Bartholomew Massacre is either completely ignored as irrelevant or downplayed by moderating Evangelicals and Baptists, or • The Saint Bartholomew Massacre is both excised from history and/or defended by church historians, who by confession are encumbered with the teaching that Rome is and has always been the immaculate Bride of Christ!
1625			John Mayer publishes *Antidote Against Popery* (London: John Grismand, 1625)	The full title page reads as such: *Antidote Against Popery: Confected out of Scriptures, Fathers, Councels, and Histories. Wherein Dialogue-wise are shewn, the points, grounds, and antiquitie of the Protestant religion; and the first springing vp of the points of Popery: together with the Antichristianisme thereof. Being sufficient to inable any Protestant of meane capacitie, to vnderstand and yield reason of his Religion, and to incounter with and foyle the Adversary.* By John Mayer, B.D. an Pastor of the Church of little Wratting in Suffolk. London: Printed by M.F. for John Grismand: and are to be sold at his shop in Pauls Alley, at the signe of the Gunne. 1625.
1653			In a way very reminiscent to monastic spirituality,	• Rom 8:1-8 (KJV) *There is* therefore now no condemnation to them which are in Christ Jesus,

~Date	Prayer, Veneration, Sacraments and Other Doctrines	Ecclesiology/Politics	Rival Churches and Movements, Named by Their Antagonists	Biblical Assessment of Rome's Doctrines and Practices
			Blaise Pascal, the Jansenist, conceives salvation as a retreat from worldly things to becoming enthralled with spiritual things.[145]	who walk not after the flesh, but after the Spirit. For the law of the Spirit of life in Christ Jesus hath made me free from the law of sin and death. For what the law could not do, in that it was weak through the flesh, God sending his own Son in the likeness of sinful flesh, and for sin, condemned sin in the flesh: That the righteousness of the law might be fulfilled in

---

[145]""The first thing that God inspires in the soul that he deigns to truly touch, is a knowledge of and an extraordinary insight by which the soul considers things [material] and itself in a completely new way.

"This new light gives her [the soul] fear and brings her a troubled [spirit] that pierces the tranquility she found in the things that gave her pleasure.

"She can no longer taste with ease the things that charmed her. A continuous unscrupulous battle in the midst of pleasure, and an internal view keeps her from finding the usual tenderness associated with [material] things or else they are abandoned with illusiveness of heart.

"But she finds even greater bitterness with the exercises of piety and the vanity of the world. On one hand, the presence of visible objects touches it with more hope than the invisible, and on the other the solidity of the invisible touches it in a greater way than the vanity of the visible. And in this way the presence of the one and the solidity of the other argue against her affection; and the vanity of the one and the absence of the other excites her horror; in this way there is born in her a disorder and confusion that...

"She considers the perishable things as perishable and even as already perished; and the sure fact of the destruction of everything that she loves, she fears this consternation, seeing that every moment the pleasure of good is being taken from her, and that which is the most dear flows away at all moments, and at last a day will come when she will find naked all the things in which she had placed her hope... In this way she will perfectly comprehend that her heart was only attached to things that are fragile and vain, her soul must find itself alone and abandon itself to the ends of this life, as she did not have the care to join herself to a true good which is self-substantial, that can sustain it during and after this life.

"From that point she begins to consider as nothing all that must return to nothingness, the heavens, the earth, her spirit, her body, her parents, her friends, her enemies, her goods, poverty, disgrace, prosperity, honor, debasement, adulation, infamy, authority, destitution, health, sickness, and life itself; hence anything that will endure less than her soul is incapable of satisfying the desire of this soul which seriously seeks to establish itself with a happiness just as lasting as itself.

"She begins to become astonished at the blindness in which she lived. And she considers on one hand the long time in which she lived without considering the great number of people who live likewise, and on the other hand the constancy that the soul, immortal as it is, will never find felicity among perishable things, that will at least be taken from her at death, she enters into a holy confusion and in a bewilderment which will bring a truly salvific perplexity.

"For she considers that whatever the great the number of those who grew older in worldly thinking, and whatever the authorities that this great multitude may have as examples of those who place their hope in this world, it is a constant nevertheless that when the things of the world would have any firm pleasure, that which is considered as false by any number of infinite experiences so dooming and so continuous, it is inevitable that the loss of these things, or finally of death will deprive us of them.

"In this way, by a holy humility, God reveals [himself] above the greatness, she begins to raise herself above the common of humanity. She condemns their conduct, she detests their maxims, she cries at their blindness. She directs herself to seek true goodness. She understands that there must be two qualities, one which endures as long as she [the soul] and that cannot be taken from her without her consent, and the other that there is nothing else worth loving.

"She sees in the love that she had for the world, she found in it the second quality of her blindness. For she recognized nothing more lovable. But in this she did not see the first [principle of eternity], she knows that it was not the guiding goodness. Therefore she seeks it elsewhere, and understanding that by a completely pure light that it is not in things that are in her, nor outside of her, nor in front of her, she begins to seek it above her.

"This uplift is so imminent and transcendental, that it does not stop in the heavens: there is not enough to satisfy above the heavens, nor with the angels, nor with other more perfect beings. She traverses all the creatures, and cannot stop her heart until she arrives at the throne of God, in which she begins to find her rest and the goodness that is such that there is nothing more lovable, and that can be taken from her without her own consent.

"For even if she does not feel the charms by which God rewards pious habits, she understands nevertheless that the creature cannot be more lovable than the Creator, and her reason assisted with the light of grace shows her that there is nothing more lovable than God and that he can be taken only from those who reject him, because to desire him is to possess him, and to refuse him is to lose him.

"Hence she herself rejoices that she has found goodness that cannot be ravished from her as long as she longs for it, and of which there is none higher.

"And in these new consternations she enters with new insight into the greatness of her Creator, and this with deep humiliations and adorations. She annihilates herself in his presence not being able to consider an idea of herself that is lowly enough, nor able to be able to conceive of a great enough revelation of this true sovereign, she makes new efforts to subjugate herself to the lowest abyss of nothingness, in considering God in his immensities which she multiplies; finally in his revelation, that saps all of her strength, she adores in silence, and she considers herself a vile and useless creature, and by these considerations reaffirmed, she adores him and blesses him, and would want to forever bless and adore him.

"Next she recognizes that it was grace that manifested to her his infinite majesty to such a worthless worm; and after a firm resolution to be eternally grateful, she enters into a confusion for having preferred vain things above this divine master, and in a spirit of compulsion and penance, she falls back on her piety, to quench her anger the effect of which appears dreadful in light of his immensities...

"She makes ardent prayers to God to obtain his mercy in light of that which he revealed to her, that it may please him to show her how to live and how to know the ways to get there. For because it is God to which she aspires, she aspires to arrive there only by the means which come from God Himself, for she wants that He Himself be her guide, her object, her endpoint. Following these prayers, she begins to act, and finds among those...

"She begins to know God, and desires to arrive there; but as she is ignorant of the ways to achieve this end, if her desires are sincere and true, she uses the same methods that another person who wanted to go somewhere to another place, having lost the way, and recognizing her waywardness, took recourse of those who perfectly knew the way of this road...

"She resolves to conform her will the remainder of her life; but in accordance with her natural weakness, being accustomed to her sins wherein she had lived, reduced her to powerlessness to arrive at this felicity, she implores his mercy to achieve him, to attach herself to him, to be eternally affixed to him...

"In this way she recognizes that she must adore God as [she is] a creature, give him thanks as a debtor, satisfy him as a guilty party, and pray as being impoverished" (Blaise Pascal, "Sur la Conversion du Pécheur," in *Pascal: Œuvres Complètes*, Louis Lafuma, ed. (New York: Macmillan, 1963), 290-91; translation by Thomas P. Johnston).

~Date	Prayer, Veneration, Sacraments and Other Doctrines	Ecclesiology/Politics	Rival Churches and Movements, Named by Their Antagonists	Biblical Assessment of Rome's Doctrines and Practices
				us, who walk not after the flesh, but after the Spirit. For they that are after the flesh do mind the things of the flesh; but they that are after the Spirit the things of the Spirit. For to be carnally minded *is* death; but to be spiritually minded *is* life and peace. Because the carnal mind *is* enmity against God: for it is not subject to the law of God, neither indeed can be. So then they that are in the flesh cannot please God. One must change the hermeneutic of Rom 8:1-8 in order to come up with the Grecian or monastic philosophic approach to salvation espoused by Pascal. When Paul speaks of the flesh, or salvation by the works of the Law, one must reinterpret that as referring to worldly possessions and passions. When Paul speaks of walking by the Spirit through faith, one must reinterpret that as meaning longing for "spiritual things" rather than worldly things. This reinterpretation is absolutely central and necessary to understanding the monastic view of salvation, and to understanding how Roman Catholic salvation very quickly became a Christianized Stoicism about the time of Gregory I's writings about [St.] Benedict's life and his vows of poverty, chastity, and obedience.
1683	"Rosary prayers played a role in the victory over the numerous Moslem invaders at Vienna"		The Arab Muslims drove all the way to Vienna, they were defeated and driven back across the Danube River	This defeat of the Muslims saved the Austrian power in Vienna, that also was at times the seat of the "Holy" Roman Emperor
1685		French King, Louis XIV, signed the revocation of the edict of toleration, which gave limited rights to the French Huguenots in 1598, the Edict of Nantes of King Henry IV. Freedom of worship and civil rights were not restored to non-Catholics in France until Louis XVI signed the "Edict of Versailles" in 1787.	The revocation (Louis XIV's Edict of Fontainbleau) made it illegal to be a Protestant in France. It has been preceded by a series of increasingly restrictive laws against the Huguenots, and led to further persecution and a mass exodus of French Huguenots from France.	
1708	The "immaculate conception" of Mary was promulgated by Pope Clement XI in *Commissi Nobis Divinitus* on 6 Dec 1708; and finalized as it is believed today by Pope Pius IX in 1854. Therefore, based on this dogma, Mary was said to be conceived and born without Original Sin. She was thus sinless, and able to live in sinless perfectionism in order later			Contra Psa 51:5.

~Date	Prayer, Veneration, Sacraments and Other Doctrines	Ecclesiology/Politics	Rival Churches and Movements, Named by Their Antagonists	Biblical Assessment of Rome's Doctrines and Practices
	to be prepared to carry Jesus, the Savior of the world. The origination of this doctrine appears to have its roots in the 5th and 7th Centuries in the Eastern Church.			
1713			In 1713, Clement XI in his Constitution *Unigenitus Dei Filius* condemned 101 heresies of the Jansenist Pasquier Quesnel, refuting errors in his commentaries published variously in 1671, 1687, 1693, and 1699. Note three of the statements that Clement XI deemed to be heretical errors: "80. The reading of Scripture is for everyone. Acts 8:28. "81. The holy obscurity of the Word of God is not for lay people a reason to be exempt from reading it. Acts 8:28. "84. Tearing the New Testament from the hands of Christians or holding it closed to them, by removing from them the means of comprehending it, is closing the mouth of Christ to them."[146]	
1716	[St.] Louis de Montfort died; credited with enrolling over 100,000 members in the Confraternity of the Rosary; Pope Clement XI extended the Feast of the Holy Rosary (October 7) throughout the Church			Calling the Rosary, the "Holy Rosary," is calling a prayer "holy" that is not found in the Bible. Praying in the name of anyone other than that of Jesus goes against the NT's admonitions only to pray "in the name of Jesus": John 14:13-14; 15:16; 16:23-24, 26; Heb 4:15-16; 7:25; for Jesus is the only middle-man, intermediary, advocate, or lawyer, since He is the only ransom or "propitiation for our sins": 1 Tim 2:3-7; 1 John 2:1-2 Decreeing special feast days, which days are not a part of the New Testament church, which follows the sin of Jeroboam (1 Kings 12:26, 33)
1761	Clement XIII's *In Dominico Agro* (14 June 1761) wrote: "The faithful should obey the apostolic advice not to know more than is		In the same encyclical, Clement XIII explained the fine balance between condemning their enemies without appearing to turn their backs on them:	Again, many teachings and examples of Scripture enjoin all of its readers to constantly deepen their knowledge of God and of His Word: • 2 Tim 2:15 (KJV), "Study to shew thyself approved unto God, a workman that needeth not to be ashamed, rightly dividing the word of truth."

---

[146]DS 2480, 2481, 2484.

~Date	Prayer, Veneration, Sacraments and Other Doctrines	Ecclesiology/Politics	Rival Churches and Movements, Named by Their Antagonists	Biblical Assessment of Rome's Doctrines and Practices
	necessary, but to know in moderation."[147]		"It is very difficult to cautiously balance our speech between both enemies in such a way that We seem to turn Our backs on none of them, but to shun and condemn both enemies of Christ equally."[148]	• Acts 17:11, "These were more fair-minded than those in Thessalonica, in that they received the word with all readiness, and searched the Scriptures daily *to find out* whether these things were so" • 1 John 4:1, "Beloved, do not believe every spirit, but test the spirits, whether they are of God; because many false prophets have gone out into the world." • See the long list of other passages, related to freedom of conscience in A.D. 397. All of these teachings are denied to Christians by the Pope's long-standing theologically-motivated attitude of keeping rank and file Catholics ignorant, Mary's humble submission to the will of God being their quintessential example. The admonition in Deut 17:18-20 for the king to write for himself with his own hand a copy of the Book of Deuteronomy in a scroll shows that God did not segment insight into His Word only to priests and their hierarchies (see the "Jesuits axioms", promulgated in Cologne, A.D. 1560)
1766		Clement XIII's *Christianae Republicae* (25 Oct 1766) denounced Protestant writings as "evil books"[149]	Clement XIII's *Christianae Republicae* (25 Oct 1766) called for propagators of such evil to "burn in the fire and perish" and calling on the sword of the state "to vigorously rout those accursed men who fight against the armies of Israel"[150]	

---

[147]"3. The faithful—especially those who are simple or uncultivated—should be kept away from dangerous and narrow paths upon which they can hardly set foot without faltering. The sheep should not be led to pasture through trackless places. Nor should peculiar ideas—even those of Catholic scholars—be proposed to them. Rather, only those ideas should be communicated which are definitely marked as Catholic truth by their universality, ambiguity, and harmony. Besides, since the crowd cannot go up to the mountain [Exod 19:12] upon which the glory of the Lord came down, and if whoever crosses the boundaries to see will die, the teachers of the people should establish boundaries around them so that no word strays beyond that which is necessary or useful for salvation. The faithful should obey the apostolic advice not to know more than is necessary, but to know in moderation [Rom 12:3]." (Clement XIII, *In Dominico Agro* [14 June 1761]; available at: http://www.ewtn.com/library/ENCYC/C13INDOM.HTM; accessed: 8 Sept 2004; Internet).

[148]"2. It often happens that certain unworthy ideas come forth in the Church of God which, although they directly contradict each other, plot together to undermine the purity of the Catholic faith in some way. It is very difficult to cautiously balance our speech between both enemies in such a way that We seem to turn Our backs on none of them, but to shun and condemn both enemies of Christ equally. Meanwhile the matter is such that diabolical error, when it has artfully colored its lies, easily clothes itself in the likeness of truth while very brief additions or changes corrupt the meaning of expressions; and confession, which usually works salvation, sometimes, with a slight change, inches toward death" (ibid.).

[149]"2. Therefore since the Holy Spirit has made you bishops to govern the Church of God and has taught you concerning the unique sacrament of human salvation, We cannot neglect our duty in the face of these evil books. We must arouse the enthusiasm of your devotion so that you, who are called to share in Our pastoral concern join together to oppose this evil with all energy possible. It is necessary to fight bitterly, as the situation requires, and to eradicate with all our strength the deadly destruction caused by such books. The substance of the error will never be removed unless the criminal elements of wickedness burn in the fire and perish. Since you have been constituted stewards of the mysteries of God and armed with His strength to destroy their defenses, exert yourselves to keep the sheep entrusted to you and redeemed by the blood of Christ at a safe distance from these poisoned pastures. For if it is necessary to avoid the company of evildoers because their words encourage impiety and their speech acts like a cancer, what desolation the plague of their books can cause! Well and cunningly written these books are always with us and forever within our reach. They travel with us, stay at home with us, and enter bedrooms which would be shut to their evil and deception" (Clement XIII, *Christianae Republicae*, 25 Oct 1766 [online]; available at: http://www.ewtn.com/library/ENCYC/C13CHRIS.HTM; accessed 22 April 2001; Internet).

[150]"Since you have been constituted ministers of Christ for the nations, in order to make holy his Gospel, exert yourselves and do everything in your power both by word and example to cut down the shoots of falsehood. Block up the corrupt springs of vice. Sound the trumpet in case as their leader you have to account for the souls who are lost. Act according to the position you hold, according to the rank with which you are vested, and according to the authority which you have received from the Lord. In addition, as nobody could or should avoid sharing in this sadness and insofar as there is one common reason for everyone to grieve and to help in this great crisis of faith and religion, call to your aid when it is necessary the time-honored piety of Catholic leaders. Explain the cause of the Church's sorrow and arouse its beloved sons who have always served it well on many occasions to bring their help. Since they do not carry the sword without cause, urge them with the united authority of state and of priesthood, to vigorously rout those accursed men who fight against the armies of Israel.

~Date	Prayer, Veneration, Sacraments and Other Doctrines	Ecclesiology/Politics	Rival Churches and Movements, Named by Their Antagonists	Biblical Assessment of Rome's Doctrines and Practices
1769		Clement XIV's *Cum Summi* (12 Dec 1769), proclaimed: "5. Whatever pertains to religious worship, to moral training, to right living can be found in the two fold instrument of scriptures and tradition"		Placing the tradition of men as equal or interpretive to the Word of God limits, or in fact, cancels the ultimate authority of the Bible to the interpretation of men, cf. Matt 15.
1769		Clement XIV's *Inscrutabile Divinae Sapientiae* (12 Dec 1769) offered the ordinary indulgences normally reserved for a Jubilee, as well as the commutation of vows, using the following language: "He may also commute any vows (except those having to do with religious life and chastity) to other pious and salutary works, having enjoined, however, in all the above cases, a salutary penance and other acts according to the decision of the same confessor"		The breaking of vows, especially to heretics, was encouraged and even commanded by Popes, beginning in 1073 with the absolution of fealty from a temporal lord who was not "catholic", for example Pope Gregory VII (1073-1085), formerly Hildebrand of Sovona, published, *Extra, De Haereticis, cap. Ad abolendam*, "Holding to the institutions of our holy predecessors, we, by our apostolic authority, absolve from their oath those who through loyalty or through the sacred bond of an oath owe allegiance to excommunicated persons: and we absolutely forbid them to continue their allegiance to such persons, until these shall have made amends" (quoted in Aquinas, *Summa*, SS, Q[12], A[2]); Innocent III repeated a similar measure in 1208; the Fourth Lateran Council (1215) repeated a similar provision, encouraging rebellion against a heretical prince; Innocent IV repeated this measure (1243); repeated in the Council of Constance (1415); repeated by Innocent VIII (1487), including the absolution of all contracts or debts with heretics; abstinence from all commerce with heretics; and freedom to pillage all the belongings of the heretics
1775		Pius VI's *Inscrutabile* (25 Dec 1775) condemned the missions and evangelism work of Protestants "which is worse than the very darkness," as well as the concept of republican government. It also encouraged every bishop to found a college in their diocese (or assist in a neighboring one), following up on the statement of Clement XIV in his Encyclical epistle of 1741		Pius VI's *Inscrutabile* (25 Dec 1775) showed what he felt of the U.S. Constitution (and its Bill of Rights), and the soon to come "Rights of Man" as voted by French Parliament in 1789, as a part of the "French Revolution": "7. When they have spread this darkness abroad and torn religion out of men's hearts, these accursed philosophers proceed to destroy the bonds of union among men, both those which unite them to their rulers, and those which urge them to their duty. They keep proclaiming that man is born free and subject to no one, that society accordingly is a crowd of foolish men who stupidly yield to priests who deceive them and to kings who oppress them, so that the harmony of priest and ruler is only a monstrous conspiracy against the innate liberty of man." Controlling and monopolizing education is the way

"It is principally your duty to stand as a wall so that no foundation can be laid other than the one that is already laid. Watch over the most holy deposit of faith to whose protection you committed yourselves on oath at your solemn consecration. Reveal to the faithful the wolves which are demolishing the Lord's vineyard. They should be warned not to allow themselves to be ensnared by the splendid writing of certain authors in order to halt the diffusion of error by cunning and wicked men. In a word, they should detest books which contain elements shocking to the reader; which are contrary to faith, religion, and good morals; and which lack an atmosphere of Christian virtue. We manifest to you Our great happiness in this matter that most of you, following the apostolic customs and energetically defending the laws of the Church, have shown yourselves zealous and watchful in order to avert this pestilence and have not allowed the simple people to sleep soundly with serpents" (ibid.).

~Date	Prayer, Veneration, Sacraments and Other Doctrines	Ecclesiology/Politics	Rival Churches and Movements, Named by Their Antagonists	Biblical Assessment of Rome's Doctrines and Practices
				to effectuate change in a democratic society over time!
1816			Pius VII wrote regarding "The Translation of the Bible" to the Archbishop of Mogilev, Belarus in 1816: "This is why the heretics with their biased and abominable machinations had the custom, in editing Bibles in vulgar tongue (of which the astonishing diversity and contradictions results that they accuse and tear each one the other), to seek to insidiously impose their respective errors by wrapping them of the magnificence of the most holy divine Word."[151]	
1832			Greece, seat of the Greek Orthodox Church, received its independence from Muslim rule, with the military aid of England, France, and Russia	
1844			In 1844 Gregory XVI's encyclical "*Inter Praecipuas Machinationes*" specifically decried the translation work of Bible Societies.[152]	
1846			In 1846 Pius IX wrote the encyclical "Qui Pluribus", which condemned the Bible Societies and their free Bible distribution programs[153]	
1854	**"Immaculate conception**			Contra Psa 51:5.

[151]Pius VII, Letter "*Magno et Acerbo*" (1816) to the Archibishop of Mogilev [Belarus]; *DS* 2710-2712. In this letter, Pius VII cited "the celebrated [1199] letter of Innocent III to the faithful of Metz," as well as writings of Pius V, Clement VIII, and Benedict XIV, also mentioning Clement XI's condemnation of the Jansenist teaching: "79. It is useful and necessary at all times, in all places, and for every kind of person, to study and to know the spirit, the piety, and the mysteries of Sacred Scripture" (Clement XI, *Unigenitus* [1713] [online]; available at: http://www.papalencyclicals.net/Clem11/c11unige.htm; accessed 30 June 2003; Internet).

[152]"You do not ignore finally what diligence and what wisdom are necessary to faithfully translate into our languages the words of the Lord, because nothing also is so easily produced as the very serious errors introduced into the multiplied translations of the Bible societies, and which stem from the stupidity and deception of so many translators; and these errors, the great number even and the diversity of the translations are concealed for a long time to the detriment of many. These societies themselves bring little or not at all that by reading these Bible translated into the vulgare languages that men fall into such errors rather than others, given that they accustom themselves little by little to turn for themselves to liberty of thought concerning the meaning of the Scriptures, and to despise the divine traditions guarded in the Church on the foundation of the doctrine of the Fathers, and to reject the hierarchy of the Church herself" (Gregory XVI, "*Inter praecipuas machinations*" [8 mai 1844] [online; also from *DS* 2771]; accessed: 8 Nov 2008; available at: http://www.catho.org/9.php?d=bw2; Internet. My translation from the French).

[153]"This is what the very cunning Bible societies who, renewing the old trickery of the heretics, translate the books of the divine writings into all of the vulgar languages, against the regulations of the very holy Church, interpret them with the help of explanations that are often perverse, and do not cease to distribute them freely, to give them to all sorts of people, even to those who are less cultivated, with the result that rejecting the divine tradition, the doctrine of the Fathers, and the authority of the Catholic Church, all interpret according to their private judgment, turning aside its meaning, and in this way fall into far greater errors. These societies... Gregory XVI... reproved, and We wish likewise that they be condemned" (Pius IX, "Qui Pluribus" (online); from *Denzinger*: 2784; accessed: 8 Sept 2008; available at: http://www.catho.org/9.php?d=bw2#elo; Internet).

~Date	Prayer, Veneration, Sacraments and Other Doctrines	Ecclesiology/Politics	Rival Churches and Movements, Named by Their Antagonists	Biblical Assessment of Rome's Doctrines and Practices
	of the Virgin Mary, **proclaimed by Pius IX"** (Boettner, #40); see also 1708.			
1858	The Rosary was said to have played a central role in the apparitions to [St.] Bernadette at Lourdes			Contra Gal 1:8-9.
1864	Pius IX's "Syllabus of Errors" (Sec IV) condemned the "Biblical Societies" [Bible Societies] as pests[154]	**"Syllabus of Errors, proclaimed by pope Pius IX, and ratified by the Vatican Council; condemned freedom of religion, conscience, speech, press, and scientific discoveries which are disapproved by Roman Church; asserted pope's temporal authority over all civil rulers" (Boettner, #41)**	Pius IX's "Syllabus of Errors" (Sec 5) reaffirmed the infallibility of Rome, its unilateral authority over all aspects of human government, disallowed the forming of any "national churches" (such as the Anglican Church)	Contra 2 Thess 3:1-2; Contra Jesus said, "My kingdom is not of this world" John 18:36; cf. Luke 17:20-21.

1870	**"Infallibility of pope in matters of faith and morals, proclaimed by the Vatican Council"[155] (Boettner, #42)**	Nine killed and over 100 injured as Irish Roman Catholics attacked the Irish Protestant Orange Parade in New York City		Contra Rom 3:10-12; 1 Cor 10:13 Several passages may be leveraged to come up with this view:
				• God raising up a prophet, "listen to him" (Deut 18:18-19), which refers specifically to Jesus, and not broadly to the "Vicar of Christ";
				• The high priest (Pontifex) who prophesied the need for the death of Jesus (John 11:51-52), which occasioned his plotting to put Jesus to death (John 11:53); not a great precedent;
				• The power of the "anointing oil" of the Sacrament of Holy Orders:
				  "This sacrament configures the recipient to Christ by a special grace of the Holy Spirit, so that he is able to serve as Christ's instrument for his Church. By ordination one is enabled to act as a representative of Christ, Head of the Church, in his triple office of priest, prophet, and king" (DS1581).
				  "It is the same priest, Jesus Christ, whose sacred person his minister truly represents. Now the minister, by reason of the sacerdotal consecration which he has received, is truly made like to the high priest and possesses the authority to act in the power and place of the person of Christ himself (*virtute ac persona ipsius Christi*).
				  "Christ is the source of all priesthood: the priest of the old law was a figure of Christ, and the priest of

---

[154]"IV. Socialism, Communism, Secret Societies, Biblical Societies, Clerico-liberal Societies. Pests of this kind are frequently reprobated in the severest terms in the Encyclical 'Qui pluribus,' Nov. 9, 1846, Allocution 'Quibus quantisque,' April 20, 1849, Encyclical 'Noscitis et nobiscum,' Dec. 8, 1849, Allocution 'Singulari quadam,' Dec. 9, 1854, Encyclical 'Quanto conficiamur,' Aug. 10, 1863' (Pius IX, "Syllabus of Errors" (online); available at http://www.papalencyclicals.net/Pius09/ p9syll.htm; accessed 8 Sept 2004; Internet).

[155]"When the Roman Pontiff speaks *ex cathedra*, in other words when, fulfilling his charge as pastor and doctor of all Christians, he defines, by virtue of his supreme apostolic authority, that a matter of faith or of morals must be held by the entire Church, he enjoys, by virtue of divine assistance which was promised to him in the person of Saint Peter, of that infallibility which the divine Redeemer desired be endowed to his Church when she defines doctrine on the faith or on morals; by consequence, these definitions of the Roman Pontiff are irrevocable in themselves and not by virtue of the consent of the Church.

"If anyone, to the displeasure of God, has the presumption of contradicting our definition: let him be anathema" (DS3074-3075).

~Date	Prayer, Veneration, Sacraments and Other Doctrines	Ecclesiology/Politics	Rival Churches and Movements, Named by Their Antagonists	Biblical Assessment of Rome's Doctrines and Practices
				the new law acts in the person of Christ" (DS1548)
				• Therefore, Rom 3:4 (DRA), "But God is true; and every man a liar, as it is written, That thou mayest be justified in thy words, and mayest overcome when thou art judged"
				Raising up the word of the Pope to the level of the Bible, brings down the unique authority of the Bible for several reasons:
				• It causes the words of the Pope to be equal in authority and spiritual power as those of Moses, Jeremiah, Paul, and yes, even of Jesus Himself!
				• It causes the word of the Pope to be the most valid interpreter of the Bible:
				o Moving authority from the Holy Spirit to a man in an office
				o Making the man, the Pope, the only proper interpreter of all of historical interpretation
				• Making the word of the Pope infallible:
				o Must needs make him infallible, when he receives this office
				o Must needs make him the only man in the world truly and perfectly led by the Holy Spirit
				Truly, the infallibility of the Pope is a pernicious doctrine.
1871		The Irish Protestant 12th July Orange Parade originally prohibited in New York, then allowed, leading to 62 civilian, 2 policemen, and 3 soldier deaths and more than 100 injured		Herein was the beginning of the loss of control of "White Anglo-Saxon Protestants" on "Puritan America" The immigration policies of Rome had worked to begin to swing the political fortunes of Rome in the U.S.
1884	Spiritual Testament of Cardinal Lavigerie, founder of the White Fathers [The White Fathers is an order formed to re-evangelize and re-colonize Equatorial Africa; which feat by the way, they accomplished] *"In the name of the Father, of the Son and of the Holy Spirit* *So may it be.* "This is my spiritual testament. "I begin it by declaring, in the presence of eternity that will open itself before me, that I want to die with the same convictions in which I have always lived, that being obedience and devotion without limits to the Holy Apostolic Seat and to our Holy Father the Pope, Vicar of Jesus Christ on the earth. I have always believed, and I believe all that they teach and in the sense that they teach it. I have always believed, and I believe that outside of the Pope or against the Pope, there can be in the Church nothing but trouble, confusion, error, and eternal loss. He alone was created as the foundation of unity and as a consequence [of that] of life, and all that regards things of salvation. "I have the signal honor of remaining very close to the Holy Apostolic Seat by my character of priest, bishop, and by my title of cardinal of the Holy Roman Church. Without a doubt these honors which are strongly above my misery and my weakness are done to confound me, in this moment that I ponder my presence before the tribunal of God, but I want to see in it even greater gratitude and faithfulness to the Seat of Peter and before our Holy Father the Pope, who has lavished me with the marks of his confidence and of his goodness. "I have served him with my best, all that I was able. Not being able to do anything now, I pray that the Lord will accept the sacrifice that I have offered Him in my life and in my sufferings that will accompany my death, for the prolongation of the precious days of Leo XIII [his contemporary Pope] and in the triumph of his magnanimous designs" (Cardinal Lavigerie [1825-1892], *Ecrits d'Afrique* [Paris: Bernard Grasset, 1966], 235-36. Translation			This influential Bishop of Algiers, Cardinal, and later Bishop of Carthage, founded the White Fathers as an order to re-evangelize and re-colonize sub-Saharan or Equitorial Africa, that had begun to be reached by Baptists and other Protestant missionaries and explorers (Livingston, Stanley, and Burton), tens of thousands of Protestant missionaries went to those lands, especially after the "Haystack Revival," the ministry of the "Cambridge Seven," and in the early days of the "Student Volunteer Movement" (approx. 1887-1910).

~Date	Prayer, Veneration, Sacraments and Other Doctrines	Ecclesiology/Politics	Rival Churches and Movements, Named by Their Antagonists	Biblical Assessment of Rome's Doctrines and Practices
	mine).			
1888		Leo XIII on Freedom of Speech and Freedom of the Press: "23. We must now consider briefly liberty of speech, and liberty of the press. It is hardly necessary to say that there can be no such right as this, if it be not used in moderation, and if it pass beyond the bounds and end of all true liberty" (Leo XIII, *Libertas Praestantissimum*: On the Nature of Human Liberty [Rome: 20 June 1888]), §23).		Leo XIII made it imminently clear what he felt about the First Amendment of the U.S. Constitution which provides for freedom of speech and freedom of worship. It would appear that the Church of Rome feels threatened by freedom of the press, and would rather suppress free discourse and control the presses, much as they did prior to the Protestant Reformation.
1893	Leo XIII in *Providentissimus Deus* three times affirmed the inerrancy of Scriptures (including the Apocryphal Books), as well as Church Tradition[156]			In this way a post-Napoleonic Pope reaffirmed all the past teachings and decrees of Rome which led to the virtual genocide of many peoples. While U.S. Protestants may ignore the Medieval Councils, Rome does not—see below on Benedict XVI's repeated mention of the Fourth Lateran Council as exemplary (both in 2000 and 2007) A reading of the current edition of Denzinger[157] (used for footnotes in Rome's 1994 *Catechism of the Catholic church*) would enlighten any Baptist, Evangelical, or Protestant on the true teachings of Rome (unfortunately the only current version of Denzinger that I have found is in French and Latin with some Greek)
1897	Leo XIII *Affari Vos* wrote against Manitoba's legislation on Catholic schools Leo XIII in his 1897 "Apostolic Constitution *Officiorum ac Munerum*: On the Prohibition and Censorship of Books" wrote against vernacular translation of the Bible[158]	The *imprimatur* affixed on the copyright page of the book was mandated by Pope Leo XIII, in his 1897 Apostolic Constitution "*Officiorum ac Munerum*: On the Prohibition and Censorship of Books."[159] Furthermore: "29. Ordinaries, even as Delegates of the Apostolic		Herein we find Leo XIII affirming that Rome is the only true church, and guiding its adherents to use every measure under Canadian Law to promote Rome's causes

---

[156]"For all the books which the Church receives as sacred and canonical, are written wholly and entirely, with all their parts, at the dictation of the Holy Ghost; and so far is it from being possible that any error can co-exist with inspiration, that inspiration not only is essentially incompatible with error, but excludes and rejects it as absolutely and necessarily as it is impossible that God Himself, the supreme Truth, can utter that which is not true. This is the ancient and unchanging faith of the Church, solemnly defined in the Councils of Florence and of Trent, and finally confirmed and more expressly formulated by the Council of the Vatican" ([Pope] Leo XIII, *Providentissimus Deus* (§20); available at: http://www.catholic-forum.com/saints/pope0256b.htm; accessed 8 March 2002; Internet).

[157]Heinrich Denzinger, et al., *Symboles et définitions de la foi catholique: Enchiridion Symbolorum*, 38th ed. (37th ed., Freiburg: Herder, 1997; Paris: Cerf, 2005).

[158]"7. As it has been clearly shown by experience that, if the Holy Bible in the vernacular is generally permitted without any distinction, more harm than utility is thereby caused, owing to human temerity: all versions in the vernacular, even by Catholics, are altogether prohibited, unless approved by the Holy See, or published, under the vigilant care of the Bishops, with Annotations taken from the Fathers of the Church and learned Catholic writers.

"8. All versions of the Holy Bible, in any vernacular language, made by non-Catholics are prohibited; and especially those published by the Bible Societies, which have been more than once condemned by the Roman Pontiffs, because in them the Wise Laws of the Church concerning the publication of the Sacred Books are entirely disregarded" (Leo XIII, *Officiorum ac Munerum* [Rome: 25 Jan 1897], §7, 8)

~Date	Prayer, Veneration, Sacraments and Other Doctrines	Ecclesiology/Politics	Rival Churches and Movements, Named by Their Antagonists	Biblical Assessment of Rome's Doctrines and Practices
		See, must be careful to prohibit evil books or other writings published or circulated in their Dioceses, and to withdraw them from the hands of the faithful."[160]		
1898	The last of several encyclicals by Pope Leo XIII extolling the Rosary were written	Leo XIII *Caritatis Studium* urged Catholics in Scotland to found good schools for Catholic youth		The same measures encouraged by Pius VI in 1775 were repeated
1907		Pius X, in *Pascendi Dominici Gregis*, established "Councils of Vigilance" in every diocese: "charged with the task of noting the existence of errors and the devices by which new ones are introduced and propagated" … "to extirpate the errors already propagated and to prevent their further diffusion, and to remove those teachers of impiety through whom the pernicious effects of such diffusion are being perpetuated"[161] Pius X's charge is by no means unimportant to dealing with "false teachings" in other Christian faiths, such as Baptists, Evangelicals, and Protestants	This charge allows for spiritual oversight of [and if necessary infiltration into] all Baptist, Evangelical, and Protestant organizations deemed to be a possible or plausible threat to the teaching and defense of the most "Holy Faith"—using the power of "nihil obstat" Nihil obstat—or: nothing opposing—allows persons with proper exemptions and indulgence to fully participate in the religious life of any denomination or religious grouping, and be vigilant for anyone or anything potentially negative to the Bishop of Rome or its causes. See Thomas Aquinas (*Summa*, SS, Q[10], A[11]) on permission to be involved among heretical groups for a greater good (partial citation in chronological history). In 1907, Pius X mandated all his bishops to put into	As part of the pastoral charge of the Catholic bishop, he is to protect his people from false teaching and false teachers: "It is the Magisterium's task to preserve God's people from deviations and defections and to guarantee them the objective possibility of professing the true faith without error" (*Catechism*, §890). "For the bishop, this is first of all the grace of strength: the grace to guide and defend his Church with strength and prudence as a father and pastor" (*Catechism*, §1586). Nihil obstat provides the mindset by which this secretive censorship is effectuated to all levels of communication (from secular media to religious writings and teaching). By the way, nihil obstat has proven extremely effective since 1907, especially among denominations, publishing houses, schools, and leaders ignorant of Rome's agenda. Consider the massive strides that the Catholic Church has made among American Evangelicals since 1907. From Vatican II and following, it has virtually neutered any negativism towards its history and designs among mainstream Evangelicals.

---

[159]"Let the Ordinaries, acting in this also as Delegates of the Apostolic See, exert themselves to proscribe and to put out of reach of the faithful injurious books or other writings printed or circulated in their dioceses" (Leo XIII, *Officiorum*, §21; cited in Pius X, *Pascendi Dominici Gregis: Encyclical on the Doctrine of the Modernists* [Rome: 8 Sept 1907], §51).

[160]Leo XIII, *Officiorum*, §29.

[161]"55. But of what avail, Venerable Brethren, will be all Our commands and prescriptions if they be not dutifully and firmly carried out? In order that this may be done it has seemed expedient to us to extend to all dioceses the regulations which the Bishops of Umbria, with great wisdom, laid down for theirs many years ago. 'In order,' they say, 'to extirpate the errors already propagated and to prevent their further diffusion, and to remove those teachers of impiety through whom the pernicious effects of such diffusion are being perpetuated, this sacred Assembly, following the example of St. Charles Borromeo, has decided to establish in each of the dioceses a Council consisting of approved members of both branches of the clergy, which shall be charged with the task of noting the existence of errors and the devices by which new ones are introduced and propagated, and to inform the Bishop of the whole, so that he may take counsel with them as to the best means for suppressing the evil at the outset and preventing it spreading for the ruin of souls or, worse still, gaining strength and growth' ["Acts of the Congress of the Bishops of Umbria" (November 1849), tit. 2, art. 6]. We decree, therefore, that in every diocese a council of this kind, which We are pleased to name the 'Council of Vigilance,' be instituted without delay. The priests called to form part in it shall be chosen somewhat after the manner above prescribed for the censors, and they shall meet every two months on an appointed day in the presence of the Bishop. They shall be bound to secrecy as to their deliberations and decisions, and in their functions shall be included the following: they shall watch most carefully for every trace and sign of Modernism both in publications and in teaching, and to preserve the clergy and the young from it they shall take all prudent, prompt, and efficacious measures" (Pius X, *Pascendi*, §55).

~Date	Prayer, Veneration, Sacraments and Other Doctrines	Ecclesiology/Politics	Rival Churches and Movements, Named by Their Antagonists	Biblical Assessment of Rome's Doctrines and Practices
			effect this type of infiltration and clandestine censorship, with bimonthly personal oversight by the bishop himself.	
1917	Apparitions of Mary at Fatima in which the Rosary was a central action and theme			
1925	Sister Lucia of Fatima revealed the First Saturday devotions centering on the Rosary's mysteries			
1928			Pius XI condemned Protestants, as well as Roman Catholic participation in the World Council of Churches in his encyclical *Mortalium Animos*[162]	
1930		**"Public schools condemned by Pius XI" (Boettner, #43)**		It must also be remembered that in 1949 the U.S. American Library Association voted Paul Blanshard's bestselling *American Freedom and Catholic Power* (Boston: The Beacon Press, 1949) as one of the 50 outstanding books of the year. It strongly denounced Rome's political exploits to become the dominant world religion and power!
1942	Fr. Patrick Peyton began promoting the "Family Rosary"; in time he was called the "Rosary Priest"	"The Vatican Bank was founded in 1942 by Pope Pius XII to manage assets destined for religious or charitable works"[163]		Catholicizing the concept of "Family Devotions": Rather than being devoted to Bible reading, one should be devoted to saying the Rosary!
1945		Two predominantly Catholic political parties are founded in Germany: • "Christian Democratic Union, founded after World War II… has its roots in the Center Party, a Catholic political party founded in 1870" • "Christian Social Union (CSU)… a predominantly		

---

[162]"There are some, indeed, who recognize and affirm that Protestantism, as they call it, has rejected, with a great lack of consideration, certain articles of faith and some external ceremonies, which are, in fact, pleasing and useful, and which the Roman Church still retains. They soon, however, go on to say that that Church also has erred, and corrupted the original religion by adding and proposing for belief certain doctrines which are not only alien to the Gospel, but even repugnant to it. Among the chief of these they number that which concerns the primacy of jurisdiction, which was granted to Peter and to his successors in the See of Rome. ...

"8. This being so, it is clear that the Apostolic See cannot on any terms take part in their assemblies, nor is it anyway lawful for Catholics either to support or to work for such enterprises; for if they do so they will be giving countenance to a false Christianity, quite alien to the one Church of Christ. Shall We suffer, what would indeed be iniquitous, the truth, and a truth divinely revealed, to be made a subject for compromise?" (Pius XI, *Mortalium Animos* [6 Jan 1928]; available at: http://www.ewtn.com/library/ENCYC/P11MORTA.HTM; accessed: 15 July 2001; Internet).

[163]"Vatican Bank mired in laundering scandal"; availalable at: http://www.usatoday.com/news/world/2010-12-11-vatican-bank_N.htm; accessed: 24 May 2012; Internet.

~Date	Prayer, Veneration, Sacraments and Other Doctrines	Ecclesiology/Politics	Rival Churches and Movements, Named by Their Antagonists	Biblical Assessment of Rome's Doctrines and Practices
		Catholic state party in Bavaria"[164]		
1949		On the Baptism of Desire: Innocent II's letter (Apostolicam Sedem" [DS 741], see 1130-1144) and Innocent III's letter *Debitum officii pontificalis* [28 Aug 1206; DS 788] were expanded by Pius XII to include as catechumens those who "are victims of invincible ignorance"	Just months before the Billy Graham crusade in Boston, Pius XII wrote the Archbishop of Boston [8 Aug 1949] (DS 3866-3873) encouraging him to treat as having taken an explicit vow to the church some who cannot do such, but rather can only make an implicit vow to the church (especially see DS 3870)[165]	Here, it seems, that the Archbishop of Boston, who wrote "Bravo Billy!" in his diocesan paper, was rewarded for his obedience by becoming a Cardinal weeks after the Graham crusade was over. Perhaps this letter and its aftermath explain the fatal flaw in Graham's theology of cooperation in evangelism with the Church of Rome. The concept of a "baptism of desire" goes back to Gregory IX, *Apostolicam sedem* (1119-1124) and Innocent III, *Debitum oficcii pontificalis* (1206), wherein a Jewish man baptized himself, which baptism was declared valid by virtue of his desire.
1950	**"Assumption of the Virgin Mary (bodily ascension into heaven shortly after her death), proclaimed by pope Pius XII" (Boettner, #44)**			I guess this places the bodily assumption of Mary is meant to place her at the same spiritual level as Enoch (Gen 5:24) and Elijah (2 Kings 2:11)
1957	Pope Pius XII declared St. Claire the Patron Saint of television in his encyclical *Ad perpetuam rei memoriam* (4 Feb 1957)[166]			Notice that the Pius XII takes authority over any other authority in the use of television to benefit Rome and its designs; Much like the printed page (Council of Trent), it would seem that these same principles are true also for the radio and the Internet, in their use and policies. This oversight includes to important and distinct aspects: • *Nihil Obstat*—no obstacle; oversight to assure that nothing negative to Catholicism is found in movies (i.e. nothing that would cause a good Catholic to stumble from his faith); and • *Imprimatur*—official sanction; oversight to assure that what is said about Catholicism is portrayed in a

---

[164]"A Quick Guide to Germany's Political Parties"; available at: http://www.spiegel.de/international/germany/where-do-they-stand-a-quick-guide-to-germany-s-political-parties-a-651388.html; accessed 24 May 2012; Internet.

[165][DS 3867] "… This is why none will be saved if, knowing [being] that the Church has been divinely instituted by Christ, he does not accept meanwhile to submit to the Church or refuses obedience to the Roman Pontiff, Vicar of Christ on earth. …

[DS 3870] "… For in order that someone obtains eternal salvation, it is not always required that he be effectively incorporated into the Church as a member, but he is at least required that he be united by vow or desire.

"Meanwhile, it is not always necessary that this vow be explicit, as it is in the case of catechumens, but when man is the victim of an invincible ignorance, God also accepts the implicit vow, called such because it is included in the good disposition of the soul by which man wants to conform his will to the will of God" ("Lettre du Saint-Office à l'archevêque de Boston, 8 août 1949. La nécessité de l'Eglise pour le salut" ["Letter of the Holy Office to the Archbishop of Boston, 8 August 1949. The necessity of the Church for salvation"]; from *1996 Denzinger*, §3866-3372; translation mine). Pius XII then went on to cite his own encyclical *Mystici corporis* [29 June 1943], in which he distinguished between truly incorporated members of the Church and those who are incorporated to it by a vow (presumably explicit or implicit) [DS 3802-3803]. In this last section Pius XII wrote that "All life does not disappear from those who, having lost by the sin of charity and of divine grace, become by consequence incapable of all supernatural merit, conserve nevertheless the faith and Christian hope and the light of divine grace, by internal inspiration and the impulse of the Holy Spirit, are pushed to a salvific fear and [being] excited by God to prayer and repentance of their faults" [from DS 3803].

[166]"Consequently, having consulted with the Sacred Congregation of Rites, of sure science and after considerable reflection, in virtue of Apostolic power, by this Letter and for always, We make, We constitute and We declare Saint Claire, virgin of Assisi, Heavenly Patron before God of the Television, attributing to her all the privileges and liturgical honors that comprise such a Patronage, opposing everything contrary. We announce, We establish, We ordain that this present Letter be firm and valid, that it goes forth and produces all these effects in their integrity and fullness, now and in the future, to them that it concerns or may concern; that it be regularly judged and considered in this way; that from now it be considered null and without effect anything that may be attempted by whomever, in virtue of whatever authority, with knowledge or in ignorance, against the measures decreed by this Letter" (Pius XII, Ad perpetuam rei memoriam; from: http://www.vatican.va/holy_father/pius_xii/apost_letters/documents/hf_p-xii_apl_21081958_st-claire_fr.html; accessed: 26 Sept 2006; Internet; translation mine).

~Date	Prayer, Veneration, Sacraments and Other Doctrines	Ecclesiology/Politics	Rival Churches and Movements, Named by Their Antagonists	Biblical Assessment of Rome's Doctrines and Practices
				way that is agreeable to Rome and its designs
				In combination with the "Councils of Vigilance" put into place in by Pius X's *Pascendi Dominici Gregis* in 1907, we can estimate that the diocese where films are produced (e.g. Hollywood) are given strategic oversight over the films produced in their diocese.
				Could it be that this encyclical provided legitimacy and finances to fund overt and covert Catholic lobbying efforts in Hollywood and elsewhere in the world?
1960		The Roman Catholic John F. Kennedy elected President of the United States of America		Protestants, such as Billy Graham's father-in-law, L. Nelson Bell, expressed grave concern over the election of an adherent of the Church of Rome as President of the U.S. (L. Nelson Bell, *Protestant Distinctives and the American Crisis* [Weaverville, NC: Presbyterian Journal Book Room, 1960])
				Likewise Lorraine Boettner published *Roman Catholicism*, 1st edition (Presbyterian and Reformed, 1962) in response to questions and concerns about the Church of Rome
1962		In Boettner's *Roman Cathocism*, he included a section titled, "Contrast Between British-American and the Southern European-Latin American Cultures." In this section he wrote: "How are we to explain the glaring contrast that over the centuries has developed and which continues to manifest itself so prominently between Protestant and democratic Britain and the United States on the one hand and the Roman Catholic countries of southern Europe and Latin America on the other? The former are known for the stability of their governments, the latter for the ease and rapidity with which they overthrow their governments. Mr. Howard[167] has given an explanation that is for the most part unknown even to Protestants, but which we believe gets to the very heart of the matter. ..."[168]		Is Mr. Boettner within his right to make this point or is he being ugly and anti-Catholic? Consider Deut 29:18-23: Deut 29:18-23, "So that there may not be among you man or woman or family or tribe, whose heart turns away today from the LORD our God, to go *and* serve the gods of these nations, and that there may not be among you a root bearing bitterness or wormwood; and so it may not happen, when he hears the words of this curse, that he blesses himself in his heart, saying, 'I shall have peace, even though I follow the dictates of my heart'—as though the drunkard could be included with the sober. The LORD would not spare him; for then the anger of the LORD and His jealousy would burn against that man, and every curse that is written in this book would settle on him, and the LORD would blot out his name from under heaven. And the LORD would separate him from all the tribes of Israel for adversity, according to all the curses of the covenant that are written in this Book of the Law, so that the coming generation of your children who rise up after you, and the foreigner who comes from a far land, would say, when they see the plagues of that land and the sicknesses which the LORD has laid on it: 'The whole land *is* brimstone, salt, and burning; it is not sown, nor does it bear, nor does any grass grow there, like the overthrow of Sodom and Gomorrah, Admah, and Zeboim, which the LORD overthrew in His anger and His wrath.'" Or consider: Prov 24:30-34, "I went by the field of the lazy *man*,

---

[167]George P Howard, *Religious Liberty in Latin America* (Philadelphia: Westminster, 1944), 103-05.

[168]The quote continues, "He first calls attention to the difficulty that people in southern Europe and Latin America have even today in governing themselves, and points out that the political institutions in those countries are largely servile copies of Anglo-Saxon models. A constitutional monarchy such as existed for a time in Spain and Italy, the republics of France and Portugal, or the federal governments in Latin America are only imitations, and poor ones at that, of the contstitutional forms found in Great Britain and the United States. The Anglo-Saxons have been able to carry forward and strengthen political institutions which the Latins have found almost unworkable" (Lorrain Boettner, *Roman Catholicism* [Phillipsburg, NJ: Presbyterian and Reformed, 1962], 442-43).

~Date	Prayer, Veneration, Sacraments and Other Doctrines	Ecclesiology/Politics	Rival Churches and Movements, Named by Their Antagonists	Biblical Assessment of Rome's Doctrines and Practices
				And by the vineyard of the man devoid of understanding; And there it was, all overgrown with thorns; Its surface was covered with nettles; Its stone wall was broken down. When I saw *it*, I considered *it* well; I looked on *it* and received instruction: A little sleep, a little slumber, A little folding of the hands to rest; So shall your poverty come *like* a prowler, And your need like an armed man"
				For surely the Church of Rome frames itself as the seat of Western culture and the reason that Western culture has prospered and does prosper.[169]
1964		Vatican II's pronouncement "Lumen Gentium" which 3 times calls non-Catholic Christians "separated brethren": "67. ... Let them assiduously keep away from whatever, either by word or deed, could lead separated brethren or any other into error regarding the true doctrine of the Church." "69. It gives great joy and comfort to this holy and general Synod that even among the separated brethren there are some who give due honor to the Mother of our Lord and Saviour, especially among the Orientals, who with devout mind and fervent impulse give honor to the Mother of God, ever virgin" After "Preliminary Note of Explanation, Part 4": "N.B. Without hierarchical communion the ontologico-sacramental function [munus], which is to be distinguished from the juridico-canonical aspect, cannot be exercised. However, the Commission has decided that it should not enter into question of liceity and validity. These questions are left to theologians to discuss- specifically the question of the power exercised de facto among the separated Eastern Churches, about which there are various explanations."	In a secretive meeting in November 1964 in Crêt Bérard, France, Eugene Nida of the American Bible Society, Olivier Béguin of the Bible Department of the World Council of Churches, and the Jesuit Cardinal Bea, rector of the Rome's Pontifical Biblical Institute met together to discuss cooperation in translating the Bible. It appears that Eugene Nida penned the first draft of what was to become the 1964 and 1968 "Guidelines for Interconfessional Cooperation in Translating the Bible"[170]	In this 1964 document, apparently penned by Eugene Nida, 200 years of Protestant and Evangelical translation work was about to be turned over to the control of Rome (see 1968 and 1987).

[169]E.g. Father Brian Van Hove, S.J., "Beyond the Myth of The Inquisition: Ours Is "The Golden Age"; available at: http://www.catholiceducation.org/en/controversy/the-inquisition/beyond-the-myth-of-the-inquisition-ours-is-the-golden-age.html (online); accessed: 30 Nov 2014; Internet.

[170]Edwin H. Robertson, "Author's Preface," in *Taking the Word to the World: 50 Years of the United Bible Societies* (Nashville: Nelson, 1996), 114.

~Date	Prayer, Veneration, Sacraments and Other Doctrines	Ecclesiology/Politics	Rival Churches and Movements, Named by Their Antagonists	Biblical Assessment of Rome's Doctrines and Practices
1965	**"Mary proclaimed Mother of the Church, by pope Paul VI (Boettner, #45)** Transubstantiation reaffirmed in Paul VI's *Mysterium fidei*, (3 Sept 1965) restating the confession of Berengarius of Tours required of him by Gregory VII in 1079: "I [Berengarius] believe in my heart and openly profess that the bread and wine which are placed upon the altar are, by the mystery of the sacred prayer and the words of the [our] Redeemer, substantially changed into the true and life-giving flesh and blood of Jesus Christ Our Lord, and that after the Consecration, there is present the true Body of Christ which was born of the Virgin and, offered up for the salvation of the world, hung on the Cross and now sits at the right hand of the Father, and that there is present the true Blood of Christ which flowed from His side. They are present not only by means of a sign and of the efficacy of the Sacrament, but also in the very reality and truth of their nature and substance."[171]			
1968		UBS and SPCU since the "Guiding Principles for Interconfessional Cooperation in Translating the Bible," including the following: C. ORGANIZATIONAL STRUCTURE For the most adequate development of a translation program, there is need for three groups: 1. a Working Committee, 2. a Review Committee, and 3. a Consultative Group. 1. *Working Committee* Consisting of 4 to 6 persons equally divided between Protestant and		In this UBS and SPCU agreement, about 200 years of Protestant and Evangelical translation work worldwide was essentially signed over to the Church of Rome, at least on paper.

---

[171]Gregory VII, "Profession of Faith given to Berengarius" [1079]; from Mansi, "Coli. Ampliss. Concil." XX, 524D; cited in Paul VI, *Mysterium Fidei* (Rome, 3 Sept 1965); available at: http://www.papalencyclicals.net/Paul06/p6myster.htm (online); accessed: 11 Dec 2014; Internet.

~Date	Prayer, Veneration, Sacraments and Other Doctrines	Ecclesiology/Politics	Rival Churches and Movements, Named by Their Antagonists	Biblical Assessment of Rome's Doctrines and Practices

		Roman Catholic constituencies and possessing four essential characteristics:
		
		  a. equal standing,
		
		  b. complementary abilities,
		
		  c. mutual respect, and
		
		  d. capacity to work together.[172]		

1979	John Paul II affirmed that the Vatican II Counsel (1964-1968) did not change the Church of Rome, in his "Mexico Ever Faithful"[173]			

1987	John Paul II's *Redemptoris Mater* focuses on the Mother of Christ:
	
	• "In this way Mary's motherhood continues unceasingly in the Church as the mediation which intercedes, and the Church expresses her faith in this truth by invoking Mary 'under the titles of Advocate, Auxiliatrix, Adjutrix and Mediatrix.'"[174]
	
	The same added one more time around the rosary for "the Mystery of the Church"
		A revision of the 1968 "Guiding Principles" was published and place on the Vatican Website. The revision changed the above quoted portion as follows:
		
		2.3. ORGANIZATIONAL STRUCTURE
		
		  For the most adequate development of a translation program, there is need for three groups: 1. a translation team, 2. a review panel, and 3. a consultative group.
		
		2.3.1. *Translation team*
		
		  Consisting of not more than six persons of high competence from the Roman Catholic and other Christian constituencies and possessing four essential characteristics:
		
		  a) comparable qualifications,
		
		  b) complementary abilities,
				This encyclical by John Paul II reaffirms all Rome's preceding doctrinal developments related to Mary; it is a very sad read for anyone who does not affirm that Mary is the Mediatrix of all the graces of God through Christ
				
				The revision of the "Guiding Principles," at least on paper, allowed Rome to gain control of the entire translation work of the United Bible Society and its many auxiliaries, allies, and partners. Of particular note:
				
				• "Protestant" is changed to "other Christian constituencies" (this pattern is duplicated in 17 of the 19 1968 uses of the word "Protestant");
				
				• "Capacity to work together" would eliminate conservative Evangelicals who would feel it necessary to separate from the Church of Rome, especially when it comes to Bible translation;
				
				• "Equal standing" is changed to "comparable qualifications," as the 1987 revision calls for a "Translation Consultant" to oversee the entire work.[176]

---

[172]"Guiding Principles for Interconfessional Cooperation in Translating the Bible" [Pentecost, 1968], from Thomas F. Stransky, C.S.P., and John B. Sheerin, C.S.B., eds. *Doing the Truth in Charity: Statements of Pope Paul VI, Popes John Paul I, John Paul II, and the Secretariat for Promoting Christian Unity 1964-1980.* (New York: Paulist, 1982), 166.

[173]"The Second Vatican Council wished to be, above all, a council on the Church. Take in your hands the documents of the Council, especially "Lumen Gentium", study them with loving attention, with the spirit of prayer, to discover what the Spirit wished to say about the Church. In this way you will be able to realize that there is not—as some people claim—a "new church", different or opposed to the "old church", but that the Council wished to reveal more clearly the one Church of Jesus Christ, with new aspects, but still the same in its essence" (John Paul II, "Mexico Ever Faithful," *Osservatore Romano* [5 Feb 1979], 1. The "old" and "new" language has been regularly used by the Roman church to equivocate on the role of Vatican II [e.g. John Paul II, *Tertio Millennio Adviente* (14 November 1994), §18]).

[174]John Paul II, "*Redemptoris Mater*—Encyclical on the Blessed Virgin Mary in the Life of the Pilgrim Church" (Rome: Vatican, March 25, 1987); available at: http://www.knight.org/advent/docs/jp02rm.htm (online); Accessed: 20 May 2005; the citation in the quote is from "Second Vatican Ecumenical Council, Dogmatic Constitution on the Church, *Lumen Gentium*, 62."

~Date	Prayer, Veneration, Sacraments and Other Doctrines	Ecclesiology/Politics	Rival Churches and Movements, Named by Their Antagonists	Biblical Assessment of Rome's Doctrines and Practices
		c) mutual respect, and d) capacity to work together.[175]		
1988			Pope gathers non-Christian religious leaders for prayer	
1993			"Pontifical Commission on Biblical Interpretation," chaired by Cardinal Ratzinger, vilified what it called "Fundamentalist Interpretation," defining Fundamentalist by the five fundamentals of the 1895 Niagara Bible Conference.[177]	
2000	Joseph Cardinal Ratzinger (now Benedict XVI) in *Dominus Iesus* affirmed the Fourth Lateran Council (of 1215) in footnote 82: "The famous formula *extra Ecclesiam nullus omnino salvatur* is to be interpreted in this sense (cf. FOURTH LATERAN COUNCIL, Cap. 1. *De fide catholica*: DS 802). Cf. also the *Letter of the Holy Office to the Archbishop of Boston*: DS 3866-3872."		Perhaps the most shocking portion of *Dominus Iesus* was in section 17, where the Ratzinger affirmed the following: "On the other hand, the ecclesial communities which have not preserved the valid Episcopate and the genuine and integral substance of the Eucharistic mystery, are not Churches in the proper sense; however, those who are baptized in these communities are, by Baptism, incorporated in Christ and thus are in a certain communion, albeit	Another footnote reminiscent of the *Catechism of the Catholic Church* §192 citing Pius IV's 1564 *Iniunctum nobis* (DS 1863) (see above) Here Benedict XVI shows that he affirms the virulent council that led to the extirpation of the Albigensian so-called "Cathars." The letter to the Archbishop of Boston, happens to be written several months before the Billy Graham crusade in Boston where Graham read "Bravo Billy!" in the diocesan paper following his crusade (see 1949 above). Putting these two items together sends a rather strong message to those who know Rome's history.

---

[176]"Translators are normally employed by their churches and not directly by the Bible Societies. This is necessary because after the completion of the translation project the translators will generally return to the work they had done previously. All conditions of service should, however, be established in consultation with the national Bible Society and the translation consultant involved, as the supervision of the overall program requires that a balance be maintained between members of the translation team, who come from different churches. In most cases also the translation consultant will be the person most directly involved in training translators and proposing the approval of the final text of the translation for publication. ...

"...The translation consultant should assist the translation team in designing a set of principles that are applicable to the particular translation being considered.

"...The translation consultant should take the responsibility for editorial supervision." (ibid.).

[175]"Guidelines for interconfessional Cooperation in Translating the Bible the New Revised Edition Rome 1987"; From: http://www.vatican.va/roman_curia/pontifical_ councils/chrstuni/general-docs/rc_pc_chrstuni_doc_ 19871116_guidelines-bible_en.html; accessed: 8 Sept 2007; Internet.

[177]"The fundamentalist reading has its origin, from the period of the Reformation, in a preoccupation with faithfulness to the literal sense of the Scripture. After the Enlightenment, she presented herself, within Protestantism, as a safeguard against a liberal exegesis. The title 'fundamentalist' is directly related to a American Biblical congress that was held in Niagara, in the state of New York, in 1895. The conservative Protestant exegetes defined there 'five points of fundamentalism': verbal inerrancy of Scripture, the deity of Christ, His virgin birth, the doctrine of vicarious expiation and the bodily resurrection at the Second Coming of Christ. When the fundamentalist reading of the Bible propagated itself in other parts of the world, she gave birth to other types of readings, equally 'literalistic', in Europe, Asia, Africa, and South America. This type of reading finds more and more adherents, during the last part of the twentieth century, in religious groupings and in sects as well as among Catholics. ...

"The fundamentalistic approach is dangerous, for she is attractive to persons who are looking for biblical answers to their life problems. She can trick them by offering them pious but illusory interpretations, rather than telling them that the Bible does not necessarily contain an immediate response to each of these problems. Fundamentalism invites, without saying it, a form of intellectual suicide. It places false sense of security to life, for it unconsciously confuses the human limitations of the biblical message with the substance of the divine message" (Commission biblique pontificale, *L'interprétation de la Bible dans l'Église* [Quebec: Éditions Fides, 1994], 48, 50; translation mine).

~Date	Prayer, Veneration, Sacraments and Other Doctrines	Ecclesiology/Politics	Rival Churches and Movements, Named by Their Antagonists	Biblical Assessment of Rome's Doctrines and Practices
			imperfect, with the Church."[178] In this statement, the concept of "separated brethren," touted Vatican II conciliatory phrase, was notched back to coincide with historic Roman Catholic doctrine.	
2002	John Paul II in *Rosarium Virginis Mariae* added 5 new "mysteries of the rosary"			
2005		George Bush is the first U.S. president to attend the funeral of a Pope.		
2006			Note some of the points from the report on the "Inter-religious Consultation on 'Conversion—Assessing the Reality," affirmed by the Vatican and the World Council of Churches, on 12-16 May 2006, in Lariano/Velletri, Italy: 3. We affirm that while everyone has a right to invite others to an understanding of their faith, it should not be exercised by violating other's rights and	This statement, with its apparent antagonism to the "obsession of converting others," does relate directly to New Testament evangelism. Interestingly, the World Evangelical Alliance's general secretary Rev. Dr Geoff Tunnicliffe apparently signed off on this "Inter-religious Consultation" in 2007.[181]

[178]"The Catholic faithful *are required to profess* that there is an historical continuity — rooted in the apostolic succession[53] — between the Church founded by Christ and the Catholic Church: 'This is the single Church of Christ... which our Saviour, after his resurrection, entrusted to Peter's pastoral care (cf. *Jn* 21:17), commissioning him and the other Apostles to extend and rule her (cf. *Mt* 28:18ff.), erected for all ages as "the pillar and mainstay of the truth" (*1 Tim* 3:15). This Church, constituted and organized as a society in the present world, subsists in [*subsistit in*] the Catholic Church, governed by the Successor of Peter and by the Bishops in communion with him' [SECOND VATICAN COUNCIL, Dogmatic Constitution *Lumen gentium* (*LG*), 8]. With the expression *subsistit in*, the Second Vatican Council sought to harmonize two doctrinal statements: on the one hand, that the Church of Christ, despite the divisions which exist among Christians, continues to exist fully only in the Catholic Church, and on the other hand, that 'outside of her structure, many elements can be found of sanctification and truth' [*Ibid.*; cf. JOHN PAUL II, Encyclical Letter *Ut unum sint*, 13. Cf. also *LG*, 15 and the Decree *Unitatis redintegratio* (*UR*), 3], that is, in those Churches and ecclesial communities which are not yet in full communion with the Catholic Church [The interpretation of those who would derive from the formula *subsistit in* the thesis that the one Church of Christ could subsist also in non-Catholic Churches and ecclesial communities is therefore contrary to the authentic meaning of *Lumen gentium*. 'The Council instead chose the word *subsistit* precisely to clarify that there exists only one "subsistence" of the true Church, while outside her visible structure there only exist *elementa Ecclesiae*, which — being elements of that same Church — tend and lead toward the Catholic Church' (CONGREGATION FOR THE DOCTRINE OF THE FAITH, *Notification on the Book 'Church: Charism and Power'* by Father Leonardo Boff: AAS 77 [1985], 756-762)]. But with respect to these, it needs to be stated that 'they derive their efficacy from the very fullness of grace and truth entrusted to the Catholic Church' [*UR*, 3].

"17. Therefore, there exists a single Church of Christ, which subsists in the Catholic Church, governed by the Successor of Peter and by the Bishops in communion with him [Cf. CONGREGATION FOR THE DOCTRINE OF THE FAITH, Declaration *Mysterium Ecclesiae*, 1: AAS 65 (1973), 396-398]. The Churches which, while not existing in perfect communion with the Catholic Church, remain united to her by means of the closest bonds, that is, by apostolic succession and a valid Eucharist, are true particular Churches [Cf. *UR*, 14 and 15; CONGREGATION FOR THE DOCTRINE OF THE FAITH, Letter *Communionis notio*, 17: AAS 85 (1993), 848]. Therefore, the Church of Christ is present and operative also in these Churches, even though they lack full communion with the Catholic Church, since they do not accept the Catholic doctrine of the Primacy, which, according to the will of God, the Bishop of Rome objectively has and exercises over the entire Church.

"On the other hand, the ecclesial communities which have not preserved the valid Episcopate and the genuine and integral substance of the Eucharistic mystery [*UR*, 22], are not Churches in the proper sense; however, those who are baptized in these communities are, by Baptism, incorporated in Christ and thus are in a certain communion, albeit imperfect, with the Church [*UR*, 3]. Baptism in fact tends per se toward the full development of life in Christ, through the integral profession of faith, the Eucharist, and full communion in the Church [*UR*, 22]" (*Dominus Iesus* [16 June 2000; 6 Aug 2000;]; available at: www.vatican.va; accessed: 1 Sept 2008; Internet).

[181]"Christian code of conduct on religious conversion wins broader backing"; available from: http://www.oikoumene.org/en/news/news-management/eng/a/article/1634/christian-code-of-conduct.html (online); accessed: 24 Sept 2009; Internet.

~Date	Prayer, Veneration, Sacraments and Other Doctrines	Ecclesiology/Politics	Rival Churches and Movements, Named by Their Antagonists	Biblical Assessment of Rome's Doctrines and Practices
			religious sensibilities. At the same time, all should heal themselves from the obsession of converting others. 4. Freedom of religion enjoins upon all of us the equally non-negotiable responsibility to respect faiths other than our own, and never to denigrate, vilify or misrepresent them for the purpose of affirming superiority of our faith. 5. We acknowledge that errors have been perpetrated and injustice committed by the adherents of every faith. Therefore, it is incumbent on every community to conduct honest self-critical examination of its historical conduct as well as its doctrinal/theological precepts. Such self-criticism and repentance should lead to necessary reforms *inter alia* on the issue of conversion. 6. A particular reform that we would commend to practitioners and establishments of all faiths is to ensure that conversion by "unethical" means are discouraged and rejected by one and all. There should be transparency in the practice of inviting others to one's faith. 10. We see the need for and usefulness of a continuing exercise to collectively evolve a "code of conduct" on conversion, which all faiths should follow. We therefore feel that inter-religious dialogues on the issue of conversion should continue at various levels.[179] "A finalised code is expected by 2010"[180]	
2007	Benedict XVI's *Spe Salvi*			Now seemingly more bold than in 2000, as Pope,

---

[179]"Report from inter-religious consultation on 'Conversion – assessing the reality'"; available from http://www.oikoumene.org/index.php?id=2252&L=0; accessed 2 Nov 2007; Internet.

[180]"Evangelicals back other Christians on cconversion code of conduct"; available at: http://www.eni.ch/featured/article.php?id=1118 (online); accessed: 24 Sept 2009.

~Date	Prayer, Veneration, Sacraments and Other Doctrines	Ecclesiology/Politics	Rival Churches and Movements, Named by Their Antagonists	Biblical Assessment of Rome's Doctrines and Practices
	(Rom 8:24) [8 Nov 2007], again affirmed the Fourth Lateran Council [1215], this time in the text of §43.[182]			Benedict XVI revealed his interest in Innocent III and the Council called by him in 1215, the Fourth Lateran Council. Benedict XVI, in his approval and espousal of images [statues and the like], goes so far as to call the rejection of images "atheism"!
2011		The Pontifical Council for Justice and Peace published "Towards Reforming the International Financial and Monetary Systems in the Context of Global Public Authority" (25 Nov 2011) which advocated the forming of a "world political Authority" following the organizational structure exemplified by the Church of Rome[183]	If a political system is developed which is for "the common good" of all people, it appears that evangelism will be nullified and so will disagreement with Rome (if it becomes the one world church)	This proposed "one world government" appears to be similar to that which is prophecied in Revelation 13: Rev 13:3-7, "And I saw one of his heads as if it had been mortally wounded, and his deadly wound was healed. And all the world marveled and followed the beast. 4 So they worshiped the dragon who gave authority to the beast; and they worshiped the beast, saying, 'Who is like the beast? Who is able to make war with him?' 5 And he was given a mouth speaking great things and blasphemies, and he was given authority to continue for forty-two months. 6 Then he opened his mouth in blasphemy against God, to blaspheme His name, His tabernacle, and those who dwell in heaven. 7 It was granted to him to make war with the saints and to overcome them. And authority was given him over every tribe, tongue, and nation" Notice that even though the world is saying "peace, peace," it will be a time of wars and rumors of wars. Hence, the cry for peace will be illusory: Jer 6:14, "They have also healed the hurt of My people slightly, Saying, 'Peace, peace!' When there is no peace" Mark 13:7-10, "But when you hear of wars and rumors of wars, do not be troubled; for such things must happen, but the end is not yet. For nation will rise against nation, and kingdom against kingdom. And there will be earthquakes in various places, and there will be famines and troubles. These are the beginnings of sorrows. But watch out for yourselves, for they will deliver you up to councils, and you will be beaten in the synagogues. You will

[182]"43. Christians likewise can and must constantly learn from the strict rejection of images that is contained in God's first commandment (cf. *Ex* 20:4). The truth of negative theology was highlighted by the Fourth Lateran Council, which explicitly stated that however great the similarity that may be established between Creator and creature, the dissimilarity between them is always greater [citing DS 806, "Fourth Lateran Council, Chap 2, The False Doctrine of Joachim of Flore." This section dealt with the great dissimilarity between the Creator and the created]. In any case, for the believer the rejection of images cannot be carried so far that one ends up, as Horkheimer and Adorno would like, by saying "no" to both theses—theism and atheism. God has given himself an "image": in Christ who was made man."

[183]"The establishment of a world political Authority should be preceded by a preliminary phase of consultation from which a legitimated institution will emerge that is in a position to be an effective guide and, at the same time, can allow each country to express and pursue its own particular good. The exercise of this Authority at the service of the good of each and every one will necessarily be *super partes*: that is, above any partial vision or particular good, with a view to achieving the common good. Its decisions should not be the result of the more developed countries' superior power over weaker countries. Instead, they should be made in the interest of all, not only to the advantage of some groups, whether they are formed by private lobbies or national governments. ...

"In the tradition of the Church's Magisterium which Benedict XVI has vigorously embraced, the principle of subsidiarity should regulate relations between the State and local communities and between public and private institutions, not excluding the monetary and financial institutions. Likewise, on a higher level, it ought to govern the relationships between a possible future global public Authority and regional and national institutions. This principle guarantees both democratic legitimacy and the efficacy of the decisions of those called to make them. It allows respect for the freedom of people, individually and in communities, and allows them at the same time to take responsibility for the objectives and duties that pertain to them.

"According to the logic of subsidiarity, the higher Authority offers its subsidium, that is, its aid, only when individual, social or financial actors are intrinsically deficient in capacity, or cannot manage by themselves to do what is required of them. Thanks to the principle of solidarity, a lasting and fruitful relationship would build up between global civil society and a world public Authority as States, intermediate bodies, various institutions – including economic and financial ones – and citizens make their decisions with a view to the global common good, which transcends national goods" (Pontifical Council for Justice and Peace, ""; from: http://www.radiovaticana.org/en1/print_page.asp?c=532223 [online]; accessed 7 Nov 2011; Internet).

~Date	Prayer, Veneration, Sacraments and Other Doctrines	Ecclesiology/Politics	Rival Churches and Movements, Named by Their Antagonists	Biblical Assessment of Rome's Doctrines and Practices
				be brought before rulers and kings for My sake, for a testimony to them. And the gospel must first be preached to all the nations"
2014			Rome calls for a "Global Covenant of World Religions" arbitrated by Rome as a "neutral party." "There are bits and pieces and streams of interfaith laws that talk about protection of people and religion but in fact it's not working"[184]	See 2006, and the "Code of Conduct" related to evangelism.

---

[184]"Call to action for 'Global Covenant of World Religions'"; available at: http://en.radiovaticana.va/news/2014/10/23/call_to_action_for_global_covenant_of_world_religions/1109296 (online); accessed 27 Oct 2014; Internet.

CONCLUSION

Thomas M'Crie described the sad realities of society's that slumber under the deadening spiritual influence of Rome:

> "The consequence of this, under the corrupt form in which Christianity everywhere presented itself, was the production of a spirit of indifference about religion, which, on the revival of learning, settled into skepticism, masked by an external respect to the established forms of the church."[163]

Some possible questions emerge from this study:

- When did the Church of Rome appear to become a one-issue-church,[164] that being "yea or nay" on the absolute submission to the teachings of the Supreme Pontiff? (or "unity in Christian Charity," as per Augustine); e.g. are you cooperative with us or non-cooperative?
- When did the veneration of and prayers to Mary become a denial of the doctrines of the deity of Christ and the Trinity?
- When did Rome's adherence to sacramentalism [sacerdotalism] become incompatible with New Testament evangelism, the new birth, and justification by faith alone?

Baptists and Evangelicals would do well to consider these questions prior to emphasizing points of commonality between the two theological [religious] systems.[165]

If the reader would allow, it appears to this author that some concluding deductions may be appropriate. First of all, it appears that there were a number of competing factions in the Fourth Century Latin church. It appears that one of these factions was more Sacramentally-oriented and another was more Evangelically-oriented. In the mix of the Fourth Century ecclesial politics and through the late Fourth and early Fifth Century writings of Augustine, the Sacramental faction of the Latin Church won political preeminence, gaining control of the bishopric of Rome. If this deduction holds true, then the Sacramental Church of Rome has maintained in adversarial relationship with Evangelicalism for over 1500 years. This deduction coincides with uses of the word "enemy" sprinkled throughout the centuries in question. Likewise, Rome has absorbed the fruit of Evangelical labors century after century, gaining from its spirit and adapting to and absorbing its innovations. Concurrently it progressed down a slow but ever-increasing Sacramentalism, in complete opposition to Evangelical salvation. By the time the fires of Inquisition burned, it gave vent to its true spirit. That same spirit being curbed for a time to accommodate republicanism.[166]

Second, until very recently, the Bible used by Rome appears to have remained relatively unchanged since Jerome's Fifth Century Latin Vulgate—the only version deemed authoritative, infallible, and inerrant. This very strongly held viewpoint was recently modified by John-Paul II's approval of the 1982 Nova Vulgata. This revised edition of the Vulgate has adopted significant changes, both coinciding with the recent Nestle-Aland critical editions of the New Testament and advancing Rome's theological causes. Even the Lutheran Adolf von Harnack was surprised that the writings of Paul remained up until his day, being that Paul had caused so much religious ferment in the history of the churches.[167] Again, the

---

[163]Thomas M'Crie, *History of the Progress and Suppression of the Reformation in Italy during the Sixteenth Century* (Edinburgh: William T. Blackwood, 1833; London: T. Cadell, 1833; Elibron Classics, 2004), 41.

[164]Consider this interchange from the Anabaptist Martyrology titled, *Martyr's Mirror*: "First Jelis was brought forth, who, as he was going to death, said, among other things: 'Because I believe that Jesus is the Christ, the Son of the living God, born of the Virgin Mary, I must die.' Thereupon a monk, who walked at his side, instantly said, 'You lie.' Jelis further said, concluding his remark, 'And because I believe that the pope is the antichrist.' (From "Jelis Strings, with Pieter and Jelis Potvliet, A.D. 1562"; in van Braght, *The Bloody Theater or Martyrs Mirror*, 657).

[165]The last paragraph of a book on this topic reads: "Billy Graham has set the example for evangelical cooperation with Catholics in mass evangelism without compromising the basic gospel message. Despite ecclesiastical and doctrinal differences (see Part Two), there are some important things many Catholics and evangelicals hold in common not the least of which is the good news that Jesus died for our sins and rose again. Thus, there seems to be no good reason why there should not be increased ways of mutual encouragement in fulfilling our Lord's Great Commission (Matt. 28:18-20). Catholics and evangelicals do not have to agree on everything in order to agree on some things—even something important. We do not need to agree on the authority of the church before we can cooperate in proclaiming the power of the uncompromising gospel (Rom. 1:16)" (Norman L. Geisler and Ralph E. MacKenzie, *Roman Catholics and Evangelicals: Agreements and Differences* [Grand Rapids: Baker, 1995], 428-29).

[166]"Tinctured with Gallicanism through his early association with the Sorbonne, Lavigerie modified his views during his stay at Rome, and his attitude at the Vatican Council is fully expressed by the promise he made his clergy 'to be with Peter'. When Leo XIII, by his Encyclicals 'Nobilissima Gallorum gens' of 8 Feb., 1884, and 'Sapientiæ æternæ' of 3 Feb., 1890, directed the French Catholics to rally to the Republic, he generously put aside other political affiliations and again 'was with Peter'. A great sensation was created when at Algiers, on 12 Nov., 1890, he proclaimed before a vast assemblage of French officials the obligation for French Catholics of sincerely adhering to the republican form of government. The famous 'toast d'Alger' was the object of harsh criticism and even vituperation from the monarchist element. With his usual vehemence Cardinal Lavigerie answered by his 'Lettre à un catholique', in which he not only impugned the pretenders—the Comte de Chambord, the Comte de Paris, and Prince Napoléon—but even hinted that monarchy was an outgrown institution. In this he may have gone too far, but in the main point it was proved later by Cardinal Rampolla's letter of 28 November, 1890, and Pope Leo's Encyclical 'Inter innumeras' of 16 Feb., 1892, that Lavigerie had been the self-sacrificing spokesman of the pope" ("Charles-Martial-Allemand Lavigerie"; available at: http://www.newadvent.org/cathen/09050d.htm [online]; accessed 8 Nov 2005; Internet).

[167]"2. The origin of a series of the most important Christian customs and ideas is involved in an obscurity which in all probability will never be cleared up. ... But the greatest problem is presented by Christology, not indeed in its particular features doctrinally expressed, these almost everywhere may be explained historically, but in its deepest roots as it was preached by Paul as the principle of a new life (2 Cor. V. 17), and as it was to many besides him the expression of personal union with the exalted Christ (Rev. II. 3). But the problem exists only for the historian who considers things only from the outside, or seeks objective proofs. Behind and in the Gospel stands the Person of Jesus Christ who mastered men's hearts, and constrained them to yield themselves to him as his own, and in whom they found their God. Theology attempted to describe in very uncertain and feeble outline what the mind and heart had grasped. Yet it testifies of a new life which, like all higher life, was kindled by a Person, and could only be maintained in connection with that Person. 'I can do all things through Christ who strengtheneth me.' 'I live, yet not I, but Christ liveth within me.' These convictions are not dogmas and have no history, and they can only be propagated in the manner described by Paul, Gal 1. 15, 16.

labors of the Protestants are being used to further Rome's quest for primacy. Meanwhile Rome was given a beachhead into almost all Evangelical translations and New Testament Greek classes via the 1968 "Guidelines for Interconfessional Cooperation in Translating the Bible" signed by the UBS and the SPCU.

Third, it appears that much of that which is taught as "Church History" up until the Reformation period is primarily "smoke in mirrors" from an Evangelical point-of-view—quite tangential to the proclamation of the Gospel and a theology of conversion. Even following the Reformation period, there has been a careful winnowing of issues to allow the focus to shift away from an analysis of Rome's theological deviations to the differences between the Protestant, Evangelical, and Baptist groups (à la Jacques-Benigne Bossuet). Thus the obvious differences between the theologies of conversion of the sacramental system of Rome and justification by grace alone through faith alone are almost ignored, while the differences among Protestant and Evangelical groups are highlighted. Furthermore, a general ignorance of the polemic writings between the Huguenots and Catholics in 18th Century France (e.g. the writings of Brousson and Jurieu virtually unavailable in English) makes this winnowing quite clear.

The concluding words of Jacques Blocher from his book *Le Catholicisme a la lumière de l'Écriture Sainte* ["Catholicism in light of Holy Scripture"] seem fitting to provide a conclusion to the very sad progression these pages have delineated:

"In the course of our attentive studies of Roman Catholic doctrines and practices, we have always discovered the same fundamental conclusion: the visible Church, organized in its forms and hierarchy, replaces Christ on earth; she takes His place. This seems to us a dangerous substitution. Instead of guiding toward Jesus, she distances [people from Him]. There is therein an intolerable usurpation. The human institution has become like a screen between God and man. ...

"To have arrived to this point, the Catholic Church appears to us as having deviated, from the apostolic church of antiquity, by a progressive and slow abandonment of primitive simplicity. The greatest blow borne by the Church was the massive entrance of pagans and of their customs, after the edict of Milan, in the 4th Century. The Church holds a great part of the truth, but it is often deformed and masked by practices that distort it. The great sin of the Church, is to have wanted to take the place of Jesus, under the pretext of being His body; it is unduly placing the emphasis on the outward practices and having forgotten the spirit of the Gospel. The Church therefore appears to induce men toward error: one can only be saved in it *in spite of* [or *apart from*] its practices and teachings. It is therefore a question of making watchful, with love, those who have strayed toward these doctrines that are so foreign to true Christianity, to that of the New Testament.

"We believe, in fact, that Christianity is not a 'religion' among others; it originates from a unique phenomenon. Men, women, coming from all classes of society, are internally grasped by the Spirit of God, and live together in brotherly communion. They experience the joy of salvation, for they have recognized Jesus Christ as their Savior who died and resurrected to wash them from their sins and to give them eternal life. They have the same faith in Christ the Savior. They differentiate clearly themselves from the world in which they find themselves. Certainly, each remains in his career: businessman, farmer, homemaker, but their life is new, their words, their thoughts, their actions, their behavior are totally new.

"They are mocked, then they are persecuted because they present themselves to society as a body of strangers. Little by little, their faith radiates, their joy, their love make an impression on those who surround them: attempts are made to imitate them, thinking that in doing such one can possess their secret. When several generations have elapsed, numerous children of the Christians who, by veneration of their parents, repeat their actions and take on their words, without however sharing their intimate convictions. It is in this way that a Christianity of façade develops, which is a true homage, but is no more than an appearance. They wear the mask of joy, on a face ravaged by anxiety.

"Christianity has become a sort of 'religion,' established, respected, but that is no more than a gathering of formalities, words, and customs."[168]

"3. It was of the utmost importance for the legitimizing of the later development of Christianity as a system of doctrine that early Christianity had an Apostle who was a theologian, and that his epistles were received into the canon. ...

"But Paulinism especially has had an immeasurable and blessed influence on the whole course of the history of dogma, an influence it could not have had if the Pauline Epistles were not received into the canon. Paulinism is a religious and Christocentric doctrine, more inward and more powerful than any other which has ever appeared in the Church. It stands in clearest opposition to all merely natural moralism, all righteousness of works, all religious ceremonialism, all Christianity without Christ. It has therefore become the conscience of the Church, until the Catholic Church in Jansenism killed this her conscience. 'The Pauline reactions describe the critical epochs of theology and the Church' [note: See Bigg, *The Christian Platonist of Alexandria*, pp. 53, 283 ff.]. One might write a history of dogma as a history of Pauline reactions in the Church, and in doing so would touch on all the turning-points of history. Marcion after the Apostolic Fathers; Irenaeus, Clement and Origen after the Apologists; Augustine after the Fathers of the Greek Church [note: Reuter (August. Studien, p. 492) has drawn a valuable parallel between Marcion and Augustine with regard to Paul]; the great Reformers of the middle ages from Agobard to Wessel in the bosom of the medieval Church; Luther and the Scholastics; Jansenism and the Council of Trent:--everywhere it has been Paul, in these men, who produced the Reformation. Paulinism has proved to be a ferment in the history of dogma, a basis it has never been [note: Marcion of course wished to raise it to the exclusive basis, but he entirely misunderstood it]. Just as it had that significance in Paul himself, with reference to Jewish Christianity, so it has continued to work through the history of the Church" (Adolf Harnack, *History of Dogma*, a translation of the 3rd German ed. [Constable: London, 1900; Dover: New York, 1961], 132-33, 135-36).

[168]Jacques Blocher, *Le Catholicisme a la lumière de l'Écriture Sainte* [Catholicism in light of Holy Scripture], 3rd ed (Nogent, France: Institut biblique, 1979), 169-171; translation mine.

www.ingramcontent.com/pod-product-compliance
Lightning Source LLC
Chambersburg PA
CBHW062039090426
42740CB00016B/2956